MARRIAGE

CONFIDENTIAL

MARRIAGE

CONFIDENTIAL

The Post-Romantic Age of Workhorse
Wives, Royal Children, Undersexed
Spouses & Rebel Couples Who
Are Rewriting the Rules

PAMELA HAAG

HARPER

An Imprint of HarperCollins*Publishers*
www.harpercollins.com

Names and identifying details of some individuals have been
changed to protect their privacy.

FIRST EDITION

Designed by Jo Anne Metsch

Library of Congress Cataloging-in-Publication Data has been applied for.

ISBN: 978-0-06-171928-8

11   12   13   14   15   OV/RRD   10   9   8   7   6   5   4   3   2   1

CONTENTS

INTRODUCTION

Marriage on the Edge

ANDY IS AN ACQUAINTANCE of my husband, John. He is in his early forties, very smart, inquisitive, and witty, and has a wonderful stay-at-home wife who looks after their two children. With my husband, however, Andy often drifts into frank comment about his marriage. When he does, he says things like this: "What I need is an afternoon in a hotel room with a strange woman!" But, of course, he doesn't take the steps to do that. Or he'll say, "Sometimes I ask myself, how am I going to get through the day without running over this woman?" He looks at John intently before adding, "And I *mean* it."

But of course he doesn't mean it, not really.

Despite his melodramatic outbursts, Andy is anything but a wife abuser or a nasty, hostile spouse. More accurately, he's dutiful and attentive, if a bit henpecked. His marriage is, by all accounts, functional, settled, and content. But at the same time, it is wistfully deficient in other ways, and glazed over with ennui. If pressed, he would say that it works well enough for him. But there are moments when Andy pensively, almost philosophically, wonders out loud: "Is this as good as it gets?"

My friend Laura, who has been married for over ten years, is similarly ambivalent. On one evening, she will ruefully ponder if she stays in her marriage only because she lacks "the courage to divorce." On another, she will affirm her love and affection for her husband and speculate on the marriage as a "gift" of "the constant" in life; on another occasion she will reconstitute her sense of realism and duty, and say of marriage, "For some of us, marriage is for better or worse. And if it's worse, then it's worse. That's what you get."

Millions of wives and husbands have these feelings each day. They privately ask themselves a variation of the question Baltimore Orioles manager Earl Weaver used to put to his future Hall of Fame pitcher Jim Palmer, when Palmer was struggling in a game: "Are you going to get any better, or is this it?" They don't have an answer, but secretly they are troubled by a feeling that there is something in their marriage that doesn't work, possibly cannot be made to work, and that it is not going to get any better. As far as their marriages are concerned, they fear that this is, indeed, it. These spouses are sad more than miserable, disappointed more than chronically unhappy. As psychiatrists would say, their marriages are "melancholy": They have a brooding sadness about them that often lacks an obvious, tangible cause.

These melancholy spouses may not remember the dream they once had for marriage, but the dream remembers them. It tugs at them hauntingly. They know it's not their spouse's fault, per se, or even their own. After several years, a Marriage is more like a third character, with its own personality and life. It's not reducible to the sum of its all-too-human creators, any more than a child would be.

I know these people well, as their thoughts are mine. If you too happen to be someone who has come to this uncomfortable realization about your marriage, you also know the drill that follows. You shadowbox with yourself. In quiet moments when you ask yourself, "Is this all it is?," you simultaneously beat up on yourself for asking the question at all. You accuse yourself of being selfish to want more than you already have. You feel guilty thinking about lost or deferred dreams, and you wonder whether it is noble or useful to demand more from a marriage than the good things you have. You might even question your desires. Perhaps the longing for more out of marriage is just the vestige of a callow, self-defeating romantic ideal that you don't even entirely trust anymore, but can't entirely purge from your mind.

A few years ago I started casually asking women and men about their marriages, all the time. A common reaction was for a wife or husband to say, "I'm pretty satisfied with my marriage, but . . . ," or "I'm happy, but . . ." The gently inventoried deficits and suspended dreams that came after the "but" often sounded fairly serious and meaningful. It wasn't a matter of the toilet seat being left up, or of easily remedied flaws, but a collusive, ineffable shortcoming such as withered passion, boredom, lack of connection, lost affinities, or a world-weariness that beset their married life. Even so, they also felt, and I believed them, that they were more or less satisfied. They weren't contemplating separation, despite the absences and the longings in their marriages. Those missing elements weren't enough, apparently, to count as a source of legitimate unhappiness—although they seemed serious enough that, after a while, I began to wonder why they didn't.

Mostly you live with genuine ambivalence and indeterminacy: One minute, you feel that your marriage is a good, solid thing; the next, you resent it and you think, how can I live with this person anymore? One minute you can't imagine staying; the next, you can't imagine leaving.

||||||||

I'm married to the prototype Great Guy and Wonderful Father to our child. And he really is. You'd like John. Everybody does. He's an aggressively inoffensive man, with the soul of a mother hen in the body of a jock. On winter mornings, before dawn, he wakes up, jumps on his fancy German-designed stationary bike with electromagnetic resistance, and rides for hours. I can hear the bike roaring and humming so loudly from the floor below that you'd think he intended to heat our house on the exertions of his famously sculpted legs. "I was talking about your calf muscles with the mechanic at Joe's garage the other day," a neighbor tells him. Remarkably, things like this are said to him by other married men.

Perhaps because he is a triathlete, a distance runner, and a long-distance cyclist, John understands endurance, and carries the slow-metabolizing, long view in his head. His life is paced to withstand discomfort and suffering over protracted stretches. Doubtless, this skill has come in handy in marriage.

John fixes things, mechanical and human. He does this even in his sleep. His dreams lean toward intricate capers in which he helps political prisoners escape from behind enemy lines or deploys technical ingenuity to outfox villains. His eyes light up when I present him with a loose cabinet hinge or a computer glitch he can solve for me. Sometimes he inquires after problems that I've complained of ephemerally in the past. "Did you ever get that keyboard drawer installed?" he'll ask hopefully. By disposition and profession he is an engineer, now a financial engineer who devises mathematical models for a commodities trading firm.

If the term wasn't so conceptually threadbare from successive self-help regimes, I would tell you that John is an "enabler" in the meritorious sense of that term. He helps you be better at whatever it is you want to be. At a cocktail party you would be charmed by his unpretentious midwestern amiability, a happy ideal of the politician, and he is reliably the tallest, broadest, and often the most handsome man in the room. You'd intuit that you were in the presence of an actual grown-up, probably the most grown-up person there. As I often do, you would feel momentarily quelled by his company, and safe. Now the problem will be solved, action will be taken, something will get *done*, you might think.

Being a rules-following and driven person, John takes more generic satisfaction out of the *idea* of marriage than I do, although he has ambivalent feelings about it, too. It's a state of being that suits him, because it orders unruly elements and imposes a routine on life. John likes order. At a cookout, he will arrange four hot dogs geometrically on the grill, into a perfect square.

We love each other, but love expands to contain so many tender and modified meanings over years that it stops really meaning or containing anything. Unlike our vivid love for our son, which has such crisp, precise angles and ultimatums (we'd both of us *lay down our lives* for him), marital love means everything and therefore nothing. It's just the atmosphere. We entrusted the care of our lives to each other, and John is one of my favorite people in the world. I have a nice marriage, a lovely husband. He likes me, too.

But you never know. On other days, and in other moments, I think that this could very well be the last year of our marriage.

Of the more than one million divorces that happen in the United States each year, the majority come from a population that we know little about, can rarely spot, and whose problems are invisible and inscrutable to acquaintances, friends, and even family. Not long ago, I discovered that the semi-happy marriage constitutes its own distinct species in the annals of scholarly research. I learned this while browsing the pages of the august *Journal of Marriage and Family*. There, in 2001, the prominent marriage researcher Paul Amato published an article on the "low-conflict," low-stress unhappy marriage. Amato estimates that up to 60 percent of divorces come from its ranks.

In contrast to the "high-distress," high-conflict marriage, which might involve abuse, violence, addictions, fistfights, chronic arguments, projectile shoes and dishes, or other conspicuously dysfunctional habits that lead to divorce, the low-stress, low-conflict marriage is not, according to scholars, anywhere near "that bad." However, that elastic phrase "not that bad" slyly and unavoidably ratchets down our expectations to prepare us for what comes next. "They are just not ecstatic marriages." As Amato explains it, in these "good enough" marriages, "the choice is not between . . . being miserable or bailing out. The choice is . . . between being moderately happy . . . or getting a divorce." And yet, such marriages lead to divorce more often than any other kind. The Utah Commission on Marriage concluded in 2003 that 70 to 80 percent in the state "get divorced, *perhaps unnecessarily*," from "low-conflict marriages" and for "soft reasons"—presumably, for reasons such as boredom, ennui, soullessness, or other non-high-conflict sources of unhappiness. Researchers find this—us—puzzling, from the outside looking in. As scholar Alan Booth muses, "There are no studies of parents who seldom disagree or fight, yet end their marriages in divorce, a seemingly incongruous marital outcome," he notes, "but one that appears to be fairly common." Indeed.

It's not just scholars who scratch their heads and wonder why such marriages are unsatisfying enough to cause the parties to separate. So do friends and family. To the outside observer, there is nothing "really wrong" with these low-stress, low-conflict marriages—as if we were married not only *by* a piece of paper, but *on* a piece of paper, and by résumé; as if marriage were something well cast, rather than well lived. But honorably intentioned, mutually agreeable people who find themselves mired in the scholar's confection of the low-conflict, low-stress unhappy marriage struggle—often privately—with this dilemma: is this yearning "enough" of a reason to get divorced, or separated?

My first goal in this book is to give voice to this yearning, and to the low-conflict, melancholy marriage, and to show the millions of us who are in these ambivalent marriages that we're not alone. I want to provide consoling moments of self-recognition, and to satisfy curiosity about the secret life of these marriages by taking you inside them. The noncelebrity marriage is a concealed institution, even in our privacy-loathing age. Its failures, as well as its quirky, improvised revisions, are too often hidden from view. My aim is to lift the curtain and create a collective portrait of these marriages—how we get there, what decisions propel us into ennui. This book quibbles, tacitly, with Leo Tolstoy's adage: Maybe all unhappy marriages aren't all unhappy in their own unique ways; maybe in a lot of cases they're unhappy owing to choices, attitudes, and sensibilities of our time that we share. I'm after the souls of these marriages, usually, more than their quantitative indicia, or the facts about how these couples arrange chores or work.

If you are in one of these marriages—if you're a spouse with vague feelings of discontent; if you're a spouse married to someone who feels this way, and you're confused, if not heartbroken, as to why you're not "enough" for them; if you have a spouse like this in your family, or your circle of friends; if you're close to a marriage that seems cranky and frazzled, or lethargic and droopy, and, each time you leave its company, you wonder to yourself why aren't they *happier* when it seems they should be—then, for you, I aim to put a face on the melancholy.

At first glance, it surprises me that the flock of low-conflict unhappy marriages, mostly drawn here from the cohort of people in their late thirties, forties, and early fifties, is as large as it is. This suggests a paradox that interests me throughout this book: We have more marriage freedom, choice, and latitude than ever before—the old marriage imperatives and consensus views don't weigh on us—yet many of us, even with relative privilege and latitude, end up as melancholy, and as orthodox in our views of marriage, as were generations of married men and women before us. Often we feel more comfortable breaking the marriage rules than condoning a revision of them. Even though we have both the means (the freedom) and the incentive (the melancholy) to bring about change, we don't really use that freedom to figure out how marriage might evolve—substantively, not superficially—into something better and more satisfying.

To that end, my second goal in this book is to equip you with a new way of thinking about the plight of a stable but melancholy marriage. It may not be you, it may not be your spouse. It may be the institution of marriage itself. It's not my sense, or proposition, that marriage is obsolete, as others have suggested, but I do feel that it sometimes needs to evolve to new forms.

From reading much of the vast research literature on marriage it's obvious to me that not only can the estate of marriage change, it will change. It's a question of how, not if. In her groundbreaking book *Marriage: A History*, Stephanie Coontz describes how in transition from the 19th to the 20th century, marriage changed from a sturdy social institution, a duty and an obligation, to a more unstable, spindly bond based on romantic great expectations of love, affection, emotion, and intimacy. If, as Coontz suggests, the 19th century belonged more to "traditional" marriage, defined as a social institution and obligation, and the 20th century belonged to the romantic, I'm interested in the next paradigm of marriage, the 21st century's, which is gradually replacing the romantic one.

I call it a post-romantic spirit. It doesn't abide by either the romantic or the traditional scripts for marriage that came before it; it dismantles romantic premises and ideals around career, work, lifestyle, childrearing, or sex in marriage, to different effects and with different degrees of mindfulness. Sometimes we're drifting into a post-romantic age without thinking about it. In other cases, and marriages, we're deliberately dismantling and subverting both the traditional and the romantic scripts.

You may not find yourself in sympathy with all of the marriages described here, but my ambition isn't to recommend or endorse any particular path or marital lifestyle (this is by no means an advice book), only to jog our thinking out of the familiar rut of Divorce or Sticking It Out, and to propose that we enlarge our sympathies, reduce our judgments, and think in a spirit of open-minded adventure, curiosity, fun, and imagination, about where marriage might go, either our own marriages, or the estate of marriage. Sometimes, in a quest for common denominators of our discontent, I take the stance of the empathetic contrarian and question some of the ways that we, and I, think about and "do" marriage today. Sometimes I ask if this is all we should want, or expect. At other times, I take the stance of a marital agent provocateur and search for the queer traditional marriage and new patterns of thought about marriage to replace the familiar, perhaps obsolete, ones.

These new ways of thinking, by definition, aren't the norm or the mainstream, yet. I hope you'll get a sense of where marriage might be headed, not according to the broad-brush census statistics that capture the most tectonic shifts, after the fact, but intimately, according to marriage pioneers on the front lines who stretch the limits of the possible in marriage. These pioneers have Oreo marriages—traditional on the outside, untraditional on the inside . Often they faced the same dilemma and yearnings, but they opted for a third way. They changed the rules in one form or another, or they challenged an element of marriage orthodoxy. Some would call these marriages eccentric and weird, and I can understand that. But it can be hard to tell where "eccentric" ends and "vanguard" begins.

Just sixty years ago Americans didn't really imagine procreation and marriage as separate, or even sex and procreation as separate; they probably didn't imagine an age of widespread tolerance for premarital sex, "living together," or interracial marriage, to say nothing of same-sex marriage; they couldn't have imagined marriages with stay-at-home dads and female breadwinners. After Title VII passed in 1964, outlawing sex discrimination in the workforce, an airline personnel executive fretted in the *Wall Street Journal*, "what are we going to do when a gal walks into our office, demands a job as an airline pilot and has the credentials to qualify? Or what will we do when some guy comes in and wants to be a stewardess?" Things just as inconceivable today could be tolerated, even a norm, in the next half century.

Eccentric, vanguard marriages risk being judged for their improvisations, and sometimes they do them in secret, for that reason. There's a social reward attached to sticking it out and reconstituting the traditional marriage; there's shame attached to changing the rules, leaving a marriage, refusing to marry, or going for your ambitions—even if it may make for a happier marriage, or life, to do just that.

||||||||||

A word on organization and method: After a first chapter that sets the stage and context, this book moves straightforwardly into three thematic parts that tackle the main elements of any marriage: work, career, and money; children; and sex.

To try to understand the melancholy, *Marriage CSI* style, I've done a variety of things and used eclectic techniques. Sometimes to figure out the secret life of marriage, you need to go to secret places, so I've eavesdropped, both in person and in cyberspace; I've interviewed; I've joined online discussion groups and social networks where people share in that bewitching chimera of anonymity and intimacy. I've conducted two surveys, reviewed the popular commentary, and I've taken undercover field trips to places both online and in the real world. I'm most grateful to the more than fifty people that I've interviewed, either in person, by phone, or by correspondence, to get a feel for real marriage today. In some cases I let these wives and husbands talk at length; in other cases it seemed better to aggregate or synthesize voices from across sources to demonstrate one sentiment.

An important disclaimer: I don't profess to describe or analyze all of the factors, character traits, and decisions that contribute to any of the marriages described here, including my own. As I've said, my premise is that each marriage is entirely unique and that each is, also, in one or many ways, a product of our times. Readers will hear and discern in the material any number of themes. My intention isn't to analyze each marriage's multifaceted complexity, but to present stories that illustrate one or two major traits, moods, or broader trends of interest in a particular chapter.

Although this isn't an academic book, I've made use of my scholarly background. I was trained as an historian, so I share the occasional perspective on what's changed over time. I also reviewed some, but by no means all, of the research on United States marriage trends. That research is a foundation upon which I build here, and on which I arrived at some of my insights and conclusions. Usually it's just summarized or, more often, nested within a story, in the main body of this book. But I found much of it so fascinating, and a solid basis from which I could speculate, range around, and explore, that I've cited and described it more thoroughly in the Notes section.

On a few occasions, I also reflect on my own marriage or share a conversation from it, because my marriage was the incandescent spirit behind this project in the first place. I also do this because, obviously, there is no marriage that I can hope to know more about, or more intimately, than my own. Candor about marriage has been received from others as a gift—and is offered, by me, in the same spirit. For his consent and bravery in the matter I'm most grateful to John—who doubtless has come to rue that he ever married a nonfiction writer.

CHAPTER ONE

THE DILEMMAS OF A SEMI-HAPPY MARRIAGE

Why We Settle for Ambivalence

J OSIE IS ONE of my oldest and dearest friends. I've known her for years now, and she lives in a New England city. She is perceptive and brave, an accomplished nonprofit executive, confident and perky in appearance and disposition. Josie and some of my other friends would occasionally play a game of metaphoric description: "If this person were a tree, what kind would they be?" and that sort of thing. The animal Josie evoked was always a playful, clever, outgoing one—an otter or some such.

When she was in her late twenties, Josie got married, although not formally in the eyes of the state, since her partner was a woman. She had two children, adopted with her partner, Rory. What she prized in this relationship was having a home base, and a sense of security not always present in her childhood. Once, early in her marriage on a new spring evening, she gazed out the window at the meadow and river across from her house and marveled to us that she couldn't believe this was her life; it was so true to the domestic idyll she had dreamt of.

It didn't stay that way. When the children arrived, with their usual chaos, her marriage became a matter of "surviving another day," she lamented. Her home became a place where she felt alone, where Rory didn't make the effort to connect, physically or emotionally. They took pride in never raising their voices or arguing in front of the children. They ran an efficient, calm household, but Josie didn't feel rejuvenated or truly seen in her marriage. "I know what it feels like to be *alone* in your own marriage," she says.

As with other halfhearted marriages, nothing discretely terrible happened to push it toward melancholy. Whatever their problems together, there was nothing "wrong" with Rory in any definitive sense. She was, and is, a decent, interesting, and accomplished person. The forensics of the marriage's deterioration are murky. To me, it always seemed that Josie tried too hard to please Rory in the beginning, in the quest for domesticity. She subordinated her own preferences and character too much, and hewed her life too closely to Rory's style. Eventually, Josie's resentment over what she came to see as her generosity in comparison to Rory's self-absorption seemed to build up within her. And a lot of us, including Josie, perhaps, end up wanting most what we least know how to secure for ourselves in marriage. Josie wanted, and wants, that stability, but it is hard to reconcile with her experience. The restless soul who grows up without family stability just wants to settle down; the one who grows up witnessing a marriage of passionless, frigid stability just wants to run with the wolves. Maybe it's simply the human condition—to be perpetually but futilely lured in marriage by the mystery of the code we've never managed to crack.

Josie first disclosed her discontent to us tearfully over margaritas one night at the beach, during a makeshift girls' retreat. She'd kissed someone else at a happy hour, and this felt like the start of a marital slide. Josie was tormented by the idea of leaving her marriage. She is profoundly devoted to her children and household, and as an advocate for gay and lesbian marital rights she felt a special burden to make the marriage work. In some ways she felt as if she and Rory had become the equivalent of a model home or a spec house for happy lesbian domesticity. But she'd spent enough years carrying water for the directive of habituated stability and the less than joyous pragmatism of a low-conflict, low-stress unhappy marriage, which was precisely what she had. No easy path suggested itself. But she wasn't content, and she couldn't put up a front with us anymore.

I'll pick up Josie's story below, but her dilemma up to this point illustrates the mood. The country is honeycombed with halfhearted marriages like this. I ask my online survey of nearly 2,000 to respond to the statement "Most of the marriages I see aren't really that happy." Forty percent express mild to "entire" agreement, which seems quite high to me. I'm even more interested to learn how many see marriages as inhabiting a neutral, ambivalent range. So I next ask them to react to the statement "Most marriages aren't really happy or unhappy." The statement yielded a high uncertain value, with 38 percent saying they neither agree nor disagree, since we can't ever be sure about other people's marriages. But almost 30 percent agree that "most" marriages are somewhere in limbo between happy and unhappy.

Kyle was one of them. In an interview he says, "I interpret that question to mean that people are ambivalent or in the middle, and I think that's true. Lots of people get married out of societal pressure. But it's so much ingrained that people don't really think about it. They're probably relatively faithful, they get by, they trudge along. But they're not quite living their ambition."

There's a unique feel to this semi-happy marriage. It's different from the "you made your bed and you lay in it" resignation in my parents' day. This melancholy is also distinct from the old chestnut of Sticking It Out. We still have plenty of those marriages, and the economic crisis that began in 2008 has only swelled their ranks, because many couples simply cannot afford to get divorced. Or, if they get divorced, the dramatically deflated value of their home makes it hard to unload, since neither spouse wants it, and they can't sell it at a good price. Stick It Out spouses follow the Aristotelian ethic that we should choose virtue over happiness. They know full well that they're unhappy, and choose to stay together for the children or the house. In one researcher's restrained coinage, they are "as unhappy as it is possible to be without seeking relief through divorce."

The marriage I'm describing is more genuinely ambivalent than that. Often, in my own case, I really can't tell if my marriage is woeful or sublime. Maybe I'm just so profoundly content that it *feels* like unhappiness, because nirvana is *dull* in this way, it lacks frisson. Buddhist wisdom tells us that the end of desire is the end of sorrow. Maybe marital contentment is a place of stillness and solidity where nothing happens, a vacuum with no conflict or disheveling passion. I often feel that I'm "grounded." But does that mean that I'm stalled on the tarmac, before my journey has even begun, or that I've arrived, firmly if jejunely settled in the life we laid down roots for, the peaceful destination we sought?

Such an indeterminacy of emotional extremes would have been inconceivable to me in my twenties. Unlike the father of a friend of ours, who unequivocally declared the state of marriage to be "so boring" that he would "slit his wrists" if he had to stay in it one minute longer, the low-conflict, low-stress melancholy marriage has a muted palette. It's a marriage extinguished, as Robert Frost might have agreed, by ice, not fire. This marriage doesn't explode, it implodes. You contemplate your escape, or relief through flight, in a nonargumentative, tranquil, well-ordered, high-functioning household where screaming matches with your spouse are largely fantasized intrapsychic events. In exchange for bliss you gain stability, comfort, routine, decorum, convenience, and some sense of accomplishment in Being Responsible for your child.

You develop tricks and skills in a melancholy marriage. In my own, we have learned and perfected the marital screensaver function on each other: the half-conscious, half-asleep demeanor of the habituated spouse. Out of the densely knotted tangle of our marriage, we've learned to pluck at the conversational strands and themes most likely to produce alliance, stimulate agreement, and keep the harmony between us. By way of sublimation for my marital gloom and worries, I've gotten more obsessed with work and drink more red wine; John exercises whenever he can (his version of "fun") and has cultivated a fulsome hyperagreeability, designed to keep marital equilibrium. He has developed a case of Ed McMahon Syndrome: "You are *correct*, sir!" He tries with an almost flailing earnestness to be an innocuous, agreeable partner-sidekick.

Yet even as we do these things the marriage has its own CNN-style ticker at the bottom of the screen, scrolling a fractured mental subtext of unarticulated grievances, deferred fulfillments, and lost ecstasy. When you get frustrated you might fantasize yourself a boozily confrontational Elizabeth Taylor ("If you weren't already *dead*, I'd divorce you," she hisses at Richard Burton in *Who's Afraid of Virginia Woolf?*). But in your life you do the laundry, pack the lunches, make the carpool line on time, and pay the bills. You accept with quaking reverence the prescriptions, however internalized, that you must avoid divorce. And you're not entirely sure that divorce is even what you want. There are no pure choices to be had; no obvious decisions to make.

To have marital yearnings and ambitions like this in an otherwise pleasant marriage is to live out of phase with your times. In a faint echo of Betty Friedan's "mad" housewives, who "should" have been happier than they were in their comfortable, well-furnished marriages, the melancholy spouse gets told today, directly or indirectly, that they should be happier in the marriage, and more sanguine about it, than they actually feel.

For one thing, if you are, or ever have been, in a low-conflict semi-happy marriage, then you're in the crosshairs of the self-named marriage movement in the United States. The marriage movement is a loosely confederated group of researchers, advocates, and "pro-marriage" forces (some also oppose same-sex marriage) who first stated their principles at a conference in June 2000. They hope to revive a culture of marriage, to encourage "marital interdependence" (that is, a gender division of labor in marriage), and to promote government policies that are explicitly pro-marriage rather than marriage-neutral. They want the traditional marriage model back, not the romantic one. It's my feeling that these political stances, cultural moods, and our

friends' opinions and even their marriages really do affect us personally, even when we don't entirely share their views, mostly because
they subtly or not so subtly shape what we expect or ask of our marriage. The marriage movement's advice is to try to make marriage
work, halfhearted or not, for the children, if nothing else. Those in
the marriage movement might have advised Josie that she felt unfulfilled because, romantically befogged, she expected too much out of
marriage in the first place, and as a solution should recalibrate her
desires toward more pragmatic realism.

David Popenoe, a prominent marriage researcher at Rutgers University and a former head of the National Marriage Project (also the
son of *Ladies' Home Journal*'s iconic "Can This Marriage Be Saved?"
columnist), finds that many people's "view of marriage may be so
unrealistic"—romantic and narcissistic, he specifies—"that they're
doomed to failure."

Romance has acquired an avowed enemy with the marriage movement, difficult as it is to fathom taking up arms against the fluffy, me-
ringue dream of true love. Kristina Zurcher, a scholar at Notre Dame,
summarizes the movement's view that marriage ideally should be
"stronger, more lasting, and about more than romantic love," which
is, after all, a highly perishable good. As evidence the marriage movement could point to the preponderance of American divorces in the
first five to ten years of marriage. Researchers surmise that romantically enthralled newlyweds with unrealistic expectations tend to be
quickly disillusioned and to divorce early on, as the froth wears off
(which makes me think that lacy, romantically frilled wedding gowns
like Princess Diana's might be sartorial omens of divorce). Marriage
defenders therefore talk of "surviving" the first years, as if they were
discussing cancer morbidity rates or loan amortization tables.

But this romance backlash is widespread, and not confined to
defense-of-marriage forces. You can't even skim newspaper commentary on marriage without encountering romance-desecrating headlines like "Marriages Take Hard Work," a Man in the Gray Flannel
Pajamas approach to going to work in your marriage. "Many enter

marriage with false hopes, that romantic notion of living happily ever after," a *Houston Chronicle* columnist explains, characteristically. "To avoid divorce, we must prepare for marriage not with the glazed look of fairy tale expectations but with the unwavering gaze and the realistic knowledge that it takes lots of effort." Conservative *New York Times* columnist David Brooks vividly opines that we'd be better off if we saw marriage "as a social machine which, if accompanied with the right instruction manual, can be useful for achieving practical ends." If the Romantic muse of marriage was the poet, his is the engineer. To stay married, "you just have to communicate until your knuckles bleed," a woman in marriage education explains with characteristically gruesome imagery. And maybe this idea of marriage as a well-geared machine, or hard labor, promises, if not happiness, then a kind of satisfaction in the solace of heroism, and the achievement of valor if not ecstasy. You're battling on the front lines, which is gratifying—so long as you choose the right metaphor and think of your marriage as a war story and not a love story, more as *The Longest Day* than *Casablanca*.

The romantic jeremiad seems to be getting internalized: A 2001 Gallup survey found that 80 percent of single respondents in their twenties anticipated marriage as "something that is hard and often difficult."

Shirin is unmarried, in her late thirties, and runs her own business in Los Angeles, after having been a "corporate slave for many, many years." Her feelings toward romantic marriage typify the larger ambivalence. "I think marriage is passé in this time and age," she first tells me. "It doesn't jibe with the way we've evolved as people. I think it will become extinct or rather unusual at some point. Since the practical need is no longer there, what else is left? Love, love, love. I feel every decision in our life is practical. If we can't have one aspect be somewhat magical, then what is the point?" So Shirin sees herself partly as a defender of the romantic faith, and follows the progression that Coontz describes, from marriage as a practical need to an emotional, romantic bond. But Shirin ventures further. "Now that I've read every self-help book Barnes & Noble has to offer," she concedes, "I see that there is no such thing." The "ones who make your heart flip" are just "romantic love, not *real* love. I kind of believe that now." Shirin allows that the romantic ideal is probably an illusion, but it's her illusion all the same, and not easily dislodged, however quixotic. "It seems a no-win situation," she concludes wistfully. Like others our age, Shirin was born into the romantic dream and grew up in its twilight, imprinted with a romantic archetype that she no longer entirely trusts.

I'm of two minds about this true-love backlash. Many vernacular romantic ideals are probably better off discarded in marriage. It's wincingly naïve, I think, to hope for ongoing and conflict-free happiness, or for a spouse who telepathically knows your needs and satisfies you fully, or even for a psychologically "undamaged" spouse. Good luck finding one. A realist hopes instead for a husband with neuroses that complement and mesh smoothly with her own.

But aren't there some yearnings, not necessarily "romantic" at all, such as feeding your soul in a marriage, or having a marriage that enriches your life in ways that matter to you, or having an animate, alive marriage that you don't have to tirelessly buttress with duty, or a marriage that makes your life bigger than it would otherwise be, well worth fighting for? Is any marital ambition just a version of foolish romanticism? It feels in some of this backlash that "romantic" has become a catch-all invective against any marital dream that ventures beyond stable, nonviolent persistence. The abridgement of romantic naïveté seems reasonable enough to me, but not the abridgement of marital hope, or even greed.

If the romantic heyday is waning, its ideal wilting under the heat of criticism and experience alike, a new mood is taking shape to challenge it. It seems that marital stability, even mediocrity, is getting promoted almost as an ideal. This is an improvised, secret marital experiment: What happens if you replace the dream of being adored with the dream of being stable? In this mood, some marriages seek equilibrium over drama; intimacy over romance; the stable over the sublime; low stress over high passion. They nudge stable pragmatism from normal (what lasting marriages often *are*) to normative (what they ideally *should* be). If romantics saw marriage as a setting for the gem of passion, these spouses see marriage and passion as antinomies, and elementally incompatible.

I hear stirrings of this post-romantic ideal in conversation and interviews. "Personal happiness isn't the most important thing to me in marriage. I'm not a fun-seeker," declares Maggie, who is in a long-term committed relationship. "A woman after my heart," condones John when I share this with him.

Beth, my best friend from college, reflects, "It's just *unrealistic* to think that the person you talk to about hiring a plumber is going to be your big love affair." For her, despite the shortcomings and a crisis or two in her marriage, it's "the grit" she prizes in marriage, and its consolingly reliable traditions and routines on a day-to-day basis. No matter what dramas or setbacks, she says, "at the end of the year, we'll be lighting that Christmas tree together." You don't see Hallmark anniversary cards in homage to grit, but this is Beth's expectation in marriage, and it's not an uncommon or incomprehensible one.

Shirin lives on the wavering frontier between the romantic and post-romantic but has many friends who are "more practically oriented." She observes that what they most seek, and desire, is the experience of a "'next stage' of life"—marriage and children—more than "fireworks." Around these friends who have "gone the practical route," Shirin feels as if she's been "zeroed in from another planet. I think it's a combination of personality and (to be very frank) friends who are more concerned with being comfortable financially and safe emotionally." They quest after stable, middle elements of the periodic table over the unstable ones at the extreme. "In this day and age, people want the guarantee and the security. If you take the risk of choosing only love, you can come out empty-handed, a chance I am taking right now."

A more pronounced, literal version of the "practical route" is evident in what I abbreviate as the Marry Marriage mood. Don't nitpick the guy, embrace the institution; if you're married in a vaguely discontented way, trade bliss for the larger comforts of Marriage. The idea meshes with but is by no means confined to the marriage movement. Lori Gottlieb wrote a bestselling book on the idea of giving up the quest for Mr. Right. It's a couples society; overlook minor flaws in mates and choose marriage. Gottlieb invited women who professed a life of happy singledom to inspect themselves in the mirror and find disingenuousness staring back at them.

As part of what seems to me an amorphous but pervasive campaign to convince us that men are big dumb idiots, so just pick one and marry him and don't expect too much, right-wing radio host Dr. Laura (Schlessinger) has asserted that all that men truly want from women is "sex and someone to make them a sandwich." There are terms for women who provide these services: *prostitute* and *maid*. In addition to wanting sex and the sandwich, the men I knew when single also had brains, talents, ambitions, hobbies, and political causes that they wanted to share with their eventual wives. At a time when marriage has the potential to be anything but banal, it's rhapsodized for its banality.

Playfully, the cultish love for emperor penguins among school-age girls might have roots in this newfound affection for fantasizing husbands as loosely interchangeable and blandly dutiful, too. Girls still imbibe the Princess dream, but they also adore the fairy tale of penguins. A few years ago young girls in my neighborhood became habitués of online "penguin chat rooms" and adored the *March of the Penguins*, which grossed $77 million. They consumed penguin chic paraphernalia. But if you think about it, penguins are nothing if not prototypes of the entirely fungible, and stable, McHusband. They all look and sound and act and "dress" exactly alike, the Men in the Gray Flannel Suits, or tuxedos, as the case may be, of the animal world, and each penguin is just like another. They don't stray. They have no prospect, really, to fall in love with a more attractive, younger penguin. They return to the same spot every year, and waddle dutifully through the sometimes fatal tragedies of their domestic, good-provider script.

Adults, meanwhile, are growing fonder of arranged marriage and matchmaking, a pre-romantic Marry Marriage practice that has taken an improbable journey from barbaric to vogue in this post-romantic century. Like emperor penguins, one husband is more or less like another. A British woman who arranges marriages on a reality TV show calls the practice "very modern now." For these spouses, Mr. Right is deferring to Mr. Right Here. No more the dream of our perfect mate wandering about in the world, whom we discover by epiphany in the checkout line at Target or, as a divorced friend of mine fantasizes, "while riding on Amtrak."

Matchmaking is already very much in the mainstream, if we count eHarmony, the most wildly successful matchmaker of all time. With 20 million registered clients since its inception in 2000, eHarmony has facilitated an average of 236 marriages a day. Match.com is a virtual singles bar, which tosses applicants together online, but eHarmony is a virtual shtetl matchmaker, with the demystifying matchmaker role of the elder assigned to its trademarked "Compatibility Matching System," a meticulous five-hundred-question test. With eHarmony, as with any other matchmaker, the potential spouse entrusts the initial selections to reason over desire; method over epiphany. A go-between—the scientific system, in this case—screens and suggests mates based on clear-eyed expertise. "Who knew love and science could be so compatible?" eHarmony marvels at itself.

Robert Epstein, former editor of *Psychology Today*, published a controversial editorial in 2002 proposing that we shouldn't "fall" in love. Instead we should go about it deliberately and rationally, and then learn to have a happy marriage. He proposed a "love contract" by which he and a woman would learn to love each other through "extensive counseling sessions." Although Epstein stopped short of recommending arranged marriage (and eventually found a partner in a more conventional way), he noted in another article that "60 percent of the world's weddings are planned that way." The American "love marriage" based on physical attraction and romance, he declared, is "really, really horrible." It's a solid point. The romantic marriage with its notions of chronic dependency and emotional fulfillment wasn't, and isn't, such a tenable script, and these chapters will show ways that it's being unraveled today. Still, I do wonder if there isn't an alternative marriage muse for us, somewhere between the poet and the mechanic.

The endorsement of marital realism (or is it mediocrity?) isn't just an abstraction of marriage politics. The idea gets transmitted and reinforced every day in our own lives, through the usual capillaries of gossip, storytelling, and social opinion. Marital standards and norms are always an ad hoc conspiracy, arrived at spontaneously (in the 1970s, there was a certain social reward and approval placed on leaving marriages, in pursuit of the now-quaint elements of liberation, "self-discovery," or personal fulfillment): We must all agree tacitly that there's nothing different, or more, to want out of marriage, and then informally police those who insist on just that.

Pete comes to mind. He has three children, a wife, and a stable but unfulfilling personal and professional life. He's a smart and clever man who could probably change things. But he says to John, "This is just the way the world is," claiming the commanding mantle of the embattled realist. Later he says, "We're all angry. I'm an angry man," and urges John to "just get over" his disappointment. In a version of a lowering tide that grounds all boats, he seeks the peculiar Sticking It Out solace of feeling that we're all disappointed together, and that being a responsible adult to some extent means being gloomy, and that there's not much to be done about it. Because his capacity to accept mediocrity depends upon his sense of its universality and inevitability, Pete has a tendency to feel threatened, lash out, and even become judgmental when other breadwinning husbands and fathers try to break out of the harness. In urgently real, if odd, ways, Pete's personal equanimity really *does* have something to do with your marriage: It depends on other spouses conspiring to stay put with the same droopiness. Spouses like Pete can appear squeamishly afflicted by proxy when their friends divorce, as if a voodoo doll likeness of their marriage has been stuck violently with pins. Lily, who will appear in a later chapter, says, "Our friends were *shocked* by the divorce. Then, they think it's contagious. Friends act like it's a disease they might get." That's my impression, too.

There's a great amount of shame heaped on marital dissolution and even marital weirdness today. My inner voice and personification of that shame is a Greek chorus, assembled over years of pro-marriage, family values cant. The chorus frets, mocks, chants, and advises in my head like ambient ethical Muzak. Its composition changes, but has included conservative James Dobson, formerly of Focus on the Family, my parents, and our tax advisor. Occasionally I cast members from my son's carpool line. "What will *people think?*" the chorus exhorts me. "You're not going to *divorce*, are you? I wouldn't do that if I were you! Get over it! That'll *never* work!"

In particular, two judgments—"selfish" and "whiny"—probably do more than any others to create shame and police marital ambitions. They work like rhetorical prods that herd us into the closet with our treasonous contemplations against marriage, and make secret subversives out of us. I hear the terms frequently or, sometimes, just "selfishandwhiny," slurred quickly into one omnibus insult. They're spoken by nonjudgmental, thoughtful people, who are not religious or socially conservative in their views of marriage. There are distinct marital cultures in the United States today, divided by attitudes and class, that shape, in one scholar's phrase, different "marital stances." One America of marriage, in my shorthand, looks like 21st century Sweden; the other more like 19th century Kansas. But of the two Americas of marriages, the Bible Belt has the highest divorce rate in the country today while Massachusetts has the lowest. If marital values play into that divorce gap, then it seems that the secular selfish and whiny judgments cut as deep as the biblical and evangelical ones.

Many kinds of wives are thus accused, from a wife and mother who has a career, which is selfish (and it's odd to hear the work ethic described that way), to a stay-at-home mother who questions her marriage when she should feel lucky she doesn't have to work, which is whiny. Most of all, selfish gets applied to the wife who confronts the moment of self-recognition that something big is missing in her marriage, and decides to leave a Great Guy—a McHusband—for "no good reason," and when "there's nothing *wrong* with the marriage," as I've heard said.

Shame generically favors the surface over the depths; it favors the pretty still life. But that's especially so today, with our pro-marriage views and our perilous confusion as to the difference between looking like something and being something. And in any case, at some point in a marriage and middle age, it becomes difficult to distinguish between the simulacrum of a happy marriage and the real thing. It's as if marriage is a Kabuki performance, in which the shadow becomes the show itself.

The dilemma for a halfhearted marriage is that in these anti-romantic, and tentatively post-romantic, times, we can be genuinely confused as to whether we can even trust our yearnings. Is a partially unfulfilling but stable marriage a romantic failure or a post-romantic ideal? When you stay, maybe you have realistic expectations or maybe you're just rationalizing mediocrity; when you leave, maybe you're courageous or maybe you're just selfishly deluded. In the gloaming of the romantic age, we've valorized marital mediocrity, and called it realism; we've vilified marital ambition, and called it selfish. Consequently, at a time when marriage could be anything, we very often expect it to be less.

||||||||||

Josie didn't recalibrate her expectations, though. She divorced. She didn't divorce to seek the "big passion" outside marriage, but to seek a marriage that unifies passion and domesticity. "I want a partner who craves me and wants to throw me down on the floor in passion, but can't because I'm cooking dinner and tending to my children first, and I'm holding her off, and she finds that sexy," Josie told me after the fact.

This, for her, is a yearning for home inscribed like DNA in her soul. She explains her divorce today by saying that she had a responsibility to honor her own humanity as well as her family. The breakup was financially devastating for her, as they often are, but Josie doesn't regret it. Friends will still occasionally tell her, years later, that they hope she'll get back together with Rory some day, as it seemed like a nice life. While she and Rory are very amiable and good friends, the idea baffles and amuses her, since she chose "integrity over convenience."

Early one workday morning not too long ago, Josie calls me. "I'm fuming," she declares on the way to her office. She's often doing four things at once. She continues the conversation as she walks into her building and pushes the elevator button. Her cellphone periodically interrupts our conversation with a sound like a cow farting, to warn her that she's already talked so long this morning that its battery is dying.

Josie had been with an old friend the night before. Although her friend had complained about her marriage bitterly, she managed to leave Josie feeling judged for having divorced.

"Maybe my kids will have lasting marriages, and maybe they won't," Josie continues. "But they *will* know that when you're *unhappy*," she says, "you do something to change, you take action in your life to make it better. She just wants to vent, and then go crawl back into her unhappy marriage and feel superior about her choices."

It's true that people who divorce from low-conflict but sad marriages to Good Guys and Wonderful Wives get little sympathy in our anti-divorce age. After Josie divorced I thought a lot about her decision and the more I mulled it, the more I saw its logic. In any marriage, you have to decide what part of yourself you're willing to let go. A marriage adds things to your life, and it also takes things away. Constancy kills joy; joy kills security; security kills desire; desire kills stability; stability kills lust. Something gives; some part of you recedes. It's something you can live without, or it's not. And maybe it's hard to know before the marriage which part of the self is expendable—a callow, perhaps romantic, expectation for a marriage, usefully outgrown—and which is part of your spirit. Marriage alchemizes each spouse's character, and changes it. Eventually, though, a core element—a part of your character, or a passion, a career ambition, a dream, your faith, or a group of friends, perhaps—long dissolved within a marriage's alloy, may reconstitute itself.

In Josie's case it wasn't a childish expectation of "constant happiness" that provoked the decision to divorce but a moment of self-recognition that cut deeper. A husband or wife can realize that the part of themselves they gave up to be married is too vital and big to live without. And, at some point, through whatever random, incidental, or premeditated events in life, they can lose the capacity not to care about that loss. This probably happens to other wives as well, whose divorces are inscrutable to those who see the résumé perfection of the match. Josie was choosing her "adult humanity," she will say today, over compromising melancholy.

Josie has little patience with stories from the annals of melancholy marriages. "They chose their convenient life," she's apt to say. "That's what happens." She thinks that low-conflict, low-stress unhappy marriages smother the wives' (and husbands') humanity. "If she divorced," Josie speculates vigorously about one of my friends, "she'd lose weight, she'd have more *energy*, she'd probably go out and have a big *love affair* herself." Josie can always conjure, and liberate, a better life and a happier woman beneath the insulating layers of a mediocre marriage. She's extremely persuasive. When she talks this way, I catch a quick glimpse of the New and Improved Wife, her true spirit pleasingly disincarnated from her marriage. Ideally, things can change within a marriage, Josie advises, but if the marriage reaches a quagmire where change "becomes impossible to imagine," then it's almost a duty to your soul to divorce, and this was her decision, to take a risk for something more at the cost of the known and stable world that she had.

In these disenchanted times the melancholy spouse most often chooses from among three options. The first option is to heed the anti-romantic or post-romantic idea that we are asking too much of marriage. This enables us to view the nagging "is this it?" question as self-defeating and greedy. Still, as Shirin has found, it's maddeningly difficult to shake the shadow of your own dream, especially after you've been reminded of it.

A second option is to decide that marriage just isn't for us, and to renounce the estate of marriage in general as oppressive, futile, or archaic. Make "The Case Against Marriage," as the *Atlantic* headlined an essay by Sandra Tsing Loh in 2009. That's a more popular stance in the "post-marriage" countries of Western Europe, where, for example, a married Swedish professor and mother of four comments, "traditional values are not important to us anymore. They are something we do research on—like a fossil." France's then defense minister Michèle Alliot-Marie, who lives in a long-term unmarried partnership, dismissed marriage as a vestigial "bourgeois institution" in a 2006 interview.

A third option is to renounce your spouse, conclude that he or she was the wrong man or the wrong woman, divorce, and become a serial monogamist, convinced that the next spouse will work out better. In some marriages, divorce may very well be the life-affirming direction, however judged you may be for it.

In other cases, though, divorce doesn't feel right, either, because we *know* that we have happy marriages in some really important ways, and we wish, halfheartedly, that we could stay married, even as the other half pulls toward separation. A whole dilemma of these marriages is that they truly aren't that bad. They're just partial. Usually they have the vices of their virtues. Many sentences to describe a functioning but not great marriage begin, "If only I could . . ." or "If we just could . . ." If only our marriage came with a sabbatical; if only we could have separate spaces; if only we could save *this* part of the marriage and not *that* part. The favored tense of the low-conflict, low-stress marriage is the conditional—the tense of conjecture, wonder, and speculation. But it seems that if the marriage fails fatally in another aspect that we really care about, then we're stuck throwing the baby out with the bathwater. So we are left feeling that we have no choices but to change our marriage dreams, change spouses, or disown the idea of Marriage on principle. As my friend Beth once said, "marriage kills options"—or so it feels to us.

The remarkable thing in all of this is that we don't try to change Marriage instead. Such institutional dysfunction isn't really tolerated in the private sector. Divorce lawyer Raoul Felder marvels about marriage that "there is no product in the world (except perhaps commercial Xerox machines) that has a 50 percent breakdown rate, and is still in business."

This surprises me. We're dramatically freer to change marriage to suit our temper than any generation before us. My parents didn't have our feeling of latitude. They wed in 1952, during the heyday of the marriage consensus: a time when marriage with children was the norm, for all classes, and "everyone was pregnant," as John Updike recalled in a *New Yorker* essay. Scholar Claudia Goldin describes women who graduated from college between 1946 and 1965. In 1946, the average age at first marriage for women overall was at its earliest, at under twenty years. About 90 percent of college-educated women in this cohort married, and about 90 percent of them had children. Half of them married by age twenty-three, probably to someone they met in college. College-educated women married at the same high rate as women who attended no college at all. Economically, single women didn't have many options in jobs or professions. In 1963, almost all wage-earning women (90 percent) made five thousand dollars or less a year. The number of women graduated from all U.S. law schools combined in 1956 would have fit comfortably in a large Starbucks. Amid concerns about the Vietnam draft, Harvard Law School dean Nathan Pusey complained that for students, "we shall be left with the lame, the blind, and women." Americans married young, and more or less compulsorily. As my eighty-year old mother recalls, there wasn't much else, or better, to do. "There are worse things in life than being *bored* and unfulfilled," my mother would advise me each time I discarded another Nice Young Potential Son-in-Law with a Safely Bland Personality.

Marriage was the story starter for my parents' generation. They married each other and "built a life together" *as a marriage*, as one unit ("how's your better half?" the old greeting went). Marriage wasn't a part of adulthood. It was the woof and warp of adulthood, the fabric out of which an adult life was cut. Spouses began and built their careers, bought and furnished their first houses, discovered their sexuality (more or less), forged their social networks, established their social identity, and had children, all as a joint creation of the marriage, and this was the norm of the era.

Some look back fondly on the marriage consensus era. These spouses might have enjoyed a happiness and camaraderie, under lucky circumstances, as my parents did, of being all in it together, following the same McMarriage script as everybody else. The consensus also left many unhappy, stunted, and vulnerable. It was built on sex inequality and rigid gender roles. "I hadn't really wanted to marry at all," recalls writer Alix Kates Shulman of the early 1960s. "I wanted to make something of myself. . . . But I knew if I didn't marry I would be sorry. Only freaks didn't." Shulman also knew she'd have to marry early, before all the decent men were taken. With the consolation of consensus comes the oppression of conformity. It would take Betty Friedan's galvanizing work to expose the plight of the housewife, and the subsequent women's movement, to undo some of that damage. In either case, whether we think the consensus era was qualitatively better or worse, without a doubt the place of marriage has changed on us.

Today, we most often marry in mid-plot of our lives. This is one of the most basic and consequential marriage trends of the last four decades. We marry with many aspects of our lives already formed. We've finished our education, gotten our first job, or embarked on our career, bought our first house, built an adult social support network and contacts, maybe traveled a bit, and had sex. Many of us come to our marriages pre-loved, and pre-heartbroken. We've fallen in love, hard, before we meet our spouses. The Big Love or passion of our lives and the Husband may or may not be the same person.

My generation grew up on the cusp, between the era of marriage as an imperative and the era of marriage as an option. We came of age during the momentous rhetorical shift from *"When* I marry . . ." to *"If* I marry . . ."* The marriage imperatives had faded. We didn't need marriage for a meal ticket; we didn't need it to secure our social identity or to have a sex life; we didn't even need it to have children, as the idea of "single motherhood by choice" was just beginning to take off in the late 1980s.

This means that where marriage used to be a thick institution—one that had numerous overlapping and reinforcing imperatives, stubbornly impacted and therefore difficult to change—it's now a thinner and more spindly institution, which stands or falls on its own. But it also means that we have unprecedented latitude to define marriage in our own image, and not in our parents' image. The women's movement did the heavy lifting for us and created the options that freed us from the imperatives to marry.

In this light, it's a fascinating paradox, and one deeply relevant to the plight of the low-conflict, lugubrious marriage, that the facts, circumstances, and the shell of marriage have changed so breathtakingly in the post-liberation era, yet the soul of marriage—its dreams, conscience, ethics, and rules—hasn't necessarily evolved to keep up. Instead we follow viscerally many of the same premises and orthodoxies as our parents, as if marriage is a Procrustean structure to which we must conform ourselves, rather than the other way around. To be sure, some of those rules are worth holding on to. But maybe others are worth tweaking and reinventing. Or, at least, they may be worth reinventing in the marriages that interest me here, those that are partially satisfying but melancholy, and swirling around the drain of divorce. As the iconoclast and architect R. Buckminster Fuller urged, "do not try to change man." Try to "change his environment" instead.

By the "rules" of marriage I have in mind something different and more metaphysical than, say, gender roles. Most of us don't want our parents' "traditional marriages" in the sense of gendered chores or wifely subordination. Research in 2002 found that if women had to choose between remaining single or being in a traditional marriage thus defined, an overwhelming 80 percent would opt to remain single. (This statistic leads me to speculate, incidentally, that traditional marriage might be killing traditional marriage in the divorce-plagued Bible Belt today. Maybe marriage survives best by swaying a little with the winds rather than bracing against them.) Instead, by rules I mean more basic challenges to Marriage, but within its traditional framework—something more than chore reallocation, but less than polygamy. This might mean some secret audacity, like rethinking the expectation of lifelong marital monogamy, or the idea that marriage is structured to meet most all of our needs for intimacy, or that it is a unit for social mobility and greater prosperity, or even that marriage means, ideally, living in the same household, or that marriage is forever. Maybe a marriage could just be, by intention, a temporary parenting arrangement. There are many premises, and many possibilities. These are only a few that come to mind.

One change-impeding phrase that I come across almost as often as "selfishandwhiny" is "a real marriage." We all want a "real marriage," not some fake, off-brand marriage, but what does it *mean?* The phrase is at once emphatic and vague. Today, a marital litmus test is invoked most often from pro-marriage forces and opponents of gay marriage who campaign that a "real marriage" or a "natural marriage," as they have also coined it, can only be "between a man and a woman," and wish the Constitution would say so. Liberals reject that standard, but many of us have our own privately held gold standards of marital authenticity all the same.

One wife I talk to holds that a commuter marriage that doesn't involve the trials and intimacies of cohabitation is "not a real marriage," but a "weekend thing—marriage as a hobby." Secretly, more than one of my friends view the childfree marriage as not entirely real, because its bindings are loose and guiltlessly sundered in comparison, although they would never be so rude as to say so aloud, and confine that conversation to their spouses and to other married friends with children.

I've heard married people say categorically that a marriage stops being a marriage when it doesn't involve sexual intimacy, or when it isn't sexually monogamous. I have a friend who is very successful, worldly, secular, and not romantically florid in her marital views. Very late one evening, after a party, we kick around the topic of marriage and the matter of marital sex, or lack thereof. She speaks almost biblically of "conjugal duty." She says she might prefer not to have her body "invaded" sometimes, but she manages. She isn't talking about marital rape, she hastens to reassure me, and I believe her, but about reciprocal sexual duties, which is for her the watermark of an authentic marriage.

"What if you didn't do it when you didn't feel like it?"

"Well . . . then it's not a real marriage, is it?"

There's a standard of a real marriage lurking out there, even in secular minds not apoplectic about gay marriage. The number of reality TV shows about "real housewives" alone speaks to our anxiety about what marriage really is these days, but the thought of not having a real marriage can shame us out of trying to change marriage.

John and I develop a metaphor that the "real marriage" is like a pugilistic bully who backs otherwise goodhearted, well-intentioned, honorable, but not entirely successful marriages into the corner of divorce. Just because it fixes such a standard for what marriage *is* if you don't meet the standard, you feel prodded toward separation. John says, "We have all of these unique ways to be friends, or to do other kinds of relationships. But on the relationship that's the most unique, a marriage, we impose the most rules."

As a result we have a collective file cabinet, or maybe a Pandora's box, full of private, creative ideas for reinventing marriage. John and I have both mentally tinkered with various ideas. "Have term limits," John once suggested. "Make a marriage a ten- or fifteen-year thing. Then if it's going well, you renew the contract. The whole-life thing, it's too difficult." Maybe marriage shouldn't ideally be forever. Maybe we could have a few "successful" marriages in the course of one lifetime. The poet Jack Gilbert questions if a marriage is "failing" as it dies, or if it is just coming to the end of its triumph.

I love John's term-limits idea and I investigate it a little. As it turns out, Bavaria's "most glamorous politician," strange as that is to imagine, advanced just this idea. Gabriele Pauli is a beautiful redhead in her fifties, an avid motorcyclist who once posed for a magazine wearing long black latex gloves and motorcycle leathers. She shocked voters in her deeply Catholic state by proposing during a 2007 election campaign that marriages should come with an expiration date and automatically amortize after seven years; if the couple was still happy they could extend the marriage then. The idea went nowhere. Her party, the Christian Social Union, likened Pauli's idea to "the dirt under your fingernails," and German consumer minister Horst Seehofer, a contender for head of the CSU, called it "absurd." But he had little credibility, since he had been having a long-term extramarital affair with a younger woman and had fathered a child with her. His stance isn't unusual. We'll break the marriage rules that don't work so well anymore before we'll condone revising them.

I admire the work of Alternatives to Marriage, the only national organization that advocates against marital discrimination, but what interests me even more are alternatives *within* marriage, a way to evolve marriage to suit our times, or the changing temper of our marital love. This, to me, is the real lost opportunity and potential of my marriage generation.

It's been a lost opportunity in my own marriage, too. Together, John and I look like the sort of predictable, milquetoast couple you'd ask for directions if you were lost in a strange city. In other words, we are the straightest married couple you could hope to meet. "When you walked in tonight I thought to myself, 'Wow, there's a *straight* lady,'" a lesbian friend of a friend told me once at a party, and she didn't mean it at all unkindly.

"What about thinking outside the box?" I tease John, sometimes.

"I *like* the box," he responds. "It's safe in there; you know where everything is." We have been, John and I, a box-loving marriage.

Graham Greene once described vultures that had been laboriously trained to hang on a tree branch and persisted inertly in this habit even when set free. They couldn't think of anything else to do. In my marriage, I feel a bit like those vultures. Up until recently, I hadn't seriously entertained new rules, forging a third way between melancholy persistence and divorce. This book recounts stories and insights from a journey to understand the sources of marital discontent today, and to seek out ways of doing things differently, in a spirit of marital adventure and even risk. It begins where our marriages start: with husbands and wives who are more like each other than ever before in their education and careers. They—we—are heirs, on the surface, to the dream of a post-liberation marriage.

PART I

The New Normals
of Career and Marriage

CHAPTER TWO

"LIFE PARTNERS"

How Too Much Intimacy Killed Intimacy

N 1963, THE FEMININE MYSTIQUE brilliantly and consequentially named the "problem that has no name," the vague marital melancholy that beset author Betty Friedan's own age. I often find myself returning to her canonical, galvanizing pages in my contemplation of marriage, and the vague melancholy of our own age. Friedan reminds me of the post-liberation dream for marriage in its pristine inception, before the women's movement grew and took on more intricate, multifarious agendas and real-world complications. For Friedan, the lack of economic, vocational equality or opportunity for women and wives was at the heart of the suburban housewife's depression. Friedan worried deeply about the "stunting" of a wife's human potential and growth through lack of opportunities for meaningful vocation, work, or career. "It is wrong for a woman, for whatever reason, to spend the days in work that is not moving, as the world around her is moving, in work that does not truly use her creative energy," Friedan wrote. "Surely there are many women in America who are happy at the moment as housewives. . . . But happiness is not the same thing as the aliveness of being fully used." Keeping Friedan's words informally in mind as a touchstone, the four chapters in this part will look at what became of her dream of productive work and career for wives and husbands after liberation—after we were freed from organizing work and marriage according to the mad housewife and breadwinning husband script of the romantic era. In so many ways, the dream came true. We can arrange work, career, and marriage in any number of forms, and we enjoy more closeness and parity with our spouses in education and career than ever before. But in coming true, the dream also created new post-romantic variations of melancholy, and imbalances in the dreariness quotient of marriage that Friedan never would have anticipated.

I'm having dinner with Allen, an older, wiser friend. We're mulling marriage. He pauses thoughtfully as he considers my marital history, and says, "You and John seem like life partners to me." Life Partners? Good lord, I thought, it sounds like an HMO or a biotech start-up. I can see it embossed on promotional water bottles and pens. On further reflection, though, I think Allen's phrase is an apt one to describe not just my own marriage but many others of our day. In what scholar Barbara Risman calls "postgender" marriages, the roles of husband and wife aren't demarcated or unequal. The most basic and striking thing about a "Life Partners" marriage is that we have unprecedented equality and affinity with our spouses in education, career and work, temperaments, worldviews, life experiences, and earnings potential than ever before. On the whole this is precisely what liberation was about, and is indisputably a good thing. But it can have curious and vexing, entirely collateral effects on how we feel, and live, intimately within marriage.

Essentially, John and I married ourselves. We were part of the much larger "assortative mating" trend that underlies the Life Partners marriage. Assortative mating means that like is marrying like, with almost Linnaean precision. In a 2005 article in *Demography*, Christine Schwartz and Robert Mare documented a trend toward strong assortative mating by education level and corresponding career tracks. "Educational homogamy" (similarity of spousal education and careers) decreased from 1940 to 1960, during the romantic heyday, but starting in the 1970s and continuing into the 21st century, the odds of educational intermarriage have decreased. Such studies imply that as equality grows within marriage, because we're marrying our equals, inequality grows *across* marriages—rich marriages get richer and poor marriages get poorer. This subverts the romantic-era Cinderella narrative of marriage as a route to upward mobility, as well, for a less-educated woman.

Curious about this trend, I read the wedding announcements from the *New York Times* and the *Baltimore Sun* for the last few months of 2008. I compile a sample of 120 couples whose educational backgrounds were mentioned in the announcement and organize them on a spreadsheet. Only one of the 120 features a non–college-educated spouse, a firefighter, who married a college-educated woman. My heart sang when I saw it! There's a romantic in me *somewhere*, I guess. The couple achieved this democratic feat when Mr. Wright (yes, his real name) gave a CPR refresher course to the crew of a sailboat designed by his fiancée's company. They met there, and the world of yachting and firefighting were improbably joined in matrimony.

Aside from Mr. Wright, all—*all*—of the other announcements in my sample feature homogamous couples, by the most basic criterion that each partner has at least a college degree. Many have the same professional degrees, too. But this doesn't tell the whole story of what amounts to hyper-assortative mating.

I cross-reference my announcements spreadsheet with the controversial but deeply influential *U.S. News & World Report* college rankings for 2008. It turns out that college-educated men and women are sorting themselves microscopically according to their particular *kind* of college or university, as measured by selectivity, prestige, price tag, and rank. To use only undergraduate degrees as a point of comparison, the couples in 70 of the 120 cases (58 percent) either attended the same college or university (and researchers have noted that colleges have taken over the matchmaking functions previously reserved for churches, community organizations, and neighborhoods) or, more often, attended colleges and universities practically identical in terms of ranking and selectivity. Some managed to find soul mates from schools three thousand miles away but proximal to their own college in the ranks (for example, a woman from the University of Florida, ranked 49th, married a man from the University of California at San Diego, ranked 35th).

What variation I do find is pretty meager. In 23 cases (19 percent) the husband's college outranked the wife's, and in 27 cases (22 percent) the wife's college outshone the husband's, but rarely dramatically. Forget about zany intereducational leaps of the kind you'd see in a romantic comedy, high-school-educated bricklayers marrying spunky, beautiful lawyers. It's not even that common to find a modest, *intra*-tier mixed marriage—the woman from Harvard, for example, who got engaged to a man from the eminently respectable but not-Ivy Rutgers. More than a few of the fiancés with Ivy League affiliations married partners who attended the "honorary Ivy" colleges popularly known as the "Harvard of the [Insert Region Here]." A bride graduated from Stanford, "the Harvard of the West," while her husband got a law degree from the Harvard Harvard. Kevin attended the University of Pennsylvania and his wife, Stacey, attended McGill, "the Harvard of Canada," and so on. Harvard should sell T-shirts that say, "Harvard: The Harvard of the Northeast."

This kind of microsorting happens among graduates of the "lower tier" colleges mentioned in the *Baltimore Sun* as well. It's not just an artifact of elite *New York Times* power couples and the cabalistic Ivy League. My sample includes a smattering of interracial couples and same-sex couples—but they are not intereducational couples or, in this regard, all that unconventional. An African American man from Princeton married a white woman, also from Princeton; two men who married each other were both graduates of Ivy League colleges.

In the late 1990s, I participated in a press conference with Betty

Friedan. She quipped that at some point a woman's Ph.D. could be as attractive an asset to men as her "boobs." Although I recoiled to hear a Ph.D.—perhaps even my Ph.D.—juxtaposed with boobs as a sexual asset on the marriage market, even in a feminist spirit, her impromptu speculation is proving true. Megan Sweeney and Maria Cancian find that men today value strong earnings potential in a prospective wife as much as women always have in prospective husbands. In other words, if you want to marry a Ph.D. then get one yourself.

The shift toward assortative mating and the blur of colleague into spouse is evident even in how we appraise potential mates. Jake is a professionally successful engineer who manages complex systems. When he was a single man, he devised his own test, a "gap analysis instrument," to help him sort through his ideas about marriage prospects. He thought of every "substantive romantic relationship" he'd ever had and wrote down "what was great and what wasn't" about each one. From there he sorted the qualities into columns, looking for the positive and negative words that recurred, and "came up with four categories of things, rank-ordered by priority," that he wanted in a future marriage: "warmth, intelligence, beauty, and sophistication"—"WIBS," Jake named it, by the irresistible urge to acronym in Washington, D.C. Jake hastened to explain that by "beauty" he meant something deeper than physical appearance, a sort of beauty of the soul. He didn't rank the women he dated numerically, but when he was "feeling ambivalent" he would WIBS them and "go through the list and see if I could figure out why." The "concrete rational approach" helped when things were confusing. He assessed potential spouses by similar tests, metrics, and instruments as they would potential employees, partners, or colleagues.

It occurs to me, though, that as regards money and career, liberation from the old marriage imperatives has worked on men and women in totally opposite ways. Liberation freed women *from* having to appraise husbands as meal tickets and sources of social status—while the same liberation "freed" men *to start* appraising wives as meal tickets and sources of social status. And, as 2010 research reveals, men indeed do have more to gain today from marriage than women, since more wives are likely to have greater income and education than their husbands, in comparison to the 1970 cohort. Granted, marriage is a pragmatic institution dressed in drag as a sentimental one, but whatever hidden material motives we may have, women go to great pains to disown them, even as some men now feel liberated to *claim* them.

This new liberty for career-focused single men is exaggerated in epicenters of ambition such as New York City. I talk to several single women in their late thirties and they describe, cumulatively, something like the Panda Men of Manhattan, those who, like giant pandas, can't be bothered with the enervating, distracting rituals of arousal and mating. These women—one of whom is a beautiful aspiring actor, another, an accomplished attorney—were ditched by their serious boyfriends because, in the actor's case, he "wanted to be with someone who is more successful than you" and, in the attorney Samila's case, because her suitor "would want to marry someone who makes more money." The man who did end up proposing marriage to Samila during her single days in Manhattan was a prisoner, at Rikers Island. He had seen footage of Samila on a local evening news segment about a new technique for the management of frizzy hair. Samila was identified by name as a "Frizz Victim," and the convict tracked her down and sent her a letter. "Lots of the men in here have wives on the outside," he tantalized.

Finicky Panda Men live in my humbler hometown as well. Vanya is a charming woman who was educated in Moscow. She tells me that people need to marry younger as she did, at twenty-one, and "for passion." She herself married because she had a "strong urge to procreate," an unusually primal explanation, and one that I rarely hear in my conversations. When I ask her why she favors early marriage, she says, "These later marriages I don't understand. They are much more rational and calculating." As an example, she tells me of a psychologist she knows. He had a seemingly loving relationship with a woman and was contemplating marriage. Until he gave her an IQ test and found that she "dropped to average" in her score. He ditched her. "It was a shame," Vanya laments. "She was a warm person."

Meanwhile, if single men are now free to act more like single women in the 1950s—seeking a prosperous "Mr. Degree" in marriage, administering IQ tests, and aiming for someone who "makes more money"—then on the flip side, single women are now free to act more like men seeking a second, trophy wife. They can look for a nice "additive," in one wife's term, to an adult life whose essentials around money and career they have already built, by themselves. Like the husband who seeks a trophy spouse, these women are content to postpone marriage until they find someone who can truly complement and garnish their own independently achieved lives and accomplishments.

In any case, the trend toward marital homogamy will probably deepen because of changes in dating techniques as well. The founder of Craigslist, for example, observes that some people "have gotten their entire lives, from spouse to house to car to furnishings to vacations," from his service, so who needs to advertise? Spouse selection blurs into other life purchases, from *Star Trek* memorabilia to sofas. This is news. In 1952, the way you bought a refrigerator and the way you met your husband simply weren't the same. I remember distinctly the time when the personal ads ran obscurely and ignobly in free city newspapers, one category removed from escort services and listings of places to sell eggs, sperm, and platelets. Today half of American singles use online personals to find mates. The 40 million visitors to online dating services—half of the American singles population—might well find a spouse through Match.com or its techno-kin.

By their design alone these services favor even more finely honed assortative mating. Perhaps in a single person's natural habitat—a party or a bus stop—a professional might find herself lured haphazardly by a small charming gesture, or by pheromones, and fall in love with an unlikely man. With online screening capacities, she can seek her own kind with surgical concision.

"That's true," John agrees. "Would I have chosen you online? I would have had a screen, such as, must like cycling, or must be an athlete."

"*I* would have had one, too," I say, slightly miffed to think I'd have failed *his* screen. "Must know the difference between Eve Sedgwick and Edie Sedgwick, or must not confuse *affect* and *effect*."

"Remember for our first date?" John recalls. "I asked you on a bike ride, and you wrote back and said, 'Can't we go to a bar, instead?' And I overlooked that!" he marvels.

"Wasn't that lucky for you!"

"We never would've connected over Match.com. We'd have weeded each other out on a hobby screen and ended up with someone even *more* exactly and precisely like us."

All of this intimacy, in the sense of similarity, makes for strange variations on intimacy, in the sense of closeness. One Valentine's Day not too long ago I found myself staring baffled at a blank card as 6 P.M. approached. I was trying to think of meaningful and honest words, to encapsulate the bond between us. I could hear John taking the mail out of our mailbox. *Quick! Write something!* I scrawled the next sentence-like thing that popped into my head: "Thanks for ALL that you do!" I might have been writing a corporate commercial to air on *Meet the Press*: "A.D.M.," the voice-over would boom. "For *all* that they do." John and I joke about that phrase now, deploying the marital survival skill of humorous self-ridicule.

"We have something deeper than the deficits. It's a soul mate bond," John says these days. "I really see you that way."

Privately, the American embrace, and dilution, of Eastern spirituality amuses me a bit. Even my husband does it! *Soul mate* is so ubiquitous now that it's on its way to commercials for air freshener or instant coffee. It's the new black for American marriage. In 2001, the Marriage Project commissioned a Gallup survey and found that twenty-somethings almost unanimously (at 96 percent) agreed with the statement "When you marry, you want your spouse to be your soul mate, first and foremost." David Popenoe, the marriage researcher, worries that this is an inflated and self-defeating ideal for a spouse.

Probably so. But what interests me more than the term's quixotic airiness is its lack of romanticism. This gold standard of 21st century marriage, while unrealistic, isn't, strictly speaking, a romantic idea of finding a lover or an erotic counterpoint, a yin to your yang. It's not an ideal distinguished by passion or sensuality, nor is it inherently specific to a marital bond. According to its now profoundly smudged Hindu roots, the soul mate is anyone, from a child to a hairdresser to an annoying but karmically instructive neighbor, whom one has shared past lives with and will continue to encounter in future lives. Soul mate inflation runs rampant in America. A friend of mine applies it with sloppy largesse to our favorite bartender. The intimacy of a soul mate is unisex and generic, encompassing any kind of relationship. When I hear the term, as I so often do, I imagine an out-of-body marriage that floats incorporeally, one that regards itself as deeply intimate, but not romantic per se.

Wedding vows, the crystallization of our dream at its inception, reveal similarly unisex ideals. Couples increasingly prefer to personalize their vows, as part of the larger trend toward "unique" weddings. I gather a sample from online websites of the most popular wedding vows today. If we don't select the soul mate idiom, we borrow a page from Wall Street and the corporate world and declare ourselves to be "partners." As if we were rummaging through the annals of Cold War communism, we pledge ourselves stout "comrades," or "partners in parenthood." Favorite opening lines include: "I take you to be my partner" and "You are my best friend for life." One vow begins, "I take you as my partner, my friend, and my love" (presumably in that order), and continues almost as a list of performance benchmarks: "I will seek to balance my needs with those of our community and family. I will openly draw from our combined experience. . . ." Reading these vows I think of the quintessential comradely gesture of a marriage, the fist bump that Michelle and Barack Obama almost shyly exchanged after he won the nomination.

This notably androgynous ideal for marriage contradicts the romantic one, which holds that love and passion distinguish and exalt the relationship. Marriage in the romantic heyday enjoyed a status as a sui generis bond. A post-romantic marriage shares more characteristics with other intimacies and social bonds, whether between best friends, business associates, colleagues, or partners. There's not as much marriage in marriage anymore. It would be uncouth to declare in whatever delicately euphemized terms that you were marrying your red-hot lover because he drove you mad with lust, or because she really got your rocks off. Granted, this romantic model, and the traditional model that preceded it, had their own problems. But the post-romantic style, while perhaps not quantitatively better or worse than what came before, is a new sensibility that creates its own problems and quirks, and has its own touchstones for marriage melancholia.

Paula is a chemical engineer in her early forties. She says of her marriage that she wanted to find "a *true partner*. The best thing is the comfort that brings, of having someone who sees life very similarly and who has very similar goals as myself." It's a common dream. I ask my online panel to react to the statement "Marriage is more like friendship these days than anything else." This opinion elicits one of the highest agreement levels of all of my questions, with 50 percent of respondents agreeing anywhere from "somewhat" to "entirely." Only 30 percent disagree. A kind of intimacy blur is under way, by which a spouse looks more like a friend or a colleague.

|||||||||

Assortative mating departs from most of American marriage history, and subverts the basic (although questionable) "opposites attract," yin-yang romantic assumptions. Up until the last few decades husbands and wives complemented each other more than they resembled each other as colleagues.

Complementarity in marriage was foundational to middle-class culture in the 1800s, when marriage was at its apogee as a social institution. Our most hackneyed needlepoint clichés ("There's No Place Like Home") were once bright-eyed epiphanies that asserted an alliance between heartless ambition in the economy and selfless nurturing and morality in the marriage. Historian Nancy F. Cott examined journals, diaries, letters, and other archives of the ascending middle class in the 1800s. She discovered that a marriage formed a single cultural unit with a split personality. The husband was indentured to the "pecuniary excitement and ambitious competition" of the market economy. He waged "amoral market struggles" in the nascent rat race while his wife soothed ambition's soul-crushing, morality-effacing symptoms. That was how marriage worked in theory. The husband did ruthless but profitable things at work; the wife performed emotionally palliative and ethically inculcating acts of "salvation" in the sharply distinct world of matrimony.

These weren't "intimate" marriages, at least not by prescription. Wives and husbands had so much cultural distance between them, not only in roles but in their presumed temperaments and souls, that they inhabited and governed separate domains. Their deepest intimacies tended to be with their own sex, and women were so patently unequal and constrained in their opportunities outside the home that they didn't have much choice in the matter. This is Cott's double entendre in her discussion of the "bonds" of womanhood. The bonds of oppression that created bonds of intimacy among women.

Marital complementarity persisted through the 1950s and into the romantic heyday, when it changed into a story of the spiritually bankrupt corporate man who drove his gas-guzzler from the suburbs to a downtown office to climb the ladder while his wife spent her days entombed in a ranch home surrounded by a moat of lush green lawn, bereft of vocation, waiting to tend to her husband's sexual, gustatory, libational, and emotional needs at the end of the day. Home and office still had distinct temperaments. The corporate drone or the wage slave understood that the point of work was for his employer to expropriate as much labor out of him as possible, and for him to give as little as required to secure his advancement. This equation was widely understood and accepted. The office didn't have much to do with ethics, sentiment, intimacy, emotion, or even collegiality. Those values belonged, if they belonged anywhere, to the marriage and home.

The success of the women's movement that Friedan helped to catalyze eroded the ethical firewall between the spheres of wife and husband. In the new migratory pattern of modern marriage, husbands and wives moved more frequently and freely between work and home than ever before. Women advanced into careers and the professional ranks, and men took a more active role in the family. Today, the once prescriptively distinct temperaments of work and home infiltrate each other, to curious and consequential effect.

|||||||||

John works in an almost entirely male research department with neurologically exotic colleagues. John's work environment and career are intense, nerve-jangling, and mildly deranged. John calls his office the Matrix—when you're there, you're plugged in to a humming, sentient organism that runs on money, risk, and testosterone. Something's always beeping or blinking or jittering on a screen. Dry-erase boards are covered in mathematical notation and numerical chicken scratch. In a typical office in the research department, you can't see a person sitting at his desk bathed in computer glow, because two or three supersize monitors block him from view, encircling him like a defensive techno-wall. John has to duck his head around the monitors to make eye contact with me when I visit.

And in the Matrix, John has a "workplace spouse," a growing phenomenon. These office marriages are usually platonic, the *Boston Globe* reports, rooted in "the intimacy of common goals." In other words, they're all but interchangeable with a Life Partners marriage, which is rooted in pretty much the same thing.

John's workplace spouse is his partner Gaspar—his literal work partner, that is—whom he respects and likes a great deal. Gaspar is a bald, eclectic genius with a spark-plug physique and a pugnacious, boisterous temperament. In addition to his mathematical brilliance, he's a concert pianist and a climatologist. He's obsessed, for no discernible reason, with the injustice of prison rape and will often predict to John a "lubeless prison rape" kind of day if he senses a bad temper in the markets. He's also a neophyte dogsledder who dreams of opening a piano school in the Alaskan wilderness and likes to buy huge swaths of land and create his own worlds on them with his wife and three children. I fondly envision him on his acreage in Alaska as an icy version of Kurtz in *Heart of Darkness*. From vacation on the tundra Gaspar sends dispatches to the Matrix, informing John about the temperaments of his team of huskies. With his own pack of dogs at home, he'll occasionally get down and rassle them and nip a neck or two, "just so they remember who's lead dog." When he's not on an Alaskan dogsled, he enjoys chasing hurricanes across the Oklahoma panhandle. Gaspar is convinced that the state of Maryland is impeding his freedoms.

"Your freedoms to do what, exactly?" John asks.

"My freedoms generally," Gaspar responds evasively. John has not figured out what Gaspar would be doing, precisely, in a freer state, and he thinks it best not to probe too, too deeply.

John's workplace spouse is in many tangible, sincere respects more wifely and nurturing than his spouse spouse. Gaspar understands John's brilliance as I could never hope to, since it involves numbers instead of words. Gaspar flatters him more. I remember an argument during the early years of our marriage in which I accused John of paying attention to Gaspar with much more intricacy, depth, and intensity of vision—which is the soul of intimacy—than he did me, as if Gaspar were the beloved mistress whose slightest hues of mood and whim John registered with tender regard.

We went out to dinner one night with Gaspar and his wife. "John and I, we know each other so well," Gaspar effused to me over appetizers. "We are soul mates."

Soul mates? I almost laughed out loud. Gaspar had just described his relationship to my husband in exactly the same terms that John described his relationship to me. I was to John as a wife as Gaspar was to John as a colleague. It was a demented SAT analogy question.

When his workplace spouse isn't available, John has his office therapist. John's office has been in therapy for some time now, and with good reason. This is another dimension of the intimacy blur between work and home. John and his colleagues can "work through" issues with the therapist-consultant that are as delicately idiosyncratic and nebulous as those of a troubled marriage were once assumed to be— before the tough-love vogue of nuts-and-bolts "instruction manuals" for the "social machine;" before work came to feel more like marriage and marriage more like the work of auto mechanics.

Michael Kramer had had a twenty-year career as a licensed marriage counselor before he became an office therapist in the St. Louis area. Kramer calls himself a corporate chaplain and sees his marriage counseling skills as loosely interchangeable with his corporate ones. "There's no difference between dysfunction in the family and dysfunction in the organization," he says—and quite remarkably so, if you think on it.

Shirin, my unmarried Los Angeles informant, spent years in a high-powered corporate position. She indicts work and workplace spouses as the biggest threat to marriage, and research confirms her instinct. The vulnerability for the stay-at-home wife today isn't solely financial, it's also sexual. Sex and economics in marriage are a double helix: They are distinct issues but morphologically entwined. When husbands are sole breadwinners, they have more opportunities to stray with women whom they admire collegially and intellectually. "If you want to blame something," Shirin declares, "blame business travel. Exotic travel, first-class hotels, lonely nights, colleagues of the opposite sex who spend inordinate amounts of time together chatting about common interests—everything back home seems a dream, and far away." Amusingly, but convincingly, Shirin flips the business trip into a sexy romantic tryst.

Offices are kinder, gentler places today, and more intimate. I think this is especially true as managerial orthodoxy moves toward collaboration, and as the economy shifts from a manufacturing to a service base, since the paradigm worker in a service economy is more empathic and sensitive—stereotypically feminine. While corporations are as rapacious and greedy as ever, offices themselves function more like families, tending to the moral and ethical development of their employees (witness diversity training), eschew open avarice (one wants to be a collaborative team player), viewing outright ambition as unseemly if not dangerous to an employee's health.

All this was predictable, if unintended. As wives moved into the office and husbands moved into the home, things were bound to cross-pollinate. In 2005, the same year that Judith Warner described the hypercompetitive urge for perfect parenting in the home, Marcus Buckingham described in the *Harvard Business Review* a set of softer values for the office, values inspired, literally, by the Romantic movement. Buckingham provocatively subverts decades of management aphorisms by proposing that truly great managers know how to pamper and cultivate the "individuality" of their employees. He manages to draw a parallel, for perhaps the first time in human history, between a Walmart store manager and Romantic literary masters John Keats and Percy Bysshe Shelley. Like a true Romantic, he concludes, the manager "does not try to change an employee's personal style" or shove a round peg into a square hole. Armed with her intimate understanding of the "enduring idiosyncrasies" of her employees, her family of Grecian urns, she nurtures their sense of "self assurance" and tailors assignments accordingly. Buckingham pulls off a dazzling ideological metastasis from home to office. His Romantic managerial style calls to mind a mother's appreciation for each child, all of whom she "loves the same" despite—indeed, because of—their unique personalities.

Meanwhile, back at the ranch. The aura of something familial, emotional, and spousal in the office is one facet of the intimacy blur that also creates a more collegial, comradely, even workmanlike feeling in our marriages—with ambivalent and sometimes melancholy results. While colleagues are behaving more like spouses, spouses are behaving collegially and less romantically.

Bill, a man in his late forties whom I met in an online community, seems to have a prototypical low-conflict but ambivalent Life Partners marriage. He and his wife are avowed "best friends," sexually dormant yet logistically high-functioning. "I'm in a 20-year, buddy-buddy, sexless marriage. We co-own a company and have kids, which is why we stay together. It's not too bad," he writes, "because we don't argue or raise voices and we have created a safe and secure environment for the kids. We share the same interests and split child-raising and housework 50–50." This sounds like a basic, post-romantic equilibrium. "My only complaint about the lack of sex," he continues, "is that she will not agree to an open marriage or to investigating the swingers scene, which would be perfect for us. Also she tells me that if I go to prostitutes or have an affair she will dissolve the company, kick me out of the house, and take the kids. So if I actively sought out sex with someone and got caught, I would lose *everything*, including my job, and at my age it's too late to start over."

I write in response that it sounds like a perplexing catch-22 to me, but he's more relaxed about it. "Yes, it's a drag," he admits, but "things will be fine if I can find a Buddy With Benefits"—a friend who acts as a sexual "surrogate," as it's sometimes called, for the Buddy With No Benefits wife. "Like I said," Bill concludes, "the marriage is fine—other than the no-sex thing."

Kristin's marriage might be called "The Case of a Good Friendship Spoiled." She and Ted "were *best friends*" for most of their marriage. This is the first thing she tells me. People envied their low-conflict, ostensibly thriving marriage. They had a vacation home in the mountains and went on ski trips. Now, seventeen years after these best friends married, Kristin is divorced with two children, in a new home, and struggling with attorneys, accountants, and the IRS. The two divorce attorneys who still represent the couple as they try to hammer things out are themselves adversarial, which adds another layer of anger. It's exhausting, she concedes, but you wouldn't guess that from her appearance. She has sparkly green eyes and curly reddish hair and arms toned from swimming. She laughs enthusiastically and seems to be handling the entangled cataclysms of her divorce with aplomb. I ask her how she manages. Kristin tells me that she tries to think about how she has attracted bad relationships, takes her own spiritual growth seriously, and attends an institute that encourages it. She meditates. Occasionally she also takes a Wiffle ball bat and pounds it into a pillow.

Listening to Kristin chronicle her marriage's demise, I'm reminded of an old Sicilian technique for tuna fishing, called *mattanza*, in which the tuna are maneuvered into smaller and smaller nets and compartments until they are entirely trapped in the smallest one and killed. Kristin comes from a Catholic family of eleven children, only two of whom are divorced. "We're the 'tainted' ones," she laughs. "I never thought I'd get divorced, or I wouldn't have gotten married at all." Best friends Kristin and Ted started off in a cozy, sociable neighborhood, with separate jobs and no children. Like true Life Partners with wanderlust, they didn't want to be "tied down." Then they got into sequentially tighter and more confined spaces in the marriage. The strength of their camaraderie, at each step, inspired them to do more together.

When she talks about what went wrong for them, Kristin gravitates first to the error of forming a business with Ted. "I *knew* we shouldn't start a business together," she laments. Several years into their marriage Kristin and Ted joined the growing ranks of "copreneur" marriages, in which the "life partner" is also the partner partner, business and marriage fused into one venture. There are 24 million family-owned businesses in the United States, and some estimates put the number of married business partners, specifically, at 3.6 million.

Kristin and Ted ran their business out of their home. "It was suffocating," she remembers. "We never had any time apart." Then, when Kristin was thirty-seven, they both decided simultaneously that they wanted children. "Our thinking was, we'll build on this great unit we have." They had a first child, and a second a few years later.

Ted grew enamored of the idea of living in a chic, more prestigious

ZIP code. They sold their first home in the less prestigious but more sociable neighborhood and bought a stately late-1800s house that needed a lot of work. They began remodeling it as partners in this project as well. "I didn't hold my babies on the weekends," Kristin recalls, "because we were too busy drywalling." It sounds like she didn't assert herself much in the marriage, and felt compelled by Ted's priorities and manic interests.

They loved having children, but when I ask how parenthood affected the marriage, she says "it definitely moved us toward divorce." They co-parented, in the modern manner of partnership, but they had clashing parental temperaments. They were, as in other matters, partners in conflict. "He yells. He needs to wear people down," she says, pounding a fist against her hand, "not physically, but with screaming. And I'm an appeaser. When someone's yelling at me I just let them win." Kristin believes that they shared childrearing, but "if you ask Ted, he would say I was a 'wet nurse' and he was the one who did more parenting." In either case, they were doing the parenting together, as putative equals. Their friends dwindled, they got more isolated, and eventually, Kristin admits, "no one wanted to be around us anyway because we fought all the time."

As we talk, it strikes me that there was no area in their marriage where they weren't "life partners"—not their career and business, not their remodeling, not their parenting or their social life. "After eight years or any amount of time like that, when you're married," she says, "it's too hard to *untangle* things. It's easier to stay together when you're not married." What Kristin means is it's easier to be close and content when you're less close.

Having read through two years' worth of her ex-husband's emails while they were getting divorced, Kristin now surmises that he was logging one or two hours of work a day and probably spending the rest of his time "cruising Home Depot, coffee shops, and the pool." Within minutes of divorcing, as Kristin has it, Ted started up with a woman from the pool whose husband was away for months on business. When that relationship ended he began an affair with another married woman from the same pool. Kristin and her friends call them his "pool hos."

Kristin had her head buried in the sand about money. It turned out that he hadn't been making tax payments for their employees, and that her name wasn't on the "jointly held" accounts of their partnership marriage. She is a copreneur, and is therefore just as liable with the IRS.

I'm interested in her decision about divorce, the moment when it became clear to her, and why. I keep imagining an epiphany when an answer reveals itself, but for Kristin it was more an imperceptible creep before she finally declared, in a couples therapist's office, that she didn't want to be married anymore. Their marriage was a slow circling of the drain that took more than five years but started with a bracelet. Ted had bought it for her birthday and told her beforehand that she could exchange it. When she said she wanted to, he "yelled for hours about how ungrateful I was and how nothing makes me happy. I can still remember exactly where I was standing in the room, and I thought, that's it. I realized I was so lonely."

It seems fantastically ironic that Kristin had such suffocating closeness with her husband in every aspect of life and ended up lonely in the marriage. Perhaps as lonely for being so much with and so much like her husband as Friedan's Mad Housewife was lonely for being so much apart from and unlike hers. And for Kristin the lack of intimacy was, quite simply, too big to be without, no matter the children, no matter the convenience, or the house.

Even so, Kristin shadowboxed with herself over the ensuing years, thinking things would change if they got a new boat or finished fixing up the house. She's now an object lesson in her sister's relationship classes on "how long you put up with something." "I can see why war happens," she muses. "I have all this negative energy, even though I'm pretty peaceful." If Ted is yelling at the children, "I have to tell them reasonably, 'Maybe your daddy was just having a bad day,' when I secretly feel like saying, 'Your daddy's the biggest asshole in the world.'"

Kristin let her semi-happy, and eventually unhappy, marriage continue long past the bracelet incident partly because she was dependent on Ted, not in the old style of the 1950s, but because she had spent so much time being "entangled" in partnership with his life that she couldn't figure out "how to live alone." "Integrity" is her bottom line about marriage today. You need it, she says. Kristin means integrity in the sense of honesty with your partner, and with yourself, but it might equally mean the integrity of two distinct entities, with clear boundaries.

|||||||||

Alone is the word that I come to hear consistently, almost ubiquitously, when I talk to women who made the decision to divorce from low-conflict but melancholy marriages. It's an odd way for marriages of affinity to fail. There must be a delicate sweet spot to marital intimacy, somewhere between too different and too familiar. I'm not sure that the Life Partners marriage has enough marriage in it—enough traction, or friction. For one thing, of course, ethereal soul mates don't have sex. They belong on the ceiling of the Sistine Chapel. As Beth, my friend who values the everyday "grit" in her marriage, speculates, "Maybe the problem is that we get along *too* well as friends. If that part weren't so easy we might have to try harder at being *married*."

CHAPTER THREE

"I CAN BRING HOME THE BACON"

How Having It All Became Sort of Having Two Things Halfway

MAYBE WE GET less out of marriage because we expect less. When I was growing up, this wasn't the case. I didn't think about marriage much even as a young girl, but when I did, regrettably having been schooled by television commercials, I thought I'd be the Enjoli perfume woman and Have It All. This was the vernacular dream of a post-liberation marriage between Life Partners. Like Enjoli's slinky, silver-gowned model, I'd be bringing home the bacon and frying it up in a pan after my day of triumphs in an Office, of some sort, where I pursued my Big Career, of some sort. I'd wear the glass slipper to kick in the glass ceiling and shatter it. I had no idea what "never letting him forget he was a man" was all about, but it sounded doable. I imagined myself, when I imagined marriage at all, as one half of a dual-career power couple.

Other women imagined likewise. In 1970, an American Association of University Women survey found that among the "best-educated" women, almost half still thought that a woman's major role was "wife and mother." Just thirteen years later, in 1983, as my friends and I were just graduating from high school, a stunning 85 percent of college women in one survey aspired to have it all, to be "married career women with children." For these women, being a wife and mother without a career had devolved, with remarkable speed, from the apotheosis of middle-class womanhood to a mark of failure and mediocrity.

By the time I dutifully completed college, checked off my education and career milestones, and got married, the Having It All dream had fallen on hard times. It had been beaten into ill-repute by an accidental coalition of antifeminist conservatives and exhausted, bitterly overworked spouses, including wives who felt less like the glamorous Enjoli woman and more like bow-backed Boxer the horse in *Animal Farm*, who vows always to "work harder."

That dream is sadly tattered today. Having It All, which sounds like a gift and a triumph, devolved into Doing It All, which sounds like a burden, and a chore. Shirin, my unmarried informant, summarizes, "Women are conflicted in ten different directions. They know you *cannot* have it all. You cannot have the career, the travel, the friendships, the time alone, and the family as well. Women do end up sacrificing more. Nor do many men I know really do fifty percent of anything in the house." "Everyone" knows that the dream of Having It All just makes us unhappy. However, it's worth noting that Friedan, for her part, made a crucial distinction that's so often missed in the contemporary polemics: Feminism sought equal opportunities and responsibilities for women to be full participants in life, whether or not those things inclined them toward greater personal "happiness." A woman's personal happiness was never really the main goal of second-wave feminism. Friedan conceded that there might be "many women in America who are happy at the moment as housewives. . . . But happiness is not the same thing as the aliveness of being fully used." The goal of feminism and of Having It All was closer to liberation, opportunity, and equality. Sometimes those goals might make our marriages and lives richer and more of our own invention, but not "happier," per se.

In any case, I don't entirely share the pessimistic view. John and I bring home the bacon and fry it up reasonably well, I suppose. As for never letting him forget he's a man . . . well, never mind.

Having It All's descendant dream is Work-Life Balance, a dream now so familiar that it's abridged simply to Balance. It's the mantra of weary thirty- and forty-something married professionals. Yet, for all its apparent modesty, it's proven to be cunning prey for modern marriages, which rarely report capturing it. Having It All, a suitably audacious dream steeped in America's famous manic ambition, has morphed for my generation into the meeker dream of Sort of Having Two Things Halfway.

Admittedly, I suspect that Balance is mostly shorthand for the supremely understandable and familiar sentiment in the dual-career marriage, I'm So Damn Tired, and I Need a Vacation, and who can begrudge a spouse for wanting not to be exhausted. But to the extent that it is a lifestyle or a marital aspiration, the subtle underlying assumptions of Balance perplex me. Balance makes me imagine the two foundations of life, as Freud saw it—"work and love, that's all there is"—as generic, interchangeable lumps of life activity counterpoised on the scale. When did we become such bean-counters? The opposite of balance isn't imbalance, necessarily, but passion. That passion could lead in any direction. As a marital benchmark, Balance discredits passion generally, whether it's passion for a career or passion for home, in one concisely diminishing gesture. For all of its logic, it lacks the organic quality of a life in which dreams and commitments can't really be planned or metered by schedule. Obsession and passion, for anything, provoke imbalance. And isn't there a case to be made for doing things in an exuberant, passion-driven, impromptu, half-assed way? We end up with exasperatingly tepid outcomes soon enough. Why dream of them? Why aspire to a marriage that is managerial instead of inspirational?

The war of balance against passion is more than merely rhetorical. It's a metaphor of marriage that, like all big metaphors we tell ourselves, helps shape our lives. In 1995, sociologist Karen Arnold published fascinating longitudinal research on "contingency planning" among high-achieving valedictorian women in high school. She found that these smart young women who in another era might have aspired to Have It All are often timid and cautious in their fantasies of career and marriage in deference to the impossible dream of Having It All. Before they marry, long before they have children or land their first job, they make career plans with an eye to what would be easiest if they *were* to marry and have children someday. A similar form of preemptive thinking inspired the widely discussed "opting out" women of elite universities who, when interviewed by a *New York Times* reporter in 2005, said that they planned on having a career for a few years and then setting it aside to stay at home. This is a variation on Balance, to plan on doing a little of this and then a little of that, in a schematic way. It's this pervasive retro mood about marriage that worries author Leslie Bennetts in *The Feminine Mistake*, that has sparked a much-documented "motherhood war" between stay-at-home wives and working wives, and that sporadically inspires newspaper articles about how all wives really want is a chivalrous male breadwinner-husband, a return to the romantic orthodoxy, or even the traditional one.

Some opting-out women who have heeded the skepticism toward Having It All and are planning their career lives to avoid that frustration point to what they saw firsthand in their mothers' hectic lives. "We feel a lot of pressure to succeed in the working world, but how do we do that and also succeed at home?" says a Wellesley College student interviewed by the *Christian Science Monitor.* The benchmark of "success," a term indigenous to the workplace and here transplanted to the home, makes things seem tougher than they need to be. These women might well succeed in the familiar troika of parenting from my own childhood—that we provide "food, clothing, and shelter" to our offspring and not beat on them—but they worry about failure by today's extravagantly embellished parenting standards.

"These women are right to be worried," says Elayne Rapping, a professor of women's studies. "The notion of Having It All involves a lot more than most young women anticipate. It's very difficult to negotiate within a marriage who will do what when both people have high-powered careers." Life maintenance isn't easy, it's true. In fact it can be downright exhausting. As scholar Joan Williams perceptively argues, many women are "pushed out" of the workforce more than they "opt out," because we live in a culture that persistently envisions the "employee" as a middle-aged white male with a full-time wife at home to take care of the house and children.

The workforce isn't accommodating for parents, and this is an ongoing policy and social challenge. Another challenge, more private and internal, is to be brave enough in our own marriages to resist the peer pressure toward maternal perfection, when those standards make us anxious, melancholy, or unduly timid. Maybe we can, indeed, "have it all," if we have realistic domestic goals and embrace the idea that there are just as many ways to be a "successful" mother as we imagine there are to be an unsuccessful one. Otherwise, too many wives today experience the unique, post-liberation marital melancholy of feeling either that they've failed as mothers or that they've failed at reaching their potential—or, in the worst of all cases, they feel both at once.

In that regard, where does shrewd foresight end and shortsighted wariness begin? Arnold's female valedictorians, and to some extent the opting-out group, seem to be operating under a kind of premature realism.

Sometimes, though, if you don't plan for trouble, you don't get any. It's a curious, counterintuitive lesson, perhaps, that we get more out of marriage by planning less—or, at least, by not planning on the impossibility of having it all. Take Paula, the chemical engineer. "I *never* assumed I'd get married," she declares. "The future I imagined for myself was that I would be a single woman working at a high-powered corporate job in a suit in a big city, and every morning I'd grab a bagel and coffee and walk to the office." She grew up a "bright" girl, the term of art in our day, and it was always expected, in these "I am woman, hear me roar" years of the women's movement, that she would have a career. Paula's mother encouraged the dream. A product of the marriage consensus era of the 1950s, her mother had gone from college student to wife and mother in the span of one year, at the age of twenty-one, and wasn't very satisfied with her marriage early on. As for Paula's father, his "repetitive chant was that because I was chubby and smart, men weren't going to like me and I was going to have a rough time in life, so I'd need to have a career."

But she didn't develop fixed ideas about career and marriage, nor did she "have anything against getting married." As for many of us in the late 1970s, it just wasn't a preoccupying dream for her. Later, in college, Paula didn't "contingency-plan" around a future marriage, or anticipate opting out, or think preemptively about the struggles of Having It All, or proactively *plan* to Have It All, or worry about Balance. She didn't plan much of anything, really. Instead she started out in her adult life by letting things unfold more organically. She followed her passion: chemical engineering. She now works for a Fortune 500 company in plastics, having followed *The Graduate*'s iconic career advice. Paula thrived and got promoted quickly, and found her career deeply satisfying, and prosperous. "My career was predominately my life," she says.

As Paula approached her thirties she had the familiar career girl epiphany that she had forgotten to get married and procreate. She might have fallen into the category of rueful, second-guessing career women without children or husband that author Sylvia Hewlett warned us about in her widely discussed book, *Creating a Life*, but Paula didn't despair. When she did start to contemplate marriage, she thought of it in the trophy marriage spirit of our time as something that "*had* to be additive" to the rich and self-sufficient life she had built for herself already. Then, with the soul of an engineer more than a romantic, she realized that she could "manage it just like a project," and what she calls her "Get a Life" mission began. She bought season tickets to singles-themed cultural events in Detroit and met her husband, Alex, in this way in 1999. They married a year later. When she called her parents to tell them she'd gotten engaged, her mom's response was "How's work going? Have you been promoted?"

By intention this was going to be a dual-career marriage. "I was very up front that my career was extremely important to me," she says, "and that I would not expect it to be diminished once we got married, if we got married." Alex, who works in a company with just three employees, is somewhat less ambitious. "He likes to control his projects, but he doesn't want to conquer the world. I came from a conquer the world *and* outer space perspective," Paula says with a laugh. She states unequivocally that you don't get breakthroughs "on a part-time schedule. It just doesn't happen." (That conclusion may not be fair, just, or desirable, but it is most likely our reality. Former Harvard president Lawrence Summers, notorious for impolitic commentary, hazarded the same conclusion when he commented that scientists don't really achieve greatness on the modified career devotion implied by Balance. But he mangled the insight so badly—and then sizzled on the third rail of feminist politics after stomping through neuroscience about male and female brains—that he had to resign his presidency as a result.)

If Paula didn't plan on getting married, she "sure as *heck* didn't envision having children," but spontaneity to new goals is a "recurring theme" in her life. "I'm open to stuff. I may not think the probability of it happening is all that great, but I'm game to try things." Paula decided that career and children could work symbiotically. Married and restless for a new challenge, she used a six-month unpaid maternity leave as a makeshift career sabbatical in lieu of opting out or quitting her job altogether. She was temporarily off the "corporate-promotable list" at her company, "and it was a big thing to trade in, but what really got me was that maybe this would be a better adventure."

Paula went into the career sabbatical maternity leave with an open mind. "I had *no* idea where it would shake out." Her approach is notable for the modest reason that she didn't have fixed expectations or standards of success. Other young mothers I've known had such firm prenatal convictions that they *should* enjoy staying at home with the baby, or should be able to breast-feed exclusively, or should be able to have natural childbirth, that they ended up berating themselves as failures when they wanted to work instead. (For example, one acquaintance of mine finally gave birth to her first baby only when her doctor had an epiphany and told her, "You know, you don't get a medal for doing it without medication." Disabused of the notion of a medal of *some* sort, I suppose, for doing it "naturally," she agreed to an epidural and pushed that baby right out.)

Paula's first infant was challenging. Some days were "so cool" and others "so frustrating that I was anxious for them to end." What she found she enjoyed, though, was the "opportunity to have a new project that took a lot of work to try to get the whole thing figured out." Paula's professional mind-set helped her tackle motherhood as a challenge more like an engineer than a domestic goddess.

Paula has two young children now and is back at her job. Interestingly, she sees her marriage today as "fairly unconventional. I'm not a stay-at-home mom, and I've got an active career." It's interesting that the Having It All dream so basic to the idea of a post-liberation marriage now feels a touch outré. But Paula might be right. She and other unapologetic, dual-career couples today are pioneers in a sense—not because they've invented a new dream for marriage, but because they've chosen to still believe in an old, unpopular, even ridiculed one, and to craft their marriages around it.

Paula and Alex really do have a fifty-fifty marriage, in her opinion, although not by a literal accounting of who does how many hours of exactly comparable chores (you could drive yourself crazy trying to balance a ledger sheet like that). Since Alex is currently part-time, he does more chores than Paula, who works full-time, but they are equals in sharing what I call in all of these chapters the "dreariness quotient": Each does enough unpleasant or necessary but uninspiring tasks—according to their own definitions of *unpleasant*, since a wife's drudgery can be her husband's joy—to support the household and family. The litmus test is that they don't bicker over who's doing more. Paula gets up at 4:30 A.M. to make a shift that ends at noon, and Alex takes care of the children in the morning. She cooks, he cleans. The control of money has always been crucial for Paula, so they have separate bank accounts.

Paula grew up with a "having one thing" mind-set. She believed she would probably only ever have a career, and then stumbled in to Having It All—a fulfilling career, marriage, children, and friends. The significance of her story is that she got more by not planning too timidly, or too early, to have less. Or she planned, only insofar as Betty Friedan might have hoped, to be a woman who first pursues her own muse and passion in life. The prevailing wisdom, and mood, today is to plan for less. There is a great deal of skepticism these days about that Having It All dream. But women like Paula suggest a counter-intuitive recommendation that planning for trouble may be part of the problem. It leads women, and perhaps young men as well, to curtail ambition before they've tried in marriage.

Paula would advise her own children to do pretty much what she did—follow their passion, learn how to support themselves, and wait until later in life to marry. "I was secure in my identity before I tried to get fulfillment from anybody else," she says. If they don't want to get married, she hopes they'll find a group of supportive friends, and she doesn't think she'll "advocate one way or another" for marriage. Close friendships, Paula reasons in the post-romantic spirit, can fulfill many of the emotional needs of marriage. Mostly she doesn't want her children to feel forced into marrying too early.

|||||||||

In the same *Christian Science Monitor* feature about Having It All, another Wellesley student reports that she and her friends talk "all the time" about how they will "juggle" the demands of home and work, the two elements reflexively imagined, and feared, as adversarial forces in a life. It's a pervasive view: In the dual-career marriage, version 2.0, career is a chore, family is a chore, the two are mirthlessly juggled and managed.

Having It All might be dismissed as the impossible dream. As the evidence slowly accumulates, though, it's not clear that opting out in search of balance is a workable dream, either, even if it sounds reasonable on paper and has the promise of its seeming novelty. Take the fact that women now outpace men in the completion of Ph.D.s. Today, some of these women, clearly talented and ambitious, aspire to "juggle" motherhood and career by becoming part-time, poorly paid, largely unrespected adjunct professors. According to Alison Gopnick, a psychologist at Berkeley, career-and-children-juggling moms hope that part-time adjuncting is a means to achieve balance—to keep one foot at home and one foot lightly in a career—but instead this plan seems to be consigning these women to an enduring employment ghetto. "A lot of women think they can have families and stay in the game by adjuncting," Gopnick says, but they get trapped there, and when they want to return to a full-time career, the career is not there to be had. One such woman had a very promising academic career, attended prestigious schools, and even wrote a commercial book. Then she opted for part-time teaching so that she could "be there" for her three daughters. She's now been divorced for years, and cobbles together an under-$40,000-a-year living for her family through teaching several courses at two community colleges. She never got back the career side of the balance equation, or dream.

In lieu of juggling, Amelia and Kyle found symbiosis. What interests me in their story is how they ended up using marriage to advance both of their career ambitions.

Their marriage is that rare creature that bridges the Two Americas of Marriage. Amelia grew up with the abbreviated post-romantic marital expectations typical of the secular blue-state set. "I always hoped I would marry, but it wasn't a given in my mind at all, and even when I was older, I thought maybe I wouldn't, and I started planning my life with that in mind." When she did decide to marry, it "felt like a stepping-stone. It didn't feel like the end result, it felt like we should get married to have health insurance, to have everything be easier, to have kids."

Kyle grew up in the rural Midwest in an enclave of traditional marriage expectations and social conservatism. "I never formally thought about it, but culturally, everyone did it," he remembers. "You got married right out of college and had babies soon thereafter. It's what you *do.*" When he moved to D.C., where the couple lives today, "my peers were definitely not doing that. They were waiting longer, traveled the world, had fun, and immersed themselves in careers. Culturally, I can't overemphasize the amount of pressure that was on me going back there. It was like I was being disobedient."

"I'd never *seen* that before, the level of concern about him not being married," Amelia agrees. "He was in his thirties, he had a great job—"

"People were joking at my reunion, 'Are you gay?'" Kyle interjects. "It wasn't derogatory; they just couldn't understand. They didn't know any guys in their thirties who were able-bodied and not married."

Kyle developed more progressive views about marriage, more like Amelia's and more consonant with the marriage rationales of our day: He saw a marriage as not unlike any other committed relationship, but he knew that his parents would think more highly of them if "we had a kid under the flag of marriage, but we could have had a deeply committed relationship without it." But marriage "was important to my goals," he adds, because it would give him the "flexibility that I want in life to change careers, to pursue my dreams."

When they married, Kyle had been a lobbyist in Washington for six years, and although it was in many ways a perfect job, he didn't want to be in an office on K Street, wearing a suit and tie for the rest of his life. He was fully vested, and he wanted to try a new job— creative writing classes and consulting. "I was able to do that because of the marriage. Amelia has health benefits. Getting married made it financially *feasible* for me to pursue my creative side." There are less tangible benefits, too. Kyle says that career-wise, "Amelia allows me to dream, to find things that I love. She gives me the license to do that." Amelia agrees that "allowing the partner the freedom to do what is right for them" is a big part of marital success.

By the same token, Kyle supports Amelia's career. She works at a prestigious consulting firm in D.C. and loves her job and her company. "Amelia was ready to go full steam ahead with her career," Kyle says, and she has been able to do that because his job and his teaching position at a community college have more flexibility. He works, but he also does more of the chores so Amelia can put in long hours.

Kyle would have felt guilty, and thought the marriage "inequitable," if he had downgraded professionally before he'd saved enough money, and Amelia wouldn't have felt right about it if Kyle were lounging around watching infomercials. "My one concern with Kyle quitting his job was that he would take it as a chance to do nothing. Which I'm totally fine with for a month or two," she hastens to add, "but I *did* know it would bother me if he watched TV all day and I had to do chores and have a career while he sat around."

As it is, though, Amelia's in the pleasant position of having her real marriage exceed her worriedly modest expectations. "I actually thought marriage would be way worse," she says. She had internalized the warning that Having It All never works. "It was my expectation that marriage would entail a lot of giving up, and that I'd do more housework and more of the crap work. The reality is a lot more about partnership." Amelia makes much of choosing the right husband. "Most of the women I know are pretty open, and it seems like it comes down to the husband and his willingness to have it equal. A friend dated a guy who felt like he had to 'provide' enough. The woman could work, but it was an issue." Like Paula, Amelia doesn't see Having It All as a myth. "I *do* feel like I have it all. I want to have children and things will change then, but I trust we'll work it out." The two of them have a symbiotic arrangement that uses the dual-career potential of our day so that both end up getting what they want. The marriage works to add possibilities rather than to create new hassles, burdens, or inequities.

|||||||||

I'm having dinner with a married, dual-career couple, who have two school-age children. Both spouses are intensely dedicated to their careers, in creative fields. "Balance" doesn't really leap to mind around them. They cherish their family life but Anna is uncharacteristically jaunty about her pursuit of passion over balance, in that she is unapologetic about her love of hard work, ambition, and career. "What else is there?" Anna says. "We talk about our work all the time—either that or the kids. It's what holds the marriage together." She has a work ethic for tasks other than parenthood and seems fairly impervious to the guilt-tripping tendencies against the pursuit of career, fun, nonparental aspirations, and adult prerogative in a marriage. Refreshingly, she rejects the "attachment parenting" vogue today, which keeps wives and mothers ever more tethered to their children and homes. "I'm the most boring playmate my kids could have," she asserts. "It's good if they can see me doing work that I care about."

Anna and Gordon evolved their idea of marriage and work over time. Anna is younger than Gordon by almost a decade, and he recalls that she had a "new bride" obsession, perhaps a vestige of her upbringing, that expressed itself in a craving for the latest appliances and other accoutrements she associated with married life. Anna thinks that because she was younger, she might have burdened him with the expectation that he would "take care of things." These are familiar romantic expectations. But today "it's not romance," Anna says, that makes the marriage work. Instead, over the years, they kept returning to the idea of their work, their "cultural production," as a kind of shared mission, or soldering, for their marriage. They wanted to be producers and creators together, not consumers. They seem to have worked their way, against the grain of balance, toward a marriage that affords them a chance to feel, in Friedan's terms, "the aliveness of being fully used" in life—even if they are working hard.

"I guess I'm taking two bites out of the apple," Anna says of having a career, marriage, and children. I like her comment. I like its greediness. Intensity, ambition, single-mindedness, and obsession aren't chic these days, or at least not in spouses. The parent who craves their career, who is truly happiest when pursuing that muse, tends to muffle their zeal in layers of apology. Conversely, the opting-out wife, for example, who finds that she really does have a single-minded passion for domesticity, in an organic, nonbrainwashed, non-Stepford fashion, can end up feeling abashed about pursuing it wholeheartedly and offer up her own defensive apologies for why she's not "doing anything," as I've heard it described. She might introduce herself as a "stay-at-home mom, but really a lawyer," or whatever her last known career coordinates happened to be.

Maybe that's why we've settled on a dream of balance over passion, or Having It All. The current hedging of the bets through balance seems the least objectionable, pungent, socially offensive approach to take. Who could judge us, or vilify us for such a modest benchmark? Who would criticize it as a selfish, ambitious, obsessive, or stupidly idealistic dream in a marriage? Who could accuse us of being retro, desperate housewives or "selfish" career women, if we just try to mete out a little of both and "juggle" and manage them?

It's not as if we lack any Having It All success stories. It's just that we don't trust the dream, and so these marriages are told mostly in cautionary rather than victorious tones (as Shirin says, "They know you *cannot* have it all . . ."). They come to feel like illicit, hidden triumphs in the age of Balance. This distrust of the big dream for marriage—the dream of living large in marriage—might pace the larger retreat from risk and the spirit of adventure in American culture, as we become more fretful and wary. In any case it does have consequences. It's dispiriting to see younger women plan on less, or preemptively curtail ambition, however understandable their concerns are, since nothing is easy.

Maybe the Enjoli woman really was Boxer the horse in disguise— but I want the bold, prodigious, and audacious spirit of the dream rehabilitated as a good and plausible thing to want. In that dream, marriage was a stylish locale that had passion and kick and a larky energy to it. The Enjoli model wasn't apologizing for being sexy, successful, flirtatious, hot, and so culinarily adroit that she could cook dinner in a gray charmeuse floor-length gown. No, she was flaunting it. The Having It All marriage supported a kind of gaudy excess. We should all be anti-Bartlebys, the dream proposed, we should always prefer *to* and prefer *more*. Now that the economic imperative to find a meal ticket ("will marry for food") has faded, now that the marital economy can be anything we want, why not want it to be more?

CHAPTER FOUR

THE TOM SAWYER MARRIAGE

The Plight of the New Workhorse Wife

*Tom gave up the brush and while . . . [his friend] Ben worked and sweated
in the sun, the retired artist sat on a barrel in the shade close by. When the
middle of the afternoon came, Tom . . . had had a nice, good, idle time all
the while, . . . and the fence had three coats of white wash on it!*

—MARK TWAIN, *THE ADVENTURES OF TOM SAWYER*

S OME SPOUSES, CERTAINLY, do want more, and expect marriage to be more, not less. They still pursue the marital ambition, and the big dream. Almost by intuition, or perhaps deeply
ingrained habit, they find ways through marriage to avoid "work that
does not truly use [their] creative energy," as Friedan had hoped, but
to melancholy, grumpy effect for their spouses. This is the story of
how some modern Tom Sawyers get their fences whitewashed—by
their wives.

Beth, one of my oldest friends, was something special among special women in our college because she turned down Yale, and no one
did that. When she applied to graduate programs in the sciences after
college she was admitted to all of the schools she had applied to, and
she had a chance to turn down Yale a second time, which she did.

While Beth was in graduate school she met and married Richard, a
fellow graduate student in the sciences. Rich is a charming and smart
man, with big dreams. He's enjoyable to talk to, and he defies any easy
categorization in his thinking or his beliefs. Beth had a baby earlier than
they had planned, while she was still struggling to complete her Ph.D.

Beth weathered the usual ups and downs of motherhood as she simultaneously finished her dissertation research. The family lived in a small apartment in a midwestern city as Richard pursued an intellectually exciting but characteristically low-paying postdoctoral fellowship. I visited Beth a lot in the year after the birth, during which Beth continued to wear her black maternity clothes. She recalls today that she was depressed during this year. Tensions between the two over the division of chores simmered under the surface.

Since then, twelve years ago, they have moved every few years, often for Rich's dream career possibilities, once for Beth's. Consistently, she has ended up the workhorse wage earner for the couple. She disliked several of her lucrative but unsatisfying jobs ("I write reports to sit on bureaucrats' shelves"), but Richard always had more clarity and passion about his career dreams than Beth, and sought jobs that would provide interesting challenges. On one occasion he endeavored to start his own company; on another he took a poorly paid but satisfying job as an adjunct instructor; and on another, he worked as an athletic coach. Once he explored the possibility of abandoning his primary field to become a missionary, and took a part-time unpaid position in a church. In choosing among potential jobs, Rich has followed a muse. Beth has had to follow the dollar sign. Maybe each small decision along the way made sense to her, and to them, or seemed fair or temporarily expedient, but over time they had accumulated into a life that pinioned her to a soul-numbing rat race.

On one visit, several years ago, Beth was not in a good spot. Although I wish it were not so, her life had me perplexed. I tried to be supportive, but we have known each other for so long that my discomfort, which borders on a heartfelt frustration about her circumstances, must betray itself. Rich had just taken another poorly paid teaching job at a school three hours away, which meant he was gone several nights a week. This gambit had tied Beth to sole childcare responsibilities most of the week, as well as to a job that she loathes.

We are settled comfortably on her living room couch, in that ephemeral sweet spot of red wine intimacy between good friends,

drunk enough for truth-telling but not yet so drunk that we take umbrage at it, when Beth says to me, almost in tears, "It would be nice to
have a chance to be a real mother, before they're much older."

No matter how intimate or enduring the friendship, there is hardly
a touchier domestic set of related topics among women than motherhood, parenting arrangements, and money. We trespass on this land-
mined turf at great peril. Nevertheless, her wistful poignancy rouses
me to uncommon courage and candor.

"Well . . . can't *Richard* be the wage earner for a while? Can't *he* support *you* so that you can take time off? It seems only fair." There. The
elephant has been pointed at and named.

"I know, I'm frustrated being the big breadwinner here." She pauses
to rip a chunk of bread off the baguette she has arrayed with the olives
and cheese, and chews it aggressively.

And then, in addition to motherhood, I dare to bring up all the
stray professional dreams she has shuffled since her undergraduate
days. "Do you think maybe you can make a move for your job next?
I can see you working with people in social work, or remember, you
wanted to work with large animals?" I wince to think of how much
this sounds like conversations I've had with the five-year-old girls on
my street, all of whom want to be vets or princesses.

I am heard but there's no reaction. "Rich," she calls, "could you
adjust that center light in the kitchen, over the counter? It's glaring
too much out here."

I get the hint; the conversation wanders off.

Beth asks Rich to do the dinner dishes, which I take as a hopeful
sign. It's a baby step toward the assertion of equilibrium in the dreariness quotient of their marriage. Richard does this task cheerfully, and
my mood brightens. But he misreads the unfamiliar labels and uses
dishwashing liquid instead of dishwasher liquid, and the dishwasher
overflows with suds that spill out all over Beth's impeccably selected
wood floors.

"My God, it's an *I Love Lucy* episode," I say.

They laugh. Beth cleans up the mess. I help. Richard wanders off to do something or other—check his email for business leads, perhaps, or do Google searches.

Somehow, a daughter of feminism has become the melancholy heir apparent to the Man in the Gray Flannel Suit.

|||||||||

I'm surprised to learn that Beth's case isn't all that idiosyncratic or rare. In one out of three American marriages today (33 percent), women out-earn their husbands, an increase from one in four (24 percent) in 1987. That 33 percent encompasses a variety of marriages. Certainly, it contains symbiotic, or at least benign, modern marriages in which a stay-at-home dad does the heavy lifting of parenthood and house-work, while the wife pursues a more or less satisfying career, and both feel that the arrangement works and makes them happy.

I emphatically see that arrangement as among the most unalloyed feminist success stories of our time, because the husband and wife really do transcend gender roles and operate according to their own needs, predilections, and preferences. Also to be found in that 33 percent are some of those famously beleaguered dual-career marriages where the wife may nominally out-earn the husband but both work basically the same hours, for basically the same salary, in jobs they both basically like or basically despise. These couples have a grim, exhausting parity to them—their dreariness quotient balances out. There are breadwinner women among the 33 percent, too; women who find their careers soulfully satisfying and wouldn't give them up for the world. (I chatted with one of these happy breadwinners when I saw her doing a rare drop-off at my son's kindergarten one day. "*When* do they open the classroom doors?" she kept asking me anxiously, eager to imbibe the sacred air of her corner office again. Her husband stays at home to care for the children, and they are both satisfied with the arrangement.)

But nestled within those one in three marriages is a more troubling subset that includes some of my disgruntled friends, women who are highly educated, successful, ambitious, and talented, and who inhabit low-conflict melancholy marriages today, but for distinctly modern reasons. Most of them finished college and blazed through prestigious professional and graduate programs in the late 1980s and early 1990s. They are lawyers, scientific researchers, academics, editors, and entrepreneurs.

And now they are wives who work in demanding, high-powered careers for which they have little passion or affection, financially supporting husbands who are following their own creative, artistic, avocational, or intellectual muses.

If Tom Sawyer married, this might be his life.

For workhorse wives like Beth, the high-powered career is the New Housework. Like taking out the garbage, vacuuming, or cleaning toilets, it's the thing that neither the husband nor the wife especially wants to do, but the wife does it, more as chore than joy.

Is the Tom Sawyer effect—dispirited workhorse wife supporting happy career-free husband—the extreme case of sex ghettoization? Some economists hold that a profession's prestige diminishes over time when women infiltrate it (there goes the neighborhood!), with the result that the coveted, high-status, well-paying professions dominated by men migrate elsewhere once women get a foot in the door. Power, like coolness, has a way of staying one step ahead of eager arrivistes. The most obvious example in our time is the computer science and technology sector, which really heated up just as women were dutifully completing all their years of college and professional school to constitute near majorities in the erstwhile prestigious male bastions of medicine and law. By the time a woman proudly got her M.D., a tech wunderkind of the same graduating class had started a dot-com in his parents' basement, made millions, bought real estate, and retired.

Perhaps it's not just that well-educated husbands have fled from one (feminized) profession, but that they've given up on the whole lot of them. According to economic analyst Anirban Basu of the Sage Policy Group, recent research shows that the number of men out of the workforce has climbed from 5 percent in the 1960s to almost 13 percent today, and the recession that began in 2008 has exacerbated male unemployment. That migration out of the economy, through buyouts, early retirement, disability, layoffs, or personal choice, cuts across all income levels and includes men in the professions. Attrition in this last group, Basu tells me, is a more recent phenomenon, but one already documented by *BusinessWeek* and the *Wall Street Journal*, among other business and trade publications.

My friend Gretchen has made an exceedingly dreary and taxing commute for the last fifteen years, four or five days each week. First she drives fifteen minutes to a commuter ferry at the crack of dawn, then she hops on to a subway to complete the journey on the other side. Her husband, Adam, is one of the smartest, most delightful people John and I know. So many Tom Sawyer husbands seem to have a sparkle and glow that I suspect come from doing exactly what they want to do with their talents and time. They are unfailingly interesting people to talk to. Adam has had a notably less stable, or tedious, fifteen years than has his wife. He spent most of those years fitfully inching toward a degree, which he did not complete, in an obscure humanities program that matched his intellectual passions and interests. He has taken jobs that pay a bit, but not enough to relieve Gretchen of what she bewails as an anvil of a career. For several years now Gretchen has wanted to do something that feels more like what Adam does—to find a vocation that is also a mission, where her desires harmonize with her livelihood. She has variously contemplated: opening a stationery store, becoming a journalist, producing a documentary, becoming another kind of lawyer than the one she is now, abandoning law altogether, working for a nonprofit, and teaching high school.

None of these things has happened, because among other obstacles there is the insuperable matter of a mortgage, groceries, and gas. Gretchen and Adam do not readily act. I've often thought that they would be happier if someone stamped a "Use or Freeze By" date on their lives, some arbitrary prod to compel a decision. At this point Gretchen has deferred dreams stacked up in a dusty corner of her marriage: the dream of parenthood, expired; the dream of a new house, on interminable hold; and the dream of a career that satisfies her soul, postponed.

Gretchen and Adam are self-questioning people. If the workhorse wife feels "trapped" in the breadwinner role, as Gretchen and Beth have both described their predicament, then it's not for lack of trying. When the topic first came up in conversation many years ago, she complained to me, as she had directly to Adam, that his inability to repay student loans or to "market himself" for better jobs had stymied her own life. Vicariously angered, I asked whether she didn't think it unfair that she had become the workhorse. Gretchen thought it over, and conceded an injustice. "But if I ask him to earn more money, and then he doesn't get to write his book or get his degree," she said, "it will be as if he didn't get a chance at his dream." That made sense to me. I still cannot understand why neither she nor I thought to ask after her dream that night.

But then again, many tacit deals struck between lifelong partners are so quirky that even close friends cannot grasp what might have been traded and for what. Marriages develop their own uniquely weighted scales.

Not coincidentally, both Beth and Gretchen are old-school type A characters. Beth also has a strong caregiving personality—even toward her husband, it seems. These women are strong, driven, ambitious, and shamed by failure. They have high standards of both perfection and control, so while they would like their husbands to shoulder more life maintenance burdens, and may nag ineffectively in that direction, they are also concerned that they can't perform the tasks up to their own standards. I've heard two workhorse wives complain in almost identical terms about bacteria in their toilet bowls, muse that their husbands perhaps should assume this bathroom chore, and then dismiss that notion, also in identical terms, because their husbands could not clean the toilet properly, and were apparently beyond learning. When Beth and Rich went through a rough patch in their marriage and talked about separation, the depths of Rich's acquired helplessness became clear. "How will I live?" he asked Beth plaintively. Specifically, he was flummoxed by the task of finding an apartment. Treating the husband like a charming but unreliable child seems to give the workhorse wife some satisfaction—a sort of maternal power over her husband, in lieu of spousal equality.

Beth could afford to loosen up on her standards, certainly, but the relationship holds sacred Richard's quest after a fragile, mercurial dream. Inevitably then, and without any malicious scheme or intent, the New Housework of career gets punted onto the wife. No one wants to bring home the bacon, or fry it up in a pan, for that matter. But life is not free, and somebody has to do it.

|||||||||||

In a cockeyed way, this is a pre-feminist state of affairs gussied up in post-feminist clothing. Appearances deceive. What passes on the surface for liberation—a workhorse wife's right to a career—looks underneath to be abjection, a bit of 1959 reincarnated in 2009. These wives have the shell of the feminist dream—the career, and the economic autonomy—but their husbands have the soul of it—the life with meaningful work, a marriage that supports a big, gaudy dream. Although they wield BlackBerrys and not brooms, workhorse wives are a new inflection on an old story: They subordinate their daily lives to dreariness, this time in the rat race, to support their husbands' intellectual and creative aspirations.

The plight of the workhorse wife is not so widespread or so one-dimensional as that of Friedan's housewife. But substitute "career" for "work" in Friedan's passage about housewives who spend the day in "work that is not moving, as the world around her is moving," and it describes accurately the inner plight of the wife who, in Friedan's coinage, has "forfeited self" in the service of her husband's pursuits.

In a disheartening irony, workhorse wives have taken a long, hard route to get back to where we started. In the pre-feminist era, wives worked and toiled in the home to support their husbands' careers and dreams of success. A 1963 *New York Times* article used a familiar nickname for the wife who was supporting a graduate student husband, that she was going for her "Ph.T. (Putting Hubby Through)" degree by "doing some sort of clerical work." The American mainstream recognized the wife's work as ancillary to the husband's, and performed to truss his ambitions. Today the workhorse wife does essentially the same thing with different gadgets and tasks.

Judy Syfers memorably wrote in the early 1970s that she "needed a wife"—meaning someone to tend to her creature comforts, her soul, her ego, and the upkeep of her household. If the Tom Sawyer husband were merrily playing the figurative wife to his wife, then the arrangement would make more sense and feel more just. It would be tallied as a notable feminist victory—from each partner in the relationship according to the needs and talents of each, without regard for gender straitjackets. But apparently Tom Sawyers are not greeting their wives at the end of the day with a perfect dry martini in hand and dinner in the oven. According to a recent study in the *American Journal of Sociology*, the more a woman earns and the harder she works at her career, the fewer chores her husband performs in the house. When a wife contributes more than half the family income, the husband's contribution to the housework drops; when she is the sole provider, it drops even more.

This was the case with Helen, an attractive sole proprietor of her own law firm. For most of her marriage she and her husband, Colin, had no children. She would return from work late each night, drag herself upstairs to the bedroom, and more often than not pass out from exhaustion in front of the TV while Colin brought her dinner up—such fare as marshmallows, popcorn, and Nutella. He was not much of a cook, and had never learned any of the vaunted arts of the wily pre-feminist domestic goddesses.

In a brilliant if unpremeditated jujitsu tactic of using an opponent's strength to one's own advantage, Tom Sawyer husbands have converted the sword of feminism into the plowshare of moocherism. The ones I know are all acutely, self-consciously feminist, seeing themselves as fully liberated—thoughtful, smart, open to new ideas about gender, willing to subvert the norms. It's paradoxical, that a feminist sensibility in a marriage kindles a pre-feminist inequality. But in some respects it's that sophisticated, high-sheen feminism in the Tom Sawyer marriage that seems to paralyze the wife to the point that she cannot make practical, reasonable demands upon the husband. What self-respecting feminist woman would want to shackle her husband to the role of breadwinner, or to rely on his paycheck? What self-respecting feminist man would define his masculinity around his father's jejune notions of obligation, emotional suppression, and conformity?

There is hardly a fellowship or a prestigious school that my friend Constance has not conquered. She is also beautiful, sexy, a great dresser, politically engaged, and a good friend—a perpetual-motion machine of success.

I cannot figure out how Constance's domestic arrangement works. She once confessed that it does not. Her husband, Ian, steeped in a feminist ethos himself, is a playwright, although he has not published anything. When Constance had children, she was already a professor, with ambivalent feelings about her profession but with every intention of securing the brass ring of tenure. Yet primary parenting and household responsibilities still fell on her shoulders, along with the onus of breadwinning, because Ian was writing and doing light teaching at workshops. It seemed all backward, and Constance knew this.

"Feeling resentful that I can't stay at home more," she once wrote to me after a second child was born, and "wishing it were otherwise."

But why *wasn't* it otherwise, if Constance wanted it to be at that phase of her life? I wonder if Constance's feminist sensibilities made her feel oppressively traditional about placing reasonable demands of parity on Ian. I wonder if Ian felt au courant and liberated for shirking them. Nothing requires more upkeep for the workhorse wife than a smart, dreamy, self-consciously feminist husband.

I encounter a house husband in a coffee shop, with maps of the

South Pacific and the Fiji Islands unfurled conspicuously on his table. He's not planning a trip. He's working on an adventure novel about environmental activists. His wife is a doctor.

I've no idea if his marriage has gone Tom Sawyer, because my criteria require that the workhorse wife be grumpy about her lot, and his wife may be content. Who knows, maybe he gives her a foot rub at the end of the day and smoothes her furrowed brow. Still, I do worry about the marriage's dreariness quotient. It unnerves me to think of his wife frantically cracking a chest open in an ER or stanching the carnage of Baltimore's violent streets while her unemployed, childfree, and unpublished husband happily pores over maps of remote islands and imagines being an überradical environmentalist whale-saver.

But I don't begrudge Tom Sawyer husbands their pursuit of their avocational dreams. Quite the contrary. Everybody should enjoy that sort of emancipation. It was very much what Friedan and second-wave feminism had in mind—for wives.

|||||||||||

At least our Tom Sawyer friends don't live in Malaysia. There they would be targets of a fatwa against house husbands. What a thrilling, perilous world where what passes for liberation in one culture ignites a holy war in another. In May 2006, influential Islamic clerics ruled that men who stay home to do housework (or not) while their wives work are "un-Islamic" and should be stopped. "Such a practice is clearly forbidden in Islam," declared cleric Noh Gadut. Or, if not un-Islamic, then at best a case of "shameful" sloth, according to Shahrizat Jalil, the Malaysian minister of women and family development. "The only reason males might want to stay home is probably they are just lazy or can't cope with office work."

It might appear that Tom Sawyers have compromised their masculinity, which Americans have for centuries pegged to the breadwinning role. John thinks that a lot of them have. "They're nagged," he observes, "and their wives think they're fools." Perhaps. But setting aside the minor indignity of castration by (ineffectual) nagging, such husbands are often more emboldened than emasculated by their marital arrangement. My circle of Tom Sawyer friends has fashioned a new kind of dignity calibrated by personal, intellectual, and creative freedom; the role of breadwinner is a shocking irrelevancy to their identity or self-esteem as husbands and men, neither a source of great pride nor a source of great shame.

Tom Sawyer is emphatically not a grown-up version of the notorious Gen X slacker. Tom Sawyer husbands are dreamy and quixotic, but they're not idle or lazy. On this point some of my girlfriends dissent ("They're not following any 'muses' except those leading to potato chips and football," says Laura), but I see most of them as hardworking, creative, and idiosyncratically inspired—which is to say, ambitious, in ways that do not pay the bills. They betray no particular masculine shame at not earning their keep—nothing like the brooding laid-off heroes of the average Bruce Springsteen song. They labor diligently, but theirs is a labor of love, secured for them by their wives' labor of labor.

Tom Sawyers have some genealogical resemblance to the *Playboy* swingers of the 1970s, who began to define their masculinity, social critic Barbara Ehrenreich argues, around consumption, casual sex, and fun. But Tom Sawyer pursues his unconventional masculinity in a conventional household, and with a strong, albeit quirky, work ethic intact. Tom Sawyer's closest kin may be the dilettantish Renaissance man. What a trust fund used to secure for a man, a well-heeled wife will now provide—a chance at an enchanting life off the tracks as a dabbler, amateur, and intellectual explorer.

I catch glimpses of this kind of masculinity in the obituary section of the *Washington Post*. Here you may occasionally find a flattering obituary of a handsome man, featured wearing a tuxedo at a charity function, who spent his life in philanthropy and archaeological adventures of some sort. Solidly educated, but with catholic tastes, the deceased will have achieved an obviously plush and expedition-filled life with no obvious source of income except inherited wealth.

Any intelligent, curious person would want something like that. He would prefer to spend his days writing poetry or painting rather than drinking stale coffee and writing memos. One workhorse wife I know asked her husband, "What do you want to *be* when you grow up?"

Usually, however, the oddity at the core of the marriage is discreetly elided. Identities are declared, not proven: Joe is a lawyer but has no clients; Jack is a novelist but has no publications; John is an entrepreneur but has no business. The husband pretends to work; the wife pretends to believe him. The husband creates a Potemkin village, and the wife pays to decorate it. With time and habituation, the elephant in the room—why doesn't this man *pull his weight?*—is sidestepped like any other dimly registered piece of furniture.

In a few cases I know of, workhorse wives, however disgruntled they may be, take a codependent delight in the charming, childlike dishevelment of their husbands' professional lives. Their husbands simply cannot schmooze, they will tell me with an absolving twinkle in the eye, or "navigate the workplace," or decipher office politics, or "handle authority and hierarchy." Of course, no one really enjoys handling these things, but most of us manage. To be evenhanded, some Tom Sawyers are nagged so remorselessly for their incompetence that I half imagine their mooching is a form of revenge against the hectoring.

On the point of presumed incompetence, Tom Sawyer has popularized neuroscience on his side. A bevy of experts seem to have converged on the idea that men's social skills and neurological tendencies handicap their ability to perform tasks in the vaunted new economy. The emerging wisdom about men's inferiority in school, social interactions, and even their traditional domain of the corner office makes it easier to treat Tom Sawyers as endearingly hapless figures lacking the de rigueur "skill sets" of the 21st century. Management gurus have been genuflecting at the feet of women managers and professionals for years, and perhaps that view of men's occupational obsolescence has seeped into the groundwater of marriage. Tom Sawyers happily live down to low expectations.

Whatever the reasons, workhorse wives value their husbands' dreams a great deal while they trifle with their own. The usual suspects can be corralled by way of explanation: Workhorse wives are self-defeating masochists, guilt-driven to deny their dreams, hobbled by ingrained deference, or overly defined by caregiving and sacrifice, and so on. It is a common conceit to point to women's complex inner lives today and to blame feminism for its naïve, misguided ideals, as if the problem began with espousing the dream of equality in the first place or believing that women would actually *want* careers. As the late Norman Mailer put it a few years ago, in explaining his notorious hostility toward feminism, "Men's lives as breadwinners are so dreary. Why would women *want* that?"

Of course, feminism never intended to fight for an equal right to dreariness. Missing in the workhorse wife and abounding in her Tom Sawyer husband is the basic sense of entitlement—to follow a dream or a muse or a crooked path shaped by whim and preference, to pursue a destiny of one's own choosing, freed from drudgeries performed in the service of someone else's destiny. Surely, freeing women from work and drudgery undertaken always for the sake of others—fathers, husbands, mothers, children—was the point of feminism. Wasn't feminism's deepest mission to equip women with a sense of their full humanity, and a sense of entitlement to that humanity?

Then again, entitlement is a tough nut to crack. It's proven easier to talk about choice, or what Linda Hirshman perceptively critiques as "choice feminism." Choices are things arrayed behind glass, a potential without action; entitlement suggests shattering the glass and seizing them. Too often, "choice" becomes an excuse not to remedy systemic inequalities in the workplace, instead chalking them up to women's deceptively personal decisions. For example, when feminists express concern about mothers who leave the workplace because of inadequate childcare options and inflexible hours, critics retort, "Well, wasn't feminism all about giving women *choices*, after all?" Not really. It's a costly misunderstanding to think so. "Choice" founders without entitlement, and it is the sense of entitlement that the workhorse wife does not claim easily in her own life even as she bestows it upon her husband's. It's such an extravagant gift! Tom Sawyer gets to do what he loves, unburdened by the quotidian dreariness of chores or concessions to reality.

Curiously, this places Tom Sawyer husbands among the biggest jackpot winners of feminism. They have achieved its ideal of liberation more fully than have their wives. They have unchained themselves from the breadwinner constraints of masculinity and embraced a feminist-inspired pursuit of their dreams without the artificial encumbrances and expectations of gender roles. Workhorse wives, meanwhile, are doing with a briefcase what they used to do with a dustpan: supporting their husbands' dreams and ambitions. That used to involve making soufflés, wearing cocktail dresses, and vacuuming. Today it might mean making big money and wearing tailored suits— and, still, vacuuming—but it amounts to a similar state of mind. "Life," my brother-in-law tells me, "is ninety percent maintenance—" unless you qualify for the Tom Sawyer discount.

CHAPTER FIVE

THE JOY OF FALLING

Downwardly Mobile and Mutually Liberated

NINA AND JOSH don't have the kind of marriage they thought they'd have. "Our lifestyle could have gone either way," Nina speculates. They're both in their early forties and have been married for more than eleven years. For the first of those years they were on track and on schedule for the American Dream. Nina is one of five daughters, and a second-generation Mexican American. She worked her way through college and still had about thirty thousand dollars in student loan debts when she got married. Josh comes from an upper-middle-class suburban family, and "always thought he'd marry some blond driving a BMW, and live in a high-rise condo in the Silicon Valley," Nina says. "Then he met me, the total opposite of his 'vision.'"

Early in their marriage Nina and Josh immersed themselves in the dot-com go-go years of Silicon Valley. In the mid-1990s, Nina was still in the "good grip" of credit card spending, and Josh was in the harness of the "classic rat-race lifestyle, commuting to work for an hour each way, making a lot of money and spending it faster than he realized." Like everyone around them, they glided in the slipstream of consumerism. The more they succeeded, the more their marital life-style made them melancholy. They tried to buy a house in the over-heated San Francisco real estate market, and realized they couldn't afford anything except a condo under the flight paths in the suburbs. So they made an unusual decision to pack up and move five hours north, to the rural area of Eureka, California. It started mostly as a quest for more space, but the marriage also had begun its journey toward a "simple, mobile lifestyle."

Once they moved out of Silicon Valley, simple living came more readily to Nina and Josh. Outside the frenetic habitat of Silicon Valley, they realized they wanted and needed less. But they were still working eighteen-hour days to get a graphic design business going. "We had visions of owning more real estate and some toys," Nina recalls, but another impulse competed with that one, and ultimately prevailed. They opted to fatten up the business in order to sell it. At the same time, a lot of their Bay Area married friends were "making huge sala-ries. When we would visit our friends they would show off their latest toys, new houses, et cetera, and I have to admit there were times when I did feel some of that pressure."

Instead they responded by downscaling and simplifying further, a contrapuntal move in the era of bubbles and leveraged luxury. They ditched their house. They now live and work together entirely in a mobile RV, and have for almost two years. "Some think of RVs as wasteful, but if you're a full-timer, like we are, and your only carbon footprint is your RV, it's a pretty small footprint," Nina reassures me, fearing that I might think her environmentally profligate. When they went "totally RV," they also discarded their television so they weren't "constantly comparing ourselves to the masses." Theirs is no ordinary RV. It has Internet hookups and a solar system that allows them to live off the grid when they want to, which they do about half the time. Their daily habit is to have cocktails in the trailer instead of going out, and they've met a community of like-minded nomad marriages in the RV world (it's not all old people and retirees, Nina explains). They have married friends with the same views on downward mobility and simplicity. Nina's friends "with regular jobs tend to be a little bit puzzled by our choices, and some will tell us that they are outright envious, too."

Nina and Josh have successfully run their co-owned business from "the remotest places in North America." They once went an entire year without using even a ream of paper. "There have been so many times where we'll be working from the most beautiful places in the mountains," Nina says, "yet we're still connected to the world with our Internet setup. It blows me away to think that we used to live any other way. We don't argue about money, unlike most couples. Both of us realized that material things won't make us happy, so what's the point in killing ourselves by working crazy hours for an income that's just going to make us want to spend it on stuff?" Nina and Josh are living the American Dream in reverse. They started out with a lot of money and possessions and through the course of the marriage they've shed them mindfully and intentionally, piece by piece.

The link between money and love—material wealth and a happy, thriving marriage—is one of the most basic, deeply internalized, and usually unexamined assumptions of marriage in the romantic style (and, although it didn't have romantic sources, an infamous marriage promotion billboard in Washington, D.C., some years ago promised that "Marriage Makes You Richer"). Even if we're not focused on consumer goods or possessions in marriage, most of us still assume that marriage supports upward mobility and that the economic purpose of marriage is to build prosperity. But what if a marriage played the romantic script around money and work in reverse, with an intention to redefine its material purpose? This was Nina and Josh's decision, and other marriages are experimenting in the same way.

The first deliberately downwardly mobile marriage I encountered was my sister's. At the time I thought this eccentric kind of marriage unique to my family. My sister married precisely on her fortieth birthday, escaping by just six hours the statistically apocryphal fate that a woman is more likely to get struck by lightning than to marry for the first time after she turns forty. She and her husband, who looks like a flesh-toned Papa Smurf (as he's the first to agree), have an eco-friendly home that they built and designed themselves over painstaking years. He had been married before, at the other extreme: a country club life-style with a high-pressure urban planning job that eventually left him disconsolate and sent him seeking refuge at the end of the workday in the calming mountains around his home. When that marriage ended he walked away from its trappings, the house and most of his things, and he stopped drinking.

Their house is like a day spa, tranquilly elegant and spare, crafted out of gorgeous woods milled from trees on their own lot. Their two cosseted cats, Cosmo and Lois, pad about gracefully in lieu of children. They make me wonder, not for the first time, if cats haven't begun to inch past children on the evolutionary scale as preferred domestic companions. The house lacks clutter. One Christmas, my sister jokingly recommended that I get them a gift certificate to the Goodwill, and their austerity is such that I believed her.

|||||||||

The vanguard of downwardly mobile marriages glints in several recent studies that document waning financial and career ambition, especially among college-educated Americans in their twenties and thirties. This trend of *voluntary* austerity predates the 2008 recession, and isn't its by-product. A growing number of us would prefer leisure, freedom, and time over money, big houses, and stuff. A 2008 Pew survey, among many others, found that adult Americans prize having "enough free time," at 67 percent, more than any other value listed, and far ahead of "being wealthy," at 13 percent. While not going to-tally RV, other marriages have acquired a taste for smaller, simpler, and more compact homes, as the latest architectural trends reveal.

As I've encountered them, the spouses in intentionally downwardly mobile marriages are most often college-educated and professionally employed. Many were raised in the suburbs, or, like Nina, are the chil-dren of immigrants. They can earn more but choose not to; they can afford a more opulent marriage but don't pursue it. In some cases they decide to stay childfree; in many cases they are attuned to living in environmentally sound ways; in all cases they voluntarily embrace the embourgeoisement of austerity. They rehabilitate what Barbara Ehrenreich describes as the "fear of falling"—of losing middle-class status—into the joy of falling. Their marriages are a kind of Huck Finn counterpoint to the Tom Sawyer ones.

For Ellen and her husband, bankruptcy worked as a catalyst the way an affair does in other marriages. Sometimes the most galvanizing and often estranging language in a marriage is money; sometimes it's sex. In any case, it's usually one or the other. "We are still married because I had a fit when I realized we were up for bankruptcy," Ellen remembers. "I put my foot down and said, 'No more. Get out, and if you're coming back, we're gonna dig our way out.'"

Ellen and Ron were both making good money in a dual-career marriage, but they ended up bankrupt. Harvard law professor Elizabeth Warren writes about this troubling phenomenon: the "two-income trap" of middle-class marriages that come to rely on both salaries just to support a basic standard of living. The potential liberation of having two high-income breadwinners in a marriage becomes a burdensome requirement of the marital budget. If one spouse loses a job or disaster strikes, the marriage has no backup or reserve income potential to tap into.

There was "nothing fun about the journey," Ellen admits, but now, seven years after the come-to-Jesus bankruptcy scare, they are "more in love than ever" and fiscally trim. "Folks around us assume we make a buttload of money," Ellen says. They don't. She works in nursing, Ron in IT, and they live off 48 percent of their combined salaries. They could double their salaries by working for corporations, but they don't "need or want the cash, and we each enjoy our careers and our employers who treat us well." They sprang their marriage from the two-income trap by living sparsely off a fraction of their income. They are using the historically unprecedented dual-career potential of husbands and wives to advance their security and mutual freedoms in the marriage.

Ellen says that "money is a nonissue" for them. "We find we almost always have something to chat about, and I used to worry about that." They ritualize the conversation around frugality, in the same fashion that weight watchers might fastidiously chart their caloric intake. For a decade, Ellen and Ron have sat down every January 1 to design their goals for the year. They take care of basics and then draw up a "want list" that includes very specific items for each of them, their fixer-upper cabin, and their home. Their wants have included a particular book, a woodworking clamp, a quilting tool for Ellen, a trip to Alaska to gaze upon Denali, tires, and rosebushes. Ellen and Ron live according to a pay-as-you-go rule. They save up for the "once in a lifetime" purchases and choose quality over price. They were married for seventeen years before they bought bedroom furniture, but when they did it was solid cherrywood that will last forever. They cross off and date each item as they achieve it, and "relish the successes" the next year. It sounds like money really is an "issue" in the marriage, but in a positive way. A financial crisis brought them to the brink of divorce, but now budget talk is an intimate marital code, just as another couple might bond by talking dirty in bed.

America is replete with opportunities for a marriage to try to buy its way out of sad reckonings, be it with a new frying pan or a house. It strikes me as brave, to remove that psychologically muffling layer of *things*, so that the marriage reveals itself unmistakably and starkly, with the clarity of the bone.

|||||||||

In a sense, the American Dream in the 20th century was a national rendition of the Cinderella dream: We find true love, we marry, and we live happily in well-appointed castles. We "provide for" each other—and inevitably our success at providing gets displayed in a comfortable standard of living and lifestyle. In the romantic script, love brings prosperity, not because we want it or plan it that way—gold-digging and opportunistic materialism offend the romantic spirit—but as the propitious, incidental dividend of our pure Excalibur love. The "standard of living," a mercurial, pacesetting concept first coined in 1902, entwined itself around the romantic ideal of marriage that grew up with it.

In the post–World War II decades, marriage became the natural unit and occasion for buying stuff. In his 1957 essay on the "suburban·sadness," David Riesman wrote of the American Way of Life in the postwar years, that "having had the cornucopia upturned over our heads, we feel it, if not a duty to consume, at least a kind of civil liberty to do so." Perhaps inescapably, this American Way of Life was also the American Way of Marriage. The two reinforced each other in a dense weave as the collusive lifestyle dreams of the "American century." Historian Elaine Tyler May has demonstrated the fascinating interdependency of marriage, household consumption, and Cold War politics. She found that "instead of rampant spending for personal luxury items" in the 1950s, Americans "poured their incomes into homes and family pursuits" to support what she characterizes as a "consumer-oriented family life," staged in suburbia. In the postwar years Americans binged on washing machines and appliances in a strange national cathexis of keeping up with the Joneses. The married household spurred consumption, and was its cellular unit. So much so that as Ehrenreich brilliantly argues in *The Hearts of Men*, Hugh Hefner's real genius with *Playboy* in 1953 was to liberate men as consumers. He invited single men to spend money liberally *outside* marriage, on themselves and their individual pleasures, while the airbrushed centerfolds absolved them of the stigma of homosexuality long associated with such smartly furnished and dapper bachelorhood.

Gradually, the furnishings and mise-en-scène of middle-class American marriage became its soul. The housewife grew to take pride in what May calls "her shopping list definition of marital success"; she began to think of the marriage in its marrow as a ritual of acquisition and a journey toward affluence and mobility. The massive Kelly

Longitudinal Study in the 1950s found that "consumerism and chil-dren" were the housewife's reward and raison d'être, the things that "made marriage worthwhile" to her. The husband joined the fran-chise of adulthood by being a family provider. He "could display his success through the accumulation of consumer goods" in the home. The romantic story of marriage was also the story of class mobility.

Dave is a husband in an intentionally downwardly mobile marriage, but he grew up, as did millions of middle-class Americans, according to the 20th century romantic script. He watched his mother "never sit down and read a book or just sit in peace, because my dad wanted a perfect house, so she just kept working every day. I don't think she was very happy at times. Life revolved around money and how you 'showed' how much you made." It's not an unusual story.

Dave interpreted his parents' marriage as a cautionary tale. He learned not to attach status or anxiety to material things. He wanted to grow up to be a beach bum with "a job to pay for what I needed, a little for retirement and a lot of time for fun. I didn't want Stuff." "Stuff" is often talked about totemically like this in the simple-living community, as if it were diabolically animate. When he first moved out on his own, as a bachelor, Dave rented a one-bedroom apartment near the beach, where he walked every day, rode his bike, and had a full-time job, but he only bought what could fit in his car, or furni-ture that could be hauled in a little trailer. Because of this abstemious-ness—his belongings were as effortlessly transported as a turtle with its shell—he saved a lot of money. He could "travel and move freely," and went Dumpster diving or thrifting to fill in gaps.

Then "marriage came, and Stuff accumulated." It's the next plot point in the romantic script. A woman woos an errant, free-ranging man—a playboy, a bachelor, a dreamy beach bum—and tames him into a breadwinning husband who buckles down to adulthood out of love and sheds his Huck Finn wanderlust. The whole point of marriage was to transform the beach bum into a breadwinner. (Some marriage defenders today still see the economic and sexual domestication of otherwise shiftless, rogue males as a primary social function of marriage.) Or, in a modern sequel, the husband manages to hold on to his freewheeling life, but only by mooching off a disconsolately hyper-achieving wife. The couple won't budge on their standard of living, or of toilet bowl cleanliness. They try to finance an upper-middle-class lifestyle as if they have two robust incomes, the husband's (non)salary deceiving them like a phantom limb.

Next came baby. By now Dave was "really tired, and tired of stumbling over baby Stuff and the house looking like a wreck." He and his wife had reached the next plot point—the marriage inspires hard work, and that begets prosperity, and prosperity begets more Stuff. Instead they took a post-romantic turn. They started with "a bag here, a box there." They got rid of most of their possessions in two yard sales, and have paid off all but a small amount of debt. They are "surviving" financially, and have time to spend as a family, to sit in the sun, and go back to school. Dave considers himself "an official beach bum with a family."

It's unusual, even disorienting, to see "beach bum" joined with "family" in the same sentence. The marital imagination holds loosely that in finances and career, we either live single and free or married and encumbered. Joy-of-falling couples imagine marriage differently, as a collaboration to support not material affluence but creative passions, financial sufficiency, free time, and mutual happiness. They are voluntarily deconstructing the 20th century romantic narrative, much as the Tom Sawyer marriage does, but in a different and more equitable way. In this regard the joy-of-falling marriage reads like a genuine if unanticipated feminist fairy tale of marital liberation. Both husband and wife get to pursue their passions, avocations, and freedom in the marriage, *because of* the marriage. This sort of mutual liberation sounds close to Friedan's utopian vision.

Mutual liberation has always been the better angel of the feminist nature. Only in right-wing caricature do feminists aspire to liberate and empower women by subordinating men. And it wasn't the point of feminism to stage a charivari wherein the wife swaps places with the dreary breadwinner husbands, or takes a round-trip through liberation and ends up yearning in 2010 for a retro revival of the stay-at-home wife of 1959, with all the legal, social, sexual, and financial vulnerabilities that that can entail. Nor, really, was it a feminist goal to send a dual-career couple on an exhausting journey culminating in a modest yet often futile quest for the fantasized peace of balance. These downwardly mobile marriages recommend that Friedan's dream is very much within our grasp. It doesn't necessarily entail changing gender roles, or careers, but changing the marital lifestyle goals, all the . . . Stuff.

|||||||||

These couples are marital pioneers in the sense that they are trying self-consciously to take one of the major facets of marriage in both the traditional and the romantic style—the assumption that it supports, and to some extent exists to support, prosperity—and rewrite it with a sense of adventure. It requires subtle acts of bravery. They have to resist the small, quotidian pressure to feel judged or ashamed for not having the most toys for the children, or for driving the shabbiest car in the carpool line. It cuts both ways, though. The standard of living for marriage is inherently viral. As middle-class couples see peers opting for reverse mobility, the idea drifts from the tributaries to the mainstream of marriage as a legitimate standard, and perhaps eventually a fashionable one. In a discussion online a wife recalls a weekend she spent with a well-educated professional couple that "theoretically could have been raking in the money, and instead were of very modest means and doing what they wanted in life." It inspired her to rethink her own marriage's economy.

Kiera and George have been married for five years. They get the occasional disparaging comment from Kiera's mother that their house is too small, and a real estate agent in their family couldn't understand why they didn't want to take out an exotic mortgage in 2004 to buy a bigger one. They see peer pressure in the other direction, too. They have a large number of professionally employed friends who "want flexibility, time, and energy for a wide variety of interests," Kiera says, and who think deeply about their standard of living. While these couples may not label it "simple living" explicitly, as Kiera and George do, he sees in the marriages around him "a trend toward streamlining life."

Kiera and George could easily have ended up ensnared in the two-income trap that Warren describes, or in a lopsided Tom Sawyer marriage. Kiera's a professor in a midwestern university town, and George is a freelance writer. "In honesty, our relationship started off on a bad foot financially," Kiera confesses. "George has almost always been un- or underemployed," and at one point had to declare bankruptcy. As they approached marriage, they were pursued by the four horsemen of debt apocalypse: credit cards, student loans, a mortgage, and personal debt. Kiera started accumulating consumer debt at a time when she was unhappy with her work. She grew up in the suburbs, the daughter of educated Indian immigrants, and her family "careened between cheapness and misplaced extravagance." As a child she felt "deprived," and "made up for it by buying whatever I wanted" as an adult during this unhappy time.

Things didn't seem promising. Kiera realized that if they didn't resolve the money problems, their marriage wouldn't work. George wanted to "dig out of the hole" of spending once his "life became tied to someone else" and he realized, admirably, that he "couldn't be selfish." The downwardly mobile marriage is about ethical decisions, such as respecting each other's dreams and happiness, as much as it's about the bottom line. Kiera and George had many conversations to change their marital rules and expectations. They chose austerity not out of necessity (they might have continued to stack up debt like everybody else) but out of preference. They decided that George could have a freelance career. Since Kiera's job wouldn't be flexible, it would be good if his was. But they made decisions to trim the marriage's standard of living so that Kiera wasn't disproportionately burdened with the breadwinner yoke, and to stay childfree. Neither was especially enthusiastic about starting a family to begin with.

Kiera and George swapped material ambition for what another simple-living wife refers to as the "luxury of time." That phrase intrigues me. Competition around the standard of living is hard to outwit in American marriage. Even when we go downwardly mobile, standard-of-living ambition has a way of regrouping and smuggling itself back in. We want to acquire and display our "luxuries."

For these marriages the coveted "luxury" items aren't cars but time, personal liberty, creative freedom, and professional latitude. I can imagine a day when middle-class marriages compete over the possessions of "lifestyle," "freedom," and "leisure time" as enthusiastically as they once competed over bigger homes and designer shoes. But for now, joy-of-falling husbands and wives are marital pioneers. Their improvised ideal, as one engaged woman explains it, is that neither "my fiancé nor I need to work like mad. We have enough stimulating work, enough time to pursue our interests, enough skills and enough grit to turn the resources around us into something that can sustain us. We have enough."

PART II

|||||||||||||||||||||||||||||

Parenting Marriages

CHAPTER SIX

THE HAVE CHILDREN– WILL DIVORCE PARADOX

How Parenthood Inspires Marriage and Then Steals It

THE REPRODUCTIVE IMPERATIVE of marriage is over. We can have children, by choice, without marriage, and in many but not all communities, that is an accepted choice if it's done responsibly and with dedication. Conversely we can be married without children. Of the nearly 105 million households recorded in the 2000 U.S. Census, only 55 million were composed of married couples; only 25 million were nuclear families with children. The romantic life cycle—falling in love, getting married, having sex, and having children—has been disrupted and fractured along each of its points, which no longer follow sequentially according to edict or convention. A single mother by choice might run the whole life cycle in reverse. She might have a child with donated sperm and a turkey baster, then have a passionate sexual affair, then fall in love, and then get married much later in life.

Our freedom from what amounts to compulsory parenthood— the idea that all marriages should be fruitful, and that this is a wifely duty—surely must free us and make us more content in marriage. Thinking broadly, that feels indisputably true. Because of the women's movement, birth control advances, and the evolution in women's identity, it's not a social death sentence to be childfree, or to reproduce insufficiently, and what's more, we have some control over these decisions in the age of optional parenthood.

Strangely, though, while the imperative to have children has waned, for many of us parenthood now feels like the one remaining imperative to get (and stay) married at all, in that parenthood is the one thing we can't honestly imagine doing just as easily on our own.

Chris, an acquaintance, knows of my interest in unexpurgated husbandly views of marriage. In that spirit, he tells me that he went on a weekend ski trip with a group of eleven husbands, "just the guys." Late that night they wandered, uncharacteristically, into a frank conversation about marriage. His companions were melancholy, but committed. One of them asked how many in the group would still be married if they didn't have children. Only two said that they would.

As recent research has concluded, while children give many of us a reason to marry, they may also make us unhappy in marriage, and even push us toward divorce. This is one of the paradoxes of the parenting-centric marriage, in which parenthood is both the inspiration for the marriage and its apparent downfall. As an aside, I'm not sure if the research on divorce, happiness, and parenthood measures the most pertinent emotion. I think children bring to your life and your marriage something more profoundly consoling and pleasingly solid than happiness—something to die for, a place in the world that's fixed and unchanged, a private religion, the capacity to have your heart broken and repaired. Children may not consistently make us happier but in my experience they make us more alive, and in my opinion feeling more alive is better than feeling "more" happy.

In any case, though, the paradox remains that parenthood can inspire and then kill a marriage. A "Mother's Index" in 2010 from Save the Children found that the United States ranked a dismal 28th, behind even debt-besieged Greece, on a list of the best places to be a mother. The chapters in this part will dissect that paradox, and seek the modern origins of our melancholy in the parenting marriage, in an age of optional parenthood. It will also look at some marriage pioneers who have found alternatives.

When my acquaintances describe the "transition to parenthood" in marriage, they gravitate to the language of trauma (It goes without saying, I hope, that they love their children. Love and devotion to children is a constant, it seems to me. Only the mothering fashions and politics change). A friend of mine described her child's baby years as "an emergency"; another friend, who is an award-winning teacher and knows plenty about children, called them an "ongoing crisis." Paula, the optimistic chemical engineer, says that early parenthood is like "jumping into cold, deep water. How do you get to the surface and breathe, and then how do you keep both of you afloat? It feels an awful lot like treading water a lot of the time. *Everyone* I know with young children feels that way." When our child was an infant, I privately emended the old anti-drug commercial to describe our plight: "This Is Your Marriage. This Is Your Marriage on Children." In another conversation with John I likened having a baby, psychologically, to a state of terrorism, because you never know what's going to happen next, or when, and you have no control over things.

In that sense, do we feel more like parents or hostages to our babies and toddlers? And, if we're hostages, then do we have a case of Stockholm syndrome?

Granted, today, I'm more a Subway Parent than a Helicopter Parent—a pneumatic car, zipping as quickly and surreptitiously as possible through the boisterous world of my child's school and letting the professionals do their jobs. The "transition to parenthood" has mellowed over time from a tragedy to a light, comic farce. We have an imaginative and easy child today, and he's pretty much his own helicopter anyway, an exquisitely attuned and conscientious child who worries about sugar consumption, trans fats, lightning strikes, McDonald's, and rare flesh-eating bacteria in the Chesapeake Bay.

But at the start, my mentality was very different. I didn't have an "easy" infant. Then again, no infant would have been easy for me unless he had been born reading Balzac and content to sit quietly in

a corner meditating. The maternal temperament didn't come effortlessly to me as it does to some other women. And for many women
who came of age in the early 1980s, children often weren't loosely
around in our lives before we had our own, so for me the baby was the
most central being in the marital ecology, the muse for its existence,
and the most alien. I was probably exceptionally oblivious, true. The
closest I'd come to motherhood in my thirty-four years, since I have
no nieces or nephews, was the occasional feminist-postmodern critique of "the (m)other," or the ambient cranky baby on an airplane.
I didn't absorb motherhood tricks by osmosis. In lieu of babysitting,
I burnished my college application by pursuing internships where I
performed tasks such as locating pictures of great American historic
bridges and dams for a preservation society.

What did come easily to me, almost naturally, were my good
student, type A professional skills. The decline in marital happiness
linked to new parenthood is probably exacerbated by the metasta-
sized professional temperament many of us bring to it. It's more than
professional "skill sets": It's an entire disposition. In the early 1970s,
second-wave feminists advocated for "Displaced Homemakers,"
mothers and housewives who found themselves bereft of financial
and social support when their husbands died or divorced them. I was
more like a Displaced Professional, suddenly bereft of an office and
looking for a rat race. It's another, and baleful, element of the intimacy
blur between work and home, colleague and spouse, parent and professional: The muse of the nursery is shifting, from Madonna (biblical,
not musical) to Donald Trump.

Being a displaced professional, I missed my old habitat, which I
could navigate with such brisk, intuitive competency. John's job got
reoriented in my mind as an unfair freedom or privilege, which I re-
sented, since it was a known world for me, sometimes frustrating but
at least familiar in its frustrations and governed by theoretically rational people able to use the toilet. Each workday, I'd clock-watch with
beseeching patience for the official transfer of power, the handover
moment when I could foist the squalling newborn onto John when he

returned from what now appeared to me the vacation of being in his office, doing the halcyon work of trying to wrestle multibillion-dollar global commodities markets to the ground and predict their future seizures and mood swings.

This handover ritual that I thought was my own desperate tic is a surprisingly idiomatic complaint from husbands in the parenting marriage, the marriage that defines itself largely by the project of having children and is the focus of the following chapters. When the wife is on maternity leave, or is a permanent, stay-at-home mom (and it's probably the same for stay-at-home dads), the breadwinner comes home from a challenging day of breadwinning only to have plastered onto him, before he's even changed his clothes, one, two, perhaps three children who are fighting, soiled, surly, or crying. There is something not only desperate but almost accusatory in the gesture (and I would know) because the spouse has "gotten" the luxury of going to work all day, and now must pay for it.

In Oprah Winfrey's entire career, up to September 2002, the most responses she had ever received to a single show was when feminist author Naomi Wolf came on to expose "the conspiracy of silence" around the dark undertow of motherhood. I read the transcripts for the show, and note that Wolf and her allies in the audience consistently referred to motherhood as "hard work," or a "job that sucks 80 percent of the time." Several other mothers took indignant umbrage, denouncing Wolf's profane view and her feelings, odd as it is to judge someone for her feelings, as—you guessed it—"selfish" and "whiny." Not me. The professional idioms she used about motherhood felt intuitively right. In earlier times, the work of childrearing has been perceived as anything from a religious act of stewardship to a creative art to a mystical experience to a nonchalant assumption to a random crapshoot. Somewhere along the way, for some of us, the child shifted from Member of the Family to Project to Be Managed.

Of course, if we were all willing to be "good-enough" displaced professional mothers who performed "good-enough" mothering—psychoanalyst D. W. Winnicott's outdated benchmark, and maternal absolution, of the 1950s—then we might escape this soul sickness. We'd be content to be goldbricking professionals, at least, who knew how to game the system to secure our peace of mind and happiness. Author Nora Ephron tells us that she can remember the day before "parent" was a verb. But we set much higher and self-defeating performance goals for ourselves today, as Judith Warner has described vividly and accurately in *Perfect Madness*.

Perfection is one parenting fashion; "attachment" is another. Combined, the fashions of perfection and attachment don't really predispose us toward an easygoing, nonchalant marriage once we opt for children. Attachment parenthood seems to have gotten more pronounced since the days when I had an infant, at least within the progressive, relatively prosperous classes. Principles of attachment—a mother isn't doing the best job to bond unless she carries her baby constantly, sleeps with her children, breastfeeds exclusively, and so on—keep wives effectively tied to their children and to their homes, if the prescription is to be followed precisely. The net effect is that the mom-child dyad swamps other adult roles for the mother.

It's tempting to see attachment parenting and natural motherhood as a return to the wifely domestic confinement of the 1950s, but post-millennium mothering is different from that. In the romantic-era marriage of the 1950s, the middle-class housewife, however limited her sphere, had all sorts of roles and sources of social approval, in addition to her children and motherhood (more on this in the next chapter). And these post–World War II housewives believed—for better or worse—in the great American gods of appliances, technology, electricity, bottle-feeding, clever gadgets, the new miracle of television, plastics, Twinkies and other sugary treats with which to bribe, fast foods, the Cocktail Hour, and other notions to make domestic life easier.

The closest kin to the attachment or natural parenting fashion is perhaps more an 18th century, pre-industrial American domesticity, given our current emphasis on extended breastfeeding; the idealization of unmedicated childbirth; the return of the Colonial-era snug family quarters, with the "family bed" in which maternal bonding occurs; the use of cloth diapers; the home preparation of baby foods; the constant carrying of infants in baby slings; wariness toward vaccinations and modern medicine; the revival of home gardening; the momentum toward home schooling; the rejection of babysitters and daycare; the enthusiasm for do-it-yourself arts and crafts projects with children, such as spending hours laminating hearts on Valentine's Day goodie bags or hand stitching a Frankenstein Halloween outfit; and the repudiation of television, media, computer games, or anything else that might be plugged in to a wall to provide a reprieve from the otherwise remorseless interactivity of motherhood. If we added home butter-churning demonstrations and Colonial bonnets and buckle shoes, we could have the "living museum" of historic Plymouth Plantation reconstructed in our 21st century parenting prescriptions.

To be accurate, I've yet to meet a mother who attempted with earnest masochism to follow each and every one of these prescriptions for perfection and/or attachment. But the extent to which one is willing to be swallowed whole within the whale of motherhood does become an informal benchmark in playground conversations among mothers, in an age of insecurity, as Warner describes, around marriage and parenthood alike. More often, I hear uneasy confessions from women that they've not done all of these things to spec (for one example, a few acquaintances tell me that they "felt like a failure" because they had C-section deliveries), as if their reasonable exercise of common sense constituted a breach of maternal devotion and sacrifice.

This might account for something I hear anecdotally from wives my own age, but less so from those of my mother's generation. I've been told by my contemporaries that their experiences with their second child was qualitatively better than with the first, in part because they felt more competent the second time around, but also because the exigencies of having more than one child at a time logistically impeded the quest for flawlessness.

In 2006, I published an essay in which I stated that I was a mediocre mother and unashamed of it. It felt bold at the time to assert even such an intuitive proposition. After all, by statistical law alone, most of us inhabit the vast, mediocre middle of being neither awesome nor wretched for any task at hand.

I hope it's not just wishful thinking, but I do hear stirrings of a marital shift, or perhaps an outright rebellion, against the pervasive-parenting philosophy. *New York Sun* columnist and author Lenore Skenazy and others champion "free-range" parenting. I sense it as well in women who are coming out of the closet about their own guiltless maternal imperfection. This is the vanguard of the Happily, Unapologetically Laid Back, and Middling Mothers, and it really amounts to a dusting off of the psychoanalytic chestnut of the "good-enough mother."

But, for now, the imperfect ideal is still a promising but minor chord in motherhood. "Helicopter parents" can be ruthless in their pursuit of that perfection. There's no ambitious, competitive "I" in *teamwork*, the collaboration-obsessed, nurturing Romantic office manager will tell you, but there most definitely is one in *family*.

Toy marketers, to pick one example among so many, cater to the exacting standards of the displaced professional mother. To have a baby in the 21st century is to be thrust into a world where Fun dares not venture forth unaccompanied by Learning. Do some "laughin' and learnin'," a random baby toy enticed; "have fun *while* learning," another promised. Lamaze churns out developmentally appropriate toys for babies, devised by Ph.D.s who apparently have strong psychedelic affinities. Our favorite was a squeaking monkey named Max with a black-and-white checkerboard chest and a red pom-pom belly button, clutching a yellow triangle and a banana with its feet. High-contrast colors, evidently, boost brainpower and intellectual output.

I laugh now at my earnest devotion to all the advice manuals, and the pop neuroscience—the kind of neuroscience whose conclusions fit on the side label of a cereal box or a toy—but the funny bone is the first thing to fail us, I've heard it said, and I took these recommendations seriously at the time, as if my baby would end up blind and stunted without the stimulation of black and red objects and a prodigious bounty of breast milk.

Each moment counted toward baby enrichment. I could almost imagine my son's neurons withering because I wasn't talking enough or pointing out interesting, edifying, neuron-forging things to look at (one of the most indelible but apparently deeply simplified, if not apocryphal, bits of pop neuroscience is that the "first three years" are make-or-break for a brain, so you need to be trailblazing as many neural connections and pathways for your child as you can with Mozart and pre-birth fetal stimulation apparatuses).

Like most babies today, mine got toted around in the royal palanquin of his car seat. Many days we'd make a pilgrimage to the organic supermarket Whole Foods, which I sometimes imagined as a 3-D performance art installation on the parenting fashions and cant of the American middle and affluent classes. Up and down the aisles, parents would narrate to their babies, who sat in specially padded grocery carts to keep their rears comfortable. Like garrulous color commentators tasked to fill the lulls in a baseball game, they'd exclaim, "That's an *orange*," their laughin'-and-learnin' words echoing in the cavernous, artfully restored warehouse. "That's a *kiwi*, see how *green* it is!" Everything was an occasion for edification. This parenting, fulsome and relentless, had a bizarrely ostentatious quality. One day I heard a young mother ask a cashier if they had organic formula and then apologize, since it "must not be popular here." She was genuinely worried about being judged for her baby-feeding decisions by a twenty-something checkout guy, or from eavesdropping shoppers such as me. Oddly, my overwhelming feeling in those days was one of intense self-consciousness, and this characteristic seems the most different from my parents' era: Has a generation of parents ever been so acutely *aware* of itself as parents? Almost as if we were performers onstage—susceptible to bad reviews, and always being appraised.

The parenting marriage is exquisitely, even morbidly attuned to its own performance and parenting standards. This tends to undercut whatever happy nonchalance or blasé view we might have managed

in an earlier age, when kids were pretty much compulsory and therefore part of the marriage scenery. Oddly, there might have been a kind
of collateral freedom in the idea that children were just there, and
nothing all that special or even chosen in a marriage. When I think
about the melancholy parenting marriage today, I am reminded of
Alaskan salmon who die in the act of succeeding at their deepest and
most sacred purpose, of spawning.

Alice is one story among millions in the Have Children–Will
Divorce statistic. She was a wife in a low-conflict melancholy marriage who divorced a Great Guy—and her ex-husband Peter is, by all
indications, a lovely person. Alice's marriage fits the paradox. A desire
for children inspired her to marry Peter, and, when she had a child,
she was inspired to divorce. As their bonds as parents strengthened,
the marital bond faded over three years into an inoffensive but wispy
irrelevance. I think of Alice's marriage as the case of the "Eunuch
Barbie," a phrase she herself uses to describe her postpartum identity
as a wife.

To understand her parenting marriage, she tells me, I have to know
a few things about what came before. Alice was in the midst of a gruel-
ing surgical residency in a southern city when she met the big passion
of her life. "He was a bad boy, and I had the best sex of my life, and it
was so irresponsible." He was never interested in marriage. "When I
was with him I remember thinking that he would drive off with the
baby seat on the roof of the car. So part of me said, don't make this a
permanent thing, but I was in a total addiction." The demon lover was
also impossible, she says, because he was rough-hewn and a Latino and
"I could never bring him home to mother. I've got a totally conservative right-wing father who would basically not allow him in the house."

The second important antecedent is that Alice went to medical
school late in life, in her waning twenties. Before then she was a personal fitness trainer. A beautiful, lithe woman with iridescent eyes,
she emanates a bouncy energy and enthusiasm, but she also has the
methodical and focused mind of a doctor. It's hard to imagine her
glumly vanquished by circumstance.

Alice would have been in her early forties by the time she was done with her surgical residency. That left her wondering how she'd find a husband. She always assumed she'd marry. "To me it was more about wanting to have kids," she says, "and I could never do the one without the other. It never, *ever* occurred to me to be a single mom. It was *so* unacceptable. It would be like announcing to my parents that I was an artist, or that I was gay. It just wouldn't fly." For her, parent-approved childrearing was very much the imperative of marriage.

She cast about for role models. She knew a female trauma surgeon who had beautiful, thorough hands—and a husband who was having an affair with his secretary. Another surgeon, in her early forties, had lost her husband to cancer, and was going out into the dating scene. "With being a surgeon and her age? It was *zilch* in terms of her marketability." Alice was in the fateful second year of her residency when she decided to leave the surgical specialty, which was extremely hard, because she loved it. "But it was the kid thing, the mid-thirties and living in a city" where she didn't think she'd meet good candidates for marriage. She moved back to her hometown of Cleveland, where she still lives, to pursue a new medical specialty. "And there is Mr. Peter!" she laughs. "Handsome and of European extraction and a doctor, and he came to my home and my parents *poured him a glass of wine.*" The spectacle filled her with "orgasmic" delight. "Wow, it is possible to have a relationship that involves my parents. It was all so acceptable. It was *dry-cleaned* for me."

Peter made sense in every on-paper way. He's a warm, funny, and kind person, and he was finishing up a fellowship in Alice's new specialty of endocrinology. He became an invaluable, generous career mentor to her, and when they moved in together they created an elegant mise-en-scène, largely because of Peter's aesthetic sophistication. Today, he'd fit the profile of a metrosexual—a decidedly heterosexual but style-conscious single man. "Our apartment," Alice recalls, "was a lot about cooking, drinking wine, listening to music, watching foreign films, and having people over." During the surgical residency she had been "fighting fighting fighting, and I felt like I wasn't fighting anymore." And in comparison to the demon lover, "the threat level or stability was better. You want to have a block of amplitude" with the man you marry; "you don't want it all over the map." It's quintessentially post-romantic, to marry with a dream of being stable dancing in our heads.

Although Peter's integration into her family filled Alice with orgasmic excitement, their sex life didn't. She later had an epiphany that she'd married the dapper but neuter Planters Peanuts man, Mr. Peanut, whom Peter vaguely resembled with his long legs, striped shorts, and slight paunch. "I would say that sex was relegated to a very small, low part of the relationship," but "he was okay about it and I was, too, because look what I was getting"—a career mentor, a family-approved mate, and a lovely habitat.

They got engaged, and it's clearer to Alice in retrospect what she wanted: a child. "Here's the deviousness which at the time I didn't recognize, but now, OMG, it's so obvious, because of course we had a microscope in our apartment for work. . . ." So one night, after they'd fooled around, Alice obtained a sperm sample from Peter and rushed over to confirm his sperm count and motility. She was reassured of hassle-free conception in her future.

"Maybe he had the same agenda, to get married in order to have a child," I propose.

"I wish that were true," she responds. "I'd feel less guilty."

The couple's desire for a small wedding yielded to parental pressure. In the end they had a two-hundred-plus wedding reception at Alice's parents' house, with her parents' friends, the night after the wedding. She recalls the wedding as quite beautiful but underwhelming. As a general principle it seems that the wedding predicts the marriage, and this one blurred drowsily into their daily life. After the ceremony, Alice and Peter slipped into their regular clothes and wandered off, at Peter's suggestion, to cruise cookie-cutter bars in a town dominated by strip malls and office buildings. "I felt like saying to the bartender, 'I just got married tonight. Isn't this *weird*?'" Peter got drunk and fell asleep on the hotel room floor. The next morning they went home to do laundry.

Just after the wedding, they didn't have sex much, but on one occasion Alice stood on her head to facilitate conception. During the pregnancy there was no sex at all, "even in the second trimester, when you're horny," Alice remembers. "But it was okay because you're going through all the excitement and you feel the baby and you see the ultrasound. Sex takes a backseat. I think women can just turn it off like that." The baby was already supplanting whatever emotional spot Peter might have occupied as a husband.

The delivery was an epic saga, with a lot of damage because the baby's head was huge. But once Perry was born, "suddenly, you have this object beyond any love you've ever known."

Alice was enveloped in love for her son, but the transition to parenthood was a lonely, treacherous one. "The highlight of my day was closing the bathroom door and crying and having a sitz bath to soothe my tattered perineum. I remember having dreams that my old Barbie doll was like any other, except between the legs there was this big, carved-out gash. Like all of my sexual organs were gone, carved out. . . . I was the Eunuch Barbie."

In Alice's case the carved-up Eunuch Barbie has literal antecedents in her battlefield birth experience, but it's a telling metaphor of modern marriage with children, the sexual organs and the couple's erotic life excised by the baby. "He was the whole focus," Alice says, and like me, she credits some of the "hellish" transition to the competitive coercion to breast-feed and to judge a woman by how much milk she stores in the freezer. "At the end of the day," Alice reflects, "it ensures that you have nothing else left." It's the baby and you.

The marriage, Alice says poignantly, was a "diaphanous thing. It wasn't all there." That seems to have been true even before Perry, but it faded steadily after he arrived and all the energy and focus drained from the marriage to motherhood—Alice's muse for the marriage in the first place. Alice doesn't think she rejected Peter, and says he probably doesn't feel that he rejected her. They were cordial, they slept in the same bed—"*slept*, that is." But she had high performance standards for herself as a mother, and "it was all the baby, everything was about the baby, everything we talked about and did."

They didn't have sex for three years, from the pregnancy through to Perry's toddlerhood. Alice was "not capable of sound-mind situations," as a parolee once memorably pleaded before a judge acquaintance of mine. Alice imagines that Peter may remember the whole "first two years" as "a blip, except for having a strangely anxious wife." There wasn't a lot of communication or fighting in the marriage. It was low-conflict, low-stress in the extreme.

When Perry was a year and a half old, the couple went to a resort in Texas to vacation with Peter's family. Everything was easier there— they had community, and help with the baby. One day at the beach "I said to him, 'This is not working. We haven't had sex for *years*.'" Peter said some "generic, noncommittal stuff, and I finally had my shit back together where I could convey a thought, and I said, 'There's no way this will work. I've got no connection with you in *any* way.' And maybe at that point, I told myself: This is my mate. This is the person who is implicated in the crime of having a child with me."

Another year went by. "Nothing. Zero."

"Did *you* ever throw him down or make a pass?"

"I never had that 'grab his arm and smack him and bite him' thing, no."

And a year after their first conversation on the beach, they had the exact same conversation, in the same spot. Time conspires against the child-centric, sex-free, Eunuch Barbie marriage. Before you know it, you've gone years without any (or any meaningful) sex, you've gone a year without even mentioning the problem. Then you arrive at the same milepost—an annual vacation or holiday—and the cycle repeats.

But that year, Alice stumbled across the demon lover, who had moved to the area where she and Peter were vacationing. She arranged to meet him one night. In person, and over the phone, Alice had a feeling "not of wanting to *be* with him, but of having that connection with the wild me again, all that stuff I left behind."

The demon lover reminded her of her old self. But he also clarified for her, indirectly, what the marriage was really about. Alice had the two-year-old Perry in her arms, and he was "the cutest thing you can imagine." And the demon lover was late, as always, and left the car running as they talked. "I thought, this is why I did this, for Perry. This never would have worked with him." In one rekindled connection with the demon lover, Alice achieved clarity about why she had married and why she could no longer stay married.

Others in melancholy parenting marriages might Stick It Out, or they might make accommodations to their discontent. But in another number of cases, a sometimes incidental or sometimes premeditated epiphany of all that's been lost makes it impossible to stay. Peter wasn't a bad guy, not at all. He just wasn't, for Alice, a presence in the marriage who made her the person she wanted to be. This was all before social networking, but with the advent of Facebook, which gift-wraps your romantic past and delivers it to your doorstep—you don't need to find trouble, as it comes and friends you—we can expect many such stories in which the ghosts of past relationships come back like Hamlet's father to catalyze change in a marriage, provoke divorce, spook the marriage into revelation, incite an affair, or just remind us, to trivial or consequential effect, of the parts of ourselves that we may have let go when we married.

Alice and Peter slipped into divorce as calmly as they had gotten married. She didn't "break up" the marriage so much as she let it decompose. When Perry was still a toddler, they bought a house. Peter put her name on the deed with his, but generously said that he'd pay the mortgage alone. Consider it a Christmas present, he told her. "It was his way of acknowledging divorce," Alice thinks, an old soft-shoe out the door. So much of marriage seems to transpire through real estate today—the bonds it forges, the way it solidifies or dissolves commitment. Alice moved out of the house, and into a small but charming cottage. The first night she flung the windows wide open and reveled in "getting back myself."

She has no regrets about the divorce, because she and Peter are quite close now. Alice has a sharp sense of humor about the foibles of her married life, but they both clearly esteem and respect each other. She has a boyfriend in another town, and no desire to remarry, although she'd like a monogamous long-term relationship. In Kristin's case, described in chapter 2, a wonderful friendship transmogrified into a bad marriage, but in Alice's case a bad marriage morphed into a rich friendship and co-parenting relationship. "We're as focused on the child as you can be," she says. Perry was always the fulcrum of the marriage, her husband a wispier figure, and now there's no internalized social pressure on them to be anything more than what they mostly were together: co-parents.

||||||||||

During the years of early parenthood my marriage began to waver, too, and in some of the same ways as Alice's. Precisely when the marriage had fulfilled its biggest imperative, and we had a beloved child, it started to founder. Looking back, this is when I first began to think of myself as maritally melancholy—the moment when I decisively joined the fraternity of the low-conflict, low-stress semi-happy marriage.

I don't spend a lot of time at spas. Relaxation like that unnerves me, and it's expensive, to boot. Oddly, though, both the marriage proposal and the first intimation of divorce occurred at spas, the first in 1997 and the second in the early 2000s. With a two-year-old at home, it was not a convenient time for me to be discontented about marriage.

Just as the first utterance of the word *marriage* inescapably reorients a dating relationship, there is something incantatory and materializing, like a spell, in uttering the word *divorce* for the first time, earnestly. It makes things happen, makes them seem possible. A feral dread is tamed in the act of saying it.

I was with my oldest friend, Eva, at a day spa in California in the early 2000s. Wrapped up in white towels, we were lounging in chaises on the deck of a thermal pool, with cucumber slices over our eyes. Eva asked me about John. She's fond of him. She once commented, and I agree, that if "all men were like John, we'd have this masculinity problem worked out in one generation."

In lieu of the stock responses to her question, I said something real.

"We don't connect anymore intellectually," I mused, just on the polite side of complaint. "We're not close or intimate. The parts of me he understands, and the things I liked about him at first? The things that were positive? I don't care as much about those things anymore."

"But . . . you're not thinking of *divorce*, are you?" The word echoed in the hollow, tiled pool room. The cucumber slices still covered my eyes. My head snapped in the general direction of Eva's voice before I remembered to take them off. Eva looked alarmed, or perhaps baffled. She stared at me probingly.

"No!" I said frantically. "Not really . . . *divorce*." Eva wrote an ingenious parody of an Edgar Allan Poe poem as a toast at our wedding; I've known her since we were twelve, before sex, before desire, long before compromise. Recalling that whole unsullied world "before" made me wistfully ashamed of the nonbliss in my marriage—and to such a Great Guy!

"It's okay! It's just complicated. Or . . . not complicated, dull."

"Be careful," Eva said, wrapping the towel around her tighter, "or you two could end up really hating each other."

Once the word is spoken, divorce becomes a Damocles' sword over the marriage. A recklessly destructive anti-romanticism even attaches to the idea: You can *do* this to each other. You can unmake each other, and your world—just the very same way you made it.

Nothing discretely terrible happened in our marriage to provoke that moment with Eva. I'm sometimes inclined to portray John as a cartoon of a perfect husband, and he does have wonderful qualities. But inevitably we conspired in our drift toward cordial estrangement, and our marriage like all the others I've encountered is vastly more complicated than the sum of its two Wonderful Wife and Great Guy parts. John's narrow emotional band was soothing and comforting at first, and then became frustrating. Often he didn't listen or observe very closely, preferring appeasement to truth-telling; preferring an appearance of contentment and agreeability to a slog through a gnarled mess; preferring to tell me what I'd like to hear instead of what he really thought. I was writing in my journal one day, and thought that perhaps I should tuck it away in a private corner when I finished, but then I had the jolting insight that I could leave it anywhere in the house, with confidence that John wouldn't look at it. Not because he respected my privacy, per se, but because he wouldn't really be that curious anymore, if he ever was. The brisk competency that I prized in him at first came to appear founded on bland incuriosity, invidious denial, perhaps laziness, or even an antisocial retreat from the risks of feeling and intimacy. Our virtues can turn on us in marriage, since the virtues and flaws are so often Janus-faced. The hypothermia of early parenthood, in which we pulled deeply into ourselves to "survive another day," in Josie's phrase, made us even less inclined toward fruitful insurrection against familiar roles. We had trouble seeing each other's full humanity through the efficacious caricatures we turned ourselves into during the "ongoing crisis" of parenthood.

Even when the crisis passed, we didn't shift back. After the tumult of early parenthood, the simple solace of order and a hallowed routine when our son was a toddler, and then in school, felt like a cup of hot liquid that had to be balanced carefully lest it spill on us. So in these years we became much more deeply habituated—more entangled with each other—while becoming much less intimate. I wouldn't have thought habituation without intimacy possible, before I married. It's my impression that marriage can introduce previously unimagined variations or compromises on intimacy.

For a fair percentage of high-functioning but discontented couples, the turn toward melancholy, one-dimensional dispassion occurs first and most literally around sex and the loss of desire. In *The Sex-Starved Marriage*, Michele Weiner-Davis estimates that almost one in four marriages are essentially sexless. Former secretary of labor Robert Reich even had a pet acronym for it: DINS, for "dual-income, no sex." Dagmar Herzog, an historian of sexuality, writes that the sexual "crisis" that he diagnoses in the 21st century has extended beyond premarital sex to postmarital sex, "its quality, its quantity, . . . indeed its very existence. . . . Never before have so many Americans worried so much about whether they really even want sex at all." A bachelor friend once told me that he couldn't imagine it would be *possible* to be in the same bed with a woman he fancied and not want to have sex with her. Now, married, he understands. It feels almost as if passion exsanguinates from a marriage. As far as erotic charge goes, one day you're sleeping with a lover-husband, and the next you might as well be in bed with a toaster.

Some research suggests that early in parenthood the withering of lust even may be evolutionarily preordained and biologically normative. The oxytocin that used to go toward bonding with the sexual partner gets transferred to the baby. I think it's natural for desire to wane anyway, and a noble man-made effort when it doesn't. It's rarely a case of attractiveness, apparently. According to a 2008 study, only 12 percent of unfaithful spouses felt that their lovers were more attractive or in "better shape" than their husbands or wives. I know that marital-bed death can be corrected if caught in time, and that many advice books can help, but marriages often let things slide, and, in any case, this isn't an advice book.

Josie and I talked over the general theme of marital sex, as we slumped on her futon sofa on a summer night. She has a sensible-shoes, foot-soldier view that I've heard other wives share. Marriages simply need to do it. "Just have mercy sex," Josie comments. "Just look at it like the Eisenhower years. It's a wifely role." Josie was by now in the throes of no-mercy sex with an exciting but tormenting new girlfriend, Donna, who was maddeningly evasive and mercurial, and wouldn't commit to the relationship through the bond that the joint purchase of a center-hall colonial house in a tony neighborhood would have represented.

By this point I'd grown to distrust any well-intentioned sentence about a marriage that begins with the imperative *just*. It's not that easy, and the sacrifice or compromise that the word *just* heralds often feels too impossibly hard to make, for whatever reason. Just leave if there's no passion. Just have sex more. Just put up with everything happily, and don't be Selfish and Whiny. "Just" is the one thing that a low-conflict semi-happy marriage emphatically is not. You don't enjoy the fixed celestial navigation of just.

In my own particular case, the most troubling contemplation, but perhaps the truest, is that passion, depth, surprise, and multifariousness died because in some grimly cunning way we wanted it dead. If disenchanted companionability wasn't what we "wanted," it was in a deeper sense, perhaps, what made us comfortable and safe. Alice's yen for a stable "block of amplitude" speaks to me. A deep irony, but, in retrospect, a preordained one, and one that's not limited to our marriage, as the research on children, divorce, and unhappiness indicates, is that our parenting-centric household flourished as the marriage withered.

This inverse pattern can't have been an accident. The pruning of marriage's other, nonparental, imperatives and reasons for being leave parenthood at the center of things, alone. What the child-centric household loves, the marriage hates: the no-sudden-moves banality, stability, predictability without surprise or digression. In a word, charmlessness. Charm means many things, but mostly the capacity to be surprised, enriched, transformed, delighted, and nourished in the ways that matter to you. Maybe the happy marriage isn't so much about realism, responsibility, or pragmatism, of which John and I have more than enough to gladden the heart of the marriage movement, but about the opposite. Being happily married in the long run may require living under a private magical spell or even falling perpetually for a trompe l'oeil. By a trick of the eye the trite can become new, shocking, even thrilling; a mystery long ago solved is revived, and you feel that you knew nothing of your spouse after all, that your feeling of habituation was a grave conceit. A marriage under the seductive,

rejuvenating spell of charm slips out from under the hubris of famil-
iarity or habituation as if it were a kaleidoscope composed of simple,
obvious elements in endless patterns and variations. Charm must be
the deeper wellspring of desire, alacrity, sexual intimacy, and other
perishable elements of a long marriage. Somewhere in these years, I
suspect that John and I lost it.

It was around this same time that we first floated the terms *divorce*
and *trial separation* seriously, although we spoke of it aloud only rarely
and I don't remember the first conversation. The idea settled in subtly
and gradually, like a new season. Still, the more you say the word, and
think it, the more it's defanged into harmlessness. We should have
insisted in these years that we live truthfully, not conveniently, in
marriage, but we chose competent habituation. We'd begun our own
low-conflict spiral into amiable disengagement.

||||||||||

Dan is a marriage therapist whom I chat with informally for research
purposes (and not "on the record" as an expert). Dan has practiced
marriage therapy in Baltimore for more than three decades. When
I meet him for coffee, he wears a scruffy beard and a fishing cap and
has a gentle, optimistic air. He's my ambassador for the regenerative,
self-healing powers of an injured marriage.

"There's no divorce after a child," Dan tells me emphatically. He
might have added that there's not much *marriage* after a child, either.
Dan means that in all but the most lopsided or treacherous circumstances you end up having to deal with your spouse anyway, through
the joint custody laws. As part of his note-taking with new clients,
Dan will create charts to remember the family structure. These charts
used to be simple, and drawn vertically on the page. They depicted
generations of married-for-life people producing the next generation
of married-for-life people. "Now, I turn the sheet of paper horizon-
tally," he says. It's easier to diagram complex, blended families and
stepfamilies that way.

If Dan were to diagram John and me, he might want to do it with a circle—as a galaxy of two planets, each in its own orbit but with beloved child as our gravitational pull from the center, alone. It's a rich paradox: We are less encumbered by the idea that marriage means having children than any earlier generation. But we may end up the most defined by parenthood, once we do make that choice.

CHAPTER SEVEN

CHILDREN: THE NEW SPOUSES

How the Strength of Family Values
Became the Weakness of Family

OUR MARRIAGES WOULDN'T necessarily feel this defined by parenthood if other marriage imperatives competed with it—and even occasionally won. As a child, I sat in a rickety folding chair at holiday dinners. I was a fledgling eavesdropper into the obscure machinations of the grown-up world from my perch at the children's table, a humble artifact of a vanished marital civilization. Most all of my friends remember sitting at the battered, modestly adorned children's table, exiled to the hinterland of the dining room. There you ate with the other nominally civilized children while the adults enjoyed adult amusement and repartee. The children's table conveyed a sense of proportion and order. We were integral to the family, but we were cogs in the machine, not its center. Again, marriage was a thick institution. It had numerous overlapping obligations and agendas. Necessarily—and fruitfully, I contend—these occasionally clashed with each other. Being the corporate wife might mean putting your dinner guests ahead of your children, who would have to scramble off to amuse themselves. A wife *as* a wife had her own value and identity; a husband *as* a husband had his. An acquaintance of mine expresses mixed, ironic nostalgia for the "pre-Friedan housewife" days, when a wife could get credit socially for, say, being a great decorator, arranging flowers nicely, baking a cake, throwing awesome cocktail parties, dressing stylishly, organizing charity drives and/or knowing how to set a formal table or play a mean game of bridge. A wife could get social recognition or status, that is, for something other than her children, or for being a mom. The strongest double bond, as chemists might say, was often between the spouses. Children today occupy the center of a marriage with fewer if any rivals because marriage has been pruned of its other imperatives. Children aren't *an* imperative so much as *the* imperative. The oppressions of the romantic script of husbandly and wifely roles are familiar and hardly need to be rehashed here. What interests me is the post-romantic, topsy-turvy world that has taken its place—the child's migration from folding chair to throne.

||||||||||

Some research concludes the opposite, that children in the 21st century are less central to marriage than ever before. Whereas most Italians today see having children as the main purpose of marriage, 70 percent of Americans, according to a 2007 Pew Research Center poll, think it's some version of mutual happiness or fulfillment instead. And, to judge by the number of couples who opt to remain child-free—not child*less*, they say, which implies a lack—marriage is indeed more adult-centered. Deliberately childfree marriages are a small but steadily and robustly growing marital trend. Fully 18 percent of married women in the United States were childless at century's end; more than four million reported in a 1995 survey by the National Center for Health Statistics that they were voluntarily childless. A 2009 Census report finds that only 46 percent of households have children, down from 52 percent in the 1950s. The website for No Kidding!, an international social network for childfree couples, tantalizes with pictures of an adult-centric utopia—couples lounging by pools, enjoying white-water rafting trips, and flirting at costume parties.

Those in childfree marriages say that they occasionally get judged for being selfish and immature in choosing to do nonparental things like buying expensive cars or going on safaris. But when we look at the reasons behind many childfree marriages, it seems that the protracted family values campaign that began in the 1980s has been internalized brilliantly, and to richly ironic effect. My generation grew up in the divorce heyday of the 1970s, and then came of age in the divorce back-lash and pro–family values spirit of the 1980s. That legacy has left its mark on us. The family values movement may have killed the goose that laid the golden egg. It sets such strict child-first standards that type A parents, concerned about success and doing the right thing, might understandably decide to stay childfree. When researchers ask why people don't have children, they are often told that it's way too much responsibility, that it's too hard to do a good job of it, that it's too big an "investment" and a "financial burden"—as if only the wealthy and affluent can succeed at it. By the same logic, perhaps, one-child marriages have more than doubled since the 1960s, and are one of the fastest-growing family types in the United States.

Childfree couples are imagining children differently, more acutely and dauntingly, than in the days when it was assumed they followed naturally and almost compulsorily from marriage. The agitprop that children are a huge responsibility, such hard work, and such a pro-found commitment has been so deeply internalized that the childfree can be forgiven for thinking it's better not to risk botching it. Their logic sounds like a hyperinflated case of family values spooking the marital imagination. Some childfree marriages pour their nurturing impulses into friends instead, whose upkeep is vastly less expensive—usually discharged by a few glasses of wine or the occasional sushi lunch—and who do not require toilet training (or "toilet learning," in the new enlightened argot).

Likewise, decades of warnings about divorce and its deleterious effects on children might unintentionally persuade a financially self-sufficient woman to sidestep the risky business of marriage altogether and pursue single motherhood by choice, another powerfully growing vanguard. One in three babies is born to a single mother today. While the number of unwed births among teens has decreased steadily, it has risen just as steadily among college-educated women in their mid-thirties and forties.

Defenders of traditional marriage do not condone these Murphy Brown families, without fathers in the household. But in a way, the single-mother-by-choice thinking simply follows the family values logic to a distant conclusion that family values advocates would loathe: If children alone matter, you might as well just have the children. The husband *as* a husband, the marriage *as* a marriage is relegated to an ellipsis between parent and child. It's another example of the queer improvisations and twists that "traditional marriage" ideals can accidentally kindle in untraditional minds.

A 2006 study directed by Barbara Dafoe Whitehead found that spouses, far from being unduly focused on children and parenthood, are more "adult-centered," and the world more adult-oriented, as we live longer and have fewer children. "It's almost as if raising children, which used to [be] the common lot of most adults, now has become more of a niche in your life rather than one of the main features of adult life," Whitehead says.

Perhaps for this very reason, that parenthood is a unique niche in life, the focus becomes child-centric in an almost Copernican way once a marriage does opt to have children. So marriage in general may be both less child-centric than ever before and fanatically more child-centric than ever before, at the same time. When marriages start out as or become parenting marriages, the couple pours everything into doing right by the choice to have children. We see it in the childhood drowned in privilege that Madeline Levine describes in *The Price of Privilege*; in the "overscheduled" child that Robert Coles worries about; and in the infamous helicopter parents that most of us encounter firsthand in our parenting adventures. I suspect that many in the liberal "marital stance" of America today marry more like 21st-century Italians: Once we choose to have children, most of us really do think that the unique task of the marriage is to raise them.

Optional parenthood has this ironically subordinating and coercive effect in the ways it pressures the marriage. Every ten-year-old has argued the QED "I didn't ask to be born." Our choice in the matter—the withering of the imperative that marriage be fruitful—has lashed us tightly to that choice. We *did* ask the child to be born; we *did* choose parenthood.

In this respect, the strength of family values is the weakness of marriage, once it opts to have children. By this I mean that marriage *as* marriage, rather than as a synonym for "parents" or "parental responsibility," has withered into a forgotten or at least ancillary bond. Marriages may either be adult-centered or child-centered, but fewer are truly family-centered in the sense that they harmonize marriage, parenthood, and adulthood.

By way of contrast, one of the things I admire about the "Christian marriages" I encounter, for lack of more finely calibrated shorthand, is that they seem to maintain a nonchalance and a genuinely noncompetitive equanimity around children. They don't display the level of anxiety I see in affluent, secular marriages, so their exercise of "family values" has a different effect. Children are there, flawed or not, and they unfold according to some divine will, I suppose, and in my wanderings I've yet to hear a devout family agonize over whether a child would get into the top professions or schools (well, perhaps that owes to their fear of evolutionary theory), or worry about their children's intelligence or savvy. This kind of marriage is a refreshing enclave of parental fatalism, in its way. It's also an example of parenting relations that don't swamp the marriage or other adult roles. Maybe there's a subtle narcissistic hubris in imagining ourselves so influential over, and hence so burdened by, our children's fates. Maybe children find themselves happy or unhappy, successful or not, of their own accord. But these are marriages circumscribed and defined by evangelical faith, whose consolations are inaccessible to me.

118 MARRIAGE CONFIDENTIAL

To be emphatically clear, I'm not disputing the prime directive of parenthood, and the care of children. I'm not arguing that children shouldn't be the priority. Nor am I imagining a zero-sum calculus, whereby marriages gain only if children lose, and one role—wife *or* mother; husband *or* dad—must be chosen over another. I'm proposing that a harmonious compatibility of adult priorities and children's well-being should be possible, as it once was—and that this is what *"family* values" really should connote. Ideally, a "family" is a place where every member learns the tools of accommodation, deference, compromise, and the harmonious resolution of conflicting priorities, needs, prerogatives, and demands.

But under the ideologically distinct but deeply reinforcing regimes of perfect parenting and family values alike, children are so much the prime directive, the only thing that really matters, we are told endlessly and remorselessly, once you opt to have them, that the richer and more authentic concept of "family" as a complex unit, in which *all* members negotiate and get to have priorities, has weakened substantially. We feel this in the melancholy of our marriages. Having become parents, it's hard to be anything but parents.

In the show *Supernanny*, a British nanny attired to resemble Mary Poppins—the visual icon for good parenting—stages an intervention in a disordered American family. Details vary, but in most cases the family suffers because the children rule the household with mad despotism. In one memorable but not unusual episode, the couple has a pampered pet pig living in the house, the toddler rules the household, and the children "sleep" (not) in the parents' bed by routine. The mother comments poignantly at the beginning of the show, "We're not husband and wife anymore. Just parents."

What this housewife says in despair, some Western European couples say happily. They're proudly not husband and wife anymore— just parents. It's as if they've cut out the middleman of marriage and gone directly to parenthood as the real bond. "We have little commitment to the institution of marriage, that's true, but we do have a commitment to parenthood," explains a sociology professor at Norway's

University of Trondheim, who was interviewed by a *New York Times* reporter. Eric Larrayadieu, a Scandinavian photographer, explains that in wedding photos, children sometimes occupy the central position. He's not married to his girlfriend, although they've lived together for years and have a young child, a more widespread and much more socially accepted pattern in Western Europe than in the United States (moreover, Western European children measure ahead of American children in several international studies of well-being). "The two of us are together and we made a very good wine, and it's called Marius. Probably the child is the best wedding we could have together."

I find it unsettling and even perhaps creepy to imagine a child transitively as a marriage, or to position the child as the focal point of a wedding ceremony. But it's an apt metaphor, even for marriages in the United States. Our marital disequilibrium goes beyond the breezy and often unheeded advice that parents "make time for each other." Children hold a different place in the inner life of a marriage today. As we become "just parents," children are in some ways the new spouses. They occupy the psychological and sometimes literal space previously occupied by the spouse, or the marriage itself. They're the ones to whom commitment is made, the ones around whom intimacy is defined, the inviolable bond, the affective and even romantic focus of the family. Paula, introduced in chapter 3, summarizes the inner life of a parenting marriage succinctly, and characteristically: Children are "the driver of the marriage. I clearly see marriage as a way to create a stable environment for kids."

Incidentally, legal opinions in opposition to same-sex marriage buttress the idea that marriage is fundamentally an arrangement for procreation and a "stable environment" for children—that this is the state's interest in marriage. A 2007 Maryland Court of Appeals ruling, *Conaway v. Deane*, upheld as constitutional a statute limiting marriage to a man and a woman. In the ruling the court asserted, as have other benches, that marriage enjoys its "fundamental status" in large part because of "its link to procreation." The fundamental right to marriage is conferred, they clarified, not because couples "actually procreate" but "because of the possibility of procreation" occurring in a biologically accidental and nonassisted fashion. In this example criticism of same-sex marriage pushes "traditional marriage" into more reactionary, obsolete definitional corners, as an institution defined by the theoretical possibility of biological conception occurring accidentally through an act of vaginal-penile intercourse.

More broadly, as legal scholar Ian Smith notes, courts have come to interpret marriage and family law almost exclusively to mean "children's law" and parenthood. A "family" means children. Candace, a childfree wife, notices this anecdotally, in everyday discourse. "When I refer to my family, people seem baffled," she comments. "They say, 'I thought you didn't have kids.' I absolutely consider my husband and myself a family, but other people don't."

Once the decision is made, children become, in legal parlance, the last surviving "status" intimacy, as opposed to "contract" intimacy. That's something I experience viscerally and psychologically. Children have always created an enduring, fixed status bond, but now they provide that inner solace almost exclusively, because the frail and attenuated roles of husband and wife certainly do not. My wedding felt more like an "I Can't Believe It's a Wedding!" cocktail party with some vows attached, but on two occasions over the last eleven years I've had wedding-like moments that felt like an inviolable bond had truly and instantaneously been forged between John and me. The first was three months before our wedding, when we bought our house. It involved vastly more quantification and certification than marriage, fitness tests of our financial worthiness, personal history, and character, and reams of more documentation. America takes real estate very seriously. You can't run off to Vegas and buy a house in ten minutes from a banker dressed up as Elvis. The second was when I stood in the smallish bathroom of that house on a black, freezing cold early February morning of 2001 and watched happily as the line on a home pregnancy test emerged and turned blue. At that moment we really and truly were bonded to each other, for life.

Now that marital roles have diminished as status relationships, parenthood provides that one fixed orientation point of an inviolable bond in life, our own personal true north. It offers refuge from the vertiginous discomfort of boundless choice that psychology professor Barry Schwartz describes.

Social workers and scholars have noted this in low-income communities, where children are coveted for the psychological succor they promise, as imagined anchors in an uncertain life. Nisa Islam Muhammad, founder of Wedded Bliss and a marriage defender, recounts that she once asked a classroom of inner-city girls how many wanted to be mothers. Almost all raised their hands. When she asked how many wanted to be wives, none did. What added value, identity, or consolation, after all, does being a wife possess on its own?

Maybe children get used, subconsciously, as anchors like that in our lives, in both the positive and negative senses of the term *anchor*. We can hide from other aspirations, dreams, and adult ambitions by becoming mothers. My friend Lucy debated with herself for years about whether to have a child, and eventually decided not to. When we discussed the pros and cons she gravitated to the idea that once you had a child, you didn't have to worry so much about professional ambition, or identity; you could *relax*, to use her word. That idea puzzled me at first. What could be less relaxing than a two-year-old? Now I understand it. Children can function as a socially sanctioned Get Out of Jail Free card, or an alibi, for the other parts of your life. You can let yourself fail or slack professionally, or give up on old ambitions, or lighten up on exercise goals or your social life. You can hide behind being a displaced professional mother who pours everything into researching the best approach to foreign language instruction—and you'll win social approval for it.

We can also use children, and especially the en vogue perfection and attachment standards, to hide from our marriages. A wife with a tenuous marriage, but with unsparingly brave clarity about her own psyche, admits that she deployed her baby and young child almost like "a shield," in her telling term, so that she wouldn't have to deal with intimacy with her husband. Her body and bed belonged almost entirely to the children, a living barrier around the brittle attachments of the marriage. Again, the strength of family values can become the weakness of marriage.

"If you have a child," a childfree married friend of mine once observed in a similar vein, "that's all you need to do." Like Lucy, my friend imagined a certain unburdening from worldly matters and expectations in the practice of burrowing into motherhood. If this is a small little secret of modern motherhood fashions, that there is perhaps a psychological relief or escape from other anxieties in becoming an anxious hyperparent, then it's certainly an understandable one to me. It's not easy to handle the post-liberation conditions of freedom, opportunity, and a surfeit of lifestyle choices, desirable though these things obviously are. This sort of freedom can be daunting and demanding. Contemporary motherhood, done a certain way and with a certain intensity, can indeed shield us from having to make difficult and risky claims on our marriages, or from having to pursue other dreams, talents, ambitions, careers, creative muses, and nonfamilial service that our educations and backgrounds have equipped us to fulfill. We can "relax" from the strain and anxiety of having other ambitions.

In these ways and more, children occupy a complex and dense place in the conscience of a marriage. They are "all that matters" under the regimes of perfect parenting and family values, and for that very reason, they have enormous, uncontested power in the family, which naturally could produce ambivalence about them. Do we owe our children all of our lives, after all? But how can we express that ambivalence openly? It would seem a betrayal of our children, and of our encumbering choice to have them, if we articulated the nuances and the tedious undertow of parenthood in realms other than comedy and the occasional lugubrious memoir. At the first meeting of No Kidding! in 1984, one husband told a bracingly honest cautionary tale of how the decision to have a child had made his marriage a "daily hell." In order to please (and keep) his wife, he went along with having a child, and "we have regretted it since the day our son arrived."

You don't hear parents today talk like that. What this husband confessed so candidly, other parents may experience much more mildly or ambiguously, or in mute secrecy. We fear our children's vulnerability, we want to protect them, and deploy all our professional competencies and displaced competitive instincts to advance their well-being. After all, we asked them to be born. So shouldn't we be able to forgive ourselves for sometimes feeling overpowered or harassed by our own children, or perpetually "underwater" in our parenting?

Popular culture, tapping into this private ambivalence of love, fear, and resentment, tends to represent children in antithetical ways. On the one hand, pink-doused Princess parties thrive, (doing errands one day, I see a bumper sticker shaped like a pink ribbon that says, "Her Spoiled Highness on Board"), and material marketed to children displays a belligerent imperiousness ("Kids Rule!" "Girl Power!"). Peggy Orenstein and other feminists have thoughtfully criticized the Princess phenomenon for its regressive sex roles, but it's also a reinforcement of the unisex royal prerogatives of children generally.

On the other hand, popular movies depict children as omnipotent monsters—Chucky the Killer Doll, for example, or the devil-child in the popular 2004 horror film *The Ring*. ("You were all I ever wanted!" the mad mother scolds her evil-spawn daughter as she drops her into a dark well in a futile attempt to murder her.) More recently we had the demonic girl-child in the movie *Orphan*. Cinematically, we like to see children go demonic and deranged on us almost as much as we like to see major cities destroyed by tidal waves, or blown to smithereens by aliens. In 2007, CBS aired a reality TV show called *Kid Nation*, an updated *Lord of the Flies* in which children ranging from elementary to high school age created and presided over their own society as quasi-adults. I wonder if the show appealed because it was so weird in its premise or because it was so familiar, a playful extrapolation on an inner state of mind that is all too common in the parenting marriage: Kids Rule!

. . .

Children can also colonize the literal space of the spouse, or at least the center of the home. The more extreme interpretations of attachment parenting encroach on the sacred marital bed, which becomes the family bed. The child, as a matter of habit rather than nightmare-inspired exception, occupies the position of the spouse literally and with Oedipal verisimilitude. If you want to have sex, go to the laundry room, the parents are advised. You've lived for decades, gotten your education, accomplished so much, but know your place: the laundry room with the cat box and the lint balls. Such is the indignity of adulthood.

The children's table has been put in storage. Chances are, if you have dinner with parents, the child will be sitting at the table with you. The child may monopolize the conversation, or adult badinage may come to a startled halt when a learning moment approaches and all eyes turn to the child, expectantly. I'd like to have T-shirts printed up that say, "I Am Not a Learning Moment." Table manners have always been the ritualization or instantiation of civil society and family—both an illustration and a tool of the accommodation and compromise required among all members, of family or society. Their demise paces the larger disequilibrium of the parenting marriage.

P. M. Forni, a professor at Johns Hopkins, writes extensively on manners and civility. He marveled when he had Italian guests whose children managed to sit quietly at the table, in deference to the setting. As for American children, their disruptive behavior isn't surprising, he says, since they are "trapped in a cage of narcissism we have built for them."

Sometimes you can peek through the windows at an otherwise opaque marriage and catch its hidden truths peripherally. As far as I can tell, it's the best way to get an unexpurgated view of marriage (another way is to accidentally pick up scenes from your neighbors' marriage through an overlapping channel on a baby monitor, like a car radio on the "scan" function). My son's "favorite *girl* to play with" is a charming, weedy eight-year-old. Emily loves to play "family," and in this game, she ventriloquizes her parents' marriage with what sounds like chilling concision. My son, being a sunny and domestically oblivious child, plays happily along while I listen enthralled, my ear planted gluttonously against my closed bedroom door.

"Honey, are you *driving*?" Emily prods with tired nasality.

"Sure!" he says appeasingly, almost frantically. (He learns his role quickly!)

"HONEY, I *told* you to put the bags in the car. Where are my *keys*?"

When Emily exhausts even herself with her pretend nagging, she relents and apologizes to her pretend henpecked husband in her household's fashion: "Oh, don't mind me. I'm just getting my period."

I've noticed that when all the kids on the block play grown-up, they play "family" almost exclusively. When John and I were growing up, we played at careers and work. John, his sister, and a neighborhood friend would play "city people," and be veterinarians, construction workers, and doctors. I would play schoolteacher (my mother's job) or real estate agent (my father's job, after his stint as a minister). The roles that signify adulthood for our children almost exclusively in their play are the roles of parents. Mostly, what they've seen their parents doing unapologetically as adults is be parents. Even the quintessential adult act of breadwinning is sometimes discussed as nothing but a guilty necessity that distracts from "time with the kids."

Some of us still have the recessive instinct to reclaim adult spaces and prerogatives from the captor of parenthood, though. We try to reconcile parenthood and adulthood.

Tim is a likable and witty man who lives in my neighborhood. He and his wife are professionally accomplished, and they have two healthy children. Although I don't know him well, he seems to be the index case of "family responsibility." For social diversion, when his children were around three and five, all Tim wanted was to play pickup basketball for two hours on Thursday nights with some old friends, but he didn't want to upset the children by leaving the house and asserting this priority. He'd be taking time away from them, and didn't want to say as much, so he'd feign going "grocery shopping" for the week—an excusable absence, I suppose—and sneak off to play basketball instead, coming home with some token bags of "groceries" borrowed from his own kitchen beforehand as a decoy.

Tim applied as much ingenuity to disguising his basketball game as a treacherous husband spends disguising his love affair. I wondered if he *was* having an affair, his alibi seemed so implausibly ornate to me, but John played with him once, and can vouch for it. Tim told me a few years ago that he and his wife had only gone out to dinner alone once in the five or more years they'd had children, which made me want to weep in empathic despair.

In Japanese, the word for "hell" translates loosely into "no space." Husbands and wives slake the hunger for solitude, dignity, avocation, and quiet as best they can. Their covert quest for adulthood may lie behind three discrete trends in the prosperous middle class. First, consider the dramatically rising popularity of distance and marathon running over the last decade. Running USA's State of the Sport report for 2008 boasts that running, and, in particular the half marathon, has "reached new heights." What the organization celebrates as the "Second Running Boom" continues strong. The Boston Marathon grew from 17,000 participants in 2002 to 25,000 in 2008, after it relaxed requirements for runners forty-five and older. Distance running devotees get up as early as 4 A.M. to sweat their way under the streetlamps in the blue light of their iPods like a vanquished race on the lam.

One of those midlife converts to marathons lives near me. She has a demanding full-time job and three ambitious, talented children (one Halloween, her oldest son carved the initial of his top-choice, top-tier college into a pumpkin, and her daughter graphed out her trick-or-treat candy by type). "I feel like I'm losing myself," she told me. A year later she started the marathon running, and, through this avocation, got her "self" back, she says.

Then there's the behemoth bathroom. Bathrooms keep getting larger in home designs and remodels. They're more like cavernous sepulchers. According to plumbing-fixture trade publications, bathroom size has grown steadily over the last three decades, so that today's average bathroom is twice as large as a bathroom from the mid-1970s.

Item three: the bizarre affection even for commuting to and from work. A nonprofit business group found in 2002 that for 59 percent of adult Americans the commute, even when it's a long one, is "the best part" of the workday.

The popularity of running, the supersizing of bathrooms, and the perverse solace of the commute all carve out makeshift spaces of adult prerogative in the shrinking territory of adulthood, spaces that children simply cannot infiltrate. After all, what ogre would make their five-year-old run twenty-five miles with them at the crack of dawn on a January morning? The website Nouveau Bathrooms elaborates that "large bathrooms are in," because they're "not just a place to get clean" but "a place to rest and relax." Clients make room for "chaise lounges and special bathroom furniture," and install "televisions, sound systems, and special reading areas." As for the commute, a woman interviewed in the *New York Times* about train travel saw it as an impregnable adult bivouac: "It's the best part of the day. The kids aren't bothering me, and the telephone isn't ringing." Another train commuter says fondly, "It's the only social life I have during the week."

As adult spaces dwindle and marriage gets pushed to the margins like a species with an endangered habitat, we seek sanctuary where we can find it.

CHAPTER EIGHT

MAN-CAVE IN THE PROMISED LAND

How Spouses Reclaim Their Adulthood
by Acting Like Children

M Y HUSBAND MIGHT well be one of those makeshift sanctuaries of adult, nonparental life that we guiltily seek. Married men love John. Not literally, or, at least, not to my knowledge. At first I thought they were on a quest for masculinity by proxy, without the fuss of actually spending two hours a day exercising, or maintaining an "exercise log" as John does. But it's more of a mystique than that. They boisterously imagine themselves in cigar bars with him or doing *he-man* things, like going on cycling trips.

Most of these husbands are middle-aged and middle-management. In one case, the husband and wife were both acquaintances because our son was friends with their daughter, a preternaturally sophisticated, rambunctious five-year-old who watched *Sex and the City* with her mother before bed and announced blithely that "when you go out with a boy, they expect you to spend the night." Her dad was a hail-fellow-well-met with an open, boyish face. When tasked to look after his daughter, he once took her to Hooters for the afternoon, where the waitresses fell in love with her, and had a group photo taken with her. He always had a touching reverence for John's masculine prowess.

John is a frequent object of what ESPN Radio dubbed a few years ago a "man crush," or a "bromance." (In 2010, the *Oxford English Dictionary* welcomed the term *bromance* into its canonic pages, so I guess the concept is here to stay.) These are crushes among avowedly heterosexual men. The energy is not homosexual but homosocial and fraternal. Eventually, I realized that John is where husbands go to escape their marriages with children. They dream of all-male expeditions with him and call to make plans. Often they don't materialize, but they enjoy the mental exercise of planning them.

Ray is the declared envy among many husbands in his office. He's almost a parody of the bachelor life. He *was* engaged, once, to a woman who "just wanted to settle down," but, all the while, she lived like a cyclone, while in contrast Ray is the most "settled down" person you can imagine. He's eaten the exact same dinner of spaghetti and peas every Thursday night for about fifteen years. The engagement broke off. Ray's a tournament-winning billiards player, an avid cyclist, a golfer, and a rabid football fan with season tickets on the fifty-yard line. He has a beach home for the occasional retreat and takes weekend trips to the mountains with "just the guys" once in a while. His usual companions are husbands on momentary furlough from their marriages. They complain to Ray most often, when they do, about the lack of affection and appreciation in their marriages, and although the grass-is-greener fallacy applies here as everywhere else, they envy the prospect of an all-male Saturday night shooting pool and drinking Scotch with an old friend.

Ray's a good one to ask about the secret social life of husbands and their rebellious retreats to their own worlds. "I see a kind of perverse equity in many marriages," he tells me. "Not only must all tasks be shared equally, but any time spent away on an individual activity must be made up in kind to the spouse. It's like there's this mental calculator that sounds a warning whenever one partner is enjoying himself too much." Fun and marriage are on tense terms these days.

As a parable of the No Fun Allowed marriage, Ray recounts a visit to a dear friend who is married in the sexless, Life Partners manner. The child is the undisputed fulcrum of his friend's marriage—its shared, and sole, devotional practice. Ray gives me an almost anthropological description of the precise machinations in the marriage's social life. "On the first evening of the visit we planned to see a movie," he recalls. "That is, he and I planned to see a movie, and that posed a bit of a problem. We sat in the living room discussing plans with his wife for a good half hour." Ray felt uncomfortable, sitting there "watching the mental machinations those two went through as they tried to exert control, but in a passive-aggressive way to avoid open conflict.

"First my friend offered the obligatory invitation to his wife in the hopes that it would be declined. That fulfilled his major responsibility: never forget the wife. His wife, realizing that the offer was insincere, said she *was* interested in going. With the ball now in my friend's court, his next maneuver was to say that he had some interest in seeing *Mars Attacks* (knowing his wife would hate that choice) but we could discuss other possibilities if that didn't seem appealing. They proceeded to examine all the possible movie choices in a pretend exercise at accommodation. This was more about control in the relationship than anything else, as my friend already knew what movie we'd see and his wife already knew that she wasn't going. Back and forth it went. They each tried to guilt the other in such a way as to ensure that neither would be happy with whatever decision was ultimately made. Finally, she relented and informed him that she would stay at home.

"As my friend and I walked out to the car, momentarily released, he said, 'I'll really owe her for this.'" And sure enough, "the first stop we made on the way to the theater was to a department store where he bought her a gift. Is it any wonder that the prospect of seeing a rotten movie with an old friend offers a momentary escape and that husbands and wives seek their own kind?"

Adult prerogatives and pleasures such as a fun, playful social life aren't easily wrested from marriage with children. I ask my online panel if they agree that "working married couples don't have much time for social life." This statement elicits a very high level of agreement, among the three highest, at 54 percent, with respondents agreeing somewhat (42 percent) to "entirely" (12 percent). No wonder so many bridesmaids end up in petulant tears.

Liam is a reluctant member of this secret tribe of husbands. He lives with his wife, Rachel, and their four children in a leafy enclave called Heathercroft, just minutes from the city in a stately first-ring suburb with beautiful stone homes built in the late 1800s. There are suburbs like this outside most of America's older cities. Many of Heathercroft's husbands work in banking, business, and finance, some in medicine. It's a conservative neighborhood in temperament and in its Rockefeller Republican political leanings. The men favor button-down shirts with suspenders; heavy crystal tumblers and carafes are displayed in their homes, and they grill expensive meat on expensive gas grills. Many of the wives—80 to 90 percent of them, Rachel estimates—are of the retro marriage variety, new stay-at-home moms with a lot of time and talent and education on their hands, along with their two, three, or more children who keep the task challenging. A disproportionate number of the wives, it seems to me when I visit, are blond and clad in Lilly Pulitzer.

Liam and Rachel don't entirely fit that mold. Rachel works as a teacher and loves her job. They have a penchant for truth-telling and self-questioning, and for a third, they are liberals in a conservative milieu. Liam is a wickedly witty Englishman with salt-and-pepper hair. He works in public relations and seems like the rough-and-tumble type who might once have enjoyed rugby. I talk to him over beers one evening about the social life of married fathers, and he tells me about a neighbor of his who became the accidental Pied Piper of the roving fraternity of Heathercroft husbands on the lam.

This neighbor, a middle-aged father prominent in law, with an artistic, sensitive streak, wanted a place to make music at home—"it's bizarre music," Liam notes—so he had a decorator retrofit his garage as a kind of adult reservation. He designed it in a tiki torch décor and with posters of rock stars and football players on the walls. He invited a dozen or so other husbands from the neighborhood over to behold his refurbished man-cave in the promised land, and they became the guests who wouldn't leave. Provided with a makeshift fraternity house, a room of their own, in which to drink keg beer and consort with each other, they stayed until late into the evening, many evenings. Two of the husbands once had such a vehement fight over an NFL quarterback's statistics that the one locked the other out of the tiki club until he apologized for his ignorance. Eventually, Heathercroft's wives pulled the plug on the tiki soirees. Their husbands were coming home too late, too drunk, and too regressed.

Sometimes the band of husbands rendezvous at a faux ethnic neighborhood pub in a nearby shopping mall. "They peg it to a sports event," Liam explains, which "breaks up the conversation" and usefully prevents the eruption of heartfelt discussion. They include enough men—"two is intimate, three is voyeuristic, four is safer"— to remove any potential stigma of homosexuality. They subsist on the basic food groups of tap beer, nachos, chicken wings, and fried mozzarella sticks. Their attire anachronistically conjures a masculinity in search of a derring-do mission: "They don North Face jackets and vests worthy of scaling Mount Everest, and boots for Arctic exploration, and they drive SUVs and off-terrain vehicles to go to the . . . mall."

"Are wives *ever* there?"

A few, Liam says, but they don't stay. A wife once dropped her husband off at the faux ethnic pub, but kept her car keys ostentatiously visible, reassuring them all, " 'Don't worry, I'm leaving.' It's like dropping your toddler off at the ball room at Ikea," Liam laughs, and the chauffeur wives like "the security that their husbands are in that one place for a while" without a car at their disposal.

Wives are present only through the iPhones and cellphones amassed like a technological centerpiece in the middle of the table, as if the husbands are "prisoners under house arrest who must wear ankle bracelets at all times." Periodically a wife calls and a device lights up, chirps, or buzzes to life, and the husband might gesture at it with a knowing look of irritation or stoic passivity. Honest conversation about wives or marriage is "strictly off-limits," Liam emphasizes, because the whole point is to "maintain the illusion of the not-marriage." Most of all, the husbands are "obsessed with reliving their days at university."

"What does that really mean to them?"

"No obligation. Fun. And conversation that has no obligation or *point* at all."

In 1956, Grace Metalious's scandalizing potboiler *Peyton Place* exposed the secret, edgy life of sexual affairs, incest, and illicit passion that roiled under the superficial rectitude of the suburban marriage. But the husbands of the Heathercroft tribe and other neo–Peyton Places are more apt to seek marital escape and rebellion with other men, through retro fraternities. Although Liam is occasionally entreated, futilely, by the other husbands at the faux ethnic pub to lure young college women over for light flirtation and to witness male chest-thumping (the men imagine that his British accent makes him a chick magnet), he's pretty confident they aren't having serious or even casual affairs.

Their husbandly subversions are just as likely to get channeled into quasi-infatuations with other men. Maybe the Metrosexual has killed off James Bond as the iconic alter ego of the husband and father.

I'm not proposing that it would somehow be preferable if husbands had secret sexual affairs like their late-1950s predecessors, known mostly today through the blockbuster television series *Mad Men*, instead of guffawing with a bunch of other exiled husbands in a refurbished garage over of a bucket of chicken wings. And of course there are plenty of cheaters among us, as always, but we don't hear much about the Tomcat Husband as a guiltily celebrated marital idiom. Instead we hear more about these nonfamily social lives that are chastely homosocial, abstinent, virtuous, backward-looking to the days of fraternities and collegiate capers, and decidedly post-romantic. A friend's husband once spoke seriously of the "blue team and the pink team" in marriage.

Heathercroft isn't an atomized suburb. It's more like a social hive in which wives and husbands move synchronously with their own sex.

The wives have their sororal equivalent, punctuated by monthly book club meetings, lubricated with copious box-wine drinking.

"What books do you read?" I ask Rachel.

"I can't remember many. Mostly the wives gossip about teachers and trash their marriages or talk about their husbands. The book doesn't figure much into it."

There are also "girls' nights out," as well as a bustling calendar of declaratively all-girl social events that have emerged in the last decade. These, too, are homosocial affairs but not lesbian gatherings, which is what I recall "all-girl" implied and euphemized when I was in college. There's the ladies' wine tasting night at a local liquor store; the Stitch and Bitch store, which sells yarn and holds all-girls' knitting nights; the all-girls' wine-drinking and pottery glazing events at another establishment, and—although it's not formally all-girl, of course— the neighborhood pool on summer days. When Rachel went to the pool during the 2008 election season, she "never heard the wives talk about politics. They talk about real estate, what they're doing to their houses, and their kids" and their accomplishments. "After a while," Rachel sighs, "it wasn't any fun. I just had to stop going."

The sororal world of wives may shade into the erotic, very much as it did in the pre-romantic era of the 19th century. I read in March 2009 of what may be an emerging microtrend of women who leave husbands for other women, in midlife, and express openly their crushes on women such as Bravo TV's sculpted fitness expert Jackie Warner, who gets fan mail galore, she says, from "straight housewives in middle America" with crushes on her.

In these ways husbands and wives look wistfully to the same-sex sororal and fraternal days of their youth, to its relationships of fun, tinted sometimes with the safely homosocial intimacy of the bromance, or the lighthearted frisson of the girl crush.

For Kay Hymowitz, a scholar at the Manhattan Institute, as well as for scholars such as Michael Kimmel in *Guyland*, the fixation on adolescence among other populations—especially bachelors in their twenties—is a source of social concern. Hymowitz worries about the "child-man," whom she aptly characterizes as "passionless." The child-man hangs out only with the guys, plays video games, still makes stupid toilet jokes, and has little professional or romantic ambition, and less interest in marital commitment, or even serious relationships. Hymowitz sees marriage as one palliative, a key station of the cross, as it were, on the journey to adulthood, and imagines it might prod these commitment-averse men to evolve out of their protracted, dilated adolescence. Marriage is magic elixir: it can add ten or fifteen years to you just like that!

I understand Hymowitz's annoyance. But getting married and having children may not have the desired sobering results. Guyland and Girl-land are the preferred social worlds in many marriages, too. The husbands and fathers who re-create fraternities in their tiki garages just find ways to return to the homosocial, collegiate comforts that marriage was supposed to cure them of. And it's not that they have refused to grow up, at all. It's more like they've done too much growing up already and that grown-upness is the cause of their bromance subversions.

"These are men who play by the rules," Liam reminds me. "When asked to run faster they run faster, they jump higher, they kick farther, they tackle harder."

"Are they happy in their marriages?"

"No. I think if you asked them and they answered honestly, they'd say they feel penned in." Liam generalizes them, in short, as classic low-conflict, low-stress semi-happy.

"Why stay married, then? Why not change the marriage?"

"They'd never improvise" by getting divorced or changing the rules, Liam explains.

They and their wives follow what critic Hymowitz flags in another article as the whole point of marriage: "to raise the next generation." That adherence to family values—no infidelity and no irresponsibility—pretty much smothers the rest of their adulthood. Adult fun, prerogatives, and privileges have been marginalized if not discredited in the parenting-centric family, so we go underground with our selfish desires. Of course, insofar as "selfish" means an awareness that we have a *self*, and that that self has needs and desires, even if the self happens also to be a parent, then a little bit of well-placed selfishness wouldn't be a bad thing in melancholy marriages today, swamped as they are in responsibility.

Liam's tiki garage makes me think of *American Beauty*, a brilliant cinematic meditation on a desiccated marriage. It offers the husband, played by Kevin Spacey, two roles: to live either as a sexless, soul-crushingly dutiful and henpecked husband, or as a pot-smoking, self-absorbed adolescent who lusts after the high school cheerleader. There is no authentic nonparental role for him in between, no option of being a multifaceted adult.

Liam and Rachel's neighbors shoulder adult responsibilities, but they don't enjoy the older privileges of adulthood. They don't have the social prerogatives and license that traditionally sweetened the toils of being grown up, and of being responsible parents. The "fun-loving husband" or the socially "freewheeling wife" isn't such a tenable position today. To describe someone that way sounds almost like a slur—a veiled accusation of selfishness, alcoholism, or sexual promiscuity. We don't have good role models for a responsible married adult who has meaningful, complex friendships, passions for civic causes or other nonmarital, nonparental engagements, and who feels entitled to assert those prerogatives. In a sense, the tiki garage husbands and their wives claim an adult social prerogative through the nostalgic ruse of "being childish."

A semi-happily married friend of mine has parents with an enviable marriage. Marriage Envy these days usually does attach to geriatric couples, whose ancient marriages are handled gingerly, like relics, in the features sections of local newspapers. And there's little more dispiriting than the realization, as another friend of mine had, that her parents might well have a better married sex life than she does. Rarely do I encounter women and men my own age who profess envy for any of their own peers' marriages. One day, my friend's mother, she of this enviable, zesty, and long-lasting marriage, asked of her daughter's queasier marriage, "How are you guys when you're on vacation?" She meant, when you actually decide to have fun, enjoy a marital social life together, and tend to your pleasures and priorities, can you feel martially contented then? And it dawned on me: her parents' enviable marriage felt the way that my friend's marriage felt only while on vacation *all the time*.

This retreat to the "childish" is a remedy to a particular strain of melancholy that intrigues me. Liam describes it as a "penned in" discontent among his peer husbands, a sense of having no room for maneuver or prerogative. Some of it may come from trying to live out the anachronism favored in the Heathercrofts of America. This is a group that got married in the 2000s, came of age in the 1970s, and opts for the 1950s in its family arrangement. They try earnestly to live by the rules of another day and age grafted on to this day and age, with all of its different options and circumstances. It can make for an awkward and sometimes unhappy transposition.

I think of their marital melancholy as a collective case of You Can't Go Back. One evening I talk to Lily, a hip forty-four-year-old with stylish eyeglasses and long, dark hair with highlights of blond. When I meet her for drinks, she's wearing combat pants and a blue-rhinestoned Bebe T-shirt. She's a lawyer by training and now a Realtor, but she looks like an artist or a rocker girl. For more than a decade Lily had the classic low-conflict "front" of a great marriage, as she calls it. "We entertained well to the bitter end," she sighs.

She and her husband Mark lived in a neighborhood that has similar mores to Heathercroft. Like the majority of Liam's neighbors, Lily and Mark aspired to a traditional (and romantic) marriage in terms of breadwinning and childrearing. Lily gladly set aside her career to raise their two children. "I was happy to do it," she says. "I really think in today's world it's hard. If you can afford to stay home, it's easier. It's better for the children." Likewise Mark self-consciously desired to be a "throwback," as Lily says, and "go back to the 1950s. He was the Breadwinner. He'd say, 'The guys in my dad's generation [in the late 1960s and 1970s] just messed things up.'" Lily and Mark's self-conscious, and prescriptive, nostalgia is noteworthy on its own terms. Although I may be wrong, I doubt that American marriages in the 1860s pined self-consciously for a return to the exemplary marriages of the 1820s. In a country that prizes the forward momentum of progress, it's odd to look backward for marital inspiration.

Despite their earnest affection for the 1950s division of labor in their marriage, Lily also simultaneously, and probably inescapably, envisioned herself and her husband in the fashion of the 2000s as co-parents. After their first child was born she immersed herself in what she calls "baby boot camp," single-minded about "doing the whole mommy thing, and that's *it*." This also sounds like a typical parenting marriage of our time—the childrearing imperative unleavened by other spousal roles or priorities—and Lily tells me that she, like many of us, married very much with having children on her mind. Meanwhile, Mark was the sole Breadwinner, true, and a responsible one, but after their first child was born he began a metamorphosis into Spouse: the New Child. When they were contemplating a second child he told her, directly, "We don't want to have number two because then I'll be number three."

"He didn't see any *shame* in positioning himself as a child?" I marvel aloud.

"He was on a quest for more attention. And I said, 'Wait a minute, we're being parents *together*, not you *being* a child.'"

Over the ensuing decade Lily and Mark's marriage settled into the familiar "worn record groove" of low-conflict melancholy. With each year the marriage became "more real," Lily says, yet left her feeling "empty and numb," sounding very much like the heir to Friedan's housewife, seduced and abandoned into discontent by the feminine mystique, or, as author Leslie Bennetts brilliantly calls the opted-out sequel of the 21st century, the "feminine mistake."

But their melancholy had new twists and sources. The marriage had the same hybrid evident in the man-cave: the responsible 1950s Breadwinner "throwback" husband who wants only to be Child No. 3. Whatever masculine affirmation Mark might have imagined receiving for being the breadwinner, he would have preferred to trade it in for the privilege of being his children. This is an interesting notion, since historically children have been the least powerful, least privileged, and most hassled members of a family, the role one sought to grow out of, not into.

Lily returns to this theme a few times in our conversation, the confusion of Mark's husbandly role vis-à-vis their children. Lily elaborates: "His father's father's generation—they were 'men.' They infantilized their wives, making them like children, but now the women are the moms and have it all together, and the men are making children out of themselves."

When Lily finally proposed separation, Mark declared that he "didn't believe in separation," and wanted to go straight to divorce while they were still young. "He didn't want to divide everything equally, either," she continues, and Lily would be the one, eventually, to move out of the home that she had created and fostered for the family. "He would have been happy if I'd left with just the clothes on my back. His view was, 'This is what I offered you.' In his mind he gave me everything I wanted—the house, the attention, the kids, and stability. Now *you* don't want it, so *you* go away."

I realize that I've heard this before in melancholy retro marriages, the idea of the breadwinning as a "gift." I don't know that a vintage 1950s husband would have figured it that way or described his role as a gift. Maybe he thought he had no *choice* but to provide for his ("infantilized") wife and his children. Maybe he thought, as the Kelly Longitudinal Study of the 1950s revealed, that marriage and children were the pacesetter that gave him a sense of "purpose and responsibility" in the first place, and that their care defined his masculinity. Maybe he saw that masculine role as more pleasurable and privileged than the adolescent role. Maybe he thought the gifts reciprocal, and therefore not gifts at all—just a marriage.

But Mark knew he didn't "have" to do these things. They could have both worked; he could have been a hardworking stay-at-home dad; he even could have slyly devised a Tom Sawyer marriage for himself. Anything is possible, after all. No longer dictated or prescribed, the retro arrangement felt like a gift to Mark, not a division of labor, an inescapable social obligation—however odious, at least consoling in its ubiquity and its masculine affirmations—or even a gender role.

And for that gift, what was he getting in return? His family, to be sure, and his children, but vastly less attention, as the children, in the post-romantic mannerism of the parenting marriage, had bumped him down to Child No. 3. Unlike Liam's comrades, who beat a nostalgic retreat to the fraternal consolations of the tiki garage, Mark still did yearn for the social companionship of his wife in the party and club scene. But, very much like Liam's neighbors, he intuited that that kind of pleasure and attention-getting privilege seemed only to persist honorably in the role of the child.

And what was Lily getting for her sacrifices, of her career and her nonparental life? The pleasure of her children, of course, but not really a co-parent, so much as a third child who clamored for attention and was jealous of their children and Lily's tight-knit birth family alike. The stay-at-home mom was pretty much what she was in the marriage, and that was her entire focus, unlike the more multifaceted, albeit oppressive, wifely roles of Friedan's day when you could get credit for throwing an awesome party or being a wonderful dresser and decorator, or the more heady, liberated roles embraced by the Having it All wife in the 1970s that some of our own mothers enjoyed.

It seems that for Mark, his "gift" cost too much, and for Lily, it gave too little.

The way out isn't to reimpose the consensus of the romantic heyday, when mothers and fathers were straitjacketed into their roles whether they liked it or not. But at least in this case, the anachronism of a marriage that opted earnestly to embrace a 1950s childrearing arrangement in a milieu of post-millennial options, sensibilities, and attitudes, didn't work so well, either. I ask Lily if she knows of things that might have solved the problems. She's not sure. Maybe if they had gone for something offbeat, like a marriage sabbatical, some "growth time" apart, they could have stayed married. Then again, maybe nothing would have saved them. At one point in our conversation, she says, with matter-of-fact resignation, and with no particular anger, "Men are kids."

CHAPTER NINE

MARITAL HABITATS

Being Married with Children in Public Again

SCANT MAJORITY OF American married couples still reside in the suburbs. Some of the new subdivisions and developments, infamously, are named for the bucolic idyll they've bulldozed—Fox Crossing, Verdant Meadow Way. Their discrete features—a yard, a garage, maybe a prim fence—conjure an image of marriage in the collective American unconscious. Here the houses tend to be isolated. The vivid lush green of the lawns encircling them seems almost a sentient, pulsing thing. Life here is less self-consciously hive-like than in Heathercroft, for example.

Through the preschool social whirl, we were once acquaintances with a married couple whose fresh, youthful faces make them seem eternally seniors in high school. They'd be most themselves, I used to think, looking for a keg party on a Saturday night. Sally literally sells shit. She's a manure and fertilizer saleswoman. When we first knew them they lived in a cozy house in an Olmsted-designed Baltimore neighborhood. Then they moved to a large home, enveloped by an expansive lawn, in a subdivision in an outlying suburb. I'll call it

Elysian Fields. The move surprised me, as it seemed discordant with their social nature.

We dropped our son off for a playdate at the new digs. When Sally came to the door, she apologized abashedly for still being in her pajamas in mid-afternoon. She hadn't had occasion or the need to breach the domestic ramparts that day. Presumably, she had laid in an adequate supply of provisions earlier in the week. Sally gave us a tour of the house. The last stop was the main area of the basement, an as yet unchristened, full-scale, functioning replica of an English pub, including a wooden bar, a tap, bar stools, a dartboard, and pub tables, all put there according to the developer's blueprint, and not on Sally's specific request. The point of a pub, of course, is to convene people socially, outside the home, people who do not live together. Jarringly, the domestic space had cannibalized the social space that the pub iconically connotes.

The parenting marriage is, by and large, conducted in isolation. The flip side of distrusting "children not included" pursuits as selfish is an inward, solipsistic focus on the family as a contained social unit. This inward focus characterizes family life in a variety of communities, both urban and suburban, although it might have been otherwise. In its germinal dream of itself, the postwar American suburb aspired tenderly to the sort of civic life that it is now more often charged with having obliterated. That suburban world, where husbands and wives had their adult pursuits, pleasures, and civic duties, and children had their own worlds, was criticized in the 1950s for its very *lack* of family privacy, and its dense, homogeneous social life (built, it has to be noted, on segregation of various forms). Critic David Riesman called it "likemindedness." But this neighborly intensity and conformity had its dividend in the provincial coziness of belonging. William Whyte wrote an ambivalent critique in his 1956 book *The Organization Man* of married couples in the corporate ranks who move to the suburbs and are swiftly "integrated" and "plunged into a hotbed of participation." Other couples "will help them unpack and around suppertime some of the girls will come over with a hot casserole and another with a percolator full of hot coffee." Wives have babysitting co-ops, and shared appliances and other household items. In a few short days the children have playmates, the wife sunbathes with the other "girls like an old timer," and the husband joins the poker club. "Their relationships with others transcend mere neighborliness," Whyte writes. The group was a tyrant but it was also a friend, a source of "warmth." Neighborliness, however, warred against another dream that eventually prevailed— a dream of isolation ("spaciousness," as Riesman characterized it), and the seduction of historical weightlessness. Loren Baritz writes of the "claustral" world of the suburbs in the postwar years, where "the move away from family customs and from sights and sounds of the city produced a thrilling feeling of liberation, of floating."

Robert Putnam's signal work, *Bowling Alone*, contends on the basis of an exhaustive meta-analysis of research that the drift in the early 1900s toward "hyper" civic engagement had reversed itself by the 1980s, when we began to recede from social life. An ethnographer who lived in a suburban New Jersey community in the 1980s observed a culture of atomized isolation, self-restraint, and "moral minimalism." Suburban marriages "kept to themselves, asking little of their neighbors and expecting little in return." Urbanist Lewis Mumford trenchantly argued that "the romantic suburb was a collective attempt to live a private life."

The culprits behind civic disengagement, Putnam concludes, range from expanding commute times to the dual-career marriage and the demise of the extended family. But social disengagement is also a story (and the collateral damage) of marriage in the romantic style. In the romantic ideal, marriage recedes from society and keeps its own counsel. It's one of the most powerful but largely unstated and unchallenged facets of the romantic marital fashion. The idea of "togetherness" within the family, memorably coined by *McCall's* in 1954, grew stronger as social vitality waned in the last half of the 20th century.

The romantic ideal of family self-sufficiency and togetherness placed unprecedented emotional demands on marriage. Baritz, among other writers, notes the anxious, insatiable "psychological dependency" in the postwar suburban marriage and family. Architecturally, the metaphor of the castle in the air, a citadel apart, conveys a key axiom of the romantic marital script: The closer you are to your spouse, the less social you "need" to be, as if the point of seeking society is to compensate for family and spousal deficiencies. Conversely, the more antisocial and emotionally reclusive the family, the stronger the love—sequestration becoming evidence not of social paucity but of romantic plenitude. This ideal of the self-sufficient marriage was reinforced by the family values wisdom of the 1980s that we should look inward, take care of our own, and think more about personal than social responsibility.

Advertisers to this day extol the carceral idea of the all-inclusive marriage capable of becoming the world to each spouse: "What diamond is good enough for your best friend, lawyer, confidant, lover, girlfriend, tennis partner all rolled into one? . . . What do you buy for the woman who is *everyone* to you?" Like an understaffed cast of extras, the spouse rushes to and fro, fulfilling many roles to create the appearance of a crowd.

The Marriage as Bomb Shelter lifestyle may be more common to my generation, which got married after the suburban migration and before the connectivity revolution of the Internet. John Cacioppo reports in his 2009 work on aloneness that 60 million Americans perceive themselves as lonely, a 30 percent increase in two decades. The Social Science Surveys found in 1984 that Americans had an average of three "confidants"; in 2004, the most common answer was "none." Putnam found "startling evidence" of a decline in sociability and an "extraordinary" decline in neighborliness from the 1970s to the late 1990s.

That retreat from society in family life, or, to phrase it as a romantic ideal, the marital dream of self-sufficiency and dependency, seems embedded in our marital habitats. Architects often criticize subdivisions like Elysian Fields for their aesthetic thoughtlessness, but their design actually reveals premeditation, and resonates with a dream for family life. Urbanists and many intellectuals tend to caricature suburban communities, a plump target for cultural criticism, as tasteless outposts for philistines, but suburban communities have an obvious, enduring appeal for marriages with children that cannot entirely be explained by safety or school systems. These developments are the very architecture of the romantic ideal of marriage castled snugly within its solitude. New suburban developments tend to follow two antithetical but spiritually similar design trends. In the first, the houses are exactly the same, lined up in rows like Monopoly houses. Visual monotony encourages social incuriosity, as no variation draws us to peek inside with the lure of something different that encourages us to make a social connection. James Howard Kunstler, a subdivision Jeremiah, deplores these places as "sinister barricades" that leave us in a "neurobiological slum" because they violate innate human needs and patterns of "aliveness," proportion, and scale. The "dead patterns in these enclaves," he warns, "infect the patterns around them with disease and ultimately with contagious deadness, and deaden us [until] isolation and loneliness broods across this land." The developers describe it differently in their sales brochures, of course.

In the second suburban trend, the houses are ornate, personalized, and much larger. These McMansions are entirely singular in their design, oblivious to the style or scale of the houses surrounding them. While the Monopoly suburbs have a socially deterring disregard for variation, McMansions are nothing but variation. They defy affinity: No coherent field of vision suggests a coherent community. Both the numbingly homogeneous and the extravagantly idiosyncratic suburb inhibit social connection. Their designs, with their lack of proportion, reinforce a lack of proportion in our lives. It's more than an aesthetic problem. It's a Marriage with Children lifestyle problem.

If communities reflect our marriage ideal, marriages and families also conform themselves subtly to their habitats, or so it seems to me. In that spirit, some marriage pioneers are seeking ways to do marriage with children in communities again, and are rejecting the "you're the world to me" romantic impulse toward self-containment and privacy.

Lauren and her husband, Oliver, for example, made a decision to try marriage in the city. They're part of a modest trend of families opting to live in the city even after they have children. They choose apartment living, or the more dense housing of city neighborhoods. These urban couples are interesting because they are zealous and emphatic about being a family in the city. It's not a default position but a self-conscious lifestyle decision. I visit an urban mother's group one morning and get a sense of the appeal. Two things come up repeatedly: First, the marriages feed on the "hustle and bustle," as one mother tells me. These couples thrive on always having something new to contemplate or look at; they're energized by the kinetic, random tableau of "people, horns, sirens, and dogs," another says. Second, I'm struck by the number of mothers here who grew up in suburban communities and are making a deliberate reverse migration in search of something more than what two wives describe in almost identical terms as a "typical suburban childhood." It's as if they perceive their own upbringings and lives as having conformed to an easily encapsulated script of the romantic heyday. These urban, middle-class families have been dwindling from cities for decades, but may be returning today, drawn to neighborhoods that offer some "sense of community," as another urbanite describes it.

The post-romantic experiment in these cases is to have a marriage that acknowledges happily, without defensiveness or umbrage, that the spouse and children aren't "enough"—that, as Kurt Vonnegut once wrote, none of us can be a hundred people to each other in marriage, and maybe that isn't a failure, but a reality to be accommodated, with changes in the marriage script and mise-en-scène. Obviously there are unhappy marriages in the suburbs and cities alike. Marriage in the city as I'm thinking of it is a state of mind as much as a housing location. You can have a cloistered marriage in the city, and a socially engaged one in a subdivision. But it's a marital temperament that values propinquity and social life, and a temperament that cities uniquely attract. If you don't like chance encounters, contact across differences, people, random activity, or the possibility of mystery and

coincidence, you move away. What interests me in these urban examples is the spirit of embedding marriage and family in social life again,
to redistribute some of the emotional burdens placed on marriage in
the romantic picket fence idyll.

Lauren and Oliver live in a renovated early-1800s townhouse in
a boisterous neighborhood near Baltimore's harbor. Both own their
own businesses, and Lauren built her clientele for her family portrait
service right from the immediate neighborhood. They have four children, all under the age of five, but they don't feel cramped in their
smallish home, since they have four finished levels.

If Lauren and Oliver didn't both live and work in the city, "I'm not
entirely convinced that I'd have this many children," she says. "If I'm
having a rough night, it's easy to call and say that I'd like him to come
home to help out, and it's not a question of getting in the car and
driving thirty minutes. It helps keep resentment from breeding, and I
think that's key." It also helps to have access to the spouse, the stores,
and work all within a few blocks. "At eight o'clock, if we are out of
milk (and that is huge for us), I can send my husband on a five-minute
walk to get it."

But trace the life cycle of that same gallon of milk in an exurban subdivision and you see its distant perturbations in a marriage. A gallon
of milk is just a gallon of milk—until the act of retrieving it after the
husband and wife have both worked full days and driven home becomes a half-hour chore that involves getting back in a car. The gallon
of milk becomes an onerous duty, one short step away from resentment, and from there, a metaphoric distillation of real and perceived
inequities in the marriage's dreariness quotient. Next time—and there
is always a next time with children—a fight erupts over who has to get
the goddamned gallon of milk and who did it the last time. Or maybe
not a fight, just a slight ripple, borne philosophically, with quiet but
simmering stoicism. Long after it's been consumed, the milk lives on
as a marital weapon, a symbolically condensed narrative of selfishness,
disregard, or bossiness, and good fodder for a marriage therapy ses-
sion. ("Then there was that time you wouldn't get the milk . . ." There's

no apparent statute of limitations on these bleats.) The resentments accrete into something obdurate and intricately fraught. It's not the *milk*, you understand, it's "the principle of the thing," the "attitude" it connotes.

Then again, maybe it really is the milk. It's the hidden tax levied on the inconveniently arranged life, where home is a distant citadel from other activities: Marriage takes place *here*, and everything else takes place *there*.

I see Kunstler's point. Subdivisions kill. On the drive home from Sally's Elysian Fields manse with its in-house pub, I discovered that by a morbid synchronicity my affable, endlessly tolerant husband and I had both been brooding over domestic violence during our tour ("If I needed help, who would hear me?") and over JonBenet Ramsey's murder ("Her body was found in an unused faux wine cellar just like this"). These gruesome phantasms were conjured, we speculated, not by the customary good grace and humor of our hostess, but simply by the experience of being in a large, sequestered, socially deterring domestic space that seemed, in some elemental aspect of its design, to be insane.

In the ongoing metamorphosis from the socially enmeshed to the romantically antisocial mind-set, the next malingering phase almost makes a pathology out of neighborly social relations. A U.S. Census Bureau study finds that many of us fear our communities. Nearly half of all parents worry that their neighbors may be a bad influence on their children. It's precisely this atmospheric dread of neighbors and society that agitates Lenore Skenazy. She suspects that the statistically irrational paranoia about the ax murderer lurking in the tree is part of what keeps parents homebound or helicoptering to protect their children from bogeymen. Skenazy stirred a media tempest in April 2008 after she wrote a column on allowing her nine-year-old, at his request, to go home on his own from Macy's, equipped with a New York City subway map, a transit card, twenty dollars, some quarters, and his common sense and wits. Skenazy's column and her decision were in their own way courageous—"Nine-Year-Old Rides Subway!" the headlines might have read—but she wonders how letting children play outside until the streetlights come on got to be "as brave as going shark hunting in a hamburger suit."

Skenazy was both praised and flamed, she tells me, for her apparently subversive act. She received a few thousand emails. Some accused her of letting her son ride the subway as a publicity stunt. One critic branded her "America's worst mom." Readers from abroad wrote in surprise. "They couldn't believe it. They said, 'We thought Americans were brave and strong, and it turns out you're totally wimpy and scared of your own shadow.'"

Skenazy believes that "there are a lot of people waiting for someone to say you're not a crazy, irresponsible parent for thinking" that children do not need to live inside, and isolated, for protection. "Ladies, you're bored and scared, and you're stuck in your homes, and there's no reason—so come on out."

Researchers Naomi Gerstel and Natalia Sarkisian inform us that marriages today are self-centered and absorbed, as well as "greedy." They published a scholarly paper in 2007 that analyzed two nation-wide social surveys and concluded that married people are less likely than singles to call, write, or visit with friends, neighbors, or extended family. They're less inclined to offer emotional support and practical help to neighbors or friends, and less connected to them. "Marriage and community are often at odds with each other," Gerstel and Sarkisian concluded. Critics such as Kay Hymowitz disputed their findings, citing other studies that have shown strong volunteer rates among married people. She also disputed their logic. "The purpose of marriage is to raise the next generation. And to call that greedy is just an astounding use of the term," she opined.

Parenthood grips our adulthood so tenaciously that other social obligations and pleasures are pried away only through a fair amount of regression to the Lifestyles of the Adolescent and Febrile. We struggle to conceive of a symbiosis, a right order and a sense of proportion, between family and social obligations—a genuinely and unapolo-getically multifaceted adulthood. Marriage is touted as the "building block" of civilization. But what civilization, if all we do is tend to our own, important though that is? We'll end up with a million building blocks and no foundation.

|||||||||

An intriguing alternative to the isolated, self-contained marriage, in addition to urban family life, is the microtrend of co-housing, a living arrangement first introduced in 1988. Currently there are ninety co-housing communities in the United States, with thirty under way and scores more in the exploration stage. These are deliberately inter-generational and usually nonsectarian communities, and most are non-urban. Members engage in some collective decision making and typically share some meals, but they own their own homes. Co-housing is what the American suburb first imagined and wanted itself to be— and to some extent was. It's even more popular in Western Europe, where it is associated with walking "lightly on the earth," and with freer, less circumscribed notions of intimacy, family, and marriage.

In revising marital habitat and community, co-housing inevitably revises romantic assumptions about marriage. "My husband and I are geeks," Jen tells me straight off. They met while at the Massachusetts Institute of Technology and attended graduate school in Chicago. There they began discussing the dreaded matter of career-life balance. Her husband, "had a vision," she recalls. "Get together with three other couples, buy land, build houses on it with a shared backyard and playhouse, and all take turns watching our kids. If each of us took one day off, we'd have the kids covered." He imagined, essentially, a form of co-housing. They attended every meeting of an aspiring co-housing group that never got off the ground, until they were able to buy a house in a Massachusetts co-housing community in 1999.

Jen and her husband nestled their marriage into that community. They had significant fertility problems. The community saw them through two devastating miscarriages, and threw them an enormous baby shower when they successfully conceived. After their babies were born they never had to cook a meal. The community organized a meals rotation for the first month of each of Jen's daughter's lives. Hand-me-downs still appear spontaneously on their doorstep. Now that her oldest daughter is five, she's part of "kid mob." She can walk through the "coho" to a friend's house on her own, and the parents have a plan to call as the child arrives and leaves. "Our kids range free, and secure," Jen says. I imagine a marriage whose weight is dispersed across a social load-bearing wall.

Co-housing isn't utopian, Jen hastens to add, and its goes without saying that there are semi-happy marriages galore in cities and suburbs alike. The benefit for Jen isn't that she likes everyone there, but simply that her married life is satisfyingly "complicated" and "fertile." Maybe marriage needs this denser habitat of people, scenes, and activities to lessen the burdens on the spouses, to remain capable of perpetual reenchantment.

Sarah values this same complexity for similar reasons. She and her second husband have lived their entire marriage in co-housing. They can remember themselves as multifarious adults in their marriage through the "complex and always-changing social combinations of people" that help them learn about themselves in new ways. Sarah and her husband both had "typical suburban childhoods." Self-consciously, they realized that they wanted to replace the default romantic cocoon with a default social life. "We're very much in love," she says, "and we both love our solitude as well. We recognized that this was a combination that might benefit from some 'stretching,'" so they chose co-housing.

Elaine and her husband stumble into social life just by leaving their house. Like Sarah and her husband, they self-consciously wanted to combat the ennui that might have set in without ready access to other people. The default social position of co-housing "makes us stronger as a family, since we are not always just focused on each other. We have human connections outside our marriage so we don't have to rely on each other to meet every social need we have. It's very liberating." The admission that marriage with children can't really be "the world entire" to us is in its subtle way a brave post-romantic experiment.

Sarah feels that living in a dense, vital community has refined her manners in marriage. "It has kept me mindful of how I speak to my family," she speculates, "since we have neighbors who *do* notice and are interested in how we're getting along." Sarah's daughter from her first marriage found co-housing "too public" for her, as she was accustomed to more "insulation" between the private and public faces of marriage, but Sarah and her husband "like the social coziness" of the casual but sincere, and sometimes probing, neighborly connection—a benefit in apartment-dwelling urban family life, as well.

Jen's story of the co-housing "kid mob" reminds me of our block, which functions ad hoc almost like a parenting commune that runs through a cat's cradle of social connections on our urban street of 1920s townhomes. Ours has become a "cool house" for the neighborhood children. We have Friday night pizza and movie parties for them. It hurts too much to even imagine the deliberate shredding of this interwoven social cocoon through divorce, much less to see it as a good and preferable thing, or to imagine the amputation that joint custody would necessarily entail.

As I explore co-housing marriages, I come across what strikes me as one of the best habitats for a divorce, and perhaps even for a marriage. Beth lives almost next door to her ex-husband in a co-housing setting. The persistent social web of co-housing made the divorce almost seamless for the children, who were eight and eleven at the time, when her ex bought a house just a few doors down. Their arrangement works not because Beth and her ex-husband are exceptionally amiable. "We are civil and cordial," she says, and "cooperate for parenting, but I certainly wouldn't say we are 'friends.'" It works because the social web that had cradled the marriage wasn't torn by the divorce. The children are with Beth for dinner and the night on Sunday, Tuesday, Wednesday, and Friday, and with Dad on the other nights. Beth works out of her home, so she tends to them after school. "There's no way we could have managed a schedule like this in any other setting," she says. "The girls often go back and forth between our homes several times every day." Both Beth and her ex-husband are in long-term relationships and "pretty much just stay out of each other's way."

Beth has seen other divorces in co-housing. "There's no shuttling kids between lives—they still have one intact life with two parents, in one neighborhood, with two homes. Since kids in co-housing often feel like extended family, having parents with two different houses doesn't seem so odd. It's just one more place they might be hanging out at any given time." It's hard to tell in Beth's case where a bad marriage ends and a good divorce begins. Their habitat supported a middle ground between togetherness and separation.

Beth's story gets me thinking about an enticing reengineering concept of what I'll call the divorced cohabiting couple. These couples are similar to Beth in that they maintain proximity to each other, but even more than Beth, because they still live in the same house with each other, and maintain one household. Divorced cohabitants improvise a limbo between "real divorce" and "real marriage." They're divorced but they continue to maintain a household, albeit with some private spaces, for the sake of their children and family. It's impossible to quantify how many of these couples there are, or how deeply satisfying their arrangements are over the long term. It may be that divorced cohabitation works for a little while, and then falls apart, just as the marriages did, but there isn't any research to know for certain. On the other hand, if cohabitation buys some time for the family to stay together a little longer but more happily, to raise the children, perhaps that would be a good outcome. In any case, the spouses who attempt it are usually amiable, bored with more than bitter toward each other—the classic low-conflict, low-stress semi-happy marriage. The idea fascinates me, as a marital frontier that blurs the line between spouses and exes. In a way, the divorced cohabiting couple has engineered its own divorce-marriage hybrid, or a demi-marriage, worthy of its own name or acronym, much as POSSLQ used to describe that bizarre new phenomenon of couples "living together."

Cate Cochran, a Canadian author, has written about a score of divorced, cohabiting couples in her country. They all reported that the best part of the arrangement was the return of dating and other freedoms of the divorced life, while simultaneously being able to maintain the home base. They got the advantages of both the stable household for the children and the sanctioned freedoms of the divorced couple. One husband migrated to quarters in the basement, where he could come and go as he pleased. Their neighbors thought the arrangement so peculiar that the couple eventually posted a sign on their lawn stating that the husband was fine and hadn't been imprisoned in the cellar.

I'm firmly convinced that as blended families become more common and the costs of setting up two houses rise, we'll see more homes designed for separate cohabitation, with both private and shared spaces. This is already happening, subtly, as architecture trends embody vanguard, post-romantic notions of marriage. For example, the National Association of Home Builders predicts that by 2015, a majority—60 percent—of new custom homes will have "dual master bedrooms" for spouses who want to sleep apart and have separate private spaces.

I can imagine the design trends and vocabulary, too, pushing further in this direction. What about new or remodeled homes that function more like camps or compounds, where each ex-spouse, or spouse, gets a separate, smaller living cottage or space, but with a shared area? Perhaps houses will be designed with distinct wings or modules. Spaces that are already designed for living alone, but together, such as apartment buildings and condominiums, might lucratively cater to a market of halfway married, or divorced, couples who want to be nearby for their children, perhaps, but not have to live in the quintessential romantic-era habitat of the single-family home, set off from the others.

When I describe my interest in this half-married, half-divorced hybrid design to an architect, she says, "You're thinking of the Schindler house. He lived that way with his wife in the 1920s." I look him up.

Rudolf Schindler was one of the most influential modernist architects of the 20th century. He had a trailblazing house, and a marriage that matched it. Born in Vienna, he came to the United States to work with Frank Lloyd Wright in Chicago. In 1922, Schindler moved to Los Angeles. Like other Europeans he encountered California as a "progressive Eden." He established his own practice with the ingenious design of his house, arguably the first modernist home design. As critic Paul Goldberger describes it, the house "is a pinwheel-shaped mélange of rooms and open courtyards, with a shared kitchen and private living and work spaces." Schindler lived there with his wife, Pauline, and another couple, the Chaces. Shortly after the house was completed Pauline gave birth to their only child.

The Chaces left for Florida in 1924, and another couple joined the Schindlers. In 1927, Pauline and her son moved to a utopian community founded by Theosophists in San Luis Obispo, California. Then she moved farther north to Carmel, where she edited a weekly leftist publication. She returned to the Schindler house in the mid-1930s to live in the erstwhile Chace living quarters. From that time until her death in 1977, the couple lived apart, together, in separate but overlapping domestic spaces. Their home's terraces staged performances by some of California's most prominent artists and dancers, and writers such as Max Eastman and Theodore Dreiser attended their soirees.

"The sense for the perception of architecture is not the eyes," Schindler asserted, "but living. Our life is its image." Habitats are designed in the image of the lives they contain, and of the ideals for that life. In his own design Schindler proposed a membranous domestic life without clear boundaries between indoor and outdoor space, or the private space of family and the public, social space or, for that matter, between marriage and divorce. The idea of separate houses, together, appeals to me, and I imagine it would appeal to other low-conflict, semi-happy couples with great households and middling marriages. A fair number of spouses today might yearn secretly for adjacent but separate houses. Eventually, I'm certain that domestic architecture will catch up to the ambiguous divorce-marriage hybrid in which some spouses are already living, albeit without a term, label, or an ideal habitat to match their sensibility. But, the Greek chorus would tell us, that indeterminate kind of life, a demi-marriage, a household but with spaces apart, or distance and private lives, wouldn't really count. It wouldn't be a Real Marriage, after all.

It's when I contemplate the great household–bad marriage plight that I'm most maddeningly confused about the intransigency of marriage rules. We are told by marriage defenders not to expect too much, not to have romantic delusions, and to maintain a "good enough" marriage for the children's sake. I'm left thinking that if the prime directive really is to "raise the next generation," as Hymowitz says, and to "provide a stable environment for kids," as Paula says, then why does so much else still come along with it? I have to agree with social science professor William Doherty, when he reacts to research on low-conflict marriages: "It's not for me to tell people to stay married if they're unhappy," he says, but cautions parents not to use the idea that their children will be happier if they split up as a reason to divorce. For example, Doherty says, "kids don't care if you're having good sex [and a good thing, too]. They don't even want to think about it. They just want their family together." I see his point. Isn't there a third way, though, between maintaining a semi-happy marriage on its own grumpy terms, or simply writing it off, even if it is a great household, through divorce?

Doherty's hypothetical of the not-bad but sexually frustrated marriage is an apt one. Divorced cohabiting couples get along fine as "life partners," and co-parents, and friends, after all, but they wanted to regain the sexual and intimate freedoms of single people, and so they improvised. In the more common scenario, however, the atrophy of passion, attraction, energy, and erotic connection in an otherwise not-bad marriage sends the discontented spouse in search of a new romantic object, and often from there into separate lives, lured (by lust, perhaps) into feeling themselves no longer "in love" with their spouse.

In milder cases the spouses stay together, but the erotic malaise pivots the marriage into the death spiral of melancholy. Libertarian economics professor Tyler Cowen posits that many of us are unhappy because, quite bluntly, we aren't getting enough sex. I'll turn now to marriage pioneers on the sexual, post-romantic frontier. They don't untie the marriage knot, but they unravel it by challenging what are perhaps the most deeply held assumptions of the romantic marriage.

PART III

New Twists on Old Infidelities, or, the Way We Stray Today

CHAPTER TEN

STORIES OF THE "AFFAIRS" FOLDER

The Underwhelming Crisis of Infidelity

O NE OF MY dearest friends hacks into her husband's email. She discovers that he has been having a years-long affair with a married woman. She forwards me a chain of his purple missives to his mistress, for my analysis, she tells me, and "for storage, just in case I need them in divorce proceedings." I feel shyly awkward, and ethically disturbed, to be in possession of these purloined love letters, but only for a minute or two. Then I consume each and every one of them with voyeuristic zeal.

My friend's husband tells his mistress about how he had the children in his Sunday school class rewrite the Ten Commandments, so that they could think about what rules and values were most important and sacred to them. I guffaw loudly at my desk. *If he'd stuck to the original commandments, he wouldn't be in this adultery mess!* But in another dispatch—one in which he lengthily complains about his wife—I am stopped in my tracks when he asks, *"Why* did marriage seem like a good idea again?"

Why, indeed? As the days passed, his question, and some of the scenes from his emails, kept trespassing in my mind. I found myself remembering his vivid accounts of the conflicts and mutual disregard in their marriage, which was a complicated, tangled semi-happiness, at the time, that they had very much knitted together. They both sought escapes—he through an affair, she through her own habits and rituals. Much as I maintained a pure allegiance and heartache for my friend, my empathies, affinities, and identifications began to wobble on me.

Meanwhile, as my girlfriend and I talked things through, I noted the uncharacteristic resort to cliché from a woman whose language and habits of thought were usually fresh and original. My point here isn't an editorial critique, obviously, but a social meditation. My friend seemed to be delivering her lines, threatening divorce, but all the while knowing she wasn't really going to do it. It felt like a paradox of the shocking banality. This isn't to say that the affair didn't hurt, but in a strange way the anger seemed pro forma as well. I remember thinking that despite our abstract opprobrium, there aren't many monogamy purists in the foxholes of marriage.

Then again, I have trouble following the wifely scripts. I've often thought I'd make a much better mistress than wife. I said this to John once, and he soothingly disagreed. But I suspect only because he fears I wouldn't be particularly good at the *alternative* role, either.

|||||||||

In one facet the sexual imperative of marriage is dramatically over. We can have a legitimate sex life without marriage. Premarital sex has moved from a peccadillo to a social norm. If anything, marriage threatens a good sex life (as the joke goes, if you're against gay sex you should be all in favor of gay marriage). But the converse isn't true. Monogamy is still the deeply lodged rule—or delusion—of marriage in the romantic style. The prevailing narrative about infidelity, marital monogamy, and adultery in the United States is profoundly normative. It starts from a religious, ethical, and legal ideal that sexual monogamy is broadly followed and binds a marriage together, and from there it walks backward into reality. Following this path, it launches a jeremiad in which the ideal of fidelity falters in the profane world. If we started empirically, though—if we were aliens with only our observations to guide our understanding of marital sex—we'd first note the tenuousness of monogamy and then work our way to the normative ideal of it. That ideal would seem more like art—a pleasant embellishment on the real world but not the real world itself.

We cheat. Not all married couples, obviously, but an obstinately significant percentage of them (precise figures are hard to come by, for methodological reasons and because of political resistance to funding sexuality research). Infidelity isn't normative, but it is normal. Shere Hite's 1987 report, *Women and Love*, staked out a high end of the spectrum, finding that no less than 70 percent of women and 75 percent of men who had been married for *more than five years* had had extramarital sex, an important qualifier absent in other surveys, which commingle sexually besotted newlyweds with grizzled marital lifers. By the most conservative estimates, infidelity occurs in a "significant minority" or a "reliable minority" of marriages. A few studies in the mid-1990s placed the figure at a low 25 percent of husbands and 15 percent of wives. The bulk of studies and surveys settle at roughly 50 percent of married men and 40 to 45 percent of married women, although the adultery gender gap has now all but vanished (more on that later). If we include the serial monogamists who divorce and remarry mostly because they want a new erotic romantic object, we're a majority nonmonogamous population. We don't normally mate for life after our first wedding. And as unreliable as figures on infidelity may be, they are also becoming obsolete (more on this later) because they count only physical extramarital affairs while the rest of the country goes cyber with online affairs, the Second Life game, and other forms of disembodied infidelity that elude our definitions of cheating. And it's hard to take a census of things we can't define.

We cheat—and we also roundly disapprove of cheating. A variety of polls place that disapproval quite high. One survey finds that Americans consider adultery more reprehensible even than human cloning. Other national surveys indicate that 70 to 85 percent of the adult population consistently disapproves of extramarital sex, probably assuming a situation in which spouses are lying about and hiding affairs from their spouses. According to a fascinating 1994 study, Americans are among the most infidelity-intolerant people in the world, with a near unanimous 94 percent judging extramarital sex to be "always or almost always wrong," and just 6 percent "only sometimes wrong or not wrong at all." By contrast, 20 percent of Italians and 36 percent of Russians, for example, deemed extramarital sex "only sometimes wrong or not wrong at all."

In 2001, in a speech at the National Summit on Fatherhood, President George W. Bush used a quotation from George Eliot's *Adam Bede* to praise "traditional marriage." His speechwriter, never mind Bush, must have been unaware that Eliot lived out of wedlock with a married man for twenty-four years, during which time she delivered the occasional acid critique of wifely subordination, and that her novel tells the story of a character whose one true love is deported to Australia after she murders her bastard baby. The choice of quote is deliciously if accidentally appropriate. "Traditional marriage" as Bush and his social allies (mis)understand it is a platypus creature, a monogamy ideal conjoined to fairly common nonmonogamous practice.

The official story on marital sexual ethics sounds like a simple case of hypocrisy and is often indicted as such, but it's probably subtler than that. The collectively held monogamy delusion of marriage certainly overshadows the many small, pixelated hypocrisies of each cheating marriage. And it's such easy, poor sport in any case to catch someone in hypocrisy, like fishing in a small prestocked pond. I interpret the story of infidelity less as a case of hypocrisy—a clash between behavior and belief—than a variation on what queer theorist Eve Kosofsky Sedgwick (in my graduate school days, literary theory's closest thing to a rock star) and critic D. A. Miller before her might have called an "open secret." Miller was intrigued by the ineptly guarded secrets in *David Copperfield*, where "the secret is always known—and in some obscure sense, *known to be known*," so that the "social function of secrecy is not to conceal knowledge" or behavior, "so much as to conceal the *knowledge of the knowledge.*" The open secret, as Miller defines it, resembles Freud's notion of disavowal. The patient isn't trying to hide a behavior, per se. Instead he registers and rejects knowledge that is traumatic, that he knows but does not *want* to know, in one psychic gesture.

The open secret is a more intricate dynamic than hypocrisy. We desire all day; the banality of lust, illicit or sanctified, animates the world. If extramarital lust is a monstrosity, then it's surely the most domesticated monstrosity lurking among us, in both the frequency of transgression and the bland ubiquity of the impulse that leads there. A study in 2008, cited after Tiger Woods's prodigious infidelity confessions, found that a vast majority of husbands (more than 85 percent) and a large majority of wives (65 percent) would have affairs if they could definitely get away with it. The open secret mystifies the lust behind the cheating and transforms it into something more shocking than we know it in our bones to be.

After Eliot Spitzer's disgrace I saw a magazine headline that read in part, "What Was He *Thinking*?" A women's magazine cover in August 2008 similarly promised to take me on a journey "Inside the Mind of the Cheater," and explain his weird behavior. This is how it goes with affairs: They happen all the time, and we're shocked by them all the time.

"Isn't this ridiculous? We don't really *believe* this, do we?" I laughed to John in the drugstore when I saw that cover, but he thought I was talking about the requisite monthly variation of "Secret Sex Tricks to Make Him Cry and Beg For More." I would venture that few things are less in need of extraordinary telepathic insight than the mind of a cheater.

The headline has it backward. What is a mystery to me, and a thing of beguiling beauty, is the genuinely sexually contented long-term marriage—a monogamous dam lovingly constructed to manage the wayward lusts of nature. In these cases, truly, "the dwarf bends the Titan to his will." I don't know many spouses who survive what Helen Fisher abridges to the "four-year itch" with their physical desires for one another intact, as opposed to enduring a dull monogamous sex life as a trade-off for the better good, and I don't know how these few succeed. Perhaps, as therapist Esther Perel recommends, they keep things sprightly with games of dominance and submission or role playing; perhaps they have blessedly slow sexual metabolisms. However they achieve the feat, I applaud them sincerely. This marriage deserves to be featured in the cover of a women's magazine under the headline: "What Are *They* Thinking?"

|||||||||

The worst affair story I've heard personally this year is Nicole's. A striking professor from Sweden, in her late thirties, with school-age children, Nicole has an air of implacable cool. She looks like an erudite, smart version of the ski bunny Suzy Chapstick in those old commercials. Through the stubborn reflex to see beautiful, nicely dressed women as inhabiting beautiful, nicely dressed marriages, I'm sure she's happily wed. I have marriage envy, a marriage crush, on her. By now I should know better.

I'm at a birthday party at a friend's house. We parents watch with glazed eyes as our children play a game that seems to involve the re-enactment of the Salem witch trials. Seven-year-old boys are prodding the babysitter with twigs as they tie her up to a swing set, but we've silently decided to ignore this and continue our conversations. Out of one ear I hear Nicole talking to a mutual friend just a few feet away . . . about her divorce.

Nicole's ex-husband, Sam, is a keenly ambitious rising star in heart surgery. A few years ago, she tells me, he started working late at the hospital and having patient emergencies with a frequency that belied his competence. It's a familiar question, I imagine, with the perpetually "working late" spouse: Is he seriously inept at his job, or seriously cheating on his marriage? There were other signs. "He never made eye contact with me," Nicole remembers, "and he avoided me a lot of the time. I'm not dumb. I suspected something and I asked." And each time she asked, he denied an affair.

One early evening Sam got another "emergency call" from the hospital. He told Nicole there was a problem with a patient he had just operated on. "That does happen," she says, but he didn't return until close to sunrise. She asked again, perhaps more insistently.

This time, for whatever reason, Sam confessed. He said he'd been "a bit of an asshole." He'd been conducting a years-long affair with a fellow surgeon who had relocated to their city to be closer to him. She was married, too, and had children, and she'd left her husband. She and Sam occasionally worked cases together in the OR.

"At that moment," Nicole says, "I understood the idea of homicidal rage."

With an eerie nonchalance, Sam promptly moved in with his lover. Nicole wasn't passive. She called the lover. "I asked her, do you want to be a home wrecker? I've got kids. I was pleading for a woman-to-woman connection," which never developed. She told Sam, "You're a bad person. You've done a really bad thing, and it's going to come back at you. We have a family, we made babies together and you do this." He couldn't believe that Nicole was being so blunt and angry.

"Well, how did he *think* you'd react? I mean, 'a bit of an asshole' hardly covers it."

"For years I'd followed him around from job to job. I was the trailing spouse. He probably thought I'd be meek about this, the same way." It occurs to me again that patterns for sex are often established with patterns around breadwinning. Sex and money in marriage do work like a tango, exquisitely choreographed and responsive to each other.

After Sam moved out and Nicole began her post-marriage life, he took a surly turn. Nicole hadn't been a good enough wife, he accused. She was "unappreciative" of all he'd given her. She'd failed him ("failed," that is, in all the trite, hardly worth mentioning ways that married people almost by custom or design fail each other). It was all her fault.

"He was trying to demonize you, to exorcise his guilt by laying it on you," I suggest.

It got worse. After Nicole called the girlfriend, she and Sam both thought Nicole was stalking them. The girlfriend even threatened to take out a restraining order against her. Meanwhile, Sam was spinning more elaborate, pathetic rationales for vilifying Nicole, saying that her friends and family had done him wrong by urging her to sue over the divorce—even as he was planning to move to a new state with his lover, hundreds of miles away from his children and his ex-wife.

"It's 'The Tell-Tale Heart'!"

"What?" Nicole asks.

"Edgar Allan Poe. The murderer imagines the heart of his victim beating under the floorboards. His displaced conscience drives him insane."

Later that night, I wonder if the husband's marriage-destroying conceit—that he is really and truly in love, this time with the "right" woman—isn't almost preordained by the romantic script we grew up with. Sam's tale is the devastating but familiar one of the marrying and remarrying serial monogamist: He's always convinced that he's in love with the next girlfriend, since he has such passion for her, after all, and that it will be different for them, in this marriage, this time around. It rarely is, because he is still himself, of course, in the first, second, or third marriage, but instinctively he tries to balance the scales of pleasure and betrayal like this: a profound lie in the marital bed offset by a profound romance in the hotel bed. Otherwise he'd just be a blackguard, obliterating his family and leaving his children for sheer dumb lust.

Sometimes the marriage-destroying function of the affair is less preordained than premeditated. For Olivia, in a same-sex marriage, it was the explicit conduit to her breakup. Like "suicide by cop," hers was a case of "divorce by affair." Olivia once talked of psychological "luggage" rather than "baggage," a gentrifying revision I find oddly charming. Part of her luggage is that she tends to leave relationships by beginning new, more intense, relationships. Olivia met Diana, her new girlfriend, while she was a consultant in her office.

Shelby had been distant for many years, in Olivia's view, especially after they had children. At dinner parties, if Shelby was tired or un-comfortable, she had no compunction about curling up on a sofa and falling asleep; on a few occasions she even fell asleep while attempt-ing to engage in foreplay with Olivia. Although the perpetrator of the affair often gets all the blame for "giving up" on the marriage, some-times the affair is only the last, catalyzing, entry in a thick Permanent Record of mutually bad and slothful marital behavior.

Shelby had a conversion after Olivia told her of her new love and her desire to divorce. She was heartbroken, and tried feverishly to re-engage with the marriage again. She cried; she took antidepressants; she treated Olivia to a lavish trip at an Arizona spa and ran up the credit card buying her miniskirts and bottles of wine. She even tried to have non-somnambulant sex with her. All to no avail. Olivia let her know, finally, just how melancholy she'd been, years of grievances that ranged from the picayune ("you don't take out the garbage") to the profound ("you never *paid attention*"), spewing out torrentially and in no particular order.

All because of the affair. But not really. "If I hadn't had something going on with Diana, I might have worked on the marriage. Luckily, I had Diana," Olivia says, but it sounds more like design than luck. In a low-conflict, low-stress marriage, the affair can be a grimly useful tactic as a transitional object, a bridge between marriage and divorce. Otherwise the trains run on time, dinner gets cooked, clothes gets washed, so why change? The catalyst must be ever more powerful and extreme to jolt the marriage out of its cozy but melancholy equi-librium.

Affairs can and do destroy marriages, as Nicole and Olivia and some too-sparse research suggest. On a Baltimore "freecycle" website that advertises items for barter, I note a "frozen moose head" available for exchange. It elicits interest from an aggrieved wife, who wants to use it to stage a *Godfather*-inspired revenge against her "cheating ex-husband."

I ask Dan, the marriage therapist, how his clients react to infi-delity. He tells me that he sees domestic violence and the affair as cognates, both "wounding behaviors," and intended to wound. That must be true in some cases, but I argue with him mildly about this. True, anything in married life, from an affair to poor dusting skills to water-slurping, can be turned into a weapon, the way an angry student will stab with a pencil, or a prisoner will fashion a bludgeon out of a bar of soap. Anything can be freighted with deeper, galling narrative—just ask any chronically bickering couple—but perhaps infidelity is about what it *appears* to be about: sexual ennui if not desperation in an otherwise not-bad marriage, and/or lust.

Or, if not about lust (exiled and despised as it is these days), then it's at least about something other than an instrumental wounding of the marriage. Perhaps it's about wanting to get back the complexity, depth, and richness of your character again, but within the boundaries of a marriage that otherwise "works." It doesn't seem outlandish to me.

In his earlier life, and an earlier marriage, and an earlier, freewheeling day in our history, my friend Allen had his encounters with infidelity and attempts at an open marriage. "All that happened was that we ended up making each other miserable, and getting a divorce," he told me many years ago, and I never forgot it.

Allen would probably agree with Dan. An affair, he says to me over dinner one night, "is always tethered to the marriage. If you've been in a settled relationship of *any* sort, it's almost impossible that it's not an escape fantasy. You think you're escaping your predicament, but the predicament's what fuels the whole affair."

"Like a battery."

"Yes. Like a battery."

"What about simply following your lust?"

Allen reiterates patiently, "It's a one-sided conversation—with your marriage. It's between you, and you."

I've noted secondhand, in post-affair conversations with girlfriends, a similar impulse—to see the lover in instrumental terms. In the joint retelling of the affair between spouses, the lover becomes a plot device in the story of the marriage. The lover's humanity is reduced to the role of being the Not-Husband or the Not-Wife. I understand the consolation this provides. It pulls the affair back into the narrative control of the betrayed spouse and trivializes the lover, which is a natural human impulse. It's harder to entertain the idea of the lover's humanity, and the facets of the spouse's humanity that the lover might have elicited, or the possibility of multiple intimacies.

||||||||||

In this section I tell a story of transformation that I'll continue in three parts, as it is relevant, over the next few chapters. Although a true story, and about a marriage that I've had a chance to get to know intimately and examine at a generous and exceptionally detailed length, it could be told in the style of a post-romantic fairy tale.

Once upon a time Jack and Jill had a nice, pretty marriage. They were an agreeable and handsome couple. They started a family and starting drifting from each other, for no obvious or egregious reason. The drift is less significant to the story, except to say that it happened. When you have momentum in a marriage, everything—every difficult conversation, every improvisation, every fantasy—feels possible; when you lose momentum, every simple gesture, the most straightforward conversation, the easiest and smallest movement, feels impossible. And at some point it becomes too late to reanimate the spirit and the flesh.

Then Jack and Jill drifted into separate worlds in their imaginations, and passion, although not amiability, camaraderie, or love had died between them. One day Jill was sick with the flu. Jack moved to a spare bedroom and they discovered that they preferred it that way, and slept so much better. This is a small post-romantic marriage trend. One in four couples sleeps apart, and the number has doubled in recent decades. It seemed benignly pragmatic at the time, but they never moved back. Maybe this should have been their signal that in their own low-conflict way they *were* making a decision to separate, and in fact beginning to separate, like tendon from bone. Maybe they should have acted, but they didn't.

It was a balmy summer morning. Jill was getting a child ready for camp. Jack was already at work. They were just about to step out the door when the phone rang. Normally she would have ignored it. She almost did. It's interesting that lives turn on such small decisions. Jill didn't recognize the caller ID, but she had some vague memory that she'd seen it before. Better pick up.

It was a terse conversation, very short, with an angry, bizarre-sounding man who just wanted Jill to know, by the by, that Jack had been "seeing" his wife, that it had started at least a year before, and might or might not be over.

This crisis didn't build up gradually. It was like an air bag exploded in her face, violently and terrifyingly unforeseen. Jill felt sick, almost vertiginous in a stomach-dropping way—as if she'd lost all the bearings she had in her marriage. She felt obliterated. This isn't unusual for spouses in her situation.

Jill and the caller didn't bond over their shared cuckoldry. No words of sympathy were exchanged. The only thing she clearly recalls saying is "You must be joking. That's not true." When he started to sound as if he wanted to tell her details, Jill said she didn't want to know. Then she told him very calmly not to call again, and hung up the phone.

She wasn't going to get scary and hysterical in front of her toddlers. Jill dropped them off, a five-minute journey up the road, and managed a cheery good-bye, but she must have looked so blown apart that none of the parents attempted small talk with her. The second she was alone in her car she called Jack, although it was difficult to still her trembling fingers long enough to work the small cellphone buttons. She probably shouldn't have been operating a motor vehicle.

"What an interesting phone call I just received!"

Jack didn't deny, deny, deny anything. He rushed immediately to claim that it was nothing, and that it all happened "a while ago."

What a strange defense, she thought. Oh, the Holocaust, the Khmer Rouge . . . That all happened *a while ago*, why bother about it?

"Shut up." Jill clicked the phone dead.

She'd never said that in her life. She'd never told her husband to shut up. It felt good. Jill went on with her business. She progressed through the day as if she were on an airport people conveyor. She ended up at the other side of it and had no idea how she got there or by what powers of exertion. Strangely, Jill kept to her routine. She went to seminars for a program she was participating in; she had lunch but was too ill actually to eat and she rearranged food on the plate instead. The *My Husband Had an Affair Diet*: *Lose 10 Pounds in One Heartsick Week!* At lunch Jill even laughed once or twice.

But Jill did more than move through her routine that day. On some deep level the revelation made her feel *alive*, jolted out of her sleepwalk of a marriage. As Samuel Johnson famously said of a pending execution, it concentrated her mind wonderfully. This must be true of world-shattering moments in general—getting fired, perhaps, or getting a grim medical diagnosis. Jill was keenly attuned to every quirky detail of her world of normalcy that had just been shattered. With something verging on appreciative, frantic awe, she delighted in its delicious ordinariness, the touching humanity of others who under different circumstances might have annoyed her—the humanity of blameless others, that is, who were sanctified by virtue of the simple fact that they were not her goddamned lying husband.

As the news settled, Jill realized that she was ashamed, too, although not anywhere near as much as Jack. She felt that distinct species of humiliation that comes from being obliviously deceived, from not even knowing the contours of your own marriage, which you should be able to navigate by touch, instinct, and memory alone, like a familiar room, even in the pitch black of night. She stills feel that shame, even in the retelling of it, years after the fact.

At first Jack and Jill sought the admittedly peculiar consolation of blame: Perhaps they could pin their marital problems tidily on each other.

"None of this would have happened if you hadn't given up on our sex life," Jack snarled.

"None of this would have happened if you hadn't *done* it," Jill snarled back. "You're unbelievable. You're seriously standing here blaming *your* affair on *me*. What did *you* ever do about our sex life? Do you have any idea how sick I am of the way you just *react*?" Things—walls, or furniture—might have been kicked there. She doesn't remember, and recalls only bits of the conversation.

But Jack was right. In many ways, Jill was a collaborator in her own betrayal as much as the victim. She'd given up on the sexual part. In his own ways so had he. Jill blamed Jack for hiding his true self from her and withdrawing behind his cool competence and refusal to have feelings. And she was right, too, and of course they were both wrong, because marriages drift far from the familiar coastline of blame. Of all the things Jack said about the affair, two stuck in her mind the most clearly: The first was "at least I was having *fun* somewhere"— the word *fun* ricocheted in her head like a bullet—and the second was "I was angry at you before. Then after it happened, I wasn't angry anymore."

Yes, Jill was ashamed. And she felt like a fool. She'd gotten ensnared in her own traps—her emotional laziness and even her intellectual vanity. Jack and Jill whiled away some hours "debating" as to whether he had even "cheated," because she had been pontificating for some time, at least a few years (basically, since they'd started a family), about the obsolescence of monogamy. It was a genuinely held conviction, but also she felt so wrenchingly guilty about the foundering of their married sex life—she wasn't a "good wife," and she couldn't "just" turn herself into one—that Jill had granted a kind of permission, albeit cerebrally and abstractly, to assuage her guilt.

She recalls that she posed inane, almost goading hypotheticals to Jack: "If I were in a coma, you'd explain that to a potential mistress and she'd understand, and you wouldn't feel *guilty*, would you?" As an artist, one says all sorts of outrageous things about mores, like monogamy, that should be flouted and flayed. And, as an artist, one never expects them to be taken too seriously, alas. Still, if you repeat something often enough, there is always a danger that someone you care about might take it to heart in the actual, real world, where they actually, really live.

Over time, "honesty" in marriage comes to feel more like a continuum than an absolute: Jill had tossed out hypotheticals; Jack had caught them as directives.

Jack insisted that the affair was a casual thing, and that he didn't intend to hurt her. She believed him. Even so, she said things like "I hate you," things that Jill would have thought herself incapable of, as Jack begged forgiveness, devastated. Jack is inordinately driven by his superego. Jill once described that if you drew a map of his personality, the superego would occupy everything west of the Mississippi and the wild subconscious would occupy a spot the size of Delaware. He's not devious or lighthearted about infidelity. Not at all. He doesn't revel in breaking the rules. The smugly outré bohemian who can't be bothered with bourgeois conventions was always more Jill's fantasy, not his. Jill loves that sense of honor in him. It often requires much more courage than subversion.

Weeks passed. They couldn't discuss their problems in front of family, which forced short cease-fires marked by civility, tolerable manners, and normalcy between them before they were alone again and they could continue to catalog each other's manifold failings—what a cold, castrating woman she was; what a remote and emotionally hobbled and self-deceiving man he was. Manageable things like that.

But Jill also spent some time autopsying what it was, precisely, that hurt. In a trite phrase from the annals of 1970s marriage therapy, was it "the sex or the lie" that wounded her? For most, the two blur into one episode of marital treason: We lie by cheating; when we cheat we lie. The mental exercise of trying to separate them and decant the essence of the grievance has a touch of sophistry, an angels-dancing-on-the-head-of-a-pin irritation.

The sex didn't preoccupy Jill. She didn't feel very proprietary about bodies, and she didn't feel a jealous sting of competition, especially because she wasn't trying anymore with Jack. Neither was he. They had both relinquished their claims on each other's erotic imaginations.

Jill could have pretended to understand his betrayal *less* than she did, and more aggressively contrived the oddly empowering stance of wounded bewilderment that animates the Age of the Victim. But she understood the betrayal more than she wanted to. Even from the depths of anger, she couldn't entirely make what happened *not* make sense to her.

She had to wonder, too, why being cheated on didn't hurt more. A second cliché holds therapeutically that infidelity "isn't really about the sex." It's about a deeper pathology, and symptomatic of a more intricate problem in the marriage, but one that is at least more soluble than lust. This sleight of hand distracts our attention from the banality of lust.

Life mostly went on, with the crisis compartmentalized in situ. One evening, with a close girlfriend, Jill did fall apart in an obscure corner of a bar, her sangfroid undone by a few flamboyantly colored cocktails.

"But don't you see?" her friend said with an exasperated *tsk* noise, as was her habit. "He *obviously* picked someone he didn't really care about. So it's no *threat* to you." Then she recommended Jack and Jill see a sex therapist (not bad advice), and waited what she must have thought a respectable interval before moving on to other stories. Kindly resolve your marital crisis, she seemed to imply, albeit sweetly, so we can resume our gossip about mutual acquaintances.

This friend was single and almost seven years younger than Jill, and Jill wondered, even from the abyss of her crying, if her friend's more blasé attitude wasn't a generational difference between them. Friends of her marriage generation, in the gloaming of the romantic era, still feel bound by script to express unmodified outrage against the cheater, despite their intuitions as to the more nuanced, complex realities. Maybe younger women growing up more decisively in a post-romantic mood had ditched the script.

Insofar as Jill could untangle the injuries, she will say the one that hurt most was absolutely and unequivocally the lie, not the sex. She had inhabited a life with somebody who had another (fun) life that she knew nothing about. If they were truly soul mates—well, best friends—they would actually share details of their lives with each other. What hurt much more, though, was the surprising sense of envy. Why hadn't Jill been out doing the same (fun) thing Jack was, instead of subsisting on the lean ethical pleasure of not being a liar? Eventually Jill realized that she felt cheated more than she felt cheated on.

Jill saw the sad, inner logic by which this affair had happened in her low-conflict melancholy marriage, and found she didn't care too much about it after all, and she accepted that indifference as something other than capitulation or weakness on her part, but secretly, as a more reasonable accommodation in marriage. Jill would expect Jack to extend that accommodation to her, too, and she feels certain that he would.

The crisis receded into Jack and Jill's marital history. They moved through it without letting it change them in any dramatic way. That was probably an error, or just one of the insidious seductions of the low-conflict, low-stress marriage, to let a crisis go to waste like that. Each day it got to be more work for Jill to withhold positive reconciliatory feelings—to refuse to laugh with Jack at a joke that they heard on the news, or to refrain from sharing anecdotes about their family, or asking Jack a question about his work when Jill was genuinely curious, just because the asking would make him think that she didn't loathe him for lying to her. Bit by bit they simply started being cordial and comradely again, which is the default setting of most stable, low-conflict but passionless marriages.

Less than a year after the phone call, Jack and Jill did something they'd been thinking about for some time. They bought a small vacation cottage. They must be staying married, they felt, because they entangled themselves more deeply in bonds of land and deed. The purchase proved their enduring if disfigured commitment to each other, and Jill is convinced that on some dimly apprehended level it was an offering at the altar of the marriage. Of all the currencies of intimacy, real estate and money are the two that they're especially adroit with. They are Life Partners after all.

||||||||||

In the early 1970s, the trailblazing marriage researcher Jessie Bernard predicted growing "infidelity tolerance" and wondered, "Will it mean marital relationships are so solid, so impregnable, so secure that neither partner feels threatened by infidelity? Or, so superficial, so trivial, so expendable, with so little at stake that infidelity really does not matter?" It's a good question. Is it a function of a shifting ethic not to care too much about infidelity, or just a marriage's necrotic indifference to itself?

I think it's the former, a shift toward greater monogamy agnosticism, or a generous amnesty policy for the errant spouse. A 2008 survey from Britain, for example, found that a third of female respondents had either had an affair or were actively considering one, but nearly half of these women believed that their husbands would forgive them, and more than half would take their husbands back if the latter had an affair without their prior knowledge. Monogamy agnosticism is a hidden marital world, and just slightly subversive.

Dan, the marriage therapist, elaborates that he sees wives who confess to some "shame" when they furtively admit to him that they want to work things out with their cheating husbands. He speculatively attributes this to the influence of feminism. Because they fear others will consider them weak or gullible, they're "ashamed of having positive attachments" to the errant husband, he says, and think they should leave the marriage instead. They tell Dan abashedly and apologetically that they don't really want to leave.

Dan is right that monogamy agnosticism isn't a sanctioned stance toward infidelity in the popular discourse. I remember how drawn I was to the image of Eliot Spitzer's wife, Silda, as he tendered his resignation as the governor of New York, following a sordid sexual betrayal of his marriage. Silda looked distraught, but it was clear where her loyalties remained. As soon as the very brief statement of resignation ended, the talk show pundits took over on a public radio station.

Why didn't she throw his clothes on the lawn, one asked, like "eighty percent of other wives" would do? When was a wife going to ditch the "Hillary Clinton script," a woman caller wanted to know, and refuse to stand there supportively behind her cheating scoundrel of a husband? The reaction troubled me and rattled in my mind at the time, but I couldn't figure out why.

A year later, when John Edwards was the cheater du jour and Elizabeth Edwards was accused of being an "enabler" of her husband's infidelity, it dawned on me what had been bothering me before, with Hillary Clinton, Silda Spitzer, and all the others: We weren't ever permitting these wives simply not to *care* that much. We insisted that they be outraged and stomp off, and if they didn't, we derided their forbearance as weakness, not indifference. But maybe the forgiving wife is neither stoically strong nor pathetically weak, as her critics allege. Maybe she's isn't a patsy, a sucker, an enabler, or a coldhearted careerist. Although she follows a script of condemnation and shock, maybe on another level she's just not that bothered, or, more accurately, she cares about other facets of the marriage more.

In Hillary Clinton's case, especially, I always got the sense that she was groping awkwardly to find the expected "pro-social" script about infidelity to serve up for us, one that she didn't entirely feel that deeply in her heart. I kept thinking, and perhaps fantasizing, that she might say a true thing, or what I imagined was a true thing. She'd say something along the lines of "my husband's a tomcat but he's brilliant and fascinating—and so am I—and I'm in love with him. We have a mission together, and a child, and an astonishingly exciting life and sexual fidelity isn't really the most important thing about it." But you can't say that sort of thing, not really. Even so, I think we all intuited easily enough that they had something a touch transgressive—and post-romantic—in their sexual rules of marriage. And, because we suspected this, Hillary Clinton was accused redundantly of having a "fake" marriage, a "warped marriage," and of not having "A Real Marriage," and even had to reassure voters explicitly that she did. For

Elizabeth Edwards, was it enabling or just a Life Partners collaboration, which ended in divorce only after John admitted to the less forgivable betrayal that he'd fathered a child with his mistress?

Monogamy agnosticism is perhaps the more unsettling contemplation in all this. Maybe some of us just don't *care* that much. This isn't *the* truth of extramarital sex, obviously—many marriages care intensely about monogamy—just *a* truth.

What happens in high-profile marriages happens in marriages closer to home, as even a quick pastiche reveals. I hear of a wife who opines that "everyone gets at least one free pass" in a marriage, affairwise. Another has had an episodic online affair for two years with a man she's never met in person. She considers herself a "cheater," someone who has betrayed her husband in her heart and mind, although her "body hasn't followed suit," because the man lives too far away. Her husband is being tolerant because he "sees that perhaps this is something I need to experience." It started out as a secret and has become an object of cautious forbearance between them, a private lightening of the marital monogamy burden.

One evening, sitting on our front porch, I chat with a neighbor whose husband has been working late. "I wonder if he's having an affair," she muses to me, and then adds, casually, "Oh well. If he is, he'll be happier."

One husband's infidelity with a married woman was exposed because he couldn't stop himself from taking promotional pens from the hotel where he was trysting, and leaving them carelessly around the house. Rather than divorce her pen-stealing adulterer, the wife banished him temporarily to a nearby apartment, but had him come back every morning to get the children off to school and pack their lunches, and then return in the evening to cook their dinner. This chore reallocation and servitude was a makeshift form of home-saving penance before he could be rehabilitated, as he eventually was, into the marital fold.

In cases like this it's the children and our profound dedication to them that nudges the monogamy agnosticism along. Paula, of the dual-career marriage described earlier, tells that she always thought infidelity should be "a deal breaker," until two good friends started confiding in her about their unfaithful husbands. "I had a hard time wrapping my head around how you could possibly stay with someone who could not be faithful to you, someone who could bring that betrayal into your life. But once you have children, custody most often comes with a split, so the reality that you're never really free from the person tends to be a huge factor in encouraging or pressuring people to stay together after infidelity. I was just amazed. I never thought that I would be able to see the other side, but marriage with children is *really* different than marriage without children."

John and I had known our friends Lucy and Phil for almost fifteen years when we found out that they were grappling with infidelity. Out of confusion, I reacted to their story in ways that I'm ashamed of. I wasn't a good friend.

Earlier that day, before joining us for an overnight trip, Phil had told Lucy about his "special friendship" with a younger woman, involving certain sexual intimacies. His hand had been forced because his ex-special friend had threatened to call Lucy herself (she'd managed to find Lucy's cell number). Lucy brought all this up as a crisis but talked about it as if it were a grocery list. I thought it was admirable that she didn't want to hide in shame over Phil's affair, but awkward that she presented it in front of both of us, and Phil, late at night around a campfire.

Was this something that *mattered* to her, or not? I was genuinely confused about that. When I tried to express sympathy or indignation, it was met with a clinical detachment, which made me feel foolish, as if I were hysterically making something out of nothing or impugning her husband's character. Well, all right, perhaps I was an old fogey, who took fidelity too seriously. So I adjusted. I tried a casual, tolerant approach, and then she'd take a punitive tack toward Phil, who sat there devastated, it seemed, by the sheer embarrassment of hearing his sexual transgression dissected in front of his friends.

It was an aphasic conversation. I couldn't figure out what the words meant, or find the right pitch, or script. I was so inordinately frustrated by the lack of agreed-upon coordinates in the world of marital ethics that I gave up on offering either consolation or wisdom, and just went to bed, practically leaving the conversation in mid-sentence. I'm embarrassed about my exasperation, and although it had a few sources, some irrelevant here, one of them was certainly my confusion about what I felt about infidelity.

Months later, Lucy thought the affair might have been more valuable as therapeutic fodder than it was injurious as marital betrayal. "I'm not happy it happened," she reflected over lunch. "But it helped focus our therapy and moved it along to a new level."

The muted, even blasé reaction to the extramarital affair after the fact is the first and subtlest post-romantic fraying of the marriage-monogamy knot so central to the romantic marriage. We approach infidelity with cognitive dissonance: It's the underwhelming crisis. I'd never tolerate cheating, we think abstractly, and then we make a separate peace with the inconvenient fact of it. This may be a case where we are more imaginative in real life than we are in our imaginations.

So I find myself in uneasy contemplation of the mistress, the roué, the cad, the prowler, the philanderer, the slut, the hussy, the Other Woman, the Other Man—the entire rogue's gallery encompassed by the shaming epithet *cheater*. It's a disquieting affinity. I can't condone nihilistic cheaters like Nicole's husband, who has left his children, but some others make a plausible point for themselves, and I become their (very) private apologist. There's always been a sexual willfulness to me, an insistence on seeing a social taunt like "easy" or "slutty" as emancipating rather than degrading. (My new favorite T-shirt, spotted in a Baltimore coffee shop and inspired by ancient pagan cultures, says, "They Never Sacrifice the Sluts.") A part of me loathes the damage and betrayal—and, having been the victim of infidelity in a relationship, the one thing that I find enduringly and probably intrinsically hurtful *really is* the lie. A part of me wonders if cheaters are just selfish or mundanely of bad character. Still another part absolves them, because under the deceit there is a life-affirming impulse in some affairs, a greedy effort to thread the needle of a marriage's antinomies about sex. We can't say that, not out loud, but I can't pretend not to understand the point, however hard I try.

CHAPTER ELEVEN

"I CALL IT MARRIED DATING"

The Accidental Cheater in the Age of Facebook and Google

THE MARRIAGES DESCRIBED in the previous chapter all experienced "traditional" infidelity. The affair was in secret, and it involved actual physical contact. But extramarital sex is a different beast today. Sometimes marital rule changes are something we force and sometimes they're foisted upon us by circumstance. There is a new metaphysic to infidelity, so that while we may believe in monogamy, it doesn't seem to believe in us. The forces of technology and the economy are undermining the monogamy culture in marriage, and in some ways, feminizing infidelity.

I'm out one evening chatting with a recently divorced woman I barely know. She's a friend of Josie's, and we're in a dark bar for a celebratory happy hour that invites sloppy disclosure about marriage.

"How did you know when it was really time to divorce?" I ask Tracy.

"Oh, you'll know when the moment comes. It's undeniable. Maybe you just need to get laid," she speculates, breezily.

"It's not that easy," I laugh, assuming she's joking.

"Sure it is," Tracy says earnestly. "Just go on Craigslist."

Husbands and wives who want to pursue affairs openly or on the sly have a vastly easier time of it today. In 2001, as Internet dating was just coming into its own and losing its stigma as a notorious "market for lemons," Noel Biderman, a Canadian "serial entrepreneur," came across an article reporting that some 30 percent of users of online singles dating services were actually attached, either married or in quasi-married relationships. This statistic intrigued him and his business partner. "What if we could create a service where they didn't have to lie about [their status]," a site entirely dedicated to "married dating. We bet that those people are spending the real money," Biderman explains. "We thought, there's a big business in that."

Biderman, who has a law degree and is himself married with two children, subscribes to a kind of erotic determinism when it comes to marital sex. "I'm not going to convince someone to have an affair. What I'm trying to say is that, if you're not getting what you physically want from your marriage—you could be the president or the Prince of England, and there's tons of risk and tons to lose from being caught, but you're still going to do it. I say, don't just go on a singles service and lie, and don't do it with a co-worker. And visiting a prostitute isn't a solution for a lot of people, either." So Biderman founded an online service for married dating. It caters exclusively to married people who seek to have affairs with other married people. Today his Ashley Madison service has 2.25 million members, more than 70 percent of whom are husbands ("maybe women don't need to advertise," a friend of mine speculates). Impressively, for a start-up, the service turned a profit almost within its first three months after launch. But between 2007 and 2008, it experienced a "meteoric rise," according to Biderman, and almost doubled its membership. Biderman credits some of this to more aggressive advertising, although he notes a gloomy consonance between economic woes and Ashley Madison's fortunes. "Finances are the foundation of a lot of marital discord," he says, "so our service is adopted in hard times." It is not only "recession-proof" but "maybe a recession growth business." It may also be the case that as the economy worsens, more spouses are opting to have an affair in lieu of getting a costly divorce.

You would think that something such as marital sexual fidelity, upheld immemorially as sacred, would not be as jittery and responsive to ease of opportunity and forces of market efficiency as it apparently is.

The most familiar "dog bites man" tale of social media and technology today is that it obliterates privacy and makes it obsolete. Each gesture and sometimes deeply regretted comment in online environments is recorded for eternity on a makeshift version of a Permanent Record of our lives. Meanwhile, online social environments such as Facebook introduce hundreds or even thousands of virtual witnesses into our lives. In this techno-social milieu of the 21st century, where can we ever hide? How could we secretly "step out" on a marriage in this world, at least without getting observed and caught? The less-familiar "man bites dog" story, however, is about the creation of much *more* privacy, of a sort. In the 20th century, a husband or wife could have a "private" life and a "public" life, and the two were fairly easily patrolled and distinguished. Today, it's true that we do not have a discrete "private" life in the same way that our parents did, but we can have multiple public lives and personae, through technology, and this in turn creates a new kind of privacy. It's the privacy, for those who want it or seek it, of having a layered life—multiple avatars, personae, email accounts, and online social spaces, as well as vast new frontiers through which to explore and stray under cover of a public alter ego.

It is this privacy-proliferating online potential that Biderman intuited to great profit. Ashley Madison and other Internet spaces change the architecture of adultery, its basic mechanisms. The Web subverts the closed (wedding) ring as a metaphor of intimacy in marriage. This happens in several ways. While social media create new means of eventually getting caught, they also minimize infidelity stigma and social risk (online, you can privately converse without the risk of having to meet face-to-face with a lover in public). Social media also increase opportunity. And "lack of opportunity," according to one researcher, probably keeps the infidelity rate lower than the infidelity urge. In one of the few recent studies of marital infidelity, David Atkins used income and employment as indicators of opportunity for extramarital sex, to test the hypothesis that when presented with more chances to step out, more married people will do it. He found that, indeed, "financial means are related to the likelihood of infidelity," but not for spouses earning under $30,000 a year. Married people who earned more than $75,000 a year were more than 1.5 times as likely to have had extramarital sex as those earning under $30,000, which the researchers think may "reflect a floor effect": If you earn under a certain amount, infidelity is frustratingly difficult; over a certain amount, it's perilously easy.

If exigency as much as conscience keeps us faithful, then new technologies can abrade the sexual monogamy imperative of marriage even when spouses have a sincere desire to uphold it. This wouldn't surprise Biderman. When I asked him why married people stray, he said simply, "Because they can." Celebrities and the wealthy "have the opportunity and the status that allows them to do it. If we did a study, and said, You can have an affair with the object of your fantasy and *nothing bad*—guaranteed—will come of it, close to one hundred percent would say yes."

It's true that with opportunity—freedom of movement, high income, and privacy—infidelity increases. Numerous studies from Kinsey onward have shown that the incidence of extramarital sex, ranging from swinging and open marriage to covert infidelity, rises along the income and education ladder. Husbands and wives with graduate degrees in these studies from the pre-Internet era were almost two times more likely to have had extramarital sex of some sort than those with less than a high school education. But today the Internet democratizes opportunity by extending some of the adulterous latitude of the wealthier classes to the less-affluent classes.

Here again, Biderman and his partner seem to have had a marketing instinct about their "product," as he calls it. I laugh silently to think of the affair as a product, but I suppose it is. Biderman tells me that they could have grown even faster in their first year, but "we were

cautious about how to market. We decided to go on television to attract the right people"—in other words, a broad middle-class market.
Marketing was tricky, he says. "I really wanted to avoid putting ads [in
places] that were beneath the dignity of the service. We create a community of people who understand where you're coming from, looking
to revalidate what they had once before: desirability. We didn't have
a 'cheating' brand, and I didn't go for advertising in porn magazines."
Lately, like the "Marriage Works" social conservatives in the marriage
movement, Biderman has taken to the billboards to promote his position. "Life is Short—HAVE AN AFFAIR," one of them beckons, to
murderously frustrated Los Angeles commuters.

I ask Biderman if he has any compunctions about his service, if he
gets nasty emails, and he tells me that he gets a few but not many,
and that he tries to answer them personally. "I'd be devastated, too,
if I were cheated on, but they need to look in the mirror. . . . If I were
cheated on I wouldn't blame the website, the hotel room, the workplace, or the office. I don't wreck marriages," he asserts emphatically.
"I don't believe that, or I wouldn't keep the service alive." Biderman
characterizes himself as a "freedom pursuer" and notes that the alternatives to Ashley Madison are worse, at least for husbands. Without his
service "they were going to do it someplace [riskier], in the workplace,
with prostitutes, or on Craigslist." For now, Biderman is focusing on
"spreading the gospel." I ask what the gospel is. He says, "Do we as a
nation want to have an honest and open conversation about the state
of marriage or not? Some foundations of marriage are not really as
timeless as people believe. There are other ways to do things."

||||||||||

We used to practice a default fidelity in marriage simply because of
the expense and inconvenience of an affair (though even *with* these
default obstacles, so many of us still cheated). Now the alignment of
access and opportunity on the Web invites an almost default infidelity

once you permit yourself that first exploration. Instant messaging, for example, is custom-designed for sexual rogue elements: teenagers and restless, semi-happy married people.

The conventional affair pushes like a tumor against the real life of a marriage. It encroaches on the marriage's finite, discrete terrain. The new infidelity metaphysic has no boundaries in space or time. It loosens monogamy's grip as simply the most logistically convenient and inexpensive option in semi-happy marriages.

More consequential in changing the geography of marriage than the kind of service Biderman offers is the new geography of work created by smartphones, telecommuting, email, laptops, and remote offices. On the one hand, the cheating wife or husband can always be called, always be tracked down through their electronic LoJacks. You can actually buy an iPhone "Spouse Tracker" app, for $4.99. The icon shows two gold wedding bands, entwined, and asks, "Is your spouse really at work? At the office party? Where they said they would be? Be 100% sure of your spouse's location." The app uses GPS technology to "pinpoint your spouse's exact location, and sends you an email map of it." On the other hand, technology creates privacy and possibility across space and on multiple fronts simultaneously; many of us are no longer tethered to the office during the day and the home at night, and we have more potentially free, unaccounted-for time.

The Second Life simulation game, although not at all the exclusive domain of restless married people, allows players to simulate entire identities and relationships through avatars online. "Second life" is an apt term. It's not an "other" life in a marriage but an added, unobtrusive one, a layer more than a secret. And if one life is added without rippling the surface of the marriage, then why not three, four, or five co-existing lives? It requires only a neophyte's skills at prevarication, multitasking, compartmentalization, and a few free Yahoo accounts.

Facebook makes this easier still. One of the major social functions of Facebook seems to be the sometimes mawkish, sometimes reckless trip down memory lane for vaguely discontented married people. Its original muse was a quest for dates and girlfriends, and it's evolved to support pretty much the same agendas, for single and married alike. Facebook seems to legitimate a boldness that spouses wouldn't otherwise muster. It's as if the forum allows us to go retro in our own lives, recycling the kitsch and oddities from our amorous pasts and putting them to new use. Just as our man-cave husbands re-create fraternity social life in their garages, wives and husbands regress to their old collegiate and youthful love affairs online. At first, some might reconnect harmlessly enough through Facebook friending, and then move the correspondence into the virtual private room, and space, of another email account. Facebook is a magical land where past and present lives exist simultaneously and interact with each other, as if time has been suspended or obliterated. In a sense, with Facebook and its kin, we live under a perpetual spell of the uncanny—that eerie, unsettling feeling that overcomes us when something that belongs to another day and world shows up in the here and now.

Facebook blurs the bright line between the illicit and the merely nostalgic and delivers temptation to your door. It slides the marital affair right into normal, online everyday socializing. There was always an either/or metaphysic to infidelity, which the new technologies and online spaces supersede. The either/or choice holds that moments of potential iniquity in a marriage force us to act *or* not to act, to touch *or* not to touch, to have sex *or* not. In the world of email and Facebook reconnects and online communities, no bright-line boundary of touch separates marital fidelity from marital treachery. The world isn't partitioned cataclysmically into Before and After by a fateful illicit kiss. In the cyber wonderland, infidelity has an almost imperceptibly thin razor's edge. It's the difference between a word or two in an email, or a flirtatious exchange that never even involves a touch.

It's a dramatic departure from the past, when an affair wasn't something you could just end up doing by accident.

A friend of mine passes along the story of a husband who posted wholesome, cheery pictures of his entire family—his wife and several children—on his Facebook profile page, only to receive a picture of a married ex-girlfriend in an unmistakably flirtatious pose and a skimpy bikini.

"Exes have found me on Facebook," says Shirin, my single informant in Los Angeles, "some for no reason other than to broadcast how well they thrived after the demise of our relationship, others to rekindle an old story." So she has been on the receiving end of a melancholy spouse's quest for past glory.

"Facebook is going to be the downfall of many a marriage," my friend Samila opines. I agree. As she says this I imagine marital monogamy as a frail, wispy mite of an idea, wielding a butter knife against the behemoth of Facebook and cyber lust. British data from 2009 revealed that no fewer than one in five divorce petitions that year mentioned Facebook.

"Maybe it feels less like cheating if you resurrect an old boyfriend, through Facebook affairs," I speculate to Josie one day.

She thinks, sagely, that it's "just nostalgia for the person we used to be, for the women's premarital sexiness."

Biderman agrees. "Why are women in their forties the fastest-growing part of Facebook?" he asks me. "Because they're looking for *old loves*," he says emphatically. Biderman knows they're out there, but currently on Ashley Madison, there are seven disaffected husbands for every three desperate housewives, and this dearth of would-be mistresses is his current obsession. Biderman is being forced to contemplate Freud's famous question, "What do women want?" "I spend a lot of time watching movies like *Titanic*," he tells me, "and reading romances like *The Bridges of Madison County*," all to devise new marketing and outreach techniques tailored to wives. "Infidelity features in a lot of these tales," he observes, perhaps because illicit romance promises "a removal from the mundane" for his target female audience. The name "Ashley Madison" is a compound of the two most popular American girls' names in 2001. "We wanted women to feel comfortable here," Biderman explains, "and think there was a woman behind the service." The website has the conventional visual clichés of feminine sexuality—mauve and pink tones, a lacy border. Biderman's ruse fooled me. After a first, cursory look at the Web page, I assumed his service had been founded by women, and was surprised to discover otherwise.

Biderman's marketing instincts once again jibe with broader trends. When Kinsey and others conducted some of the first studies on married sex lives in the 1940s and 1950s, adultery seemed like the prowling husband's domain, a world of male amusements knitted together by access, opportunity, freedom of movement, and autonomy in the use of money and time. Portentously, this infidelity gender gap is closing dramatically among younger generations. Infidelity appears to be rooted in the loamier soil of opportunity and logistical ease. In the 1990s, no less than five published research studies on marriage, using different data sources, found that men and women under the age of forty (or, in one study, age forty-five) showed no differences whatsoever in their reported rates of infidelity. Within the older cohorts, especially men and women in their sixties, an infidelity gender gap still exists. Most likely, David Atkins concludes, women's presence in the workforce has equalized access and opportunity and flattened out the adultery rate. What feminist ideology pushed in the late 1960s— sexual and marital liberation—is nudged quietly along by 21st century economic realities, even in a family values ideological milieu.

As the economic imperative of marriage goes, so goes the sexual imperative. The two have historically reinforced each other. Now they are falling together. Women and men under forty are marrying at a time when women no longer depend on husbands for support—the coin of the realm for the sexual imperative, and the old inducement to listless mercy sex—and in fact are often the überprofessionals, the *superior* learners, earners, and workers in the marriage. The gaining superiority of wives glimmers obliquely in the dramatic equalization of male and female infidelity rates. Biderman notes that women who join Ashley Madison even have a certain swagger about their tomcatting propensities. They talk about their adventures openly with their girlfriends, while old-school husbands keep it secret. Biderman's site makes explicit efforts to feminize the affair, but the technology and economy are feminizing infidelity, in any case, on their own momentum.

So is the medium itself. I tend to associate the Internet's sex life overwhelmingly with male-oriented pornography—the "Masturbation Superhighway"—and with horrific incidents of sexual exploitation, abuse, and trafficking, and a penny-dreadful gallery of dangers for teenage girls and children. But the porn superhighway has its feminine side, too, and can feminize infidelity. (It's worth noting that women are a robust but largely invisible audience for Internet porn, too. Recent studies find that one in three Internet porn users is a woman.) The accommodating design of the Internet allows women to shed inhibition and modesty, to liberate the inner slut, to indulge in the feminine convention of narrative and epistolary seduction, and to do it all offstage of the double sexual standard.

Simone* wouldn't say she had "cybersex" at all; it was just seduction and letter writing but more racy. Hers was like an 18th century Jane Austen courtship improbably revived in the 21st. She had never cheated in her marriage before. She wasn't cruising affair chat rooms or married dating services when she met him. They connected online in a political chat room.

He was by his own atavistic admission a man of dubious marital character. He was in his early forties and had three children and was fecklessly interested in cheating. He didn't try to rationalize to Simone, or blame his wife for it, and this wasn't the first time he'd prowled, although he said he'd done it infrequently. He was a sole breadwinner who wanted to keep his family intact, and he betrayed no inclination to fall in love and wallow in the romantic, marriage-killing delusions of the serial monogamist. He was just bored, looking for another erotic outlet while keeping his marriage intact. Although it's a strange word to choose, Simone felt there was an innocence to the lust, or an elegance in its simplicity.

They exchanged pictures through Flickr eventually, which was

---

* Simone is a composite character of two women with very similar experiences with online affairs—and is the only composite character in the book.

harmless enough by judicial standards. She loved the fact that although she and Cody described each other in their emails, they didn't exchange photos until they'd written back and forth several times. I can well imagine that other women would like this, that the appraisal of physical appearance isn't necessarily the first or even an intermediate step in a cyber affair. The first "screen" might be prose style, even spelling and grammar, if these things matter to you. We might judge and be judged by the content of our disembodied, ethereally conveyed characters. The wife with anxieties about body and beauty might seduce by other means.

Betrayal happened in small, accumulating rivulets. Simone rationalized that she would never *actually* see this person, or *actually* touch him, or *actually* have an affair, so he was no different, really, from any other married, male friend. It was just a daily (or, really, many-times-a-day) correspondence with another agitatedly bored but dutiful spouse. She clung to the word *actually* like it was a piece of flotsam in a shipwreck.

What followed was unpremeditated, and had nothing to do whatsoever with who Simone thought she was as a wife. They began spinning erotic scenarios. This kind of narrative, nonvisual erotic style isn't an inherently feminine one by any means, but it has been a socially sanctioned outlet for women's sexuality for some time, and one that many wives have internalized.

Simone's married sex life was stale, and hadn't been especially vibrant even at the beginning. She had a much richer, private fantasy life than she shared with her husband, and sexuality had always been such a big part of her identity, before she got married. It's like scaling the sheer face of a cliff to start a conversation about fantasies with your husband once you've cut a sexual groove in your marriage. For Simone, the most astonishing thing for her in the whole experience was how uninhibited she suddenly felt. She wasn't shy about saying what she wanted to do.

Words tumbled forth, in a torrent of pent-up flirtatiousness and eroticism. He wrote vividly and had a galloping imagination, and so did she. They both had a literary background, and Simone revealed even banal but shameful things she never would have in person, that she was a slob, a workaholic. Online the shy become audacious. Simone didn't have to see a man face-to-face and deal with the embarrassment. It was easier to write it. He was real but not *there*, so she felt free to release the inner slut. Give a man a mask, Oscar Wilde writes, "and he will tell you the truth."

The capacity to have more than one life, and persona, in the cyber wonderland collapses all the classic dichotomies that have defined, and constrained, women's sexuality—good girl/bad girl, virgin/whore, wife/mistress. I've long held that Americans faithfully overestimate how much husbands (and men) want sex, and faithfully underestimate how much wives (and women) do. In the past, to commit a sexual transgression, a wife had to be prepared to risk some tangible social trespass and to shoulder an unequal burden of shame and scorn if she was discovered, but the Internet in its feminist dimension equalizes the double standard because it makes the transgressions socially invisible. A wife can play both sides of the virgule, at once, and in private.

There was no coy pruning of words, or no modest compulsion to play games. Just say it, and say it again. And take as much as you want. The "affair" is an invisible make-believe pie, and infinitely replenishing.

The cyber affair, as Orson Welles once said of Los Angeles, is a "bright, guilty place."

Simone's reality is just layered, and life goes on happily and seamlessly. The whole thing is breathtakingly unobtrusive. She sat contentedly in her kitchen, working on dinner and writing letters with her laptop at the same time. In no tangible way did the abstinent affair steal time and space from real life; it occurred concomitant with it. The same was true for him. He had freedom of movement because of commuting and technology. He pecked out telegraphically seductive messages to Simone on his iPhone while driving, while in the midst of daylong business meetings in distant cities, while putting his children to bed, while in the middle seat of an airplane, from a public kiosk, on a family weekend away at a friend's house, and during conference calls in his office. She was awed that he managed to keep a straight face. Perhaps he halfheartedly continued with conversations as he typed. His clients may not have gotten their money's worth out of him, but Simone did.

Simone had trouble deciding if her activities were a dangerous marital brinkmanship or just an innocuous foray. It had the fascinating dissonance of feeling entirely routine and entirely shattering at the same time. One night she woke up with the jolting horror that she might be writing herself out of her marriage. At other times the cyber affair seemed light and shockingly easy, an invisible, well-deserved epicurean stratum under a still-placid family life.

For weeks Simone and Cody exchanged erotically charged letters several times a day. It got crazy and intoxicating. If she was going out to pick up the dry cleaning, she would write and let him know that so he wouldn't worry if she didn't write right back.

Naturally, they were frantic to meet each other, and after a month or so it was arranged. Simone made her family a casserole, made up a pretext, and left for the evening to a chic hotel bar. The man wasn't an ax murderer or a jerk. He'd represented himself very accurately, and they found each other attractive. To some extent they had the same rapport in person that they'd had online. But the energy fizzled out. As in other cases of online dalliance and connection, the erotic spark just didn't jump the synapse between cyber life and the flesh. They corresponded afterward to be polite, but their hearts weren't in it. Simone thinks it's the only really, genuinely mutual breakup she's ever had. They simply drifted off back into the ether and the still-unperturbed lives from whence they came, with no bitterness, no marriage-destroying consequences, no bad feelings. Nor does she make apologies for a harmless foray that filled a lack in her marriage without destroying it. Although no sex was involved, it was among the most emboldening sex she had ever had.

A nebulous "growing number" of Americans have had or are having avatar love affairs like Simone's. Jennifer Schneider, an addictions expert who has written on this topic, doubts that there exists any good estimate of how many married Americans are engaged in virtual cyber affairs specifically, as distinguished from anonymous erotic chat rooms and pornography. It's hard to inventory something that you can't define.

Schneider wrote a scholarly article that recounts cases of online affairs and what I think of as close encounters of the third kind—a vague, incorporeal sexual intimacy in the limbo between pornography and a physical affair. With the cyber affair, unlike pornography, there is "actually someone there," as one of Schneider's patients says, but it doesn't involve bodies or actual sex. It involves writing, talking, and sometimes computer-to-computer webcam links, but no touching. Sometimes the "lovers" never meet or even know each other's real names. This murky new frontier of avatar affairs confounds the meanings of sexual loyalty in the romantic marriage, even for those who sincerely believe in monogamy.

It's a world in which spouses, as in Simone's case, don't feel especially ashamed or fraught about their virtual dalliances. In their book about infidelity on the Internet, researchers Marlene Maheu and Alvin Cooper report that of the 20 percent of Internet users who engage in some kind of sexual activity online, some two-thirds by their estimates are married or cohabiting; others are in relationships. To me their most striking finding is that although 75 percent in their study say that they "keep secrets" from their partners about their online activity, an astonishing 87 percent report that they "never feel guilty" because of it. *Never.* Maheu and Cooper believe that the dangers of cybersex are actually overestimated in the media and that it "is much less of a problem than commonly depicted, when handled appropriately." The Internet they describe is a realm of the married and guiltlessly secretive. On the other hand, Schneider's patients felt strongly that their spouses' avatar affairs qualified as infidelity. "My husband actually cheated on me, and the virtual affair feels no different," one wife says emphatically. "He's never been unfaithful," a thirty-four-year-old woman says of her husband, a minister. "But he has had experiences from others [online]. I never know what he's thinking of when we are intimate. How can I compete with hundreds of anonymous others who are now in our bed, in his head? When he says something sexual to me, . . . I wonder if he has said that to others, or if it is even his original thought."

A thirty-nine-year-old wife, married for fourteen years, has no doubt but that her husband had affairs, "although not physically. He had *affairs of the mind*, and that to me is as much a violation as if he actually had a physical affair with someone. Moreover, in one sense I feel that having an affair of the mind is worse than having an actual partner: My husband can, at any time, have an 'affair' without leaving the house or seeing another human being." The interesting marital development here is that physical contact was once a sine qua non of infidelity—almost its very definition—and now, curiously, it's an optional feature. But the avatar affairs produced the secondary symptoms of a "real affair"—the same feelings of betrayal, devaluation, and abandonment, the same subtle transfer of attention. For them, unfaithful is as unfaithful thinks. The mental affair calls into question elemental definitions of marital fidelity. Remarkably, on this new frontier, the extramarital affair can be all smoke and no fire.

|||||||||

Thanks to Biderman's ingenuity I can conduct a search and find hundreds of prospective married lovers in the immediate vicinity of Baltimore in less than ten seconds. For purely anthropological reasons I want to explore the site. First I will need an adulterous alter ego. Lying about your name and obscuring your biography is the etiquette requirement here (although at least you don't have to commit the big lie, and deny that you're married), and unlike with singles dating sites, you are *valued* for your capacity to deceive.

I propose "Miranda" as an alias to John.

"As derived from the verb *mirar*, 'to look,' in Spanish? I like it," he says.

"I was thinking of Shakespeare's Miranda, actually, but you're right. It's a more clever choice than I thought." It occurs to me then that there's no real category in the annals of marriage counseling that embraces the affliction of conferring with your husband about your extramarital-affair-seeking personal ad.

Miranda's life, such as it is, must be vigilantly barricaded from my own, so I send a test email to John's office to make sure that there's no identifying information smuggled in on the account I've just created for her.

"Your name's right there, displayed prominently," he tells me.

"What do you mean—'displayed'?"

"I mean it says, From: Pamela Haag. All that's missing are the GPS coordinates for your office."

"I must have accidentally used my real name in the account settings."

"As detectives say, there are a hundred ways a crime can go wrong, and if you can think of ten of them, you're a genius."

Next I need to create a brief profile before Miranda can browse. I was able to do preliminary searches without creating a profile, but if you want to hunt on this site, you need to become prey as well. You must provide age, weight, height, measurements, and status. Miranda is reduced dispassionately to "Attached Female." For her greeting line, I type "Intrigued."

On my first search, nearly 250 affair-seeking husbands materialize instantly, in Baltimore, and that's before I expand my radius to include the infidelity-rich environs of Washington, D.C. I can add some of these husbands to my private "favorites" list on my account, and I can send them messages if I join. As a guest, I can receive messages from them. Finding these 250 husbands has taken all of half a second, and did not involve leaving the comfort zone of my office or incurring social risk. How many parties and PTA meetings would I have attended to find 250 prospects? How long would the affair groundwork have taken?

Ashley Madison discourages members (with uneven success, I'm sorry to report) from descriptions of body parts and too vulgar accounts of what they'd like to do with you, and asks them to think of the site as a virtual "cocktail party." It tries to create a gentrified affair ambience of an upscale soiree rather than last call at a scraggly bar on a Saturday night.

At first browse on Ashley Madison, I'm disillusioned. I'd expected something more French, I suppose, but this is not a coy site. With online spouse-finding services like eHarmony, clients describe their personalities and their souls. Here, it's right down to business. A roster of "Fantasy Guidelines" strips you down to your sexual marrow, commingling desire and bureaucracy. It's clinically nonerotic to see smoldering fantasies listed in alphabetical order, with check-off boxes, as though you were filling out a medical history form: "Have you or anyone in your immediate family ever had one of the following illnesses or conditions?" Among the listings are being in control, giving up control, observing, role playing, sex toys, spanking, talking dirty in bed, tickling with feathers, videotaping, and many et ceteras. "Conventional Sex" is even an option, which makes it seem kinky, although what in the world does it mean? Whatever our parents do?

I check my real email. My friend Samila has written back: "My jaw dropped to the floor. WOW. I can't imagine how weird and freaky it must be to be on this website with all the potential CHEATERS." I chuckle at the way she capitalizes "cheater," as if it's a taunt you'd hear on a playground, or perhaps an incantatory talisman: If we chant it loud enough and often enough, it won't happen to us.

Despite Biderman's efforts to roust women out of their domestic enclaves and Facebook flirtations, the adultery sex ratio on this site still holds true. While I find Biderman's ingenuity quite impressive, the site feels a bit as if the male sexual character had simply been slathered with a pink coat of paint to lure women in. It seems as long as I'm a faceless, featureless "Attached Female" in Baltimore, I'll never be lonely. This imposes strict market discipline, as John would say, an adaptive survival of the fittest. Imagine a bustling emporium, where husbands at each stall entice you with ever more dazzling exotic goods. "British, with the accent!" one advertises. My favorite is a liberal who shouts out a wonky fetish for "red hot conservatives." One husband, inexplicably, has posted a photo of the late conductor Leonard Bernstein in his profile. Another, perhaps hoping to cheat in order to prove a point about civil liberties, lures me with the greeting "My business is NOT my neighbors' Business." Yet another winsomely laments, "In the perfect world, none of this would be necessary." Some say they have "places" that are "right on the water"—which I take to mean affair boats in Baltimore's now-bustling inner harbor. Some of them cannot spell the sins they hope to commit.

But enough of all this online adultery window-shopping! Now it's time to pick up my six-year-old from summer camp.

I notice on the drive over how the site has given my everyday world a mystifying fourth dimension and wobbled it at the edges. All around me people are living in layered, duplicitous marriages. My brief initial visit alone lulls me into the illusion of ubiquity, that "everybody's doing it," and resurrects the queasy dread of my virginal high school years, that I'd better stop being such a square and jump over to the other side.

"The affair's not in you," Josie once told me. "Even if you didn't lie about it to John, wives with lovers live outside the law, and when did you ever break the rules?" True, I've never cheated—on anyone. I don't know if that is a triumph of conscience or just a failure of nerve. I seem to occupy that all too common semi-happy marital state of hypothetical enchantments, a world poised forever on the cusp of transgression, a world of seductive what-ifs and if-onlys. Maybe one day I'll be a bolder person, I'll let an arm rest knowingly against my own, I'll send that email, I won't be so shy; I won't be such a priss. . . .

|||||||||||

My son scurries off with his friends when we get home and I check Miranda's account on Ashley Madison. With no photo and little information beyond Attached Female, I've already got a mailbox crammed with husbands who are doing a preliminary gesture called "winking" at me. Most of them just send a standardized email with the tagline "Wink Message," for those of us who like to be clobbered over the head by our own seduction. Your next lover: It's the spam sitting in your inbox. In the several weeks that I leave my ad on the site, only nineteen earnest suitors manage to write a "Custom Message." Thoughtfully, Ashley Madison allows you to organize your account to display only those messages.

When John gets home from work I'm still at the computer.

"Hon, are you making that feta pasta dish tonight? I need carbs for my ride tomorrow," he calls up from the first floor.

"Yeah. I gotta manage my online lovers first, though!" I shout down to him.

He grunts noncommittally. Having your wife squirreled away in her office trawling for a lover online is all well and good—until dinner's delayed.

One of my winks calls himself "BORD in Baltimore." I roll my eyes. I should have put "proper spelling" and "judicious use of gerunds" in the "Erotic Turn Ons" section. I can console myself with the thought that I know how to spell the word, and that if I ever really had an affair it would unfold naturally, just like my marriage did. In that catch-all term of moral absolution, it would be more *complicated* than this. But who am I kidding. These are my people, too. We are, all of us, BORD in Baltimore.

After two weeks I weary of adultery spam. I decide to add some surly deterrents to my "profile." I never had the heart to fill out the erotic guidelines checklist in the first place, but in the open-ended section I write, "Sorry! I don't do checklists, especially about my sex life!" And "I've got no intention of leaving my husband." And "I don't know why I'm here." I should have guessed that belligerence would only increase my appeal. My sassiness is complimented. In my married years, I've forgotten that proclivity in men.

When I established my Miranda account, I also created an account for a hypothetical husband as well, "Sam," and even endowed him generously with my own handsome, athletic husband's basic measurements. When I pull the plug a few weeks later, Miranda has gotten 182 email responses. She disappears as instantly as she first materialized. Poor Sam still has none at all.

Josie must be right. The affair's not in me.

CHAPTER TWELVE

ISO (IN SEARCH OF): A BUBBLE

The Philanderer's Defense

AFTER I VISIT Biderman's online affair-finding site, I decide to try another venue, Margaret Mead–like, to broaden my sample. "You should try a more high-end affair outlet," John tossed out one day. "See what you get then."

Was he serious and if so, why? We don't remember. He doesn't repeat the suggestion, but it stays with me and begins to ferment.

I've always enjoyed reading the personal ads in the *New York Review of Books*, self-encomiums of exuberant paradox (brilliant but humble; rustic and glamorous). The world really *works* for these people, except that they're "in search of" (ISO) love. They are just as comfortable on opening night at the Met as they are in tattered scrubs following a trail of gorilla dung through a Ugandan forest. They prosper and inhabit comely dwellings, urban, bucolic, and coastal. Sometimes their ads promote real estate better than the Real Estate / Vacation Rentals ads that precede them. I'm waiting for the personal that stops at a description of the apartment and entices with free on-site parking.

As a lighthearted if patently demented collusion, a caper, between John and me, the *NYRB* personals becomes the next stop on my sub rosa "What were they thinking?" expedition into the mind of the cheating husband. I'll write a personal advertisement describing myself with high spirits—more or less honestly—a lot more "less" than "more"—as a wife looking to tryst with similarly situated men.

"Call yourself 'leggy,'" John suggests. He laughs. "That'll get all the leg men out there on the hook for you."

"I *couldn't*!" I giggle. "That's shameless."

"It's an ad. It even happens to be true."

"You're sweet to say."

"Make sure to mention the Ivy League degree; they *love* that in the *NYRB*."

"I'll say I'm 'broad-minded' and in a 'broad-minded' marriage. . . . We're broad-minded, sort of, aren't we?"

"Very," John says with a hint of sarcasm.

"Okay, in the loosest sense of the term, we're broad-minded."

"I'm so broad-minded you wouldn't believe it," he responds, with about as much enthusiasm as you get from an automated phone menu. I've heard this tight monotone before. Usually it means that he knows he's about to get dragged into more faux bohemian "Pamela stuff" that doesn't suit him. Engineers and writers really shouldn't attempt to mate.

I establish my own rules, the same rules as for Ashley Madison: I'm not going to correspond but merely gather and collect, asking the most perfunctory of follow-up questions only to elicit further information, when warranted. I'm using my avatar to bait more candid views from husbands than I would otherwise get. It's a counterbalance to the betrayed wives' narratives, which are more accessible and familiar to me. I won't indirectly help a good husband go bad. I'll just ask him to share a story, I tell John.

I set up a new email account to gather responses, and decide to keep using the avatar "Miranda," having grown vaguely fond of the lusty girl. In the six weeks that the ad runs, I will net close to two hundred rogues, mostly all husbands, a smattering of single men, and just a few husbands who say they are unequivocally in honest, open marriages. My married friends think this a dispiritingly large catch of cheaters; they'd have guessed twenty or thirty, they tell me. An employee of the classifieds section at the *NYRB* thinks it's large, too, but they don't track responses and can't be sure. They only know about Luddites who use their mailbox service.

When I finally remember to check the *NYRB* email account, feeling conspiratorial and illicit, I already have scores of responses and spam to sift through. Supply creates demand, the economist Jean-Baptiste Say theorized. But desire is an economy of scarcity. By tradition, illicit adulterous desire is especially so, a world of stolen, fiercely clutched moments. Online, though, it's an economy of abundance that encourages waste, greed, and profligacy.

I note that some husbands, perhaps tenderly guileless, use their real names despite their confessions that they're lying to their wives. They invite me to Google them, which I assiduously decline to do, on principle.

"Those husbands are fools," John intones laconically, from behind the pages of his special Tour de France issue of *Velo News*.

I have to concur. I suspect that my ad pitted a deep-seated instinct for marital self-preservation against an equally deep-seated and eventually triumphant instinct to boast about their professional accomplishments. Vanity requires indiscreet, risky disclosure.

It's bad enough that I'm a curious writer, but what if I were an aggrieved, avenging wife, or better yet, a marriage movement missionary intent on establishing a Registered Adulterer website? Cheaters beware: There are the amateur gumshoe spouses stalking the ether like they're in a film noir. Jennifer Schneider, an expert on sex and opiate addictions, has collected stories about elaborate ruses of cyber detection. "I found myself making up screen names to get him to chat with me to see how far he goes with his cyber-sex," a thirty-five-year-old wife reports. "I have also answered his personal ads with made-up information, only to find him asking for my phone number." Another wife, forty-seven years old, has assumed the role of parent to her

chronically errant husband—a Nanny Marriage. To prevent anonymous cruising she uses the parental controls to lock him out of chat
rooms and restrict his IM access, and then killed off her husband's
avatars when he couldn't handle what he calls the "smorgasbord of
women online."

It's a smorgasbord indeed. When I first look at my bulging inbox for
my secret online avatar Miranda, I cannot believe how easy it is—it
would be—to have an affair. With social risks, contact, "real" identity, and censorious context removed by the Web, opportunity *creates* the incentive; access *stimulates* the desire. The affair becomes the
small impulse buy in the checkout line, the pack of gum you don't
even know you want until you see it priced at a dollar. Technology
transforms the affair from a luxury that involves Herculean manipu-
lations of circumstance, time, and conscience to a cheap bargain buy.
If this banal ease and nonchalance isn't unprecedented in the annals of
American marriage, then it is at least remarkably more common.

So, what *are* these cheating husbands thinking? Naturally my married girlfriends ask me this question when they learn of the caper. If
we could eavesdrop on them, how would they plead their treasonous
case?

One of the first letters I read is from a man—and he won't be the
only one—who suspects a "prelude to a scam." He's married, but only
because "it's too damned expensive to get divorced." I revel in his response. It amuses me to think of myself as the Nigerian scam artist
of the affair world: "Have an affair with me! Oh, and my money is
frozen in a bank account by a dictatorial, corrupt regime . . ." Not
that the man's proudly declared skepticism stops him from writing in
hopes of trysting with me anyway.

I follow up, just to ask him why my ad seemed so implausible to him.
"Because wives don't state what they're not getting in marriage," he
writes back. It surprises me to hear that wives are still not expressing

desire forthrightly, but it shouldn't, I suppose. As a culture we still don't quite know what to do with women's appetites. "Your response only makes you sound sexier," he continues. I can't lose here!

From my haphazard sample, and at least as they tell it, most of these affair seekers are not in unhappy marriages. "Like you I'm married," one husband writes. He's one of the few who confesses that he really is hoping for divorce by affair. "It's an unfulfilling and profoundly unhappy relationship but I haven't figured out how to make my escape." He imagines me a "sweet woman," although how could I be doing anything less sweet than this? His letter is sorrowful and well written, and I feel sorry for both him and his wife, and pause before I file him in my research folder.

One unexpected word that crops up with surprising frequency in my eavesdropping is *bubble*. They want a "bubble" in their otherwise bedraggled lives, an escape "from mortgage, children, wife, and job," as one would-be Jerk itemizes with bracing efficiency. I get the sense that this list of his nonbubble aggravations sits ready on his tongue. I don't know how the concept originated or by what paths it went viral among restless husbands, but the bubble regains some charm when salvaged from the world of cascading economic catastrophes and applied to sex instead.

I find that it grows on me. These husbands seek an impervious, self-contained world, not a new family; not, on the whole, a catalyst for divorce; not a rival wife or yet more children. In a departure from many of the Ashley Madison husbands, they don't even seek the masculine affirmation of the player life, if their words are to be believed (and why would they lie redundantly, in the context of such a bolder lie?). Instead they seek a world suspended within the larger, settled atmosphere of a marriage, like a bubble that floats in that gelatinous red goop inside lava lamps. Perhaps a vacation or a spa would do as well as an affair. Many a marriage and job get ditched, I'd wager, for want of a sabbatical.

My bubble-seeking suitors strike me as bored more than unhappy, restless more than aggrieved, desperate more than deviously roguish, in marriages stalled in the vast semi-happy Gobi between "wretched" and "blissful." According to my suitors, it's not just the miserable or unhappy marriage that totters on the edge of sexual transgression; it's also the "uninspired" one, the "boring" one, the one that is "loving, in a way, but devoid of intimacy," or the "marriage without common interests, passion, or friendship." Other than that, it's a good marriage. As I've said, our standards are different these days.

A few respondents make much of "broad-mindedness." They tell me their wives are "anything but broad-minded," that "the last word for my wife would be 'broad-minded,'" or "you are more fortunate than me in the open minded spouse department." This rouses my sympathy for their "rigid" wives and I wish I'd not used so salutary a term as *broad-minded*. Other husbands congratulate me on my "attitude," my "boldness," and the "nonconformism and the courage of [my] ad, particularly for *this* side of the Atlantic."

Although I must have been blinded by the glare of the obvious not to have predicted this, it finally occurs to me that husbands are lauding my ad and my implied broad-minded agenda as "hot" and "sexy" because of the simple fact that I am already married. I'm not on a quest for marriage—and therefore I can't be using sex as a marriage bargaining chip, but must have an actual desire for it. And it's telling that several imagine correctly that I've been inundated with responses because what husband, or man, *wouldn't* want this? I feel guilty that I may be cutting into the yield on investment for honorable single women advertising in the *NYRB*.

I read on, methodically working my way down the inbox queue.

I open a letter with a subject line that is composed in Latin. How extraordinary! The letter itself is composed in an intricate, almost antiquated syntax and vocabulary. This man, who is unmarried and younger than I am, tells me he that is a navvy, and then helpfully explains that means a laborer. He dabbles in a wildly eclectic array of topics and strikes me as plainly brilliant, in an entertainingly flippant, quirky way. His letter is charming. It makes me laugh. "You made me laugh!" I write back instantly, only because it is true. I write a few lines more, inviting him to muse on why he thinks I might be a lacrosse-playing scientist. Reflexively, with no premeditation or compunction, I hit SEND.

Well, now, I suppose I've broken my rules. It took forty minutes. Personal experiments with the self-regulation of combustible pleasures like drink, greed, and lust often turn out badly like this. I go on to the next reply, vowing to do better, and reminding myself of my studious purpose, so quickly derailed. Back to the field book.

Some husbands pick pseudonyms of famously unfaithful or avant-garde figures with inconveniently wayward desires. A Proustian "Swann" tells me, "I can well imagine you've struck a nerve. Surprised? Grist for your next book?" Yipes. This one's too clever. Swann goes on to explain philosophically that he is "married, contentedly, in the European fashion—devoted to my role as breadwinner but must seek erotic connection elsewhere. And one must . . . That doesn't live in families, yet one does still need it." Agreed, very much so. By "European" does he mean that they have an open marriage, or simply that he steps out? It's tempting to ask for clarification, but instead, with a pang of conscience, I move on.

"I must warn you," another man writes, "my tender touch brings women to tears." Good grief, it's Pepe Le Pew! He must know some adept sexual fakers and dissemblers.

Several would-be treacherous husbands seem unexpectedly domesticated in their tomcatting pursuits. They promote themselves less as ideal lovers than as ideal wives for me. They entice me with paella and margarita recipes of their own design, brag of their culinary sophistication, and invite me on gustatory adventures. I'm surprised to discover that the cheating man's mind perceives a link between cooking prowess and an affair, but I guess this is progress of a sort: the Rake, domesticated and feminized. All this time the "affair" had been conjuring in my mind a scenario of being tossed across an anonymous hotel bed somewhere, not having paella grilled for me in the backyard—a backyard doubtless inhabited by my untrue lover's wife and children. Maybe these husbands have been married so long that they dutifully lug around their marital accessories and armature, even in their endeavors to transgress them.

It also interests me to see that a notable few are "sole breadwinners"—and they make it a point to say so, oddly, by way of what sounds to me like self-exculpation. One declared sole breadwinner says his wife is "a wonderful mother to our three children" but he "really really misses" the other things. I can almost feel the heavy pall of marital habit and duty for both husband and wife emanating from even this short email. The hardworking breadwinner with an opted-out wife feels, perhaps, more entitled to his bubble. He's tired, and maybe he didn't expect this role to fall to him and—well, he's earned it. And I imagine his wife somewhat out of the swim of things at home, just as bored as he is, feeling that she's made enough sacrifices herself and has frustrations of her own. It's the case of the retrosexual. The sexual habit follows the economic one.

In this secret forum, husbands reveal their marriages' secret rules. "My wife is more the 'don't ask, don't tell' sort," one assures me. I've heard *that* before! Another is in a "civilized but non-intimate marriage, no romance"—a perfect post-romantic equilibrium—and says he has license to roam and then offers the obligatory culinary bona fide: "I do like to eat out in nice places."

"There are a *lot* of arrangements out there, hon," I report to John. I notice that I say it with the fulsome enthusiasm of a huckster peddling dubious wares at a carnival. Considering the frailty of my marriage, this experiment is beginning to feel like the equivalent of sending a sick child out into the dead cold of winter without a coat.

"Ask the wives if *they* know about the arrangements," John retorts. "Why do you believe this stuff? They'll say *anything*." This must be right.

This ad was a devious and wicked little experiment on my part, for which I apologize, long after the fact, to my hopeful, misled suitors. But the joke's on me. I'm reminded of an old friend who was asked to participate in an intervention to help a heroin-addicted friend face his drug problem, but my friend ended up getting persuaded by the addict and shooting heroin at the intervention instead. And, so, in an experiment intended to expose and dissect the cad, I find myself, contrarily, thinking the bubble-seeking cads make a very fine point for themselves, and muster their defense.

|||||||||

It was two years after Jack's revelation. In the ensuing two years, nothing had changed, or happened, except that Jack and Jill enjoyed their routine, the household, their friendship and camaraderie. The family flourished with routine, too. One of the peculiar characteristics of a low-conflict, low-stress melancholy marriage is that it chews up the clock. You know you should be doing something to fix your problems, but the quotidian life of the marriage works so smoothly, and is so cherished, that you don't want to abrade it with honesty. So problems persist and accumulate in a corner and, before you know it, years have passed and you've been in the same pleasant but passionless status quo for that entire time. Jill wasn't content, nor was she miserable; Jack may have been slightly more content—or perhaps just more stoic—but he missed the intimacy, too. Still, neither mustered any force against the inertia and neither really tried to change. They did grow, if anything, more amiable and high-functioning as a household, though, which confused matters all the more.

The problem's not Jack, Jill thinks; Jack doesn't think the problem is Jill, per se. It's not them. It really, really is Marriage. They've shed the cockeyed optimism of the serial monogamist, the belief that it's all the spouse's fault, and that everything would be better with a new one. Things probably would be *worse* with a new husband. Jack and Jill believe instead that they are decent and well-intentioned and sincere people who are satisfied with each other partially but not in all ways suggested by the concept of traditional marriage, and they are attempting to live honorably in less than ideal circumstances, being mutually harassed by a third diabolically anthropomorphized entity, the Marriage, which by now has folded their individual failings together.

It was in this mood of tender exculpation toward each other that, one day (or it felt just that sudden) Jill refused to act married. In a low-stress but ambivalent marriage, you are always close to the edge, but it never feels that way until you fall over it.

And nothing she did was that bad, in a way. Jill just started corresponding, intensely, and with palpable intimations of lust, with someone she'd never physically met, or even spoken to. Like millions of other spouses do, she met him online. Mostly Jill has as many rationalizations about this as others have freckles. She's earned this, having lived dutifully through years of erotic deprivation and disenchantment, having stayed put after Jack's affair, rooted in desperation though it may have been.

Mostly she didn't worry about it, though. Unthinkingly Jill found herself going about her daily rounds whistling the B-52s song "Roam." "Roam if you want to, / Roam around the world . . ." Desire was exuberantly untethered—to reality, context, marriage, life, identity, even to bodies, the touch or the gasp, except insofar as it was written about and imagined. Her abstinent affair was just plain *fun*. It was fun in an entirely selfish, hedonistic way that she'd not permitted herself to experience for years.

Her pulse raced and she got butterflies of anticipation at the sight of . . . "Inbox (1)."

It was indeed an affair of the mind. The correspondence found time among its other meanderings about rat breeds or Walt Whitman or the difference between manners and etiquette to linger over the imagined minutiae of a future tryst.

Jill wondered if she was having an affair. There are secrets in marriage—things understood, known, and hidden—and then there are mysteries, unknown and not understood. She fancied she was like Io in Correggio's Renaissance painting, passionately caressed and gratified by the celestial lover Jupiter, who has no physical instantiation. Even her real name wasn't involved. They settled upon a mutually pleasing initial for her, and not her own. Nor was anything else that she would perhaps arbitrarily classify as part of her real life, aside from her picture. He couldn't have found Jill in the world. She could have disappeared and floated forever in the ether, a would-be mistress sitting like a fortune in a Swiss bank account waiting for a dead thief to claim it. The marital betrayal wouldn't produce the "ocular proof" Othello craved—no physical evidence that proves the act. Both the gratification and the betrayal were all in her head. Still, when she put these letters into Word files one day, it shocked her to discover that they had accreted in a month to the equivalent of 265 pages. The weights and measures transfixed her. Do sixty thousand words equal one illicit kiss? Are 265 physically chaste double-spaced pages equal to, better than, or worse than one wordless physical encounter?

She thought maybe she should tell Jack about all this. She remembered the corrosive power of his lie about cheating and she felt portentously, but vaguely, that they were doomed to divorce if she didn't tell him. One night over dinner, she tried.

"What is an affair?" she asked. "What if you just send a bunch of letters to someone and you never meet them or touch them, or talk to them. I don't mean cybersex, like those chat rooms, but just an intense correspondence, a mental affair . . . Maybe with some sexual stuff thrown into the letters."

Jack pondered the question silently for a while—as he continued eating. "I'd feel more hurt by a mental affair. With someone else in your head."

After a while he asked, somewhat more directly but still not explicitly—and still cutting his filet methodically—"Is there something on your mind?"

This was her chance to come clean. But she couldn't do it. Jill stared ponderously at the floor instead. She always thought herself capable of being a daredevil truth-teller in marriage. Now she wimpily relied on the conceit of clairvoyance in a low-conflict, long-term marriage: Surely we can't help but convey truths to each other telepathically, without the messiness of bluntly unadorned confession. The suggestive ellipsis must be the most useful punctuation in a settled marriage's discourse, its grammatical mascot.

Among would-be lovers haunting the Net there is a quest for the grail of the unencumbered passion: unencumbered not only by marriage but also by social convention, obligation, rules, and jealousy. It even has its own acronym, NSA, "no strings attached." Of course, strings get attached. In the dimly lit corner of Jill's mind, where unpopular truths skulk, Jill knew this. The baffling thing is that even incorporeal affairs, without any of the indelible etching that physical intimacy creates, get shouldered in ways that defy the sophisticated jauntiness of the NSA fantasy. Jill came to expect a certain standard of epistolary devotion. She felt petulant when there was an arrhythmic blip in the correspondence. It hadn't taken long to reach that point—a month, maybe. In these moments of disappointment, worrisomely non-NSA as they were, Jill experienced what must be a familiar Dantean affair (not) hell. As you've sinned, so shall you repent: alone in your own family, in secret, mute heartache. It sucks to have boyfriend trouble in your marriage.

Jill did discuss her strange and perturbing attachment with two close friends. She still recalls that one of them—let's call her Carly—worried that Jill had gone off her rocker, seeing as how she didn't know who this man even really was. Carly asked if Jill didn't find herself always comparing her correspondent to her husband, and Jill said she felt as if her correspondent, for the time being, was more interesting, and lively. None of that sounded too good to Carly. She speculated that perhaps the correspondent had a mood disorder, and that this might account for such prolific, manic exchanges, and even their brilliance. Jill responded only that they had joked about how maybe they were both serial killers on the prowl for their next victims. That's hilarious, Carly responded warily, "a real side splitter."

Later, Carly discussed Jill's situation with her own husband. When he asked what Carly thought would happen, she surmised that Jack and Jill probably wouldn't be married much longer.

Jill might have agreed with her. She didn't want to leave her marriage, but she seemed to be sabotaging it. She started communicating with Jack in terse compression, as if the effort of answering a simple question was too arduous, and too much to give. There's an inventive parsimony in a failing, melancholy marriage: For as little as you share, you can always find more to withhold. Scientists speak of a moment in the evolution of the human race when we came within a hair of extinction, only a few hundred of us, in the narrow, frail curve of an hourglass, bridging the past and future. These weeks in Jill's marital history, she told Carly, felt secretly like the closest she'd come to conceding to extinction.

Jill decided that she wanted to—must—meet her correspondent. The ethically unimpeachable and prudent idea of not meeting him and just letting it go never occurred to her. All she was thinking about was whether to hide the truth from Jack, or confess it.

She could meet her correspondent during an overnight business trip she'd wanted to plan for some time. The weekend before that trip, they were going to their cottage. Although the prospect sickened her, she decided she was going to tell him the bald, unvarnished truth, because she was running out of time, opportunities, and rationalizations. This felt like an act of terrorism against her own husband, Jill thought. He sits placidly in a café, and a lunatic with a bomb—his own wife—explodes it randomly into his life, and to prove what point? Jill's deepest impulse was to stay in the melancholy normal. It felt cruel *not* to lie. And what were the chances she would ever get caught? Or, Jill could get hit by a *bus* before next week, and the confession would be for naught, a moot act of stupidity, or courage, she couldn't tell which. Why confess before she'd even gotten to have sex? Jill reckoned that would-be cheaters are forever getting conveniently hit by buses in their imaginations.

Later that night, they're sitting in rocking chairs on the porch. It's very dark and they sit there staring ahead, moths circling, lost to their own gazes.

"I guess I owe you this after what happened. It's frustrating. *We're* frustrated."

She doesn't remember a lot of what was said, as it was such a frightening, death-defying moment. Jill reassured Jack that it wasn't a payback fling, that they just needed to give each other permission, because the one thing she couldn't handle was the lying, and the feeling of getting ambushed by her own marriage, her own life. She sobbed and cried about how sorry she was that their marriage hadn't worked out just as it should have; it was something more complicated and uneasy instead.

"If we have permission," Jill said, "and if we're careful about this, I can handle it." She didn't want to be divorced; she didn't want to be married the way they had been.

Jack didn't think it was such a bad idea, in the abstract. Yes, if they could formalize it into a new treaty of salutary obliviousness, things could work out.

"It's the ancient luxury of having lovers and mistresses. It's something we can do for each other. They do it in *France*," Jill continued urgently. She had a feeling, though, that invoking the French in an argument about sexual mores was loosely akin to invoking Hitler in an argument about politics—the last gambit of cornered intellectual desperation.

Jack mulled it over calmly.

They should have done this years ago! Jill thought. She marveled at their Continental sophistication. It couldn't possibly be this easy.

It wasn't. Later, in bed, in the pitch black of even deeper night, Jack remembered common sense, feelings, and the shaming incredulity reasserted itself. At this point, things went about as you'd imagine.

"We have to separate, or divorce. I can't handle this," Jack said.

"I don't want to divorce," Jill said. She liked their marriage, just not all of it.

"You have terrible judgment."

"You can't possibly think it's worse to be honest than to cheat. Or do you think you're the only one who needs things, who's unhappy? It's a lot to ask," she said. "I'm asking anyway."

"Ask all you want."

"Well, maybe I should have marched myself to *divorce* court the first time this happened but I didn't, did I, and you *owe* me."

"I don't owe you *anything*."

Suddenly they hated each other. What had seemed plausible just hours earlier now seemed an outrageous affront against their marriage and dignity, another such episode in a marriage that, suddenly, felt like a bitter chronicle of nothing but deprivation, outrages, and insults. How Jill ever could have thought she could stay married is beyond her. Jack feels the same. All their stockpiled grievances were unleashed: how neglectfully they'd treated each other, deprived each other, robbed each other of their bloom of youth. It was a hot, high-stress moment for them, but maybe no more real or true, for that, than the years of stoicism, low-conflict equilibrium, and abnegation that had preceded it. Just louder.

In the ensuing days Jack and Jill found sturdier ground; they normalized things to themselves. For as bad as this was, it was not as bad as the guilt of lying that Jack had felt and the deracination of having been lied to that Jill had felt. At least in their marriage, which has its own timbre, the wound of an infuriating, lacerating truth healed much faster than a quiet lie delivered with the sincere but confused intention of prolonging a tenuous marital peace.

This moment and conversation had been germinating for a long time. If it hadn't been that night, it would have been another; if not this catalyst, then another. In the example at hand, though, Jill needn't have bothered with any of it. She wishes she could say that her foray into marital rule-breaking had a happy ending, although she's not sure what that "happy ending" would even have looked like. Mostly the misadventure entailed smudging her ethics, finding new ways to make a fool of herself, and ending up in a state of baffled self-loathing, long past the age and station in life when she should have known better. The details are extraneous, and trite. Enough to say that nothing happened at all, by the familiar pre-Internet definitions of both *sex* and *nothing*, and that the denouement of the not-affair involved many martinis over an exuberantly reckless afternoon that ended with Jill alone in a chic but rumpled cocktail dress staring in glum disbelief at the ceiling of a moody, fashionable hotel room as daylight faded. Any enfeebled marriage probably affords chances aplenty to rediscover James Joyce's wisdom that we are all driven and derided by vanity.

She emailed Jack early the next day to let him know she was back. She was ashamed of what she'd done, and risked, and she didn't have the heart or mettle to speak with him.

"I'm not doing that again, ever," she wrote, truthfully. "It won't happen again."

"I'm glad you're home," he wrote back. "I love you very much."

There was this, still—*still*—an unusual, hard-won sanctity to Jack and Jill's marriage, secular though it was, odd though it was, imperfectly frail and melancholy though it was.

For a day or two, as she slithered back into the indeterminacy of her marriage, Jill would have preferred to stay in bed, in the fashion of the crestfallen, but breakfast had to get made and lunches packed. She focused narrowly on the steadying rituals of her domestic life. In the evening, when Jack returned from work, there were things they needed to talk about, work-related, children-related, Life Partners–related. The wrenching paradox was that the person Jill most wanted to tell about the end of the not-affair in some detail—which they emphatically agreed before the fact would not happen—and the one who in a weird way would have felt the most sad and sympathetic for her, was her husband.

Desire is a fever that runs its course and burns off, one way or another. Jill still has the entire chain of letters, downloaded into one file (they grew yeastily to some 360 pages) and tucked into an obscure corner of her laptop. She's never reread them, but they sit there, sometimes accusatorily, sometimes coyly. It was a perfectly transcribed relationship.

Marriage probably fractures predictably, like character, according to a passion incipient within it, if not along the fault lines of money, then along those of children, housework, career, sex, desire. It doesn't take anything that serious to cause the tectonic force to churn under the marriage's surface. Sometimes that can happen suddenly, because of a hairline fissure like this.

But Jill doesn't truly feel that her correspondent was merely the Not-Husband, a fungible cipher inscribed in the elegiac tale of her marriage, or a catalyst for divorce by affair. Whatever place this ill-conceived expedition had in her marriage, he was also someone interesting to know, she thinks.

Still, part of the experience was truly just about her marriage, and in that part Jill's correspondent was indeed a cipher. He might have been the Easter Bunny. For what little she knows, he is the Easter Bunny. He was a conduit through which she was reminded fleetingly of what she'd deliberately relinquished about herself in marriage. And through which she lost her capacity not to care about the loss. Jill wants a home base, for her family and herself, and she wants her spirit back, all the facets of herself that she allowed to flatline in marriage. She wants a place of enchanting intensity, with a chance for complexity or surprise. In the harness of a marriage with children it may be best—or, if not best, then safest and most expedient—not to remind yourself of the part of yourself you were willing to kill to stay married, since not wanting something is as good as possessing it. If you let yourself remember it, the big thing you lost or gave up, and it could be one of a hundred things, then you come to feel more urgently and irrevocably, as Jill did, that something has to change.

PART IV

||||||||||||||||||||||||||||

·The New Monogamy

CHAPTER THIRTEEN

"THE FIFTY-MILE RULE"

Affair Tolerators, Then and Now, or, the Don't Ask, Don't Tell Marriage

FOR A SECRET demimonde of marriages, the affair is not at all impossible, or forbidden—but it is a treaty arrived at through private collusion. The Don't Ask, Don't Tell marriage goes deeper than the monogamy agnosticism of spouses who forgive affairs after the fact. Nonmonogamy at least nicks the consciousness of these marriages, even if it's not discussed explicitly.

Scott is a married man in his early fifties who is a detective and has had a mistress for almost two years. They see themselves as lover and mistress, and use those terms self-consciously. In emails they playfully elaborate the manners of mistress and lover as if they are writing an etiquette book, and although it's a lighthearted flirtation, it helps to delimit the relationship, so that it doesn't lapse into the familiar romantic story of serial monogamy. Scott's wife has a "European" sensibility, he says, and knows that affairs are within the boundaries of their marriage but doesn't want to hear about it. They decided all this on principle earlier in their marriage. A governing fiction in a marriage can prove just as compelling, and useful, as a nongoverning truth.

So Scott constructs cover stories and practices Don't Ask, Don't Tell. Another husband in his late thirties describes the policy succinctly in an online discussion: "We have an implicit understanding. We can see other people but we don't share details. No prying questions. When we're together, we're together, and we focus on each other. When we're not, we're free to do other things. It doesn't matter."

I ask Scott, why not be completely up-front and honest, having gone this far? He reasons that it's not just a question of truth versus lie. It's a question of who spouses want to imagine themselves to be in the marriage, as much as what they'll tolerate. "If I come out openly to my wife, in the sense of telling her where I am, then she'd need to integrate that into her identity and self-concept"—and he's right, that's a much more audacious project for a marriage than Don't Ask, Don't Tell, which leaves the presumption of monogamy intact but permits covert affairs. It would mean confronting the fact that you were the "sort of wife" or the "sort of husband" who could live with knowing incontrovertibly of your spouse's affair.

Married couples in this gray zone between pure cheating and pure monogamy do "know" about their spouses' behaviors on some real but allusive level. Most long marriages have secret decoder rings like this around one topic or another, usually either money or sex. I wonder how many low-conflict marriages are held together by everyday acts of willful incuriosity.

The affair-tolerant survey their marriages and set boundaries on what kinds of trysts or experiences are acceptable. Within that perimeter they're free to roam, as if on a wildlife reserve, and to keep their own counsel.

Sometimes the boundaries are literal. An academic in the humanities and her husband have a "fifty-mile rule." By the marriage's fuzzy accounting, they can behave like "honorary single people" if they're away at conferences or on business outside the monogamous radius of home, as long as it's a casual thing. Versions of the fifty-mile rule have popped up infrequently, but more than once, in my various conversations.

Other affair-tolerant marriages set boundaries based on time, type of activity, or type of partner. Through a friend I learn of Melissa and her husband, who took a marriage sabbatical for several months. During this time she and her husband suspended certain marital rules. She lived in another city, and had a special bond with another man. But the arrangement didn't involve penetration or intercourse, only parallel acts of self-gratification and the like. A friend of John's has a fairly retro marriage, with several children and a stay-at-home wife. Paul tells John that he and his wife have "an arrangement." He's allowed to flirt all he wants by email with an attractive single woman at work, so long as he never touches her or escalates beyond the flirtation. It's their small, private queerification of their otherwise traditional marriage. I hear an equally novel story about a wife who wanted a one-time "payback" fling after her husband cheated on her. She told him about it beforehand, made her family a pasta casserole before she left for the night, and afterward the marriage went along as if the fling had never happened.

I thought I knew my long-married friend Madeline fairly well. When I described some affair-tolerant marriages to her one evening, it was clear she didn't see herself in one, or think much of the idea. Then, much later in the evening, she revealed casually, and without any hint of incongruity or reference to the earlier conversation, that she occasionally has flings with women and that her husband doesn't mind. As lovers, women evidently are seen as less of a threat to the marriage (a tolerance that also may have something to do with the fact that the idea of women together titillates many a husbandly heterosexual imagination).

Josie also tested the boundaries of affair tolerance and nonmonogamy. "When Rory and I were in the honeymoon phase of marriage," she tells me, "I most fervently believed in nonmonogamy." It seemed "oddly romantic and brightly radical" to her then. "We discussed a deal whereby if one of us wanted to have a fling, we would agree to send the other on a fun getaway," but when Rory acted on the deal, it wasn't exactly the spa weekend Josie had envisioned. She ended up at Rory's parents' house with their two young children, including her fussy, demanding newborn, who was nursing painfully and not yet sleeping through the night. "It's not that charming to the person who's changing diapers, nursing, and watching TV," she says, adding that it doesn't work when the relationship is "unequal"—as many marriages are in some critical way. "I was pretty miserable when Rory first called to ask for permission to get together with some person she had a crush on," Josie continues. "I basically said 'Whatever, fine.'" Although the fling was just a fling, Josie recalls it today "as one of the moments that put a nail in the coffin of our relationship. I know this because it makes me sad to think on it. For me it was always a theoretical freedom. For Rory it was very real, and she exercised her privileges."

Collecting all these stories, I realize that I'm a closet prude. My wifely rebellions never extend further than my numinous, "as-if" radicalism. For years I've been following the official press release about the monogamy imperative while my peers blithely pursue lesbian extramarital affairs and talk about their fifty-mile radii of honorary sexual singledom. All this nonchalance, however much it interests me in theory, surprises me, and that makes me feel frumpy and vaguely uncool. I understand what F. Scott Fitzgerald meant when he said that there are people whose lives make other lives "feel like death."

||||||||||

Running parallel to the history of marital infidelity is a subterranean history of infidelity tolerance, an artifact that's constantly being excavated, reburied, and then rediscovered like a dog's favorite bone. People think they've unearthed something new and take the liberty of naming it.

In the 1920s, Judge Ben Lindsey coined the phrase "adultery agreements." A pioneer of the romantic, companionate marriage ideal (and even obliquely of open marriage, along with Bertrand Russell), he was speaking of "couples who mutually agree that adultery is all right." He had "no doubt," he added, that in most cases "there is no candid agreement, but simply a tacit ignoring of the facts."

Four decades later, in their influential 1965 work on married lives,

The Significant Americans—"significant" defined as well-heeled, professionally employed, and financially comfortable—John Cuber and Peggy Harroff renamed these tacit pacts "adultery toleration." "Partly consciously and partly unconsciously," they write, some couples "have evolved a rather elaborate mythology which enables most of them to live comfortably with the discrepancies between action and belief." One wife they interviewed, an editor with a grown child, demoted the monogamy imperative as "merely a set of rules which one talks up on formal occasions and with people who don't really matter, anyway. You sort of wallow around in that sentimental mishmash, like Fourth of July speeches, some sermons, and college commencement speeches. No one takes any of it seriously, anyway."

Marriages like hers, although forged in the 1950s heyday of family values, didn't expect the monogamy imperative to regulate actual behavior in any inviolable way. "One outgrows adolescence," a wife in the gray zone told Cuber, "and the one and only and forever routine is sort of for the kids, don't you think?" As a secular social convention, monogamy created public order and private spaces of sexual liberty in one pragmatic gesture: Pretend you're monogamous, and we'll pretend not to know that you aren't. As another wife put it, there was a kind of "barter in contrived innocence. . . . I let the neighbors think what they want to. That gives them and me the same protection."

Cuber and Harroff's anecdotal view is corroborated by some startling data from Alfred Kinsey's groundbreaking work in the early 1950s. Kinsey found that 26 percent of married women in his sample had had an affair by age forty, and an additional 20 percent had engaged in "petting behavior without intercourse," for a total of 46 percent of wives who had had extramarital encounters. Of this "experienced" group, 71 percent reported "no difficulties with their marriages" because of it, even though half said that their husbands either knew of or suspected the extramarital sex.

A short time after Cuber and Harroff published their work, on the leading edge of the so-called sexual revolution, Jessie Bernard also described a "new kind of woman" (clearly not so new) who was "unfazed" by extramarital sex. "The norm is not to be flagrant about it," Bernard wrote. "It is being flagrant about it that violates the rule." Typical of this new breed was one who reported: "Two nights a week my husband and the neighbor's wife go bowling together [and] they usually come home around two. We don't say much about it, although everything is perfectly clear to all four of us directly concerned. . . . The neighbors? Well, by now they largely ignore it—at least we're not ostracized at any of the neighborhood social affairs. . . . I would say that I am in love with my husband and the woman next door is in love with hers. Also, of course, she and my husband are in love with each other. . . . I have not had an affair myself, simply for the reason that no good prospect came along. . . . There are many designs for living . . . and whose business is it anyway?"

In the early 1970s, researcher Gordon Clanton discovered the same pattern and rebaptized it "ambiguous adultery." In these "mixed type" marriages, "a person may know about the spouse's extramarital involvement but not be able to approve of it [actively]," so they quietly tolerate it instead. As the 1970s progressed, though, the discussion of affair tolerance took a new turn. For some of its advocates in the well-educated middle classes, marital nonmonogamy piggybacked on a headier political and social agenda of liberation. They had a much more pungently utopian, anti-institutional impulse than the 1950s affair-tolerant, who wanted to preserve the traditional marriage status quo even as they subverted its key sexual imperative. Advocates of nonmonogamy in the 1970s wanted to use the battering ram of sexual freedom and "liberation" to transform if not demolish the tenets of traditional marriage. I doubt that the quietly tolerant married couples Cuber and Harroff interviewed would have applauded Mervyn Cadwallader's 1966 cri de coeur that "contemporary marriage is a wretched institution" and "married people feel disillusioned and as caged as animals in the zoo."

Some Christian theologians, black-sheep ancestors to conservative evangelicals today, joined in the critique, championing a school of "situation ethics" in the 1960s and early 1970s. Episcopalian Joseph

Fletcher wrote in *Commonweal* in 1966 that "there is nothing against extramarital sex as such, in this ethic, and in some cases it is good. . . . If people do not embrace . . . faith (and most do not), there is no reason why they should live by it."

In the 1980s and 1990s, family values supporters launched a crusade for a 1950s marital revival, to combat the 1960s leftists, feminists, hippies, multiculturalists, and gay activists who they broadly lumped together and blamed for America's moral turpitude. But in terms of sexual ethics, 1980s family values and 1950s family values were very different. The ethic of adultery toleration in the 1950s set a modest goal: to create a governing fiction. Today's social conservatives aim for more than a consensus facsimile of monogamy for the sake of social equilibrium: They aspire to save our souls. They want to dictate behavior. Not only should you *act* as if you're a non-adulterer, you should actually *be* a non-adulterer.

Cuber and Harroff concluded in contrast that "probably a majority" of their subjects inhabited the affair-tolerating gray zone, happily and with clean conscience. They had "borne children and reared them," and they had "ignored the monogamous prescriptions about sex." This majority "eschews any attempt to change spouses, and at the same time often condones extramarital sexual relationships. . . . Mostly they practice more or less effective concealment and observe conventional pretenses." In an elaborate pas de deux, the affair-tolerant couples of the 1950s agreed to live with a presumption of monogamy. They understood sexual duplicity as an ethical standard *in and of itself,* a stance that departs notably from the proselytizing against adultery and in favor of traditional marriage that emerged in the 1980s and 1990s. Today, in the 21st century, affair-tolerant marriages are adding their own post-romantic stratum to this shadow history.

|||||||||

Karen's marriage doesn't conform precisely to the affair-tolerant model, but I introduce it here because it seems like one plucked from the pages of *The Significant Americans* and is an almost self-conscious homage to the prosperous 1950s. She and her husband live in a New England town near the water. They attended the same elite northeastern college, and they have four children and an au pair. Karen stays at home. Her husband, Charles, is an executive. She buys vintage 1950s clothing from eBay and collects aprons from the Eisenhower era. When I meet her at a mutual friend's house one summer evening, she looks adorable in a flamboyantly patterned cocktail dress, her blond hair pulled back in a wide headband.

When she was growing up, Karen's attitude toward marriage was as retro 1950s as her marriage itself appears to be. Unlike a lot of the equally smart and smartly educated women I talk to, Karen really did think about marriage. "I always wanted to get married," she remembers. "When I was in college [in the mid-1980s] and I told people I wanted to marry and have a family, some of them accused me of taking the space" of a woman who wanted to get an education and *do* something with her life. Marriage and family weren't a fashionable point of view for our cohort.

Shortly after college, Karen became the hard-hitting career girl anyway. She had a glamorous career in fashion, and lived in New York with a boyfriend, but she still had marriage on her mind. One Valentine's Day, while her boyfriend was in the shower, she got dressed up and asked him, "Do you see yourself marrying me some day?" After a moment's thought he popped his head out of the shower curtain and said, not unkindly but firmly, "No." That was the end of the relationship. But the hassles of New York real estate and apartment rental being what they are—and as decisions about real estate tend to dominate, or at least infiltrate, the romantic ones these days—they had to live together for a while longer.

Karen met someone else during these months. ("I never went two days without a relationship," she says.) Though she was young by the marriage standards of her peers, she was feeling some pressure. One of her sisters had just married, and two weeks after the wedding Karen accepted a proposal from the man, despite her doubts. He came from a vituperative family beset by the familiar demons of drink, divorce, and mental instability, whereas Karen comes from a tight-knit family. On her wedding day, as she waited outside the church to walk down the aisle, the doors about to be flung open on the church and the many guests, her father, who wasn't given to expressing his emotions, proposed that it wasn't too late to hop in the limo and drive away.

Within months of the marriage she regretted it. She recalls her first husband as quarrelsome and aggressive, "over nothing. He would take normal, innocent statements and questions and turn them into arguments." She was contemplating leaving him when she got pregnant and decided to give the marriage a chance because she'd always wanted children. After her child was born, Karen credited some of her discontent to being out of the swim of things, since her friends were all single. Her mother looked after the baby while Karen worked. As her marriage grew untenable, she had an affair with a co-worker. When she finally asked for a divorce, her husband was livid about it, but she was undeterred. Maybe it was another case of divorce by affair.

Karen encountered Charles again on her way to a college reunion, and they reconnected instantly and powerfully. They've been married for more than a decade now. When she reflects on her first marriage, she thinks "maybe we could have made it work," but now that she has "an awesome marriage with Charles," she sees how self-defeating and pointless it would have been to try. She says she and Charles have "pretty much the happiest marriage" she's seen.

I can understand why. It turns out Karen and Charles are the souls of sexual bohemia in the shell of *Ozzie and Harriet*. For one thing, they go to strip clubs together for sexual provocation and mutual interest. "Doesn't everybody?" she asks. For another, she wants to see women, and has since high school. "I wouldn't have married Charles if he couldn't handle that," she says. Her husband is impassive and unfazed by it. Charles is permitted certain dalliances, too, and tolerates, even encourages, an exhibitionist streak in his wife, who occasionally wears her vintage aprons without underwear. A friend affectionately calls her a racy Donna Reed.

Karen and Charles's openness is most consistent with the reality if not the illusion of the prosperous 1950s marriage that Cuber
described, even if they depart from their affair-tolerating predecessors in other ways. Theirs sounds like an enchantingly paradoxical
marriage. Out of college Karen had the traditional yearning just to
get married—desperate *to be* a housewife—but she got lured into the
competitive career all the same; they pursue an outré sexual lifestyle
within the confines of a self-consciously traditional and even romantic, marriage, and they are allies in that quest. Absent from their
marriage is the hostility of the sexual "acting out" affair, intended to
retaliate against a spouse, or the cranky Battle of the Sexes mind-set,
or the double standard about extramarital sex.

This sort of revision of the sexual imperative most often happens
in secret, and in private. So you have to go to secret places to find
out about it. To learn more about the demimonde of affair tolerance today, I go where everyone else goes. I join a marriage-themed
online social network and discussion, that bewitching chimera of
anonymous intimacy. These networks and cyber communities are
most likely changing mores in and of themselves. Here, wives and
husbands are having anonymous conversations about sexual ethics in
marriage, and in anonymous conversation we tend to forgive more
readily, imagine more vividly, and express opinions more expansively.
And the online conversation about sexual ethics and monogamy is
co-ed. Typically, husbands and wives discuss these ethics, if at all, exclusively with their own kind, which reinforces whatever double standards and stereotypes we bring to the conversation and encourages
the solidarity of one sex against the other. I wonder if husbands and
wives, as groups, have ever been potentially such collaborators and so
much in it together.

A woman having an affair with a married man wonders to the
group, "How many people really ARE cheating out there? I'm starting to believe this is more common than I thought. Trust me, no one
would believe that I was the 'other woman.' And if I'M doing it, I just

wonder how many others there are out there who are keeping 'the secret.'"

In response, a wife having her own affair says, "There's a lot of us . . . more than I ever imagined. Guilt is overrated. I don't feel guilty, and neither does he. I finally feel at peace."

A wife writes that her husband is "having an affair, and although I know about it, he does not know that I know. The sad/scary part is I am not sure that I mind/care. At home everything is fine, we are happy and actually have a good relationship. Our children are happy and healthy. I think somewhere along the way we became very close friends, but the desire for each other has faded. Am I wrong? Should I tell him I know, or let it go? His 'affairs' are more like passing encounters with other women. They only last a few weeks. . . . But if we are both happy with how it is going, does it matter? Or should I tell him that I know and am alright with it?"

The minority response holds that this marriage fails the real-marriage litmus test. "He doesn't care much about you," one person says. "It's not really a proper marriage anymore, is it?" Another asks, "Why doesn't it bother you? You're living a lie." The overwhelming opinion, however, is not only monogamy-agnostic, but affair-tolerant and underwhelmed. "You should just let it lie. If you're okay with it, let him be," writes one wife. "There doesn't seem much point in telling him if you're happy with the way things are," a man advises. Another wife concurs. "If you are getting what you need out of the relationship and he is getting what he needs, just let it be. . . . You could mess up your status quo, which doesn't seem all that horrible."

Another participant's wife had an affair that was betrayed by her cellphone bill. He's grappling with the same dilemma. He doesn't care that much, and he wants to know what others think of his indifference. Why should he either "have to be selfish and tell my wife, go away, I don't want you around (ask for a divorce), which isn't true, or sneak around [and have an affair myself] which isn't who I really am?" Just ignoring the situation seems a better option to him.

In lieu of outrage, the general perspective on the affair is one of simple pragmatism. These online husbands and wives speak in the dispassionate language of the "risk vs. reward calculus" of having an affair when "a house and kids are involved." They use the global economy term *outsourcing* to describe their extramarital sex lives. They liken their marriages and their spouses to their offices and their colleagues: "I depend on my co-workers," a husband says of his affair tolerance, "but I don't need to be around them all the time, and there are parts of me I would never show them."

These spouses view their marriages as successful, but by a post-romantic ideal. A husband describes himself as deeply committed to his marriage, but "we are like best friends and roommates. I think marriage, is 'just a job' to my wife." He adds that he wouldn't leave the marriage because of that, since "we have a lot of fun and need each other in practical ways." By these life partners standards, the marriages work. "There are those in the middle, for whom a relationship satisfies most needs, but still there is something missing," another man explains. "Often it is not the failing of one or the other partner. It's just that two people don't need to be on the same page all the time." I recall my conversation with Dan, and realize that attitudes in this online community couldn't be further from the intent to "wound" or the yen to be a player or a sexually sporting femme fatale. Odd though it sounds, these spouses are dedicated to preserving and thereby honoring the marriage—through tolerated extramarital sex.

As the affair-tolerant spouse sees it, why would you dismantle a marriage "just" over a sexual mismatch or an affair? This trivializing word, *just*, gets used a lot by my online compatriots. Somewhere in transit from the romantic 20th century to the 21st, passion was demoted from the sine qua non of marriage—its most dazzling authentication—to an ancillary "just," something incidental to a marriage's comradely soul.

If the romantic ideal of marriage imagines us always twenty-five years old, the post-romantic ideal imagines us always sixty-five and calibrates marital and sexual success by what would satisfy us in our golden years. "I really do not see the harm in an affair for sex only," a wife says. "As long as you and your spouse still get along and are friends. In the long run when you are both fifty, the sex isn't what matters, it's the friendship." Is this deeply wise or very silly? I'm not sure. My friends aren't, either. As she was divorcing, Josie commented to me wistfully, "This would be an ideal marriage, if only we were seventy." Laura observes that marriage is "wonderful at the beginning," when you're still enthralled with its novelty, and "precious at the end of life," when you need a partner to take care of you and keep you company. "It's just all the decades in between that are a problem."

Sociologist Jessie Bernard suggested decades ago that there may be an immanent clash between the imperatives of exclusivity and permanence in marriage. "If we continue to insist on sexual exclusivity as our marriages get longer, we may have to sacrifice permanence," she wrote. "If we want permanence in marriage, we may have to sacrifice exclusivity." A forty-one-year-old father of four, married for twenty years, endorses permanence in my online discussion. He hopes to reconcile a longer life span with a shorter sexual attention span by viewing monogamy as an ethical phase in a long marriage. It was a "good choice" for them initially, when they were raising young kids and pressed for time, but now he feels like he has the "time and energy to devote to my wife and another now." A wife endorses his view. "I don't think most people are made to stay true to one partner their whole lives. Some can do it. I think for the majority, it is just unnatural."

Jason is an academic who has been married for twelve years. He has two children and wants to stay married. "I intend to ensure that my children never experience the pain of a rancorous divorce, as I did while growing up. In most ways my life is ideal," he says—and I know exactly what he means—but his wife had an affair and he wants to have one, too. He met a happily married woman at a conference and fell for her hard. They exchanged hundreds of emails, and planned to consummate the relationship, but she couldn't go through with it. Now he is "looking to meet similarly restless women for experiments beyond the bounds of marriage while keeping our feet planted within those bounds." It sounds as if for spouses like Jason, affair tolerance isn't the product of radical thinking. It comes out of a traditional desire to stay married, and in his case, to avoid the bogeyman of divorce. These spouses are neither so romantic as to think that the atrophy of passion means they should divorce, nor so traditional as to think they must comply with the monogamy imperative at any cost. They maneuver sinuously in the middle. They persist in the traditional marriage gene pool even when they feel like jumping out—and, in the process, they evolve the institution in directions not at all intended by defenders of traditional marriage.

Americans occasionally worry that now that the sexual revolution has given single men (and it's always only men who are assumed to want sex for sex's sake) access to sex "for free," without the encumbrance of marriage, they will stop bothering to get married. Let's call it the "Money for Nothing and Your Chicks for Free" syndrome, after the Dire Straits song. But by the same logic, if *married* people can get it—extramarital sex—for free (that is, within such nondeceitful parameters as Judge Lindsey's "tacit ignoring of the facts" or its Don't Ask, Don't Tell reprise), then why would they bother to get divorced? Why end a satisfying Life Partners marriage "just" over faded sexual passion? You might as well "just" stay married.

CHAPTER FOURTEEN

"WE'RE MAKING IT UP AS WE GO ALONG"

Sexual Libertarianism and the Case Against Marital Monogamy

OTHER MARRIAGES UNRAVEL the marriage-monogamy knot even further, with explicit elaboration. Marital monogamy is fighting a multifront war against foes that range from old-fashioned infidelity to lust-inspired divorce and remarriage, discontented sexless marriage to monogamy agnosticism and gray zone affairs. The "asexual" marriage and the swinging marriage probably stake out the extremes of this spectrum of sexual libertarianism, the idea that individual marriages can write their own rules beyond the romantic orthodoxy.

Asexual marriages are a distinct genus from the sexless marriages. My laptop deems "asexuals" a typographical error. *Asexual* is an adjective, it thinks, not a subject. It is wrong. Asexuals are people who "flat out, no joke don't give an f. about sex," writes the Asexual Visibility and Education Network (AVEN) founder on its website. They claim this dispassion as a "fourth categorization" of sexual preference altogether, and as a marital style rather than a marital deficit. They reject the prioritizing of monogamous sexual love over friendship. Asexual marriage doesn't mean not being intimate, or even not having sex;

it means not wanting to have sex, and coveting an ideal of platonic intimacy. Asexuals have their own online matchmaking service, and AVEN has fifteen thousand members.

Samantha is an asexual wife and the mother of two young children. She has always been indifferent to sex. "I wondered, with every boyfriend, if maybe they just weren't the right one, because I never really wanted sex and never initiated it. When my husband and I began dating, we had sex all the time like most new couples. But really, I was fine with it not happening. I could orgasm just fine and as often as I wanted, but really, I'd rather just read or something." She sought medical advice but had a great "feeling of relief and belonging" when she found a Web community for asexuals and was reassured "that I wasn't just weird or crazy, that there are others just like me." The democratic instrument of the search engine has Googled a marital affliction into a marital lifestyle. "Thousands of people were going through more or less the same thing," AVEN says, "inventing the same word out of thin air to describe themselves and typing it into Google." Samantha distinguishes her lifestyle from celibacy, which implies "depriving yourself of something. That would be like saying someone who is straight is depriving themselves of the gay experience or vice versa. I'm not interested, so there's no deprivation."

With her new bearings in the world as an asexual, Samantha and her husband began a compromise of sex once a week as long as she could say when and where and he didn't pressure her or even mention it. That worked for a while, until he started "whining about his circumstances." When she grew tired of his complaints, Samantha proposed an open marriage. "He sort of thought it was a trick. He couldn't believe I was telling him to have sex with someone else," she recalls. "Say you like Ping-Pong," she explained to him. "I hate Ping-Pong, you love Ping-Pong, so go find someone who will play with you and have a good time doing it!" Once he realized her true "indifference" to his having extramarital affairs, they went about searching for his girlfriend. "I got really frustrated because I didn't think it should be this hard to find someone for him. But then I love him for being picky and not just taking the first thing that came along. We ended up finding a lot of couples who were interested in both of us. I wasn't thrilled with that because the idea is that I don't have to have sex. But swingers are very secure in their marriage, and there isn't any drama"—something they definitely wanted to avoid—so they gave it a try, and "it was okay for me but *awesome* for him." They moved away from that and eventually found "a girlfriend or two" for her husband.

I ask how they define their marriage. "We have two children we are crazy about, and we truly love each other *to death*. My husband doesn't want to pressure me into something I don't want to do. And I don't want him to go without something so important to him, either. You have to have compassion and understanding for the one you love," Samantha philosophizes, "something you should have anyhow, but there are so many who don't." Sometimes the preservation of the traditional marriage (to say nothing of a spouse's humanity) requires the demolition of traditional marriage, or at least one of its big rules.

"Divorce wasn't the option we wanted. We love each other and won't let something as trivial as sex stand in the way of us spending our lives together," Samantha says, and I note again that sex has slid from a foundation of (romantic) marriage to a "trivial" facet. But, she cautions, "you must banish all jealousy you may have from your mind. I know without a doubt that my husband isn't going anywhere. If you aren't sure of that—DON'T DO IT!"

I'm surprised to learn that a closeting shame attaches to abstinence, even in our abstinence-fetishizing age, and even for single asexuals. It's no easier to come out as asexual than to come out as a polyamorist. (Samantha herself isn't out to her parents because "I'd have to use the word *sex* to explain it to them," she jokes.) An essay on the AVEN website notes that "reactions range from fully supportive . . . to outright accusations of bringing shame on the family." *For not having sex?* Asexuals would find more company in Japan, where the national libido is so wan that a magazine ran the arousing headline "Young People! Don't Hate Sex!" The article worried that "love-hotel check ins were off at least 20 percent over the past five years." And many guests weren't visiting for a tryst anyway, but because "love hotels offer the cheapest access to karaoke machines and video games."

||||||||||

Like the asexual married community, the swinging community has been Googled into greater prominence in recent years. The number of swinging marriages is growing fast. Anywhere from two to four million married Americans engage in this recreational form of non-monogamy. Susan Wright is the executive director of the National Coalition for Sexual Freedom (NCSF), something of an advocacy group for sexual libertarianism as regards "safe, sane, and consensual" practices. Wright thinks the number of swingers is underreported, since some couples go to swing clubs but don't label themselves as such. But the number of swing clubs is growing exponentially, she says, and the lifestyle "is a lot more common than people think." There are more than 500 swing clubs nationally, twice as many as there were ten years ago, and up by 200 in the last five years alone. The states with the most clubs are California and Texas. Swinging, says Robert McGinley, president of the North American Swing Club Association, has gotten "organized and institutionalized" in the 21st century.

The NCSF maintains a list of "Kink Aware" professionals who understand sexually untraditional marriages. Wright founded it in 1997, after working at the National Organization for Women. She strikes me as a pioneer of third-wave feminism. NOW supported lesbians in the early 1980s, she recalls, but excluded s/m communities from its agenda of nondiscrimination. Wright didn't agree with this exclusion, or the hostility among feminists toward their unconventional peers. "Women would attack other women in leather jackets. People think s/m is so unusual," or, in the case of NOW, exploitative to women, "but I ask them, well, do you ever *spank* each other? That's a kind of s/m, too."

Swingers' gatherings like the annual Lifestyles convention in Las Vegas draw vendors who do a brisk business in photographic services and sexual tchotchkes. Swingers are willing to spend upwards of seven hundred dollars on weekend excursions to the Caribbean or Mexico (you know you're a swinger, the joke goes, if you've got thousands of frequent flier miles from traveling to Jamaica). Hotels love swingers, according to Wright. Usually a group will rent out a hotel wholesale and have a tactful icebreaker party, "nothing overt or graphic." Then the guests can go home or more likely go upstairs. "Hotels have swingers back again and again," Wright says. "We know how to blow off steam without getting out of control."

The free market in general loves swingers. Along with brides, they're an especially lucrative niche for the entertainment and hospitality industry because they tend toward the upper middle class, with lots of disposable income, although that isn't their image. A study in 1985 asked more than 100 nonswingers about their perceptions of swingers and compared them against profiles of 300 actual swingers. Nonswingers perceived swingers almost as sexual bogeymen, imagining them as pot-smoking, drug-using, alcoholic nonwhites with liberal and Democratic leanings and a need for counseling. Swingers actually tend to be long-married couples, not as many with young children, although the swinger with children typically tells the babysitter on a Saturday, "Stay all night, and don't ask questions in the morning." Swingers are "mostly a middle-aged crew," Wright says, "with lots of soccer moms." They lean conservative politically and religiously. Their profile befits the genesis of swinging not in the hippie counterculture but in tight-knit military communities in Southern California in the 1950s and 1960s. Swingers: the Republican base.

The Internet spares curious married couples the stigma of seeking out information in local adult bookstores or sex shops and makes the hidden culture easily apprehended. In the now unfathomable pre-Google years of the early 1990s, a raven-haired acquaintance of mine tried to locate a swinging party because her roommate and best friend hadn't had sex for a while and wanted to try. Caitlin would have to accompany her because Nan had no car. Nan found a flier in Video Pomposity, an artsy movie rental store, but they had to call three or four different people to get the actual address. "It was top secret,"

Caitlin recalls. "I wasn't sure if it would be like a real party, or not, so we brought a veggie tray just in case."

When they finally found the party house, a plush split-level in the distant suburbs, the hostess greeted them in a towel. She was thrilled to see what she thought was a lesbian couple at the door. All but one of the twenty or so couples inside were white, Caitlin says, and most seemed prosperous.

The party began in late afternoon, and started off like any other party, with chat about politics, volunteer firefighting, and the like. Although Caitlin got gingerly groped by the hostess when she agreed to accompany her on a beer run, she otherwise "saw no signs of people engaged in sex, and I was thinking, maybe this isn't really that kind of party." Toward dusk, the action picked up. Guests started congregating around the pool and the hot tub, disrobing, sitting in each other's laps, and exchanging what Caitlin recalls as "drunken, open-mouthed kisses." Caitlin panicked and wanted to "plot an exit strategy." She ended up cowering in the bathroom, unable to find Nan, while the towel-clad hostess knocked on the door and asked, "Are you ready to swing now?"

It was a "life decision moment," Caitlin says, because "her husband's on the bed and he's *definitely* ready to swing." Caitlin said no, and the couple retreated to their room—forced, presumably, to have sullen sex only with each other. She was "the false swinger," Caitlin confesses. She finally found Nan in the hot tub with the oldest man there, "a Morton Feldman figure with a hairy chest." Nan pouted that she hadn't swung yet and could she have a few more minutes? Caitlin extracted her and careened out of the suburb to the relative safety of the inner city where they lived. "I'm willing to do anything once. But, not that," she concludes.

"For *years* afterwards I'd get disguised mail from the swingers club, from a nondescript PO box," Caitlin laughs, "and I'd open it and ditto sheets would fall out for the next swinger party and the phone maze on how to find it." Things are so much easier now, without the cloak-and-dagger antics and phone trees. "People can network in a safe way today," Wright says. "Nowadays you just Google the name of your town and you find normal people in the community who are educating other adults about sexuality."

She's right. I task alter ego Miranda to look into swing clubs, and after a mere five minutes her search yields exhaustive results. I report back to John. Finally I've pushed my freakishly patient husband to the brink of his tolerance for my experiments.

"I'm not swinging," he says wearily. "I'm not having sex in public in a hanging cage."

"I'm not doing it, *either*. Don't *worry*. It doesn't appeal to me personally."

"These parties, do people dress up?"

"Like, a formal?"

"Sort of—tuxedos and gowns and stuff like that?"

"No, hon, that's so James Bond. Wow, what romantic fantasies you have. It's not the *prom*. If anything, think Catholic school girl uniforms and leather."

"That doesn't interest me."

"The Catholic Church must *love* it, that their uniforms are such a big prop for swingers," I laugh. John sighs apprehensively.

We're having this conversation as I'm preparing to get in touch with some of those effortlessly Googled swing clubs. There are too many choices, as with everything else. I'm intrigued to note that some are female-owned. The Farm, whose motto promises to "help me horse around," seems like it's the Harvard of swing clubs. It's among the most well-known and largest clubs in the world. It has two hundred acres of private land, dinner service, a huge bar, dance floors, big-screen TVs, and twenty-five themed party rooms. In the summer it sports a pool, three tanning decks, and RV hookups for the swinger on holiday, as well as hiking trails and picnic tables.

"You'd love this one, hon," I say. "It's got a dungeon *and* a workout area."

"What could be sexier than exercise?"

I discover that granola swingers in Oregon can enjoy a "night of quality sex in a group setting" with "no alcohol, no smoking, no drugs." The club is "health conscious" as well as "primal." Despite their erotic exuberance, most swing clubs are stridently nonsmoking environments. Imagine if Caligula were a health nut. It's the sort of club he might have. Smokers have got to be the biggest pariahs in the country. Have sex in public in a dungeon, but don't think we smoke.

A Swinging Boaters social club is for "swinging boaters to get together to share these two sensual pastimes," boating and sex. Anyone can host a rendezvous, provided they post by Wednesday or Thursday that "they're going some place that weekend." That sounds vague enough. The host nautical swinger is responsible for "monitoring the hailing channel and guiding other boats to the rendezvous." In a twist on piracy, these other boats can simply cruise on by and hail the host boat if they're interested.

"Is it yachts or sailboats?" John wonders.

"What difference does it make?"

"I just like *knowing* these things, hon."

Next I settle on a club in my area and glean details from its female owner. The club sits in a suburban strip mall. It's located behind a footwear store and is attached to the back end of a Chinese takeout restaurant. It's open only on weekend nights, like most other clubs, and has some impressive amenities: a "7-foot high elevated dance cage for the ladies to enjoy," eleven-foot dance poles, "heart pounding music on the dance floor." It's not a swingers club, but a "lifestyle experience," the website says.

"What do I say . . . ," I muse aloud to John, hesitating over my laptop. "Do you think you need to *promote* yourself when you talk to these people? Do I need to talk about how we *look*?" I'm imagining that there is a swing-worthiness standard.

"Maybe you have to audition."

Best to err on the side of caution. "My husband and I are in good physical shape," I write, feeling absurd, "and are considered to be good-looking."

The owner, Lisa, proves to be a helpful, warm sort who includes many hearts in her correspondence and reassures me that no one will make us do anything that we don't want to do. This is an "off-premises" club, she explains. In contrast to "on-premise" clubs, where members can have sex in private (or public) spaces right there, the whole night long if they wish, off-premise clubs function more like social meeting places, and "intimate activities" with other guests who catch your eye must be taken elsewhere.

Lisa tells me that Friday is the best night for "newbies." If I want to come alone, I could dress in red to signal that I'm a "unicorn"—swinging code for a single woman. (Rogue single men, alas, are not typically welcome.) There are tons of false and outdated photos on swinging matchmaking websites, Lisa warns me, but if I come to her club I'll get the extra certification of a big heart icon next to my profile.

Next I look for a house party. In 1975, a researcher found that almost half of a sample of nonswingers would "mind" if "an otherwise unobjectionable swinging couple" moved next door. Wright sees cases in which neighbors complain about swinging house parties, but it usually happens when the swingers decide to start charging admission, and then it's "an impromptu, swinging home business." In fact, a tempest along just these lines erupted in the plush Washington, D.C. suburb of Bethesda in 2009. Wright urges entrepreneurial swingers to set up warehouses instead, because one of the most negative things to befall sexual libertarians is running afoul of local zoning laws. "We need to get the message out—*don't set up businesses against zoning laws.*"

Ned, the husband in a swinging married couple, tells me how house parties work. Ned urges John and me—although it makes me giggle prudishly to even imagine us having the conversation—to be "as clear as possible" with each other before attending a party. Then "just relax and socialize," he says. "In this aspect, it's much like any other party. Any nervousness will disappear quickly." Since normal, fully clothed social interactions make me nervous enough, I rather doubt this. At their house parties, Ned and his wife usually plan ice-breaking exercises. I am reminded of corporate retreats.

Ned explains that some swingers just use parties to meet contacts, and not to "play"—an in-group euphemism—on the spot. "Now, what to do if a couple you've met asks the two of you to go upstairs with them, or 'Would you like to play?' Of course, you can only do what feels right for both of you." He reassures me that "being consider-ate and respectful of others, even when declining an offer, is a good policy anywhere." While people think that swing clubs are "a huge orgy, and everyone tosses their clothes aside and jumps into the pile," they're in error—aside from Plato's Retreat in early 1970s New York, which really was like that, he concedes.

Some couples just play with each other until they're comfortable branching out. There's a "soft swing," in which couples don't swap spouses but play with their own while another couple watches; there's the "full swap, same room" variation, and the "full swap, different rooms" option. Bob and Kate pursued swinging as a first step in their quest for a more open marriage. At the outset, they decided that they were "interested in soft swap only, i.e., no intercourse with other part-ners," Bob tells me. "This was mostly at Kate's behest, but the first time we were with another couple she was the one who wanted to throw that limit out, so we quickly became a full swap couple." The permutations make my head spin.

"They ought to put it on name tags," John suggests, "all the differ-ent options."

I thank Ned for his patient explanations and ask if he's got an up-coming party. No, he writes back. He and his wife had to quit hosting parties. His elderly mother fell ill and had to move in with them—and they didn't think it would go over too well with her.

|||||||||

Asexuality and swinging seem opposites on an imagined color wheel of married sex lives and ethics. But in a more profound way they're part of the same post-romantic mood. Both shrug off monogamy as marriage's prime directive, or even a relevancy. Monogamy is like marriage's appendix. It's still there, a vestige of earlier imperative functions such as assuring paternity, but does it still serve these purposes?

Gathering up all the stories on the continuum—from the deliberately asexual to the grumpily sexless to the clandestinely unfaithful to the tacitly adultery-tolerant to the ethically open marriage to the cheerfully swinging one—I am inclined to think that we should stop calling nonmonogamy a marital problem and call it a marital culture instead. Marital nonmonogamy may be to the 21st century what premarital sex was to the 20th: a behavior that shifts gradually from proscribed and limited, to tolerated and increasingly common.

The metaphor of intimacy may be shifting from the exclusive, closed circle of the wedding ring to the Web, with more far-flung, multiple connections and ties. The Web is a new morphology for marriage. More than once, I've heard young, unmarried twenty-somethings refer to themselves jauntily as "poly."

A legal axiom holds that fraud vitiates contracts. The more honest the terms going in, the less likely "monogamy fraud" becomes. In cutting-edge legal thought, Professor Elizabeth Emens provocatively questions why the monogamy imperative remains uncritically asserted when we have been challenging so many other bases of marriage. Her thinking fits with the larger trend toward viewing the marriage contract as akin to other private contracts. "If people could choose either monogamy or one of its alternatives, rather than being urged into automatic promises of monogamy," she postulates, "there might be fewer ugly, painful betrayals. More people who value sexual nonexclusivity might find one another. . . . It might be easier to be confident that one's monogamous partner really wants monogamy." Emens recommends that we use the law to "encourage partners to discuss and agree on relationship rules about sexual exclusivity."

My impression is that sexual libertarianism will continue to grow and lifelong monogamy will continue to lose its default status as the assumption in secular marriages. Couples who decide to marry may have to talk about monogamy deliberately, sincerely, and self-consciously beforehand. No doubt many will still choose it, but we can't know how many because, as Emens notes, we don't have a socially sanctioned way to discuss it.

Or spouses may decide to revisit the matter of sexual ethics at different junctures. Maybe they'll agree on circumstances under which they might overlook infidelity. Maybe they'll opt for monogamy during certain phases of a marriage—when raising young children, for example—but not necessarily forever and unconditionally. Or maybe they'll find themselves affirming rather than assuming that for them, sexual exclusivity and physical intimacy really *is* the joisting of the marriage. That heartfelt, explicit affirmation can only strengthen their dedication to making it work.

Something has taken the place of monogamy as the framework for the unconventional marriages described here; otherwise, like any poorly constructed building, they would have collapsed. Consistently, that replacement reveals itself to be a platonic ethical standard borrowed from friendship. As an asexual wife says, "We pursue a fundamentally different kind of intimacy with our partners. . . . We are making it up as we go along." A wife in a nonmonogamous marriage thinks about it in similar terms. "There's so much more to marriage than monogamy! There's the decision to live our lives as partners in all of our decisions. What does anybody get from a good marriage? Trust. Faith. Partnership."

In the 1970s, these couples might have divorced when passion faded. In the marriage consensus of the 1950s and earlier, they might have felt they had no choice but to stay together. Maybe in our time, and perhaps as a wildly unintended collateral effect of the family values movement itself, sexually nonconforming or troubled couples are resisting the romantic siren song and working harder to stay married.

CHAPTER FIFTEEN

"A PLACE WHERE A SICK MARRIAGE GOES TO DIE?"

The Hidden World of "Ethical Nonmonogamy"

WHAT JACK AND JILL are contemplating isn't as illicit and deceitful as cheating; as recreational and light as swinging; or as cozy and familiar as divorce. Sure, you'll be judged by many if you divorce, and that shame weighs heavily if you decide to pursue your adult humanity over Sticking It Out. But at least divorce is a well-trodden path, or a trail of tears, with now familiar trailheads and milestones. It has its own shelf in Barnes & Noble. Although its consequences may be radical for the couple concerned, it is not a radical social option. The actual practice of marital nonmonogamy isn't radical, either. You'll be judged for the affair if you get caught, certainly, but cheating is at least a cozy, ancient sin. The practice of open marital nonmonogamy, on the other hand, seems not only radical but weird. If you decided to explore it with your spouse as a new sexual ethic that might allow you to preserve the marriage, you'd probably be the object of more opprobrium than if you got divorced one day, started dating the next day, and had your new lover over to meet the kids that night.

Like most Americans, and me, my laptop is baffled by the word *polyamory*. As I type, it underscores the word accusatorily with a red squiggly line as a misspelling. It might think I mean *polygamy*, but polyamory is not polygamy, which means having multiple spouses. Polyamory is also different from cheating, obviously, and from swinging, which is recreational rather than intimate nonmonogamy. It's a more ethically evolved version of an open marriage. Although the term can encompass any number of geometries of intimacy, it essentially means, as legal scholar Elizabeth Emens succinctly writes, a form of "ethical nonmonogamy." Oddly, what makes it radical is its scrupulous standard of telling the truth, of shifting from the default setting of lying or salutary neglect to unflinching knowledge. Ethical nonmonogamy places the highest value on rules, honesty, agreement, and consent. This standard begins with you and your spouse and extends to choosing partners who are honest with *their* spouses or are otherwise available. Its other main precept is that your bond and commitment to your spouse is always and remains the "primary" bond. "Rivals are not allowed," Wendy-O Matik writes in a polyamory guidebook.

At present, ethical nonmonogamy is anomalous, but I think it's a vanguard more than a fringe. A large if not representative study by Lillian Rubin in 1990 found that 5 percent of marriages were open. A 2000 survey estimates the number at half a million. The federal government doesn't fund research on marriage alternatives, so it's hard to say. In a 2007 survey of 14,000 people on Oprah.com, a surprising 21 percent of respondents said they had an open marriage. Loving More, a national organization that supports polyamory, reports a rate of more than one thousand hits a day on its website. There are dozens of local polyamory networks and groups, including "mindful polyamory" in Philadelphia and a poly online dating site. Two academics have noted a recent surge of interest in workable alternatives to monogamous marriage, which is also evidenced by the popularity of *Big Love* and *Swingtown*. Reality TV shows like *The Bachelorette* reinforce the ideal of monogamy in that the "contestant" must choose only one man to marry, but for the entire season before that moment, we are exposed to the reality that the contestant has genuine romantic feelings for more than one man at a time. It's a nonmonogamous reality smuggled into a monogamous, Cinderella fairy tale.

|||||||||

An open marriage is strictly marital sci-fi to me, despite my theoretical affinity for it. It seems naïve. It's hard to imagine that all the delicate gearing of so many different people's lives, emotions, and neuroses would ever mesh smoothly—especially in the face of formidable romantic vestiges. For most marriages so much trust, symbolism, and intimacy is still entwined around sex and sexual possession. Then again, this isn't the age of "most marriages," the age of the marriage consensus, or the familiar marriage imperatives.

I ask my online panel to react to the opinion "It's unrealistic to expect a marriage to be monogamous for its duration." This question gets, by far, the largest disagreement (69 percent), with half who say they "don't agree *at all*." Only 15 percent agree, and 14 percent are undecided. More people think it is realistic to live monogamously for the duration of a marriage than actually succeed in doing it.

Next, to tease out differences between "cheating" and "open," I ask them to react to "Nonmonogamy could work if the couple agrees to it beforehand." This elicits a somewhat less pessimistic reaction. Fifty-eight percent disagree, and 43 percent "don't agree *at all*." I'm not surprised. On closer inspection, though, I'm interested in the 8 percent who "agree *entirely*" and the 22 percent who fall in the "agree" range. Almost one in five—19 percent—aren't sure, but they don't dismiss the idea, either. They think it might work, or have a neutral view. That makes for a fairly high ("especially for *this* side of the Atlantic") 41 percent who are at least undecided about whether ethical nonmonogamy could work or agree that it could. And 11 percent of those respondents who disagreed in the first question that it was unrealistic to expect a marriage to be monogamous think that nonmonogamy could work if agreed to beforehand.

If you're like my married acquaintances, the idea touches a nerve. It's a challenging topic, although they indulge my chatter about it. Privately, some would prefer open marriage or affair tolerance if it were socially sanctioned. Some have cheated and some have been cheated on. Most have fantasized about others and had marital crushes; many don't feel that sexually possessive toward or deeply aroused by their spouses anymore. Despite their curiosity, the most common refrain is "it never *works*." (Sparse though it is, research challenges this reflexive skepticism.) They wince at embarrassments in the collective historical unconscious, such as the wife-swapping infantilism of bored, wealthy Connecticut suburbanites so witheringly portrayed in the novel *The Ice Storm*. Many in my cohort want to believe in the happy openly nonmonogamous marriage as they might want to believe in mermaids, unicorns, and other enchanting mythologies. There's perhaps no idea that married people so dearly want *other* married people to propel into the mainstream for them than this one.

Although open marriage seems "icky" now, says one wife, she thinks it may soon evolve into a more common or benignly perceived arrangement, as has happened with interracial marriage. Ethical nonmonogamy is the most logical crazy idea around. Josie adds that queer culture has once again pioneered the idea. "Gay people have been doing openly nonmonogamous, committed relationships for decades. Why is this so *scandalizing* in straight marriage?"

A therapist tells me that he's encountered a few patients who would prefer that their spouses "take a lover" than work out the sexual issues in their marriage, which he laments. It surprises me that he sees this level of openness even as often as he does. "But, it's like being gay," he says, a prevalent enough but secret subculture.

Perhaps the queered traditional marriage is the deeper closet of our day and open nonmonogamy even harder to confess. While some formally traditional heterosexual marriages get queerer, some formally queer marriages—same-sex marriages—get more romantic. Some same-sex couples petition for their right to marry by affirming their belief in monogamy, exclusivity, and a lifelong bond of love, all the

romantic premises of marriage. Meanwhile, some outwardly traditional lasting marriages, which might be applauded by "marriage defenders" because they are legally recognized and between "a man and
a woman," are undergoing a kind of queerification. They're secretly
subverting the orthodoxy and improvising new rules outside both the
traditional and the romantic views of marriage.

As it turns out, Josie is getting married, in Connecticut, to a new
partner. "It's the ultimate act of optimism," Josie writes to me. Her
girlfriend proposed the old-fashioned way. She got down on her knees
in a hotel room with champagne and chocolates ("I was afraid she'd
passed out or tripped") and asked for Josie's hand and gave her a beautiful ring.

Josie isn't sure what to call herself now. "I don't want to say 'partner,'" she says. "That was before we decided to get married."

"But male-female spouses call themselves 'partners' now. You'll fit
right in."

But she's more romantic in her dreams than that. I receive her wedding invitation just as I'm delving into queered straight marriages. We
note this to each other, amused. "How is it possible that we migrated
into each other's worlds like this?" she wonders.

The queered open marriage has a certain audacity, in stretching the
limits of the possible within a conventional form. It subverts the strongest assumptions of the romantic marriage, its axioms that there is
only one intimacy at a time, that romantic love isn't plural, and that
jealousy renders multiple intimacies impossible. In envisioning a
marital fidelity that's grounded not in the practice of monogamy but
in ethical honesty, it's a staggering leap of faith, and anyone can be
forgiven their skepticism, even if it puts them in the not uncommon
romantic bind of living in a celibate monogamous marriage.

Neil is caught in that bind. He's been married for more than a
decade to a wife he still loves, after a fashion, but desire has flatlined.
"It gets to a point where there is no recovering what was there," he

writes to me. "I don't think my wife is really all that concerned about it. When my love life went down the tubes back at a time that I tend to forget, I had no idea where I was going, but over the last four years it dwindled from three, two, one to none." Neil doesn't want to "put his hormones on mothballs" for the rest of his life, nor does he want to divorce—nor does he trust the idea of ethical nonmonogamy. "In my mind, there is so much attached emotionally to the act of lovemaking. In an open marriage arrangement I'm thinking that if the love is not there with one person it becomes transferred to the one who is willing to give it. I envision a cold existence resulting on the one side, probably colder than the existing circumstances, but I'm sure that there are others who see it differently. I wish there was an easier way, a better answer."

An "I Live in a Sexless Marriage" forum in an online community had more than five thousand stories and exchanges when I last visited it. The posts are often amusing, heartbreaking, scathing, and wry, mostly variations on "Another Friday night and I'm not getting any." It fascinates me that the vast majority of these marriages never metamorphose into open arrangements with new rules. As much as it may distort a spouse's soul to live celibately in a marriage, it may equally distort the soul of a marriage to "open up," so no matter how elegant, logical, or theoretically incisive the nonmonogamy solution may be, the conversion never happens, or it never moves beyond glancingly hypothetical explorations. Complaints are made anonymously, advice offered, elegies for dead marital sex lives delivered tenderly, but there the spouses remain, sexlessly monogamous. It seems like a pyrrhic defense of a long-abandoned fort to live this way, but I understand the impulse.

I encountered Piper in this forum. I asked if she would ever consider departing from the monogamy expectation, to reconcile her needs with marital loyalty. "I would never ever change monogamy," she wrote back emphatically. "I don't want to share my lover with anyone else." Even though she lives celibately in her marriage and there isn't actually anything to share, she told me, "If I'd want to be with someone else, then I wouldn't be with my husband."

We're told by defenders of traditional marriage that romantic ideals are weakening the institution. The strongest of these is the presumption that sexual passion for one true love is the brick and mortar for a marriage. Ethical nonmonogamy would be deeply anathema to these marriage activists, as it doesn't comport with the ancient bases of marriage, but it's a declension, distantly yet clearly, of the challenge to romantic marriage ideals in the larger post-romantic spirit of the times.

|||||||||

"What's the biggest mistake your clients make?" I had asked Dan, months earlier. He thought about it a good long time before he said simply, "Assumptions. They make assumptions about what the other is doing, feeling, thinking."

"How would we live," I ask John, with Dan's comment in mind, "if there were no labels at all? Would it be easier if a marriage ditched the 'marriage' label entirely and lived exactly the same way—but called a relationship a jelly doughnut instead, or a structured, co-parenting friendship, or divorced cohabitation?" I kick around the topic.

"It might be," John says. "But if you're unhappy and bored at home and you introduce another person who's exciting and interesting in a way the marriage can't be . . . that's a tinderbox, just waiting to blow up. Whatever you call it."

"Maybe you're right," I concede. "Maybe an open marriage is just a place where a sick marriage goes to die." Maybe it's like hospice care, or a way station in the long, unwinding death spiral of a marriage, where you try to make yourself as happy and comfortable as you can before your imminent demise."

The idea of opening up as a Hail Mary pass on the inexorable path to defeat occurs to me again when I read Joe's story on another forum. He writes that he's been married for more than eight years.

"We complement each other nicely," he says. "We'd be inseparable best friends," but for the marriage. Joe and his wife had problems with communication and their sex life waned. Initially his wife insisted on monogamy and declared that she'd leave if Joe cheated, but then she fell in love with a co-worker who kindled passions that Joe could "only dream of." When Joe said he had a similar crush on a co-worker, his wife melted down, stopped wearing her wedding ring, and had an affair. "Effectively, our relationship became an open marriage—in a way, her decision, but one that I was obliged to support because of my firm philosophical belief that monogamy should be voluntary." Since then, the wife has had two affairs and Joe none, owing to differences in the market for wives and husbands, he thinks. Meanwhile, the marriage continued in sexual hibernation. "It seems to me that my wife is in an open marriage, while I am confined to celibacy." It doesn't sound promising.

|||||||||

Anita Wagner is a sexual activist and a sex educator for adults. She's in her mid-fifties and is in a polyamorous marriage. She comes from a conservative southern family, and has been honest to her family about her beliefs, which she somewhat has come to regret. Anita developed an interest in ethical nonmonogamy because she learned "just how destructive cheating is after having experienced it from just about every perspective."

As a polyamory educator, Anita observes that it's rare that both spouses would arrive at the idea of nonmonogamy simultaneously, or start off that way. (Although none other than famously unobjectionable, nonradical Will Smith told an interviewer in 2005 that he and Jada Pinkett Smith have an open marriage, in which they inform each other before they have a fling. "Our perspective is, you don't avoid what's natural. In our marriage vows we didn't say 'forsaking all others.' The vow that we made was that you'll never hear that I did something after the fact.") Usually "one spouse develops an interest first," Anita explains, "and they sometimes end up in poly/mono marriages," which she thinks are the most challenging relationships, for obvious reasons.

The "typical" open marriage today, as in the 1970s, is between well-educated, middle-class, or affluent professionals, usually in middle age. Anita describes the typical couple as one that sees the marriage as absolutely the primary relationship but not exclusive one. "They tend to think of themselves as autonomous people within a committed relationship," she says. "People who are emotionally dependent on others to feel good about themselves don't do very well at all in such relationships."

Warren Buffett, the second-richest man in America and a polyamorist before his time, would probably agree with Anita. For decades he maintained a marriage and a mistress, one in Omaha, one in California, both in the open, without the fig leaf of secrecy. When a BBC interviewer asked him in late 2009 how that worked, he said lightly, "You need to be secure," you need to "not be jealous," and everyone needs to be getting what they need out of the relationship. Sure, he conceded, if you polled Omaha residents his arrangement might have raised eyebrows, but he never cared about that. The three of them cared about "the three people involved."

In my explorations I detect two main profiles of open marriage. In the first, the passionate sexual intimacy isn't part of the marriage anymore, if it ever was, but the marriage still functions on other levels as a valued, intimate, even sacred, bond. In these cases the marriage opens up sexually to get what each partner needs while maintaining the marital tie, the household, and the intact family, in some cases.

Susan had been married for some years when she fell in love with another man, with whom she "bonded" on many different levels—"friendship, companionship, and sexually." She hadn't planned on falling in love and had no intention of leaving her marriage: "I adore my husband and will never divorce." But the marriage, while a committed and loving partnership, "lacked a physical element." She came to the familiar juncture of contemplating infidelity and lying to her husband. The one thing she wasn't willing to do was to leave either the husband or the lover, who "filled a void" in her life. She went on a fact-finding mission online and stumbled onto the concept of polyamory through Google and the usual, effortless online explorations. Now she and her husband are open about the arrangement, and he is even lightly cordial with her lover. "So is that wrong?" she asks. "Are we hurting anyone? I think not. We are not cheating, or being hurtful. It is difficult, and requires a mature and respectful attitude, but we are happily making the best of the situation, and are not going through the hurtful experiences of breaking up with each other because society has decided that we are not 'normal.'"

Holly has an Oreo marriage, too—traditional on the outside, untraditional on the inside—under circumstances that might prompt many other spouses to divorce. She's been married for sixteen years, to a man who "said he was in love with me and he certainly seemed to be. But not in every way I had hoped." He was trying, desperately, not to be gay. (This isn't an entirely unusual revelation in marriage. One researcher estimates that in as many as two million male-female, legally formalized "traditional marriages," one partner is gay or lesbian. Some of these marriages began that way; others evolved over time.) Holly now lives with her husband "the way I'd live with a best friend. No guilty secrets. There is nothing to feel guilty about. I am helping my ersatz husband to come out. I hope that he can find intimate companionship, too, while we remain trusted friends. I do *not* want a relationship with a conventionally possessive, insecure man who cannot understand my platonic relationship with my husband. He remains my only real family." Stories like Holly's have a familiar ring—traditional marriages, amiable and low-stress, with pockets of competencies and yearnings unfulfilled, inhabited by couples so dedicated to the idea of marriage that they let it go eccentric to keep it intact. For them, opening up the marriage is an act of going the extra mile to save the marriage, a way of honoring their marriage and their deepest selves.

Polyamory also happens in cases where the marriage has a vital and robust sexual bond, and a high level of honesty and trust. Being secure and libidinally gifted, both partners, for reasons of taste, sexual appetite, conviction, a yen for adventure, or a desire for multiple intimacies, are comfortable in opening up. Bob and Kate's marriage is an example. I get in touch with them after I read a comment from Kate in an online community: "I've posted on relationship forums . . . about wanting an open relationship and looking for advice on how to talk to my partner about it, but all the answers I got contained some kind of word that described me as a whore." Hostility toward assertive, confident, independent female sexuality persists.

Bob and Kate have been married for more than eighteen years and have known each other for twenty. They have children at home and they're in their late forties. "I think for us, we are so much in love with each other, and are best friends on top of that, that we are very, very secure in our relationship," Bob tells me. "We believe strongly in the polyamory notion that you can love (romantically and sexually) more than one person at a time."

When they got married, Kate had been exclusively in relationships with women since she was eighteen. Bob knew from the start that she was bisexual and sat "smack dab in the middle" of Kinsey's scale of sexual preference. They had a "traditional relationship" in their marriage with children, until about a decade into it, when they began "discussing the possibility of a threesome with another woman so that my wife could experience women again." Bob admits that he was "turned on by the idea," too, but it was Kate, not the husband, who was the catalyst for this conversation. She and Bob had always had been "very good at sharing our desires and fantasies with each other," and sometimes enjoyed watching girl-on-girl pornography together.

But the opportunity for a threesome never presented itself, so they joined a swingers' website. They tried swinging, mostly with other couples, and also visited clubs and resorts. It was a mixed experience for them, and through it they came to realize that they both wanted an emotional connection with other people, as well a sexual one. They redefined their interests and turned to the idea of an open marriage.

They don't have any particular limits or rules except for disclosure. They tell each other of budding flirtations, both on and offline. Kate has given Bob carte blanche with other women he meets while traveling for his work, as he frequently does. If he has a fling, she just wants to know about it later, and he's given her the same latitude. They're both open to having individual relationships, or perhaps a relationship jointly with another woman or a couple. They did have a ménage à trois with a married woman friend, but the woman decided it was too much for her to handle.

"In many ways, I think it would be good for Kate emotionally to find a girlfriend. As I said, I travel a lot, so I think she'd enjoy the companionship when I was out of town." I ask Bob about jealousy. It seems remarkable to be so accommodating toward another intimacy for his wife.

"Interestingly enough," he says, "jealousy's never been an issue for us, even from the beginning. Never once has either of us had a pang of jealousy."

That is unique in the stories and literature I encounter. Usually the "first hurdle is jealousy," one husband in an open marriage writes to me, "and I think that holds true for most newbies." In her extensive work with marriages, Anita Wagner agrees: "Jealousy is always the biggest concern" for spouses who want to try ethical nonmonogamy, and the conversion of envy into something else seems its astonishing feat.

"I'd get jealous," John said when I first shared with him this new idea I'd found. That seemed, at first, the end of the thought experiment, as if it had reached its natural terminus. Jealousy is like the weather.

In all but the most stalwart and resilient marriages, the new partner would have to be a threat to the old one—or so the tenuously monogamous wives in my set politely insist, filing the idea of nonjealous nonmonogamy somewhere between improbable and preposterous. Jealousy is considered a shortcoming or vice in all intimate relationships—except for marriage, and love, where it is almost considered a virtue. Old-school romantics assign an almost instinctual status to jealousy and interpret it as the certification, however perverse its effects, of true love and attachment. Polyamorists see it as something they can subdue through mindfulness and discipline.

Polyamorists have an alternative story about lust and new love. Instead of jealousy they speak of "compersion," a new term for me. Compersion is jealousy's doppelganger, a marital counter-ideal. Through compersion, situations that reflexively would produce jealousy in the romantic marriage produce warm feelings instead, such as "taking delight in a partner's love for another," or attempting to share in the joy a partner feels. Compersion thrives with parity and equity, and when both partners have another attachment.

Drawing on work by Dorothy Tennov (and, indirectly, biologist Helen Fisher), they manage intense, budding attachments by thinking of them not as evidence of "the real thing" but as "limerence" and "NRE," or "new relationship energy": passionate, exhilarating, combustible—and an ephemeral flare in comparison to the "matured relationship" of the primary bond. The open marriage is vulnerable in the throes of limerence, the "brain cocktail" of lust that makes us forget all others. But simply being mindful that the cocktail always fizzles out can inoculate the marriage.

I think of Nicole's husband and other serial monogamists who divorce their wives because they're "in love" with a mistress. What if they had an alternative to this romantic narrative? What if they had a narrative that there are varieties of attachment, passion, and love in which passion isn't certification of "true love"? I suspect that we end up feeling, assuming, and thinking what our prevailing stories and metaphors of marriage condition us to feel, assume, and think.

I return to my personal ad caper, to remember what some of the husbands in genuinely open marriages have to say about jealousy. Interestingly, they seem to revel in the openness and betray the opposite of possession or jealousy. One who says he hasn't himself gone outside the marriage finds that his wife's several relationships "improved our relationship—making it so much more honest and open." An artist tells me that "sexual jealousy just isn't worth it" in his marriage, and that he enjoys "knowing that she's loved by others."

The major challenge for Bob and Kate isn't jealousy but time, logistics, competing responsibilities. This is also the case for most open marriages. "How would anyone have *time* to be nonmonogamous?" one of my friends asks. She doesn't quibble with the idea morally or ethically but on pragmatic grounds. Polyamorists have a saying that "love is not a pie, but time is." Technology helps. "A common joke heard around the poly community is that the call of the polyamorist is 'everyone get out your calendars,' " Anita says, but Google comes to the rescue once again: "Google calendars, which we let our partners see and edit, are very useful" for nonmonogamists. Still, the dreariness quotient of marriage can get skewed quickly if one spouse has a torrid affair going and the other stays home to clean the gutters: "My wife went to have a hot tryst and all I got was this lousy list of chores."

Compared to a traditional, happily monogamous marriage, a discreet open marriage is indeed more challenging logistically. But then again, compared to a traditional divorce, it's more affordable and easier to organize. It's an efficient arrangement very similar to the lives of divorced cohabitants, who maintain one household for reasons of economy, their children's stability, or their affection for a companionable bond but have the sanctioned latitude of any other divorced couple. The expenses and disruptions of ethical nonmonogamy pale in comparison to breaking up a marriage through divorce; buying, establishing, and furnishing two households; paying sometimes tens of thousands of dollars in marriage therapists' and lawyers' fees; and finding childcare to cover all the times when the other parent might have otherwise been at home.

Another logistical challenge in Bob and Kate's case, particularly, is that they live in a small town and are cautious about their reputations. But they're still pursuing the life. Bob ended up corresponding with me because Kate was "off on a weekend trip with a friend who connected with a bunch of women on a website for women who are married but curious about developing relationships with other women, or some mission like that." Bob boiled it down to a "wild women weekend." You can find anything on the Web, I suppose. I'm reminded of the restless housewives of Heathercroft, or of Karen, the racy Donna Reed. Wifely bisexuality seems surprisingly more common as a version of nonmonogamy than I would have guessed.

It sounds as if Bob and Kate share more details with each other than most polyamorous married couples do. Rules about disclosure vary widely. An accomplished musician who lives on the West Coast and responded to my *NYRB* caper tells me that "some couples want to meet and get acquainted with each other's new lovers, some don't want to know anything about what's going on, and everything in between. Everyone has a different 'need to know' and you should have rules and stick to them." Many spouses want to know nothing or very little beyond the basic knowledge that a lover or mistress exists and doesn't threaten the marriage. Some partners agree to be unaccountable to each other during certain periods of time, and don't ask questions about what happens during that time, at all. A lesbian couple makes information about outside sex available but optional. In an ingenious feminization of the bachelor's little black book, "each kept a brief log of her encounters." They left record books that listed only names, places, and dates on top of the bookcase, available for their partner to check if she so desired. One partner never checked the log, and after a peek or two, the other stopped.

Others inch a bit further. A husband in an open marriage knows his wife's boyfriend of several years. "We're cordial but not close buddies. She prefers not to know who I'm intimate with but is cordial to all my female friends." For her part, Anita tells me that she prefers "that my partner not divulge intimate details about his other relationships. I'm happy knowing where they went, who they saw there, but what goes on in bed is something I consider private."

Still other mistress- and lover-tolerant marriages not only accept their spouse's dalliances, peeking at them warily through half-covered eyes, but also share more specific, nuanced details to jump-start the marriage or keep it energized sexually. This is the case in marriages where, as Anita says, the spouses "get a charge" out of details—knowing that the one is going out, hearing about what they did in bed, and so on. Another couple, the wife a financial executive, the husband a lawyer, the two children who "think we are more conventional than we are," enjoy "comparing notes, but no one—no one—understands, so we keep quiet." In a piece of research from the mid-1970s, one in four spouses in open marriages said it was a "turn on," in the patois of the time, "to discuss a potential encounter beforehand."

These marriages are rewriting the most basic rule, but within the scaffolding of marriage. They fill me with optimism, in a way. Maybe like a suspension bridge, marriage can maintain its integrity and relevance by swaying with the strong winds, and letting new attitudes and rules in rather than by bracing rigidly against them.

CHAPTER SIXTEEN

"FREE LOVE 2.0"

The New Open Marriage

S OPEN MARRIAGE any more feasible now than it was before? In the late 1960s and early 1970s, marital nonmonogamy enjoyed a certain ideological vogue, and it wasn't just the exclusive province of counterculture "hippies." A band of Christian sex radicals questioned the monogamy ethic in marriage. They included the feisty Della and Rustum Roy, authors of *Honest Sex: A Revolutionary New Sex Guide for the Now Generation of Christians* (1968).The Roys diagnosed marriage as "gravely ill," a putrid institution "enveloped by deterioration and decay." In a 1970 *Humanist* article called "Is Monogamy Outdated?" the Roys demoted marital monogamy as just one interpretation of the Judeo-Christian tradition, and an impoverishing, antihumanist one at that. They urged readers to take the biblical prescription to "love one's neighbor" more literally, and to replace the "monolithic code" of monogamy with inclusive, permeable networks of intimate relationships.

But in the 1970s open marriage was most widely known (deservedly so, some would say) through science fiction—Robert Rimmer's bestseller *The Harrad Experiment*—and through a misunderstanding or a highly selective reading of George and Nena O'Neill's classic 1972 work, *Open Marriage*. The book that lent its name to open marriage never intended to do so. The O'Neills defined open marriages as those in which husbands and wives valued communication, were flexible about gender roles, allowed each other autonomy in their friendships and social lives, and strove for egalitarianism. This ambitious ideal was successively whittled down in the retelling to the more bewitching element of sex, and the O'Neills became the accidental patron saints of "open marriage" as we think of it today.

"We had no control over the interpretation of the section dealing with sex," George O'Neill said in a 1977 interview. "We mentioned that there are a few couples who might be able to endure and enjoy outside relationships that would include sex and that a few might even bring something good back to their marital relationships as a result. This possibility was certainly not a guideline to open marriage. But people latched on to this part and ignored the core of the book, which is about being open to each other. So unfortunately open marriage has been widely misinterpreted to mean a sexually open marriage." Meanwhile, their once-daring ideas about chore-sharing, flexible gender roles, communication, egalitarianism, and intimacy have simply been mainstreamed as a "good marriage," at least for Life Partners. Marriage fashions and trends tend to drift like this, from eccentric subculture to vanguard to mainstream.

In the 1970s, the case for nonmonogamy sprang from numinous ideals of social liberation without much pragmatic foundation. The 1974 book *Is Marriage Necessary?* proposed in the heated cadence of the day that marriage was a "potential entrapment of the human psyche." Critiques of monogamy and exclusive marital sex arrived on the gusty winds of a borrowed leftist ideology denouncing property, sexual bondage, and the indignities of possession. In a prominent 1973 study of "multilateral" and nonmonogamous marriage, or "group marriage," Larry and Joan Constantine found that 18 percent of their subjects chose this lifestyle because of a political impulse to "protest the Establishment."

Nonmonogamous marriage indeed had a wispy political chic in

those years, but fewer touchstones in reality (and nothing about marriage is more perishable than a politically utopian idea about it). The opposite holds true today. Marital nonmonogamy—in all its forms, from illicit cheating to open—lacks political chic in our largely conservative marriage zeitgeist. But it is quietly gathering momentum through reinforcing trends of demography (we live longer), economics (women earn their own living), technology (we connect and find each other with breathtaking ease), and revised norms about premarital sex (we don't need marriage to legitimate our sex lives anymore). It's propelled by circumstances, not ideology. In the 1970s, some of us didn't believe in monogamy, but it believed in us; today we believe in monogamy, but it doesn't seem to believe in us.

Back in the 1970s, Anita Wagner speculates, nonmonogamy "was all about free love. The philosophy sounded good, but there was a huge lack of awareness. So people went about having a lot of sex with each other without taking much responsibility for the fallout. Polyamory is really free love grown up—or free love 2.0."

|||||||||

Anita teaches "practical polyamory." She explicitly untangles open marriage and nonmonogamy from political orthodoxies of any kind, and especially from the legacy of the 1970s. This is not your father's open marriage. "Polyamory is a solution for a lot of people," she tells me, "whether they believe in tantric meditation or free markets." It's a way, among other things, to reconcile the partially satisfying marriage with other, persistent desires. Hers is the perspective of the bohemian engineer. Ethical nonmonogamy may be subversive, but it's mostly a problem to figure out and a set of rules to establish. "It doesn't matter what your political views are—you can be liberal, conservative, libertarian (we have a fair number of those), whatever, and still be just as good at polyamory as anyone else." It doesn't "require anything philosophically, beyond good will." In the 21st century, nonmonogamy's formidable collaborators in the post-romantic milieu are less lava lamp than paycheck; less macramé than Google; less Age of Aquarius than Age of the Engineer.

Here politically opposite marriage movements and trends converge, amusingly, around a post-romantic consensus. Columnist David Brooks, to recall his vivid metaphor, thinks of marriage as a kind of engineering and design problem, something that requires an instruction manual to make the "social machine" work. He and Wagner draw from the same toolbox, albeit opposite ideologies. They believe that through practice, self-consciousness, rules, discipline, and goodwill, a marriage can survive. Neither a conservative marriage defender nor a "radical" polyamorist believes that the romantic script and its version of true love is the blueprint for a lasting happy marriage. Instead they both believe that it's something practical we can learn how to do, or do differently.

"Today, we're going to talk about *honesty*," says the host of a Polyamory Weekly podcast cheerily, by way of introduction. And as Bob Dylan wisely tells us, "To live outside the law, you must be honest."

Not only is "free love 2.0," as Anita calls it, a more practical, less ideological approach than its earlier versions in the 1970s; I'm also intrigued to discover that its ethic seems a much more feminine one. Reflexively, open marriage gets associated with wife-swapping, polygamy, the swinging culture, or as a moral fig leaf for a practice that amounted to no more than opportunistic male prowling (at a cocktail party few lines herald a lie quite like "My wife and I have an arrangement"). But just as the gender gap has closed in the world of affairs and cheating, wives are changing the open marriage ethic, too, and perhaps for some of the same big reasons: These changes might simply pace women's ascendance in the economy and in marriage. As women gain more power in marriage through their work and their earning potential, they tweak marital nonmonogamy in their own image.

For example, most all of the advice literature, instructive narratives, and guidebooks about the new open marriage that I've encountered were written by women. Dossie Easton, who calls herself an "activist of the heart," wrote a canonical guidebook for polyamorists, *The Ethical Slut*. Another surprising, and consistent, finding across several studies from the mid-1970s onward is that wives, not husbands, often drive the open marriage decision or first broach the topic. According to most studies, they also initiate outside relationships first, more often, and more intensively than husbands. Therapist Joy Davidson observes that wives see polyamory as empowering and "relish the feeling of owning their desires." This is important, and perhaps rare, since women don't easily admit what they're not getting in marriage, to recall one of my *NYRB* suitors.

And in its style and mood, the new open marriage ethic answers the question usually confined to science fiction or Marge Piercy novels: What might extramarital sex look like if it were designed by wives? What if it didn't involve the 1970s clichés of scoring, having multiple recreational encounters, boasting about conquests, and all the old clichés of male sexuality? For one thing, Anita tells me, the openly non-monogamous marriage tends to value intimate relationships over the recreational world of swinging and casual encounters. "Polyamory is no more about sex than monogamy is," Anita continues. "Our sex lives aren't any more important to us than our relationships, and for most of us the sex is definitely less important" than multiple intimacies. Admittedly scant research backs her up. In one study almost two-thirds of open marriage spouses experienced affairs "accompanied by deep friendship or affection for the partners." In a sense the new open marriage is more about dusting off the time-honored but currently disfavored social roles of Mistress and Lover, a world in between recreational and marital, in which the intimacies are real but circumscribed.

And polyamorists engage in stereotypically feminine sexual propensities to discuss and dissect feelings; to pay scrupulous attention to the deliberation about standards of conduct; to tend to their spouse's feelings. It's an ideal sexual style for the so-called process queens who enjoy therapy. Or imagine the new open marriage as the sort of marriage that a female Zen monk libertarian might have—a marriage that eschews institutions and values free will, but also cultivates mindfulness and the spiritual-marital discipline of letting go of jealousy and possessive sexual attachment. Polyamory's ethical nuances have a distinctly Eastern flavor. As one wife advises, "All you can do is live in the present. . . . Love him when and how you can. And let go of expectations. The world, as they say, is unfolding as it should."

|||||||||

Davidson observes that many free love 2.0 marriages end up "leading a double life." Being open and practicing an ethic of honesty and consent with your spouse can mean being closed and secretive vis-à-vis society. Bob and Kate are "out" to close friends, but they keep their world a secret from everyone else. "I really don't want to get a reputation as 'the Swinging Professor,'" he tells me. "Most of our close friends were not surprised to hear about our relationships. They know that we're both very sexual people. Then again, we only tell friends who we believe can handle the knowledge without freaking out. Protecting our children, my job, and our reputation has to be paramount."

As for the kids, "We simply don't want to put them in the situation where some other parent says to their kid, 'I don't want you hanging around with [their children] because her parents are perverts.'" I'd be amazed, he warns me, how many have that sort of reaction. "We live in a small town where too many people know everyone else's business, so we don't want our kids getting caught in the middle. We haven't told them about our lifestyle, because frankly they don't need to know. But we also figure they wouldn't be very surprised if they did find out."

Open marriages may be more difficult to confess precisely because they implicate the secret life of a traditional marriage. Most married people at least fantasize about being with someone besides their spouses; many married people have had lovers; others wish that they had. For that reason, Anita finds, it's difficult to predict how even the most "open-minded" and gay-tolerant of people will react to ethical nonmonogamy. Anita theorizes that "they can more easily imagine their partner developing an interest in polyamory, especially if there is a general acceptance of it societally."

It may be a threatening idea, but it is also an exhilarating one, in that it presents an optimistic option for the low-conflict, low-stress unhappy marriage. It maps out a way to think about adding to rather than exploding a marriage. Anita asks, "Why *can't* we have our cake and eat it, too?" It's the haunting question in many a melancholy marriage, where we want to save one part of it, but not the other.

This is what Jack and Jill decide they want: to reconcile their desires and their marriage, to have their cake and eat it, too. Jill came to believe that, for her, the more resonant definition of *fidelity* in marriage meant honestly abiding by the rules, not necessarily the practice of monogamy. Jack isn't as instinctively anti-institutional as Jill sometimes fancied herself to be. Better, perhaps, just to follow the rule of monogamy, even unthinkingly and morosely, if that's required, than to scribble an improvised marital life outside the lines. Better to follow the well-trod but sad path of divorce than to blaze a happy but new one. Some ideas, although pleasing to one or both spouses individually, simply clash against the soul of a marriage. The poet Jane Hirshfield writes, "The body of a starving horse cannot forget the size it was born into." But maybe ethical nonmonogamy could work. It's their firm belief in staying together for their family, maintaining continuity for each other's work and lives, enjoying the loving bond of Life Partners, and having a confidant at the end of the day—that has maneuvered Jack and Jill into these new contemplations. In an earlier age, they might have just gotten divorced, and it would have been applauded, to some extent, as an adventure of self-realization. Marriages with serious deficits are often written off entirely. But they have a different, ambivalent, and genuinely conflicted feeling about their marriage. Their very faith in their traditional marriage is turning them into marriage radicals.

For her part Jill sincerely wished to rehabilitate the social roles of "Mistress" and "Lover," which have distinct rules, manners, boundaries, and intimacies attached to them. Neither of them wanted a new husband or a new wife. The opposite. They grew to feel, under the circumstances of their own marriage, that it would be possible to be close to someone without it being a marriage, or without it threatening their marriage.

Then they devised their own rules, an informal codebook, for being or having a lover. In marriages like this, "ethical practice" and rules are the requirement. And the rules might run the gamut.

The most obvious for Jack and Jill was discretion, and that the marriage and the parental relationship had to come first.

Furthermore, they stipulated that this Mistress-Lover bond must be an entirely separate world, for each of them. They couldn't choose partners from their community, or from the pool of friends or acquaintances or colleagues. They didn't want to be indiscreet or risky. They didn't want to lie to each other, and they didn't want to be with partners who were lying to theirs, if they were also married. Jack and Jill decided that neither of them would want to know anything at all about the other's lover or mistress, or share any details or, really, even "know" what was going on, when. This was to be a known, but hidden, layer in each of their lives. They didn't want to know anything beyond the existence of a lover or mistress. They were "opening up" but in another way, they were really expanding the realm of privacy in their marriage.

Jack and Jill promised not to bring lovers into their domestic life or space. They wouldn't friend them on Facebook. From there they got more specific and delved into fine-print stipulations. Jack and Jill didn't want to see traces or relics of any kind, physical or otherwise, from the other life. And they didn't want to be talked about with the lover or mistress.

They would need to choose carefully. For marriages that want to do this there are a lot of communities, online or otherwise, where one can meet like-minded people. Or you can use the personals, or join the ranks of those in online singles dating sites who describe themselves as "happily married." You declare that you aren't leaving your marriage and don't want to lie. Many months go by. Principle is one thing, reality quite another. Through the usual means and venues they met new people. Some are available; some are in similar circumstances and similar terms with their spouses. When it so happened that they both found people that interested them, loosely around the same time, Jill found that for both of them the hardest thing was to be honest. Early on Jill got demoralized and spooked occasionally. Not over potential complications, but over the sadness that she was no longer entirely . . . wholesome in her marriage. Was Jill even a good person anymore, to be having such a peculiar (but happier) marriage? They still felt supernaturally secure that they didn't want to leave each other, and neither of them felt the sting of being a cheater or of having to deal with a cheating spouse. All the same, Jill felt wistful and even mournful for the innocence (admittedly, a melancholy and divorce-threatening innocence) of the marriage in the days when they still had the governing fiction with each other and the world that were playing by the same rules as everybody else, even if those rules are often broken. Jill wanted to be able to pass as a marital conformist again. The fantasy of romantic euphoria in marriage is stubbornly lodged, that every need gets met there, in one place, and the other, unmet needs die natural deaths offstage.

It was a challenge for Jack and Jill to admit even to themselves that they were doing a strange thing, because they aren't strange people, and their household was so ordered, harmonious, and straight-lined. Jill thought at first, and they said to each other, that maybe none of this would have a happy ending.

On the other hand, those concerns were hypothetical. Everything worked better in real life than in theory, where it shouldn't have worked at all. Jack and Jill weren't really jealous, or threatened, or not nearly as much they assumed they'd be. And jealousy dimmed even further over time. In their case, it wasn't so difficult to take it in stride, because the other life felt so unobtrusive on the intimacy of the marriage, which in their case was not a passionate one to begin with. But every time they chose not to lie, they had to confront the reality of their unusual marriage. As Jack once said to Jill, it takes a lot of work, a lot of faith, and management of feelings. He proposed that maybe it would get easier, with time. And it did.

Being jealous is something, Jill discovered to her surprise, that you can choose to be, or not. She learned to compartmentalize, even to revel, in that equipoise of having distinct worlds and subjectivities. Without the lying, it felt manageable—enriching, not corrosive, to the marriage.

Jill shared news of her marital arrangement and mistressy life only with a few very close friends. They asked, don't you slide into being attached, and being in love? And how can you not be jealous or threatened by Jack's lover? Jill told them she thought of herself as attached, but in a discrete, very limited way. She wasn't unattached, because this wasn't recreational or the swinging life. Jill esteemed her lover in the particular, unique, nonmarital fashion of the Mistress and Lover bond. For the mistress, the bonds are looser, the intimacies circumscribed, the attachments genuine but elastic. A Mistress-Lover relationship has greater tolerance or even appetite, as it must, for complex, distinct strata of reality that touch but never commingle.

Jill surmised to herself that having a mistress or a lover was like foster care. When you're a foster parent you have to get attached to the child, but you also have to hold yourself back because that child isn't going to stay around forever, and they are not "yours" in the sense of your permanent family, and marriage. The attachment is real and also partial.

Some friends envied her love life. They noted how happy Jill was— and that it had taken years off her complexion. Another friend worried that it was a dangerous brinkmanship. It may be. Jack and Jill weren't arrogant or glib about this. They may end up divorced, they know, or in love with someone else, or they may end up feeling too weird about having an unconventional marriage, and it may seem better to be alone than to own it. Jack and Jill might find they prefer to live a marriage that makes them unhappy but conforms, over what they now have. It would be easy and understandable to become reinfatuated with the romantic family fantasy that you can only love one person at a time, in one place, in the same household, in a "real" marriage. You could want to name things properly again, or live sheltered within a label, even if it's as a "divorcee."

However, it seems that no choice spares a tenuous marriage from danger. Danger stalks mediocre marriages and sad status quos. A husband Jill knew told his wife that he was unhappy and didn't intend to live that way his whole, remaining life. But for most of us it's a cognitive habit and a fallacy to perceive more risk in action than stasis. Things settled into a very discreet routine over the months and then into the next year, and by then the topic didn't come up much. They live their other lives on occasional afternoons or evenings here and there, but one life doesn't intrude on the other's time much. Sometimes they have date nights, like other married couples—only not with each other. Since they both occasionally do things with friends or work out of the house in the evenings, this isn't an unusual development for either of them. Through experience they've come to establish a curfew for each other, as you would for a teenager with a car. Sometimes Jill thinks about it as though she is divorced but maintaining a household, amiably. Or sometimes she imagines herself as a marital expatriate: American on the outside, French on the inside. Jill feels like herself again, in all her humanity. She feels more loving, and generous, toward Jack. They've even developed a sense of humor about it. When their sitter volunteers to spell them for a "romantic getaway" weekend, they joke, Would we go with each other?

What's so shocking to both Jack and Jill is that they did this. "It never works," they know, and you can't really, really change the rules of Marriage. But it does work for them, at least for now.

Jill wouldn't call hers a romantic fairy tale. She wouldn't call it a divorce story or a story of marriage martyrs who "stick it out." The question of divorce is never over, and it can all change. It all *will* change, inevitably. It's the nature of an age without a marriage imperative that the decision is replenished, revisited, and affirmed, or rejected.

But for now, they live happily ever after.

EPILOGUE

"Why *Can't* We Have Our Cake and Eat It, Too?"

'M NOT A marriage therapist, and this hasn't been an advice book, but my own philosophy toward marriage changed over the course of writing this book. When I began my work I thought of marriage, both my own as well as the institution, largely in terms of pros or cons. Many of us do, and quite reflexively. When I shared the topic of my book people would ask me, "Are you for marriage or against it?" It seems we imagine marriage oppositionally: that we must embrace marriage more or less on its terms, or reject it as a bad idea, either personally or, in some polemics, as a social institution. If you're in a melancholy marriage whose problem isn't easily solved, your choice is either to stay married on marriage's terms, or to divorce and lose all the things that *do* work in a marriage, or a family, and that you ideally want to maintain.

I came to resent that opposition and, in one dimension, this book has become an untraditional defense of traditional marriage, from a humanist point of view. Through listening to other people's stories, marriage and life seemed to have more possibilities and options than I would have imagined outside the realm of science fiction or pure fantasy. I came to admire a third way, something between staying the course in a partially satisfying but melancholy marriage or exploding it through divorce. I admired the spirit of adventure and improvisation within outwardly traditional but inwardly queer marriages that I encountered in my wanderings. These marriages found a way to preserve what really worked, while maneuvering to create the lives the couples wanted and honor their adult humanity. These couples found ways to reconcile marriage with a certain radicalism.

These post-romantic marriages followed their own muses; they weren't embarrassed or apologetic about their own preferences and choices; they tossed out elements of the romantic script adventurously; they had marital imagination and they were mindful about what marriage could be. They neither rejected marriage nor embraced its old scripts, traditional or romantic. They gave themselves permission to choose alternatives within marriage. They had the courage—sometimes declared, and sometimes privately asserted—to do something weird but successful. And giving ourselves the license and permission to evolve marriage is perhaps the unique challenge of our time.

So this has become, I suppose, a manifesto for having your cake and eating it, too. It's become a call for being just a bit greedy, gaudily ambitious, and even, where warranted, selfish about making marriage give us what we want, whether around work, career, free time, family life, or sex. It's a manifesto for living large in marriage. This latitude to reinvent marriage and to embrace an age of marriage heterodoxy is precisely the gift of our post-liberation, post-romantic age. Betty Friedan had to expose and second-wave feminism had to remedy basic legal, economic, educational, social, and cultural inequalities that made marriage all but imperative for all women. Today we have a different, secret, and often internal struggle, to make good on the promises of our own liberation. We can't convincingly blame the marital norms or imperatives for the melancholy, because we have unprecedented latitude to do marriage differently, to not do it at all, to divorce, to live apart, or to make up something else entirely. Any number of things could work. (Although if

I could distill some of what I've learned to indulge in a small bit of advice, it might be to live marriage as if you're always on vacation: Be self-consciously attuned to your own adult priorities and humanity. Imagine that your first child is your second and live your parenthood more casually and nonchalantly.)

Whatever it is, we need to take responsibility for our own contentment and adult humanity. We can't readily blame legal or economic barriers, at least if we're heterosexual couples who the state allows to marry, because there aren't that many obstacles left. The struggle is more about courage than law. It's about making fewer judgments about others or ourselves and having more imagination.

If you are in the semi-happy marriage limbo, you'll get more social approval and reward for reconstituting the old script or for following the prevailing marital and parental trends, and you may very well get called selfish and whiny for wanting more. But at what cost? Have the unthinkable conversation, or propose the zany marital lifestyle, or maybe just look at your marriage with fresh eyes and an open mind. You may well get a happier life and marriage for doing so. Or, if not a happier one, then a more alive and richer one for the trying.

AUTHOR'S NOTE

THROUGHOUT THIS BOOK, where necessary and prudent, I've changed names and small identifying characteristics to protect the anonymity of the women and men who were kind enough to talk to me about their private lives. For the time, generosity, thoughtfulness, and brave candor of the more than fifty people I interviewed, including some experts and public figures who are referred to by name and title, I'm most deeply and humbly grateful. I've also drawn throughout on informal conversation and insight from friends and acquaintances.

As part of my work I also conducted two online surveys, whose results inform these pages. The first asked open-ended questions about opinions on marriage, in hopes of eliciting anecdotes and stories. The 300 respondents were self-selected, and were directed to the survey through posts in social networks online, and through emails inviting respondents to participate. To get a larger and more representative view on marriage, I collaborated with an online quantitative researcher to conduct a modest second survey consisting of ten statements about marriage, which I describe throughout these chapters as they become thematically relevant. This researcher has an online opinion panel, which, overall, is representative of the Internet-using population of the United States, and my survey garnered 1,879 responses. Each statement expresses an opinion about marriage, and I asked respondents to rate their level of agreement with it on a ten-level Likert scale, ranging from "I don't agree at all" to "I neither agree nor disagree" to "I agree entirely."

I reviewed some but not all of the voluminous body of scholarly research on marriage, and I drew on my background as an historian to consider the historical scholarship on the subject. I consider that research to be a foundation for this book, but it is not highlighted in the main text. In the notes I summarize some of the major marriage trends in the United States and I would refer the interested reader to my website, Pamelahaag.com, for more commentary and analysis that didn't find a place in the book.

I also found it tremendously useful to review much of the popular commentary about marriage as revealed in newspapers and magazines from the first decade of this century—again, to get the broader context and view. I draw from those sources in these chapters as well.

In terms of themes and topics, I've spent slightly more time on the exploration of sexual arrangements and melancholia in marriage because it's a vexatious topic that emerges so frequently in the otherwise not-bad marriage, and because it provides some of the most striking and compelling examples of a post-romantic turn toward new sensibilities in marriage. But my purpose in these chapters is to explore a variety of sources for both melancholy and innovation within the shell of a conventional marriage. These sources range from mate selection habits, expectations for marriage, the arrangement of work and career, our sensibility about childrearing, our marital habitats, views about adult social life in marriage, and, finally, views on sex and marital fidelity. While these chapters have a point of view concerning marriage, in no case do I describe a marital lifestyle with the intention of endorsing or recommending one particular course of action, since what would work in one marriage would be a failure in another.

Instead I hope to get at the spirit of the times, show the potential for marital heterodoxy, where good marriages can take a variety of forms, and to see how far marriage can stretch and innovate, but within its traditional legal form. I take the humanist view that well-intentioned spouses in a marriage can contemplate a variety of ways to make their lives together more meaningful and happy.

ACKNOWLEDGMENTS

THIS BOOK HAD its genesis, as many do, in the ephemera of conversations and heart-to-hearts with friends and the occasional, wickedly eavesdropped moment. My deepest gratitude goes to the women and men who talked with me about their marriages. It would be ungainly to list those confidants here—and respect for their anonymity forbids it in some cases—but they know who they are. And for others who might find themselves quoted anonymously as the generic, unfailingly wise "friend" or "acquaintance" in these pages, I thank them collectively and with humility, and hope that they aren't vexed that I found their insights and comments so smart or pitch-perfect to the spirit of our times that they simply had to be included here, by way of illustration, and homage.

There are too many to single out, but I'm now embarking on a third decade of friendship and camaraderie with some remarkable and scintillating people that I've had the great fortune to meet. As I worked on this project, in particular, my life would have been vastly drearier if not downright impossible without the counsel and friendship of Elizabeth Federman, Shannon Avery, Peter Agree, Debby Applegate, and Haleh Bakhash.

After the topic of contemporary marriage first seized my interest, I started thinking about and tentatively working on this book while finishing an MFA in creative nonfiction at Goucher College. I experienced Goucher to be an uncommonly supportive and festive writer's community. I owe a special thanks to my mentor and friend there, Richard Todd, for his encouragement, gentle brilliance, and deft editorial voice as I navigated a transition from academic writing to creative nonfiction. While this project falls outside of the purview of my time at Goucher, I'm deeply grateful that I had this help as I began my work and the wisdom of other mentors and students in the program.

As the book moved from a notion to a proposal, I had the good fortune to have an extraordinarily adroit and generous agent. Susan Rabiner has fulfilled a role that far exceeds "literary agent." She's been a visionary, editor, counselor, teacher, friend, advocate, truth-teller, surrogate mother, a humorous Virgil to guide me through the strange new world (for me) of commercial publishing, and a delight to work with. She "saw" this book in its totality, and for her tenacity to get things right I'm very thankful.

Then, as the project moved from proposal to the actual work, qualitative researcher Diane Hopkins helped out with skillful, timely, and generous help with three interviews, and thanks to her son for hosting an online survey. Thanks also to Vanessa Verdine for help with my qualitative online survey, and to Joy Johannessen for reviewing an earlier draft of this book.

My friend and fellow writer Barbara Benham gets very special thanks for patiently and with impeccable equanimity sharing in the everyday details of my writerly life, which careen between the tedious and the terrifying. She followed the progress of the manuscript and generously read the final product.

Thanks to the other women in my writing group—Francine Kiefer, Emilie Surrusco, and Mary Richert—who read early drafts and bits, and shared in the process with humor and support. Thanks to my friend Mina Cheon for sharing marriage ideas and authorial support.

I'm extremely grateful to my editor at HarperCollins, Gail Winston, for her patience, wisdom, editorial guidance, and most especially for her faith in my efforts. This book has been improved through her comments and work, and it's hard to ask for more than that. Thanks also to her assistant Jason Sack and copy editor Tom Pitoniak.

In addition to other readers, Stephanie Coontz reviewed some notes, my friend and editor extraordinaire Cindi Leive pitched in with some timely and fun help with my title ideas, and, in the last phases of editing, thanks to documentarian Heidi Sullivan for giving the manuscript a read and for her great enthusiasm and excitement about it at a propitious moment.

Throughout this process, I've been grateful to all of the communities of friends and colleagues, from book groups to newly formed social circles to my neighbors, who have made the booking process that much more pleasurable for me, and who have picked up the slack as I moved toward completion. I'm grateful, as always, to my parents and family for their support, their collective sense of humor about the world, and their assistance on the home front. I feel as if I've had a load-bearing wall in my life, with the support of such entertaining, reliably thoughtful family and friends.

My deepest gratitude, love, and appreciation go to my husband, John. He is the most courageous person I know, with a big soul and a gentle heart, and through all the ups and downs, I can't imagine a better person with whom to take an adventure in life. The toll of a book falls hardest on those closest to it, and it has perhaps played the symbolic role of a sibling rival to our only child, Quincy, who delights us, gives us hope and insight, and reminds us to enjoy the moment. In the time it took for me to write one book, Quincy wrote six in his elementary school, as he occasionally likes to remind me. But I'm trying to catch up.

NOTES

xi the "low-conflict," low-stress unhappy marriage: Among marriage and family researchers, Paul Amato and Alan Booth are probably most identified with work on the low-conflict/high-conflict distinction among divorces. Amato's 1995 article looks for the interactions of the effects of marital conflict and children's outcomes after divorce in a national sample of 2,000 couples. He measured marital conflict based on parents' reports of "the frequency of disagreements, the conflict over the household division of labor, the number of serious quarrels in the past two months, and whether spouses have ever slapped, hit, pushed, kicked, or thrown things at one another in anger." Amato finds that "the long-term consequences of divorce depend on the level of parental conflict prior to separation." Children don't welcome divorce when the "overt conflict between parents is not excessive." But if the conflict in the marriage is high, they might be better off after divorce. Paul Amato, "Parental Divorce, Marital Conflict and Offspring Well-being during Early Adulthood," *Social Forces* 73, no. 3 (1995), pp. 895–913.

Susan Jekielek finds that marital disruption after high conflict in the marriage may improve the emotional well-being of children, in comparison to an enduring, high-conflict marriage. She concludes, "at a time when there is backlash against liberal divorce laws, and conservative policy reforms are an attempt to reincarnate the traditional American family," limiting divorce by the repeal of "no-fault" standards would harm children if it impeded the high-conflict marriage from divorcing. Susan Jekielek, "Parental Conflict, Marital Disruption and Children's Emotional Well-Being," *Social Forces* 76, no. 3 (1998), pp. 905–35.

The effect of this research, however it is interpreted vis-à-vis the politics of divorce law, is toward greater fine-tuning between the types of marriages that end in divorce, and a move away from viewing divorce in monolithic terms. Alan Booth and Amato refined Amato's earlier work in 2002 and concluded among other things that an unhappy marriage characterized by "mild disengagement has more on which it can build." Paul Amato and Alan Booth, "Parental Predivorce Relations and Offspring Postdivorce Well-Being," *Journal of Marriage and Family* 63, no. 1 (2001), pp. 197–212.

This is where the research becomes relevant to the politics of the marriage movement. The 2001 "Smart Marriages, Happy Families" conference in Orlando, Florida, sponsored by the Coalition for Marriage, Family and Couples Education (CMFCE), interpreted the scholarly research on low-conflict marriage to support a case for sticking it out for the children unless the marriage is high-stress, violent, or otherwise dysfunctional. Diane Sollee of CMFCE typifies the sentiment: "I would not suggest couples do this—stay in a marriage just for the sake of their kids—if I wasn't convinced that we now have new information about how to do it," and, moreover, have evidence of its desirability. Marriage movement figures Linda Waite and Maggie Gallagher argue in *The Case for Marriage* (New York: Doubleday, 2000) that most divorces are between low-conflict spouses whose children are not likely to benefit in any way from the separation, as they opined at the 2001 conference.

Eminent marriage scholar Stephanie Coontz comments in reaction, "The experience of kids growing up in an unhappy marriage or going through their parents' divorce are so variable that it's impossible to talk about 'the' costs or benefits of staying in an unhappy marriage versus divorcing." Indeed, effects are variable, and "effect sizes," the robustness or degree of the noticed differences, are not that large. Amato's own research notes that in studies of children and adults who come from divorces, the effect sizes are "modest" for lower quality of social relations and psychological adjustment. Coontz continues, "If parents who don't love each other can remain friendly and collaborative, and stay together for the sake of the kids, that is one thing. But if a low-conflict marriage contains contempt or defensiveness, or even just consistently cold behavior, the kids can be damaged by that just as much if not more than by the process of divorce." Coontz concludes that we "should encourage parents to think through their choices, but we should be careful of scaring or pressuring them into choices that may backfire down the line." Stephanie Coontz, personal communication with author, July 15, 2010; Amato, "Parental Divorce, Marital Conflict and Offspring Well-being during Early Adulthood," p. 897.

xi   **Amato estimates**: Amato summarizes from his twenty-year research that up to 60 percent of divorces occur in low-conflict marriages, which he calls "good enough marriages" that might be "salvaged" (quoted in Peterson, "The Good in a Bad Marriage," p. 8D). He develops the idea of the good enough marriage in his scholarly article "Good Enough Marriages: Parental Discord, Divorce, and Children's Well-Being." *Virginia Journal of Social Policy & the Law* 9 (2002), pp. 71–94.

xii   **Utah Commission on Marriage**: Brooke Adams, "Holy Matrimony! Utah is the Place for Couples; Marriage," *Salt Lake Tribune*, March 14, 2003, p. B1.

xii   **Researchers find this—us—puzzling**: Booth and Amato, "Parental Predivorce Relations and Offspring Postdivorce Well-Being," p. 197.

xiv   **In her groundbreaking book**: Stephanie Coontz, *Marriage, a History: From Obedience to Intimacy, or How Love Conquered Marriage* (New York: Viking, 2005).

xiv   **I call it a post-romantic spirit**: In all of these chapters, I'm referring to and elaborating primarily the vernacular, popular, and familiar meanings of "romantic" (and "post-romantic") rather than key tenets of the Romantic literary genre and movement, although the Romantic character and the vernacular romantic do occasionally overlap. I review some of these vernacular ideals and their historical sources in 20th century popular culture in Pamela Haag, "In Search of the 'Real Thing," in John Fout and Maura Shaw Tantillo, eds., *American Sexual Politics: Sex, Gender and Race Since the Civil War* (Chicago: University of Chicago Press, 1993), pp. 161–91.

xv **after Title VII passed**: "Sex and Employment: New Hiring Law Seen Bringing More Jobs, Benefits for Women," *Wall Street Journal*, January 22, 1965, p. 1.

CHAPTER 1: THE DILEMMAS OF A SEMI-HAPPY MARRIAGE

3 **honeycombed with halfhearted marriages**: In addition to my own online survey I seek out others. On the positive side of the spectrum, a 2006 General Social Surveys study found that 58 percent described their marriages as "very happy," which is by far the highest percentage I've seen in survey work. A 2007 Pew survey found that married Americans overall are happier than singles. Happi*er*, perhaps, if not necessarily happy. Psychology professor Richard Lucas analyzed twenty years of data and found that an initial boost in happiness associated with marriage recedes to pre-marriage levels *over time*. Lucas's findings jibe with what I glean anecdotally from single women. "At first you feel left out because all of your girlfriends are getting married in their thirties," a single woman tells me. "But now that I'm in my forties, I feel luckier." Pew Research Center, "As Marriage and Parenthood Drift Apart, Public is Concerned about Social Impact," July 1, 2007, executive summary, http://pewresearch.org/pubs/526/marriage-parenthood; Richard Lucas, "Adaptation and Set-Point Model of Subjective Well-being: Does Happiness Change After Major Life Events?" *Current Directions in Psychological Science* 16 (2007), pp. 75–80.

In an intriguing online survey, 30 percent of 3,000 respondents said that they wished they'd never married their spouses, and another 20 percent "weren't sure." AOL/Women's Day survey, in L. A. Johnson, "Would You Marry Him Again? Couples Here Dispute Marriage Poll's Unhappy Results," *Pittsburgh Post-Gazette*, January 23, 2007, p. C1.

A widely held assumption in research and commentary is that marital happiness looks like a U-curve: We lose happiness—and more marriages dissolve—within the first seven years of marriage, but then we get it back later on, after twenty years or so. But one of the more interesting scholarly articles on happiness challenges this U-curve idea of marital happiness, concluding that it doesn't hold true upon further analysis. Jody VanLaningham, et al., in "Marital Happiness, Marital Duration and the U-Shaped Curve: Evidence from a Five-Wave Panel Study," *Social Forces* 79, no. 4 (2001), pp. 1313–41, find that indeed the steepest declines in marital happiness occur in the earliest years of marriage, but they don't find support for the idea that marital happiness conforms to a U-curve pattern: Levels of happiness, they discovered, either stayed flat, or declined over time. They didn't increase in later years.

Interestingly, the happiness percentage might not have changed much since the 1970s. An Identity Research Institute study of 600 couples found that while the divorce rate was numerically at 40 percent nationally, in fact 75 percent of marriages were "a bust." Two researchers in the 1970s found that 80 percent of those interviewed had at some time "seriously considered" divorce, leaving that residual 20 percent who have not. George and Nena O'Neill eyeballed "happy marriages" at the same 20 percent mark in their influential work on marriage from the early

1970s. Della Roy, "Is Monogamy Outdated?" *Humanist*, March/April 1970; George and Nena O'Neill, *Open Marriage: A New Life Style for Couples* (New York: Avon, 1972).

A troubling trend, although one only indirectly related to the question of marriage and happiness, is that the suicide rate for 45–54 year olds—typically adults who have children, and/or are married—increased nearly 20 percent in five years, from 1999 to 2004. Among women in that age group, the rate "leapt" 31 percent, which "breaks from trends of the past," according to the American Foundation for Suicide Prevention, as described in Patricia Cohen, "Midlife Suicide Rises, Puzzling Researchers," *New York Times*, February 19, 2008, p. 19.

3   **"as unhappy it is possible to be"**: Peter Thompson, "Desperate Housewives? Difficulties and the Dynamics of Marital (un)Happiness," Florida International University, Working Papers (2005), http://www.flu.edu/orgs/economics/wp2005/05.

5   **you're in the crosshairs of the self-named marriage movement**: The loosely confederated, self-named marriage movement declared itself at the fourth annual Conference of the Coalition for Family and Couples Education, held in Denver, on June 30, 2000. On the conference see Cheryl Wetzstein, "Coalition Pledges to Strengthen Marriage, *Washington Times*, June 30, 2000, p. A11; Marilyn Gardner, "A Quiet Revolution in Support of Marriage," *Christian Science Monitor*, June 30, 2000, p. 2; Julia McCord, "Leaders Promote Marriage: Nebraskans Join a Movement to Fight the Trends of Divorce and Unwed Motherhood," *Omaha World Herald*, June 30, 2000, p. 19.

At this conference more than one hundred scholars and "religious leaders" endorsed the pro-marriage movement, to "turn the tide on marriage." They pledged to promote marriage so that "each year, more children will grow up protected by their own two happily married parents." They cautioned that they don't support "male tyranny, domestic violence or the denigration of single mothers." Stephen G. Post, "Communities Should Work to Help Marriage Succeed," *Plain Dealer*, July 3, 200, p. 7B.

Nor do they want "neutrality" around marriage in policy or law. Unlike Western European countries, whose social policies generally don't tie a child's access to benefits or services to his parents' marital status, the marriage movement's first principle as articulated at the convention in 2000 is to "make supporting marriages—not just marriage neutrality—the goal. Healthy marriage benefits the whole community." In other words, they *want* to discriminate—in favor of (heterosexual) marriage. Clint Cooper, "Marriage Movement Principles," *Chattanooga Times Free Press*, June 30, 2000, p. B3.

Their second principle reiterates that public policy should be pro-marriage rather than marriage neutral: "Respect the special status of marriage," it declares, echoing the 19th century view of marriage as a status rather than contract relationship (see *Maynard v. Hill*, 125 U.S. 190 [1888]). "Do not extend the benefits of marriage to couples who could marry, but choose not to."

The third principle reiterates the commitment to "reconnect marriage and childbearing." And be fruitful: "Don't discourage married couples from having children as they choose." This principle puzzles me. It's unclear to me how public policy has discouraged marital procreation—except perhaps by inadequate maternity and family leave policies, but those needs aren't addressed in the five principles.

The fourth principle states, "Don't discourage marital interdependence by penalizing unpaid work in homes and communities." Marital interdependence means a division of roles (most likely, in this case, a division of roles by sex).

The marriage movement's fifth principle urges "the promotion of marital permanence," which might entail the rollback of liberal no-fault divorce laws and the promotion of covenant marriage, although the principle is too vague to link to a specific policy.

Cumulatively, the principles lay out what looks like a blueprint for viewing marriage more as a social institution and obligation than a romantic bond—a revival of a 19th century "traditional marriage" concept in the 21st century, skipping over the marriage-attenuating romantic interregnum of the 20th. For more extensive commentary and analysis of the marriage movement, marriage politics, and aspects of the traditional marriage revival, and a discussion with Nicky Grist, executive director of Alternatives to Marriage, the only national organization that fights marriage discrimination, please see http://www.pamelahaag.com.

6   **David Popenoe, a prominent marriage researcher**: quoted in Dianna Marder, "Young Adults Looking to Marry Soul Mates," *Contra Costa Times*, June 20, 2001, p. D4. The National Marriage Project survey included 1,000 respondents between the ages of twenty and twenty-nine; Cheryl Wetzstein, "Young Singles Aim at Lasting Marriage, Study Shows Many Seek 'Soul Mates,'" *Washington Times*, June 13, 2001, p. A10.

6   **Kristina Zurcher, a scholar at Notre Dame**: Kristina E. Zurcher, "'I Do' or 'I Don't'? Covenant Marriage after Six Years," *Notre Dame Journal of Law, Ethics & Public Policy* 18, no. 1 (2004), pp. 273–301, p. 293.

6   **As evidence the marriage movement**: For a research review on happiness and marital duration see Jody VanLaningham, et al., "Marital Happiness, Marital Duration and the U-Shaped Curve: Evidence from a Five-Wave Panel Study," *Social Forces* 79, no. 4 (June 2001), pp. 1313–41. VanLaningham also challenges the idea that marriages experience an upswing in happiness in later years if they persist.

6   **"Many enter marriage with false hopes"**: Ana Veciana-Suarez, "Marriage is as Much about Work as Love," *Houston Chronicle*, October 15, 2000, p. 6. See also as an example, John Boudreau, "Telling the Truth about Marriage: Long, Happy Unions are Rare and Require Work," *San Jose Mercury News*, June 27, 2004, p. 3H.

7   **"as a social machine"**: David Brooks, "The Elusive Altar," *New York Times*, January 18, 2007, p. A27.

7   **"until your knuckles bleed"**: Blaine Harden, "Bible Belt Couples 'Put Asunder' More, Despite New Efforts," *New York Times*, May 21, 2001, p. A1.

7   **A 2001 Gallup survey**: Conducted for the National Marriage Project, Rutgers University. Cited in Jane Eisner, "For Blissful Marriage Shallow New View," *Philadelphia Inquirer*, June 14, 2001, p. A31.

8   **the stable over the sublime**: While some studies show enduring, inflated ideals of romantic happiness, others reveal humbly pragmatic expectations. Rachel Lawes discovered in her work that far from clinging to standards of romantic love and personal gratification, a good portion of her subjects favored a "realistic repertoire" about marriage and dismissed the "romantic repertoire" as existing only in "supposition" and not in the "real world." For them the romantic sublime had floated upward from an admittedly lofty goal into the stratosphere of pure myth. These realists anticipated marriages that would survive by spouses "making the effort" and "characterized by debt, infidelity, 'staying together for the sake of the children,'" and illness." Rachel Lawes, "Marriage: An Analysis of Discourse," *British Journal of Social Psychology* 38, no. 1 (1999), pp. 1–20. Scholar Ann Swidler interviewed 88 middle- and upper-middle-class couples in the Midwest and found that they weren't that romantically brainwashed but had fashioned a "prosaic, realistic understand-

ing of love." Peter Monaghan, "Berkeley Sociologist Investigates Notions of Love," *Chronicle of Higher Education*, August 17, 2001, p. 18. See also Lisa Neff, "To Know You Is to Love You: The Implications of Global Adoration and Specific Accuracy for Marital Relationships," *Journal of Personality and Social Psychology* 88, no. 3 (March 2005), pp. 480–97.

10   **Lori Gottlieb wrote a bestselling**: Lori Gottlieb, *Marry Him: The Case for Settling for Mr. Good Enough* (New York: Dutton, 2010).

11   **are growing fonder of arranged marriage**: American post-romantic interest in versions of matchmaking, arranged marriage, and marriage before love coexists with the international romantic "love before marriage" trend, which suggests an amusing and fascinating cross-pollination. I wonder if the globalized economy, the Internet, war, immigration, international sex tourism, and the worrying rise of mail order brides, among other places of contact and crossing, hasn't flattened our marital ideals, too, as Thomas Friedman proposes for the economy. India's "love before marriage" trend actually gained momentum on the currents of the global economy literally, with the software boom of the 1990s. Following the usual trade route of transmission, parts of the Asian and the Middle Eastern world are newly besotted with our exported romantic ideal of true love. See Del Jones, "One of USA's Exports: Love American Style," *USA Today*, February 14, 2006, p. 1B. This has inspired an Indian newspaper to editorialize with rousing hyperbole against the "sickening trend" toward "Western standards for marriage," those who "wallow in cohabitation and enjoyment," breathing the "air of all pervasive permissiveness and promiscuity, redolent with adultery and infidelity." It's the (waning) American way, I suppose. "So Why Bother Getting Married?" editorial, *Statesman*, June 6, 2006; "Bonding of Two Souls," editorial, *Statesman*, April 5, 2006.

Meanwhile, in the United States and Western European countries, the idea of arranged marriage and matchmaking is catching on. "Arranged marriages are very natural," says Aneela Rahman, a British citizen. "It is something Asian people do all the time and it is part of our culture." Rahman was twenty-three, thoroughly Westernized, well educated, and studying optometry when her family arranged her marriage. Now her TV series, *Arrange Me a Marriage*, involves working with friends to find suitable marriage candidates. Gillian Bowditch, "Mr. Right? That Can be Arranged," *Sunday Times*, November 18, 2007, p. 3. "Even though many of you might cringe at the prospect of an arranged marriage," writes American bride Anum Ghazipura, "I actually have no reservations about the idea. Not having the added responsibility of having to choose the man with whom I will spend the rest of my life . . . gives me a chance to concentrate on my goals." By the romantic script, of course, love and marriage *were* the goals of life. Anum Ghazipura, "My Relatives Will Choose my Husband," *Atlanta Journal-Constitution*, February 13, 2007, p. 13A.

For a more extensive analysis and commentary on arranged-marriage chic, see http://www.pamelahaag.com.

11   **an average of 236 marriages a day**: Email correspondence with author, April 28, 2009.

11   **Robert Epstein, former editor of *Psychology Today***: Robert Epstein, "Editor as Guinea Pig: Putting Love to a Real Test," editorial, *Psychology Today*, June 2002. See also http://www.drrobertepstein.com. Karen Peterson, "Falling in Love by Design," *USA Today*, June 26, 2003, p. 8D.

12   **"really, really horrible"**: Samieh Shalash, "It's All Arranged: 60 Percent of World's

Marriages Decided in Advance for Couples," *Lexington Herald-Leader,* "Lifestyle,"
May 16, 2005.

13 **"they think it's contagious"**: Surprisingly, an unpublished research paper based
on longitudinal data from Framingham, Massachusetts, suggests that divorce may,
indeed, be contagious. The study found that having friends who divorced increased
a person's risk of divorce by 147 percent. See Rose McDermott, et al., "Breaking Up
Is Hard to Do, Unless Everyone Else Is Doing it Too: Social Network Effects on Divorce in a Longitudinal Sample Followed for 32 Years," paper sponsored by the National Institute of Aging grant, www.scribd.com/doc/33986828/Social-Network-
Effects-On-Divorce.

13 **distinct marital cultures**: The hot-button, polarizing issue of same-sex marriage is
but one element in a story of two distinct marital cultures in the United States—the
"two Americas" of marriage. Political and marital temperaments show a "remarkable correlation," according to a 2006 microanalysis of all 3,141 U.S. counties. The
higher the rate of premarital cohabitation, postponement of both marriage and
parenthood, and having fewer children, the less likely the county was to vote for
George Bush in 2000 or 2004, and vice versa. A 2005 Census analysis based on more
than three million American households finds similarly that Red and Blue America
marry differently. Ron Lesthaeghe, et al., "The Second Demographic Transition
in the United States: Exception or Textbook Example?" *Population and Development
Review* 32, no. 4 (December 2006), pp. 669–98; Tallese Johnson and Jane Dye, *Indicators of Marriage and Fertility in the United States from the American Community Survey: 2000 to 2003,* U.S. Census Bureau, May 2005; for a review of some of the data
see Tamar Lewin, "Data on Marriage and Births Reflect Political Divide," *New York
Times,* October 13, 2005.

The divorce rate differs across these marriage cultures, and in surprising directions. The divorce rate in many parts of the Bible Belt is roughly 50 percent
above the national average. Baptists, in particular, have the highest divorce rate
of any Christian denomination, and are more likely to get divorced than agnos-
tics and atheists. Arkansas governor Mike Huckabee declared a "state of marital
emergency" in 1999. The place with the lowest divorce rate is Massachusetts, the
quintessential liberal state. Divorce rates are from U.S. Census Bureau, *Statistical Abstract of the United States 2010* (Washington, D.C.: U.S. Government Printing
Office, 2009). The most recent data is from 2007, with no data available from six
states. See also the Pew Research Center website, http://pewresearch.org, for current data on marriage and divorce rates in the fifty states. "Baptists Have Highest
Divorce Rate," Associated Press, December 30, 1999, accessed at Deism website
http://www.sullivan-county.com/bush/divorce; "The So-What View of Marriage," editorial, *Omaha World Herald,* April 24, 2000, p. 10; Huckabee quoted in
Harden, "Bible Belt Couples 'Put Asunder' More," p. A1.

The states ranked highest for numbers of children in single-parent families in
2006 include Arkansas, Georgia, Alabama, South Carolina, Louisiana, and Mississippi, and all but Mississippi were also in the bottom ten on births to unmarried
women in 2004. This prompted the *Atlanta Journal-Constitution* to name the South
the "single mother hub of the nation." Annie E. Casey Foundation, *Kids Count 2006,*
Kids Count Data Center, http://www.kidscount.org/datacenter, comparison by
topic: "Children in Single-Parent Families: Percent: 2006"; Dye and Johnson, *Indicators of Marriage and Fertility;* Helena Oliviero, "South Leads Trend of Motherhood
Without Marriage," *Atlanta Journal-Constitution,* October 13, 2005, p. A1. Naomi

Cahn and June Carbone, *Red Families v. Blue Families: Legal Polarization and the Creation of Culture* (New York: Oxford University Press, 2010) have occasioned debate about whether or not the unwed birth rates in blue states are low because of higher abortion rates.

These marriage patterns most certainly interact in complex ways with poverty and education. But among socially conservative politicians one response to the dismaying divorce and single-motherhood rate in traditional marriage strongholds has been to double down on traditional values as a remedy, and try to revive them through marriage education and similar programs. Oklahoma governor Frank Keating, for example, called his state's high divorce rate a "scalding indictment of what isn't being said behind the pulpit" to the 70 percent of state residents who go to church each week, and he vowed to use $10 million in welfare funds on a campaign to cut the divorce rate by one-third in ten years. Harden, "Bible Belt Couples 'Put Asunder' More," p. A1. Another hypothesis could be that insofar as values factor into different divorce rates, the Bible Belt's culture of traditional marriage is too strong, not too weak, at a time when doing traditional marriage by traditional conventions doesn't seem to strengthen it. For further analysis and opinion, see http://www.pamelahaag.com.

13   **divided by attitudes and class**: Today, marriage success and failure in the United States is tied more firmly to class. A marriage class divide—a "widening gulf," reports the *Economist*—has opened in the 21st century between the poor and working and middle classes. This is a recent as well as a striking trend. In the 1970s, marriage and divorce rates fell equally across class and weren't distinguished by education, for men or women. Today middle-class couples divorce at almost half the rate of less prosperous couples. Those couples making over $50,000 have a 31 percent chance of divorce after fifteen years, compared with a 65 percent chance for those making under $25,000. Scholar Pamela Smock describes that marriage seems to be emerging in the 21st century as a more elite custom. On the 1970s see Zhenchao Qian, et al., "Changes in American Marriage, 1972 to 1987," *American Sociological Review* 58, no. 4 (1993), pp. 482–495; Pamela Smock, "The Wax and Wane of Marriage: Prospects for Marriage in the 21st Century," *Journal of Marriage and Family* 66, no. 4 (2004), pp. 966–73.

One element of this class divide is that things that we once thought would kill traditional marriage may be associated with stronger marriages today. In the 1900s, prevailing research wisdom held that a woman's advanced education threatened her marital prospects and success. In the first post–women's-liberation cohort of the early 1970s, that might have been the case, but that trend has reversed itself in the 21st century. Joshua Goldstein and Catherine Kenney conclude that although in the past, women with more education were *less* likely to marry, recent college graduates at the dawn of the 21st century were forecast to marry at higher levels, but they will do it at a later age. Their research, they conclude, "suggests that marriage is increasingly becoming a province of the most educated." Pamela Smock, et al. also find that the "retreat from marriage" in this century is more pronounced for low-socioeconomic-status Americans. The probability of expecting to marry—in a country that just five decades ago saw almost universal marriage, across class—is now differentiated by socioeconomic position. Joshua Goldstein and Catherine Kenney, "Marriage Delayed or Marriage Forgone? New Cohort Forecasts of First Marriage for U.S. Women," *American Sociological Review* 66 (2001), pp. 506–19; Pamela Smock, "First Comes Cohabitation and Then Comes Marriage?" *Journal of*

Family Issues 23, no. 8 (2002), pp. 1065–87; Christine Whelan, *Why Smart Men Marry Smart Women* (New York: Simon & Schuster, 2006).

Among college-educated women who first married between 1990 and 1994, only 16.5 percent were divorced. Meanwhile, among high school dropouts, the rate rose from 38 percent to 46 percent in the same time frame. From 1975 up through the 1990s, divorce rates fell among women with a four-year college degree or more, but remained high among women with less than a four-year college degree. This trend suggests a "growing association between socioeconomic disadvantage" and divorce. Steven Martin, "Trends in Marital Dissolution by Women's Education in the U.S.," *Demographic Research* 15 (December 2006), pp. 537–60.

Likewise, waged work by wives now seems to support marriage, and marital success. In a 2002 work based on two waves of the National Survey of Families and Households data, the prominent marriage researcher Robert Schoen and others find "clear evidence that, at the individual level, women's employment does not destabilize happy marriages." Schoen comments that "contrary to frequently invoked . . . theories," wives' full-time employment is associated with greater marital stability. David Popenoe, who once voiced pessimism about working wives and marital stability, finds the new data that working wives stabilize marriage to be "probably correct. Working women have become the norm, and it's having a different effect today than 30 years ago." A 2002 study corroborates Popenoe's observation of a cohort difference. Bisakha Sen finds that the effect of married women's work differs by generation. Earlier it might have imperiled marriage, but for our century it may be "beneficial to marital stability." Robert Schoen, et al., "Women's Employment, Marital Happiness, and Divorce," *Social Forces* 81 (December 2002), pp. 643–62; Popenoe and Burstein quoted in Frank Greve, "Study Suggests Unions with Working Wives Last," *Houston Chronicle*, May 23, 2007, p. B2; Bisakha Sen, "Does Married Women's Market Work Affect Marital Stability Adversely? An Intercohort Analysis Using NLS Data," *Review of Social Economy* 60, no. 1 (2002), pp. 71–92.

Opinion and interpretations vary on the class divide. Some interpret it as an artifact of marriage's greater utility and value for the middle classes. "Consistent with economic reasoning," opines economics professor Tyler Cowen, "marriage is growing among groups who benefit from marriage the most." Tyler Cowen, "Matrimony Has Its Benefits, and Divorce Has a Lot to Do With That," *New York Times*, April, 19, 2007, C1.

Indeed, it's not that poor and low-income women resist marriage because they don't understand its benefits or fail to revere it. According to some research, they don't marry because it often actually *impedes* their children's or their own well-being, in material and psychological terms. Harvard University professor Kathryn Edin, in her fascinating and extensive work among single, unmarried poor women in three cities, asked poor women themselves why they would or would not marry, and she found that they feel "marriage entails more risks than potential rewards." Uniformly, women had some abstract praise for marriage. But women recognize that "any marriage is also economically precarious, might well be conflict ridden, and short lived." Without the offsetting advantages of pooled assets and economies of scale that characterize middle-class marriages, a poor woman might be better off not married because then "she has the flexibility to lower her household costs by getting rid of him." Kathryn Edin, "What Do Low-Income Single Mothers Say About Marriage?" *Social Problems* 47, no. 1 (2000), pp. 112–33.

Political defenders of traditional marriage in the United States lean toward the conclusion that nonmarriage is exacerbating if not causing poverty and greater class inequality. Kay Hymowitz of the conservative Manhattan Institute develops the idea of a marrying and nonmarrying "caste" system in America most diligently. President George W. Bush's health and human services secretary Mike Leavitt identified moving people from welfare to work and "building strong marriages" as the two pillars of the welfare-reform agenda. Nicky Grist, executive director of Alternatives to Marriage, dissents from the "Let Them Eat Wedding Cake" approach to grappling with poverty. See Kay Hymowitz, *Marriage and Caste in America* (Chicago: Ivan Dee, 2006); Robert Gehrke, "Leavitt Calls Good Marriages a Major Key to Welfare Reform," *Salt Lake Tribune*, June 14, 2006; Harden, "Bible Belt Couples 'Put Asunder' More," p. A1; Nicky Grist, interview with author, July 2008.

More liberal opinion leans toward the conclusion that we should worry about poverty and children's well-being rather than promote marriage to solve those problems indirectly. See, for example, Frank Furstenberg, "What a Good Marriage Can't Do," op-ed, *New York Times*, August 13, 2002, A2, p. 19. For further commentary and analysis, see http://www.pamelahaag.com.

13   **"marital stances"**: The phrase comes from Elizabeth Drogin, "The Marrying Types: Stances of Marriage Postponement and Pursuit among Young Adults" (Ph.D. diss., University of California, Berkeley, 2006), *Dissertation Abstracts A: The Humanities and Social Sciences* 66, no. 10, p. 3821.

17   **a more popular stance in the "post-marriage" countries**: Today, although the U.S. divorce rate has stabilized in the last decade owing perhaps to demographic shifts and/or more couples cohabiting rather than marrying at all, we marry more and divorce more than our peer nations. As marriage scholar Andrew Cherlin notes, the "sentiment in favor of marriage appears to be stronger in the United States than in other developed countries" for the 21st century. "The share of U.S. adults who are likely to marry is higher, but so is the share likely to divorce." The U.S. Census Bureau's *Marriages and Divorces* projects that about 50 percent of first marriages for men under age forty-five may end in divorce, and between 44 and 52 percent of women's first marriages for the same age group. Andrew Cherlin, "American Marriage in the Early Twenty-First Century," *Future of Children* 15, no. 2 (Fall 2005), p. 33.

Western Europe, the United Kingdom, Canada, Japan, and especially Scandinavia—in short, most of our peer, wealthy nations in the industrialized world—are the "post-marriage" vanguard. According to some sociologists they are undergoing a "soft revolution" away from old-world marital and family values. Arguably, marriage is no longer the primary social institution of these countries.

Since this century began, unmarried couples have been the norm in Sweden, Norway, Denmark, Iceland, and Finland. More than half of babies in Scandinavia were born to unmarried mothers in 1999. In Sweden, 28 percent of coupled households are cohabiting heterosexuals, compared to 8 percent in the United States. Norwegian researcher Oystein Kravdal notes a "massive drift" away from marriage in Norway, where as early as 1999, births to single mothers accounted for almost half of all births. In Iceland, it's 62 percent. Norway's crown prince married a single mother with a toddler after living with her first, and there is a county in Norway where 82 percent of first children were born to unmarried couples. France's marriage rate has plunged 30 percent over the last three decades, and 59 percent of births in 2005 were to unwed mothers. However, the French birth rate is rising and is nearly the same as the United States', and couples buy homes and raise children without marriage. Sarah Lyall, "For Europeans, Love, Yes; Marriage, Maybe," *New*

York Times, March 24, 2002, p. 1; "Sweden's 'Marriage Lite' Gets Closer Examination," *USA Today*, July 18, 2005, p. 6D; Oystein Kravdal, "Does Marriage Require a Stronger Economic Underpinning Than Informal Cohabitation?" *Population Studies 53*, no. 1 (March 1999), pp. 63–80; Lyall, "For Europeans"; Noelle Knox, "Nordic Family Ties Don't Mean Tying the Knot," *USA Today*, December 16, 2004, p. A15; Molly Moore, "More Longtime Couples in France Prefer L'Amour Without Marriage," *Washington Post*, November 21, 2006, p. A22.

In Britain, marriage has been in decline since the early 1970s. One in three Scottish women deems marriage "no longer necessary or relevant." Britain is only twenty-three years away from being a majority-unmarried nation. And in Australia and New Zealand, marriage continues its "inexorable decline," according to Statistics NZ. The marriage rate fell by half from 1987 to 2007. Russell Leadbetter, "One in Three Women Doesn't Want to Walk down the Aisle," *(Glasgow) Evening Times*, October 24, 2006, p. 12; Steve Doughty, "Women Waiting Till 30 to Marry if They Ever Get Round to It at All," *Daily Mail*, February 8, 2006, p. 29; Sarah Womack, "Married Parents 'In Minority by 2031,'" *Daily Telegraph*, October 5, 2007; Patrick Crewdson, "Wedding Bells Later and Rarer for Kiwis," *Dominion Post*, May 4, 2007, p. 8.

Canada reached the milestone in 2006 of having more Canadian adults (over 51 percent) who had never married. The most popular arrangement in Quebec has for many years been the "common law" family, and that arrangement, according to Statistics Canada, has surged since 2001. Barbara Kay, "Weddings Have Lost Their Lustre," *National Post*, September 13, 2007, p. A1.

For analysis and commentary on why people marry, or not, in our peer nations, see http://www.pamelahaag.com.

17   **"like a fossil"**: Quoted in "The So-What View of Marriage," editorial, *Omaha World Herald*, April 24, 2000, p. 10.

17   **"bourgeois institution"**: Moore, "More Longtime Couples in France Prefer L'Amour Without Marriage," p. A22.

18   **"there is no product in the world"**: Raoul Felder, from his blog, http://www.raoulfelder.com.

18   **Half of them married**: Claudia Goldin reviews these broad cohort differences in marriage in "The Long Road to the Fast Track: Career and Family," *Annals AAPSS 596*, November 2004, pp. 246–47, see also pp. 24–25 for a précis of Goldin's work. Betty Friedan's landmark work *The Feminine Mystique*, of course, dissected the age of this marriage consensus most vividly and consequentially, and Stephanie Coontz's *The Way We Never Were: American Families and the Nostalgia Trap* (New York: Basic Books, 1992) offers an important corrective to the inaccurate notions of life and marriage in the 1950s that were evident in the family values discourse of the Reagan era and its nostalgia for the pre-1960s family.

18   **almost all wage-earning women**: Thomas Fleming, "Sex and Civil Rights," *This Week*, March 19, 1967.

18   **"the lame, the blind, and women"**: Cynthia Fuchs Epstein, *Women in Law* (New York: Basic Books, 1981), p. 51.

19   **writer Alix Kates Shulman**: Quoted in Saul Feldman, *Escape from the Doll's House* (New York: Carnegie Commission on Higher Education, 1974), p. 1.

19   **we most often marry in mid-plot**: At the start to the 21st century, the median age at first marriage had increased to 26.8 years for men and 25.1 years for women, up from 23.2 and 20.8 in 1970. Eminent marriage researcher Robert Schoen summarizes the "overall trend toward earlier marriage until the 1960s, with marriage

ages rising from then onwards." Women in the United States in the 20th century had the lowest average age of first marriage just after 1945, at less than 20 years. U.S. Census Bureau, "Number, Timing and Duration of Marriages and Divorces," *America's Families and Living Arrangements* 9 (2001); Robert Schoen and Vladimir Canudas-Romo, "Timing Effects on First Marriage: Twentieth-Century Experience in England and Wales and the USA," *Population Studies* 59, no. 2 (July 2005), pp. 135–46.

There are a few explanations for the trend, including cohabitation before marriage. See Larry Bumpass, et al., "The Role of Cohabitation in Declining Rates of Marriage," *Journal of Marriage and Family* 53, no. 4, (1991), 913–27.

Claudia Goldin argues that the availability of reliable birth control partially accounts for the "soar" in age at first marriage for college-educated women, especially. "With the advent of the pill," Goldin writes, "some men and women could decide to delay marriage yet not pay as large a penalty." Marriage delay, in turn, could allow women to invest in lengthy educational processes. This results in a "thicker marriage market" for women with career potential. Claudia Goldin, "Career and Marriage in the Age of the Pill," *American Economic Review* 90, no. 2 (May 2000), pp. 461–65.

David Loughran also finds that later marriage is pronounced among more educated groups of women. He uses a model of "female marital search" patterns to show how rising inequality in male wages accounts for some of the decline of earlier marriage. He finds that rising male inequality accounts for anywhere from 7 to 18 percent of the decline in "propensity to marry" between 1970 and 1990 for white women and better-educated black women, specifically. Loughran notes that educated women search within narrow circles for potential mates. Decreases in male wages means longer search times for mates, and thus delays in marriage for well-educated black women and white women. David Loughran, "The Effect of Male Wage Inequality on Female Age at First Marriage," *Review of Economics and Statistics* 84, no. 2 (May 2002), pp. 237–50.

Internationally, the biggest predictor of delayed marriage is an increase in women's educational attainment. See Stephanie Coontz, *Marriage, a History.*

Today, couples might wait until their life is in order before they marry—for example, until they can afford to move out on their own, buy a house, have secure jobs, decide where to live, travel a bit, settle on a career or job, or earn professional degrees. Nicky Grist, Executive Director of Alternatives to Marriage, tells me that the desire to pay for the wedding itself delays marriage, the tail wagging the dog. Interview with author, July 14, 2008.

20 **Research in 2002 found**: See Kathleen Gerson, "Moral Dilemmas, Moral Strategies, and the Transformation of Gender," *Gender & Society* 16, no. 1 (February 2002), pp. 8–28.

23 **As it turns out, Bavaria's "most glamorous"**: Madeline Chambers, "Marriage Should Expire after 7 Years: Politician; Bavaria's Gabriele Pauli; Running for Leadership of Christian Social Union," Reuters, *National Post*, September 21, 2007, p. A14; "As Divorces Soar, Couples Told to Sign Up for the Seven-Year Hitch," *Daily Telegraph* (Australia), September 21, 2007, p. 23.

CHAPTER 2: "LIFE PARTNERS"

27 **beset author Betty Friedan's own age**: Betty Friedan, *The Feminine Mystique* (New York: Norton, 1963), p. 244.

28   **In what scholar Barbara Risman calls**: Barbara Risman and Danette Johnson-Sumerford, "Doing It Fairly: A Study of Postgender Marriages," *Journal of Marriage and Family* 60, no. 1 (1998), p. 23.

28   **We were part of the much larger**: Two of the more prominent studies on the trend toward assortative mating in the United States are Megan Sweeney and Maria Cancian, "The Changing Importance of White Women's Economic Prospects for Assortative Mating," *Journal of Marriage and Family* 66 (November 2004), pp. 1015–28; and Christine Schwartz and Robert D. Mare, "Trends in Educational Assortative Marriage from 1940 to 2003," *Demography* 42, no. 4 (November 2005), pp. 621–46. Sociologists Sweeney and Cancian found in their research that women's earning potential as an influence on their marriage prospects has grown over time, and continues to grow. They note that high-wage women are the ones who win the hand in marriage of high-wage men—the ones with high occupational status and high expected future earnings—more so than in the past. "Most striking," the researchers find, is the decline in the odds that Americans with very low educational levels will "marry up." Marriage is no longer a path to upward mobility promised by the romantic narrative, as a less-educated woman would be more likely to get edged out in the marriage market by a highly educated woman who attracts her peer, the highly educated man.

Schwartz and Mare note that the sheer rise in the number of Americans pursuing higher education increases homogamy, especially as colleges and universities assume the mate selection functions previously characteristic of churches, communities, and other organizations. Second, they note that in the context of egalitarian gender roles, men have started to compete for high-earning women, just as women had always competed for high-earning men. And this, too, encourages homogamy.

In 1994, Matthijs Kalmijn examined data on assortative mating from 1970 and 1980, and caught the trend toward *economic* over *cultural* propinquity. His article suggests how another major trend—toward later marriage—might interact with the trend toward assortative mating. Kalmijn concludes that in 1970, assortative mating by cultural status (that is, marrying people of a similar cultural group, ethnicity, neighborhood, or religion) was more important than marrying by the same economic status. The economic dimension, however, Kalmijn finds, is more important when people marry later in life. Hence the economic assortative mating by salary, and by the educational levels so deeply associated with salary in the United States, would logically become more pronounced as Americans overall marry later in life. Furthermore, he found that economic status homogamy got more important as the 1970s progressed, at the expense of cultural assortative mating. Matthijs Kalmijn, "Assortative Mating by Cultural and Economic Occupational Status," *American Journal of Sociology* 100, no. 2 (1994), pp. 422–52.

29   *U.S. News & Word Report* **college rankings**: I count as roughly "the same" those colleges and universities that were within 20 ranking points of each other (usually in the same category and tier) and/or within 5 percentage points in terms of selectivity—a flawed but at least precise metric of propinquity, courtesy of *U.S. News'* annual report.

31   **"freed"men** *to start*: After I completed this manuscript, the Pew Research Center released research indicating that there is a greater economic gain in marriage for men today than for women. Wives today, in comparison to their 1970 peers, are more likely to have more education and income than their husbands. See "New Economics of Marriage: The Rise of Wives," Pew Research Center, http://www.pewresearch.org.pubs.

33   **The 40 million visitors to online dating services**: Andrew Rocco Tresolini Fiore, "Romantic Regressions: An Analysis of Behavior in Online Dating Systems" (master's thesis, Program in Media Arts and Sciences, Massachusetts Institute of Technology, 2004), p. 13. The broad dating trend is away from random or face-to-face dating and toward online dating, whether through matchmaking services such as eHarmony, or mixing-pot online services such as Match.com. Some of the most interesting and rigorous work on online dating systems comes from the Program in Media Arts and Sciences out of the MIT Media Lab. Their work attests to the migration into the mainstream of online dating and mate selection. Online personals, they argue, "have the potential to shape how people attract one another, date, and fall in love." Michele Belot, et al. find that preferences get outweighed by opportunity in speed dating, for example. "Can Anyone Be the One? Evidence on Mate Selection from Speed Dating," C.E. P. R. Discussion Papers, no. 5926 (2006).

34   **twenty-somethings almost unanimously**: Quoted in Dianna Marder, "Young Adults Looking to Marry Soul Mates," *Contra Costa Times*, June 20, 2001, p. D4.

37   **Historian Nancy F. Cott**: Nancy F. Cott, *The Bonds of Womanhood: "Woman's Sphere" in New England, 1780–1835* (New Haven, Conn.: Yale University Press, 1977).

37   **the bonds of oppression**: An extensive body of historical research describes the deeply sex-segregated worlds of the 19th century American middle class, in which intimacy, camaraderie, and social life derived from relations with the same sex, even (or especially) after marriage. The most enduringly brilliant account of female intimacies in 19th century American bourgeois culture comes from Carroll Smith-Rosenberg, "The Female World of Love and Ritual," in her *Disorderly Conduct: Visions of Gender in Victorian America* (New York: Knopf, 1985). On masculine fraternal culture see Mark C. Carnes and Clyde Griffen, eds., *Meanings for Manhood: Constructions of Masculinity in Victorian America* (Chicago: University of Chicago Press, 1990) and in particular, Carnes' essay "Middle-Class Men and the Solace of Fraternal Ritual" and Donald Yacovone's "Abolitionists and the 'Language of Fraternal Love.'"
      One legacy of the romantic marriage heyday in the mid-20th century was the replacement of worlds of same-sex fraternal and sororal intimacy with the intense emotional bonds of the romantic pair. As both Michael C. Carnes and Richard Briggs Stott note, by the turn of the century (and into the romantic era of the 1900s), this ribald male pack behavior was replaced with an idea of abstemiousness, self-control, culturally stigmatized and more sharply defined ideas of male homosexuality, and a more domesticated ideal of masculinity. But now that the romantic heyday is fading, as I believe that it is, there is also evidence that the world of same-sex intimacy over marital intimacy is resurging (see chapter 8 of this book). For Stott, see his *Jolly Fellows: Male Milieus in Nineteenth-Century America* (Baltimore: John Hopkins University Press, 2009).

38   **These office marriages are usually platonic**: Kate M. Jackson, "It's a Marriage of Sorts: 'Workplace Spouses' Share Office Goals, Long Hours, and Need for Boundaries," *Boston Globe*, October 23, 2005, p. G1.

40   **Michael Kramer had had a twenty-year career**: Tavia Evans, "Counselor Helps Workers Keep Issues Out of Work," *St. Louis Post-Dispatch*, December 25, 2005, p. E1.

40   **The vulnerability for the stay-at-home wife**: For example, behavioral economist Zvika Newman found in her research that a marriage with two working partners is more stable when imperiled by "outside offers" (in other words, the temptation for

an affair or a new partner) than a marriage with only one working partner. Legal scholars note that social prohibitions that used to incentivize pro-marriage behavior and impede "opportunistic" behaviors such as infidelity have waned, which makes a housewife more vulnerable to abandonment and betrayal than in the past, absent legal contracts that delineate and specify expectations for marriage. Another scholar finds that a greater ratio of members of the other sex in the office increases the dissolution of preexisting relationships, but makes no difference in the transition from single to married. Zvika Newman, "Are Working Women Good for Marriage?" Department of Economics, Boston University, Working Papers Series: WP2006–039; Michael Svarer, "Working Late: Do Workplace Sex Ratios Affect Parnership Formation and Dissolution?" *Journal of Human Resources* 42, no. 3 (2007), pp. 383–95.

41 **Marcus Buckingham described**: Marcus Buckingham, "What Great Managers Do," *Harvard Business Review* 83, no. 3 (March 2005), pp. 70–80.

43 **"copreneur" marriages**: Statistic cited in Mary Shedden, "It Takes Two 2 Tango," *Tampa Tribune*, September 11, 2006, p. 1. Learning Express, a toy store chain, reports that no less than 87 percent of its stores are owned by married couples. National data indicate that 36 percent of copreneuer marriages are in service, 30 percent in agriculture, 18 percent in retail. Abigail Leichman, "Copreneurs Combine Marriage, Career," *(Bergen County, N.J.) Record*, September 3, 2006, p. B1. In a way, these marriages are the wired, 21st century version of the 19th century marriage and family-based American agrarian economy, perhaps the last time that marriage and enterprise overlaid so pervasively.

CHAPTER 3: "I CAN BRING HOME THE BACON"

47 **In 1970**: Cited in Toni Carabillo, et al., *Feminist Chronicles* (Los Angeles: Women's Graphics, 1993), p. 56.

47 **Just thirteen years later**: Mirra Komarovsky, *Women in College: Shaping New Feminine Identities* (New York: Basic Books, 1985), p. 185.

48 **That dream is sadly tattered**: A good majority of my online panel agrees with Shirin. I ask them to react to the statement "It's never really equal in terms of housework and chores. Wives usually end up doing more." This opinion garners the highest "I agree entirely" reaction of any of my questions, at a very robust 26 percent, and an extremely low "don't agree at all" reaction (only 6 percent). It's also got the lowest level of undecided reactions, at 14 percent. About this matter of equal housework, respondents have more firm and emphatic opinions, and overwhelmingly toward agreement, with 70 percent agreeing anywhere from "somewhat" to entirely.

49 **"contingency planning"**: Karen Arnold, *Lives of Promise: What Becomes of High School Valedictorians: A Fourteen-Year Study of Achievement and Life Choices* (San Francisco: Jossey-Bass, 1995).

50 **A similar form of preemptive thinking**: Louise Story, "Many Women at Elite Colleges Set Career Path to Motherhood," *New York Times*, September 20, 2005, p. A5.

50 **It's this pervasive retro mood**: I suspect that with the opting-out trend of the 21st century, this preemptive trimming of ambition has become more pronounced and acute. Another important factor is that social critiques of the career woman with a family grew louder in the 1980s and then through the 1990s, as Susan Faludi documented in her masterful *Backlash: The Undeclared War Against American Women* (New York: Crown, 1991).

Sylvia Hewlett's book *Creating a Life: Professional Women and the Quest for Children* (New York: Talk Miramax, 2002) is among the more prominent lamentations on the difficulties of balancing career and family. Hewlett concludes that half of the career-focused women in her study came to regret not having children and pursuing their careers. This book was much discussed, although apparently it didn't sell that well; see Motoko Rich, "Mommy Books: More Buzz than Buyers," *New York Times*, April 25, 2007, p. E6. Hewlett might have noted in a more optimistic spirit that the other half of her respondents *did* manage to pursue children and career simultaneously.

The economic toll for women individually of opting out is quite high. Leslie Bennetts, in *The Feminine Mistake: Are We Giving Up Too Much?* (New York: Hyperion, 2007), admirably documents that the stay-at-home wife and mother performs labor for nothing. Her work is worth $138,095 a year, according to compensation experts at Salary.com—and she gets none of it as salary.

Despite the risks, other researchers posit that opting out and a more romantic, chivalrous arrangement make wives happier. In 2006, W. Bradford Wilcox and Steven Nock attracted media attention, including a *New York Times* article, when they found in their work on wifely happiness "significant support" in their research for the "gender model of marriage"—that "traditional-minded women, women who did not work outside the home," and where the husband earned more money, "all reported that they were happier in their marriages." W. Bradford Wilcox and Steven L. Nock, "'Her' Marriage after the Revolution," *Sociological Forum* 22, no. 1 (2007), pp. 104–10.

Newspapers and magazines pounced. They headlined the research as a new phase in the housewife's ongoing metamorphosis from Happy to Mad and back to Happy again. "The Return of the Happy Housewife," proclaimed one headline; *Slate* reduced the upshot to "Desperate Feminist Wives: Why Wanting Equality Makes Women Unhappy" (March 6, 2006).

Unsurprisingly, the research itself was more nuanced than the headlines. In *Sociological Forum*, researcher Kristen Springer retorted Wilcox's claim that he had proven the happiness dividend of the retro marriage. She reexamined their own data and found that a large number of variables measuring degrees of traditionalism in the marriage accounted, all *combined*, for a mere *3 percent* of the variance in the wives' marital happiness—a spindly "factual basis," she asserts, for the boisterous conclusion that the "traditional" marriage is the happiest for wives. On the other hand, two variables that Wilcox used to measure a "husband's emotion work" increased the explanation of wives' marital happiness to a whopping 53 percent—"an explanatory power over 17 times larger" than measures of traditional marriage. Kristen W. Springer, "Research or Rhetoric? A Response to Wilcox and Nock," *Sociological Forum* 22, no. 1 (2007), pp. 112–17.

Behavioral economists dissect the economics of the mommy wars. In the terms of the behavior economist, the opting-out woman who forgoes career development for domestic labor has made a risky and uncertain investment at the expense of her professional investments. For this reason, as economist Ian Smith says, it's important that wives negotiate "marital terms" favorable to their heavy initial investment in the marriage, and ideally prior to marriage; "given that age, fecundity and marital investment diminish women's outside options faster than those of men, the so-called 'bargaining squeeze,' women can strike the best bargains when they are young and while love is strong and a fair division more likely." Ian Smith, "The

Law and Economics of Marriage Contracts," *Journal of Economic Surveys* 17, no. 2 (2003), p. 211.

Although the opting-out arrangement is the most nostalgically romantic marriage around today, with its chivalry and the male breadwinner, it doesn't pay for a housewife to think in romantic terms about her arrangement. Still, they most often do. In practice, wives in "traditional marriages," Smith observes, "empirically are less likely to write a marital contract, even though they apparently have the most to gain from doing so." Instead, other researchers find that they hold to (romantic) delusions of happily ever-after or, at the least, of favorable and amiably followed alimony resolutions. Lynn Baker and Robert Emery found that 81 percent of the wives in their research expected that the court would award them alimony if they requested it at divorce, and all predicted that their spouse would comply. Lynn Baker and Robert Emery, "When Every Relationship Is Above Average: Perceptions and Expectations of Divorce at the Time of Marriage," *Law and Human Behavior* 17, no. 4 (1993), pp. 439–50.

For detailed commentary and analysis of the economics of opting out, including a discussion of the work on marriage by behavioral economists such as Shoshana Grossbard-Shechtman, please see http://www.pamelahaag..com.

50 **"We feel a lot of pressure to succeed"**: Jennifer Wolcott, "Still Not Having It All," *Christian Science Monitor*, December 16, 2003, p. 11.

51 **many women are "pushed out"**: Joan Williams, *Unbending Gender: Why Family and Work Conflict and What to Do About It* (New York: Oxford University Press, 2000).

56 **"A lot of women think"**: Quoted and described in Andrew Hacker and Claudia Dreifus, Higher Education? How Colleges Are Wasting Our Money and Failing Our Kids—and What We Can Do About It (New York: Times Books, 2010), pp. 53-54.

56 **using marriage to advance both**: Spousal support for career in the dual-career marriage emerges in some research as a relatively novel basis for marital stability and happiness. It would have been moot as a marriage "skill" in the 1950s and the romantic era, when, by prescription, wives and husbands had complementary, distinct roles. Allen Bures finds that high levels of spousal support create higher levels of job satisfaction—but the relationship is moderated by gender. At a low level of support, both husbands and wives have equal stress, but husbands benefit more from high levels of spousal support for their career than do wives. Allen Bures, "The Effects of Spousal Support and Gender on Worker's Stress and Job Satisfaction: A Cross National Investigation of Dual Career Couples," *Journal of Applied Business Research* 12, no. 1 (Winter 1995–96), pp. 52–58. See also Uco J. Wiersma and Peter van den Berg, "Work-Home Role Conflict, Family Climate, and Domestic Responsibility Among Men and Women in Dual-Earner Families," *Journal of Applied Social Psychology* 21, no. 15 (August 1991), pp. 1207–17.

CHAPTER 4: THE TOM SAWYER MARRIAGE

67 **Attrition in this last group**: Anirban Basu, Sage Policy Group, Baltimore, Maryland, correspondence with author, August 1, 2007.

69 **"forfeited self"**: Betty Friedan, *The Feminine Mystique* (New York: Norton, 1963), p. 244.

70 **"Ph.T. (Putting Hubby Through)"**: Bruce Bliven, "By 1966, Half of Us Will be Under 25," *New York Times*, December 8, 1963.

70 **the fewer chores her husband performs**: Michael Bittman, et al., "When Does

Gender Trump Money? Bargaining and Time in Household Work," *American Journal of Sociology* 109, no. 1 (July 2003), p. 186.

72 **targets of a fatwa**: AsiaNews, "Fatwa Against 'House Husbands,'" May 16, 2006, http://www.asianews.it/news-en/Fatwa-against-house-husbands-6176.html.

75 **As the late Norman Mailer put it**: Norman Mailer interview with host Terry Gross for *Fresh Air*, National Public Radio, originally aired on October 8, 1991.

75 **"choice feminism"**: Linda Hirshman, "Homeward Bound," *American Spectator* (November 21, 2005), accessed at http://www.prospect.org/cs/articles?articleId=10659.

CHAPTER 5: THE JOY OF FALLING

80 **The vanguard of downwardly mobile marriages**: Richard Morin, Pew Research Center, Pew Social and Demographic Trends Project, *Inside the Middle Class: Bad Times Hit the Good Life*, released April 30, 2008, http://pewsocialtrends.org/pubs/706/middle-class-poll.

The Families and Work Institute compared the attitudes of younger workers with those of their parents. They found "a marked shift in the attitudes of both women *and* men" away from the high-powered career and toward cozier, more flexible stations in life. They are "choosing to stay at the same levels," the study found, "rather than continue moving up the career ladder." Horatio Alger is getting nudged out as icon of the American Dream by Herman Melville's Bartleby, who, when offered opportunities to advance, says simply that he would "prefer not to." In 1992, 68 percent of college-educated men wanted to move into positions with more responsibility, but only 52 percent in 2002. Ambition deflation is even more pronounced among college-educated women. In 1992, 57 percent wanted to move into jobs with more responsibility, compared with only 36 percent in 2002. Families and Work Institute, "Generation & Gender in the Workplace" (Washington, D.C.: Families and Work Institute, 2003), available at http://familiesandwork.org/site/research/reports/genandgender.

A survey by Salary.com found that almost 40 percent of workers, men and women, would prefer more time off to a $5,000 raise, a dramatic 20 percent shift in priorities from as recently as 2002.

A Radcliffe College–Harris study reaches the staggering conclusion that 70 percent of men in their twenties say they would trade money for time with their children. Radcliffe Public Policy Center with Harris Interactive, *Life's Work: Generational Attitudes Toward Work and Life Integration*, released May 4, 2000. *Fast Company* speculates that the gender gap in earnings may some day close when "the best and brightest people simply say, 'sorry, you can't pay me enough to take that job.'"

Medical students opt out of the most prestigious but demanding and time-consuming medical specialties because they anticipate wanting to spend more time enjoying their hobbies and leisure. Students gravitate toward time-bound specialties such as dermatology and shun more time-consuming specialties such as pediatrics or general practice. Associate Dean Suzanne Rose at the Mount Sinai School of Medicine admitted that she missed out on key events in her children's lives because she was striving to become one of the first female gastroenterologists. These students, she marveled, "don't want to work that hard." Julie Rovner, "Med Students Seeking Less Demanding Specialties," National Public Radio, aired October 13, 2004.

Architects report a "quite dramatic" decline in those signature exurban development features such as the grandiose entry doors, cathedral ceilings, or pala-tial windows. This trend started long before the economic meltdown of 2008, al-though exigency is doubtless propelling it forward now. Roger Lewis, a renowned architect and columnist, predicts a trend toward a "downsizing" of the American Dream. "There are more and more people than a few decades ago," he comments, "who realize that they don't need as much space and want well-designed, more compact housing" (correspondence with author, December 9, 2008). The Ameri-can Institute for Architects (AIA) Home Design Trend Survey for the third quarter of 2008 corroborates Lewis's instincts about the incipient trend toward smaller do-mestic spaces. The AIA finds that exurban subdivisions, even "with the opportu-nities they offer for recreation, open space, and more fully developed community plans—are losing ground." "Simplicity," they report, is "gaining in home styles and exteriors."

81 **"fear of falling"**: Barbara Ehrenreich, *Fear of Falling: The Inner Life of the Middle Class* (New York: Pantheon, 1989).

81 **marriages that come to rely on both salaries**: Elizabeth Warren, *The Two-Income Trap: Why Middle-Class Mothers and Fathers Are Going Broke* (New York: Basic Books, 2003).

82 **the American Dream in the 20th century**: Consumption, anticommunism, and patriotism (the freedom to buy Coke is "what we're fighting for," wartime adver-tisements told us in ennobling terms during World War II) tended to congeal, oddly, into one omnibus conceit about the "American Century" and global strength. "Thrift is now un-American," William Whyte declared in 1956. In the famous July 1959 "Kitchen Debate" between Nixon and Kennedy, the former gravitated easily toward the American household appliance inventory as proof of American geopo-litical superiority. In the postwar era, marriage fueled the consumer economy and the standard of living. Americans purchased 21 million cars, 20 million refrigera-tors, more than 5 million stoves, and almost 11 million televisions and moved into more than 1 million new housing units each year. In the five years after World War II, consumer spending increased 60 percent, but the amount spent on household furnishings and appliances, specifically, rose an astonishing 240 percent. Expendi-tures for food and drink grew by a comparatively modest 30 percent; for clothing, 53 percent; and for education, 73 percent. Elaine Tyler May details U.S. household consumption in *Homeward Bound: American Families in the Cold War* (New York: Ba-sic Books, 1988), pp. 165–66; 170–71.

By the mid-1950s, the number of shopping centers in the United States had mushroomed to 3,840. Significantly, they flanked the migratory paths of suburban families. From 1948 to 1954, suburban areas achieved retail sales, in dollars, almost three times higher than those of central cities. Richard Polenberg, *One Nation Divis-ible: Class, Race and Ethnicity in the U.S. Since 1938* (New York: Penguin, 1980), p 135; James Tarver, "Suburbanization of Retail Trade in the Standard Metropolitan Ar-eas of the United States, 1948–1954," *American Sociological Review*, 22 (August 1957), pp. 429–33, p. 431.

83 **The "standard of living"**: Marina Moskowitz, *Standard of Living: The Measure of the Middle Class in Modern America* (Baltimore: Johns Hopkins University Press, 2004). The standard of living would become the Keeping Up With the Joneses directive, intrinsically and vaguely competitive: It is defined as the "minimum of necessities, comforts and luxuries held essential to maintaining a person or group in customary or proper status or circumstances." Note how necessities slide eas-ily into luxuries.

83 **"having had the cornucopia upturned"**: David Riesman, "The Suburban Sadness," reprinted in William Dobriner, ed., *Suburban Community* (New York: Putnam, 1958).

83 **the fascinating interdependency**: Elaine Tyler May, *Homeward Bound: American Families in the Cold War Era* (New York: Basic Books, 1988), pp. 165–68.

83 **Hugh Hefner's real genius**: Barbara Ehrenreich, *The Hearts of Men: American Dreams and the Flight from Commitment* (Garden City, N.Y.: Doubleday, 1983).

83 **"her shopping list definition"**: May, *Homeward Bound*, p. 164.

84 **"made marriage worthwhile"**: Ibid., p. 180.

CHAPTER 6: THE HAVE CHILDREN– WILL DIVORCE PARADOX

91 **Of the nearly 105 million households**: Jason Fields and Lynne M. Casper, U.S. Census Bureau, "America's Families and Living Arrangements," Current Population Reports, P20–537, 2000; For more on single parents and cohabiting parents see Pamela Smock, "First Comes Cohabitation and Then Comes Marriage," *Journal of Family Issues* 23, no. 8 (2002), pp. 1065–87; Pamela Smock, "Cohabitation in the U.S.: An Appraisal of Research Themes, Findings and Implications," *American Review of Sociology* 26, no. 1 (2000), pp. 1–20.

92 **while children give many of us**: Diane Sollee, a researcher and key figure in the marriage movement, finds in the research that "seventy percent of couples experience a huge drop in marital satisfaction once their children are born, and that doesn't return until the kids leave home." Quoted in John Boudreau, "Telling the Truth about Marriage," *San Jose Mercury News*, June 27, 2008, p. 3H.

The link between the arrival of children and marital unhappiness and dissatisfaction isn't entirely new, and has been documented in several research studies, dating back to the 1970s. More recent studies have found an association, including Jay Belsky, et al., "Stability and Change in Marriage Across the Transition to Parenthood," *Journal of Marriage and Family* 45 (1983), pp. 567–77; Lawrence Kurdek, "Developmental Changes in Marital Satisfaction," in Thomas Bradbury, ed., *The Developmental Course of Marital Dysfunction* (New York: Cambridge University Press, 1998); and Kenneth Leonard and Linda Roberts, "Marital Aggression, Quality and Stability in the First Year of Marriage," in Bradbury, ed., *The Developmental Course*, pp. 44–73.

Although it's a persistent link, I'm more interested in this chapter in some of the attitudes about parenthood today that might exacerbate the melancholy, or give it a new twist. For example, there is evidence that while children trouble marriage, the sentiment toward "sticking it out" for the children is growing, so that they become the glue that simultaneously holds us together in marriage and increases our marital unhappiness. A Time/CNN poll in 2000 found that "more people think parents should stay together for the sake of the children." Fully 33 percent surveyed responded this way, in comparison to 20 percent just twenty years ago, in 1980, before the conservative resurgence of "family values." Survey cited in Abigail Trafford, "Second Opinion: The Case for Marriage Isn't Open and Shut," *Washington Post*, October 17, 2000, p. Z7.

And, unlike in earlier decades, when children were one of a few compelling marriage imperatives, they are today more often the sole inspiration or imperative for many marriages. Marriage traditionally has been held strongly to be the "preferred context" for raising children—and it still is, according to research by R. Kelly

Raley, in "Increasing Fertility in Cohabitating Unions: Evidence for the Second Demographic Transition in the United States?" *Demography* 38, no. 1 (February 2001),
pp. 59–66. But today, this imperative or preference in marriage faces little or no
competition from other imperatives, and thus weighs more heavily in a marriage.

Furthermore, an interesting finding from the Pew Research Center in 2007
suggests that today, the sources of fulfillment for parents, as individuals, and the
sources of fulfillment for parents in marriage may be disjointed around the question of children. The study found that children rate very low on the requirements
for a "happy" marriage, but the same study also found that they provide the highest
source of "*personal* fulfillment" for parents. Pew Research Center, "As Marriage and
Parenthood Drift Apart, Public Is Concerned about Social Impact," July 1, 2007,
executive summary, http://pewresearch.org/pubs/526/marriage-parenthood.

Cumulatively the research presents a confusing picture, in which children increase marital unhappiness but perhaps contribute to our personal fulfillment and
our reasons to marry in the first place. We have a greater "sticking it out" commitment to staying together for children than we did a few decades ago, but fewer if
any other marriage imperatives to encourage sticking it out.

92   **"Mother's Index"**: Save the Children, "State of the World's Mothers," May 5, 2010,
      http://www.savethechildren.org.
93   **"transition to parenthood"**: Jay Belsky and John Kelly, *The Transition to Parent-
      hood: How a First Child Changes a Marriage: Why Some Couples Grow Closer and Others
      Apart* (New York: Delacorte, 1994).
95   **"the conspiracy of silence"**: "What Your Mother Never Told You About Mother-
      hood," *Oprah*, September 17, 2002.
96   **But we set much higher**: Judith Warner, *Perfect Madness: Motherhood in the Age of
      Anxiety* (New York: Riverhead, 2005).
99   **"first three years"**: For a critique of the popularized neuroscience in infant brain
      development, see John T. Bruer, *The Myth of the First Three Years: A New Understand-
      ing of Early Brain Development and Lifelong Learning* (New York: Free Press, 1999).
108   **almost one in four marriages are essentially sexless**: Michele Weiner-Davis, *Sex-
      Starved Marriage: A Couple's Guide to Boosting the Marriage Libido* (New York: Simon
      & Schuster, 2001).
109   **"dual-income, no sex"**: Quoted in Kathleen Deveny, "We're Not in the Mood,"
      Newsweek, June 30, 2003, p. 40.
109   **"its quality, its quantity"**: Dagmar Herzog, *Sex in Crisis: The New Sexual Revolution
      and the Future of American Politics* (New York: Basic Books, 2008), p. 3.
109   **"better shape"**: Jessica Ramirez, "How to Keep Him from Cheating," *Newsweek*,
      September 25, 2008, www.newsweek.com/2008/09/24-how-to-keep-him-from-
      cheating.html.

CHAPTER 7: CHILDREN: THE NEW SPOUSES

114   **Whereas most Italians**: "The Frayed Knot," *Economist*, May 26, 2007, pp. 23–25.
114   **70 percent of Americans**: Pew Research Center Publications, "As Marriage and
      Parenthood Drift Apart, Public Is Concerned About Social Impact," July 1, 2007,
      http://pewresearch.org/pubs/526/marriage-parenthood.
114   **Fully 18 percent of married women**: "Childless by Choice: A Survey of Women on
      Having Children," *American Demographics*, October 1, 2001.
114   **survey by the National Center for Health Statistics**: Described in ibid. See also
      Madelyn Cain, *The Childless Revolution* (Cambridge, Mass.: Perseus, 2001). Cain

says that the idea is being embraced "by more and more people with each generation," and that women in their thirties at the start of the 21st century "feel very
little social obligation" to have children. "We're probably the largest and least recognized group in Western society right now," says a thirty-nine-year-old, happily
childfree husband in Maryland.

114 **only 46 percent of households have children**: U.S. Census Bureau, "America's
Families and Living Arrangements: 2008," Current Population Survey (CPS) Reports, http://www.census.gov/population/www/socdemo/hh-fam.html#cps.

115 **But when we look at the reasons behind**: I've come across more research on marriages that stay childfree in non-U.S. contexts and our peer wealthy, industrialized
nations than in this country. A U.S. study from 2008 found that no less than 20
percent of Americans perceive that children are "too expensive" to have, which indirectly attests to higher standards, as if nonaffluent or poor parents can't succeed
at it. See "One in Five Women are Deciding Against or Delaying Having a Child
Because of the High Cost of Child Care and Preschool, Poll Shows," http://www.
prnewswire.com/cgi, August 14, 2008. In Germany it's a similar story: Forty-seven
percent say a child "would be too much of a financial burden," while 27 percent
say that "children are hard to raise" and they don't have the strength for it. See Al-
lensbach Institute, "Influential Factors in the Birthrate (translation)," March 2004,
http://www.ifd-allensbach.de/pdf/akt_0407.pdf. In a Canadian study, 8 in 10 respondents cited "Being able to afford children" as important. See Vanier Institute
of the Family, 2007, http://www.vifamily.ca/library/future/4.html. A study from
the Australian Institute of Family Studies, undertaken in response to an alarm-
ingly diminishing birth rate, asked wives why they wouldn't have children. A fair
number of responses pointed to the idea that children require too much work, too
much money, and too much perfection. "I love kids but they are too much responsibility"; "we cannot afford to have children"; "I would prefer not to have kids unless
I was comfortable financially"; "I would have to find more money."

All of these responses concerning money are noteworthy, because even in
countries with much more tightly knit social welfare nets than the United States,
the childfree express an assumption that good parenting equals affluent parenting. Poor parents succeed at parenthood, too, all the time, but in these women's
imaginations it would take massive financial and emotional resources to do the
job right.

Not uncommonly, respondents also noted that they were too "selfish" to have
children. One in the Australian study explains, "we'd rather get ahead ourselves."
That's an understandable idea, but it betrays a subtle, underlying assumption that
parenthood is incompatible with any personal advancement or self-interest or "selfishness." Certainly we haven't come to believe that parents can *only* be parents?
But that worry glints in some of these responses, which imagine a basic, fundamental incompatibility between adult pleasure and vocation and parenthood. Ruth
Weston and Lixia Qu, Australian Institute of Family Studies, "Men's and Women's
Reasons for Not Having Children," *Family Matters* 58 (Autumn 2001).

It would be interesting to know what standards of "responsible" and "unseflish"
inform these concerns.

115 **one-child marriages**: According to the U.S. census and the National Center for
Health Statistics. See Lauren Sandler, "The Only Child: Debunking the Myth,"
Time, July 19, 2010, www.time.com/nation/article/0,8599,2002,382,00, and Susan Greenberg, "The Rise of the Only Child," *Newsweek*, April 23, 2001, www
.newsweek.com/2001/04/23/the-rise-of-the-only-child.

116 **While the number of unwed births among teens**: Rosanna Hertz, "And Baby Makes Two," *Christian Science Monitor*, October 30, 2006. Hertz wrote *Single by Chance, Mothers by Choice* (New York: Oxford University Press, 2006).

116 **"adult-centered"**: Quoted in Sharon Jayson, "Society Switches Focus Away from Children: Not as Much Adult Life Spent with Kids," *USA Today*, July 12, 2006, p. 1D. A 2007 Pew Research Center study finds that while Americans are persistently troubled by the "delinking" of marriage and parenthood, just 41 percent say that children are very important to a *successful* marriage. That's compared with 65 percent who felt that way as recently as 1990. Pew Research Center, "As Marriage and Parenthood Drift Apart, Public Is Concerned about Social Impact," July 1, 2007, executive summary, http://pewresearch.org/pubs/526/marriage-parenthood; Ruth Padawer, "State of America's Unions is Ominous," *Milwaukee Journal Sentinel*, June 29, 2003, p. 4L.

116 **We see it in the childhood**: Madeline Levine, *The Price of Privilege: How Parental Pressure and Material Advantage are Creating a Generation of Disconnected and Unhappy Kids* (New York: HarperCollins, 2006) on the material abundance and emotional impoverishment of middle-class children today, and Dr. Alvin Rosenfeld, et al., *The Over-Scheduled Child: Avoiding the Hyper-Parenting Trap* (New York: St. Martin's, 2001) on the overparenting trends that Judith Warner captures in *Perfect Madness*.

117 **"I didn't ask to be born"**: An extension of "not asking to be born" is the phenomenon of children suing their parents. Children in the U.S. have sued for abuse after recovering suppressed memories of sexual abuse; parental mismanagement of their inheritance money or trust funds; for the malfeasance of earnings entrusted to them, as in actor Macaulay Culkin's case; and for "divorce." On parental separation see Bart Greenwald, "Irreconcilable Differences," *University of Louisville Brandeis Journal of Family Law* 32, no. 1 (1993–94).

The emerging trend with children suing parents concerns "wrongful life," in which children sue their parents essentially for letting them be born, even with severe disabilities. Or, to project into the future, ethicists wonder if children might sue for parents who "failed" to screen pre-implantation embryos or embryos in early pregnancy for genetic disorders or even simply "imperfections." Might they come to sue for parents' failures to rectify or enhance their genetic blueprint before birth? Tony Fitzpatrick notes an "increase in children who sue their parents for the inheritance of conditions that could have been eliminated"; see his *Applied Ethics and Social Problems* (Bristol, England: Policy Press, 2008), p. 173. For my purposes, these genetic testing cases are most relevant for the premise of a legal claim to the best possible outcomes, and for their articulation of parental culpability, retroactively, for the lives and happiness of children, even after they become adults.

117 **Maybe there's a subtle narcissistic hubris**: Parents who hyperparent are trying conscientiously to do the best thing for their children. But research and insight are not clear on the idea that hyperparenting is any better for children, or, more accurately, that it makes much of a difference one way or another. A fascinating review comes from *Freakonomics: A Rogue Economist Explains the Hidden Side of Everything* (New York: William Morrow, 2005), by economists Steven D. Levitt and Stephen J. Dubner. They reviewed the research on educational outcomes and found that the indicators that did matter in parenting were those that describe "things that parents *are*" (p 161). The less influential list described "things that parents *do*"—things like reading more stories, or taking more field trips or enrichment programs. "For parents—and parenting experts—who are obsessed with child-rearing technique, this may be sobering news," they conclude. "The reality is that technique looks to

be highly overrated. But this is not to say that parents don't matter. Plainly they matter a great deal. Here is the conundrum: By the time most people pick up a parenting book, it is far too late. Most of the things that matter were decided long ago—who you are, whom you married, what kind of life you lead. . . . It isn't so much a matter of what you *do* as a parent; it's who you are."

From another perspective Judith Harris argues in *The Nurture Assumption* (New York: Free Press, 1998) that adolescents are influenced not by nurture over nature, but by nurture over nurture: They are far more influenced by their peer groups throughout adolescence than they are by their parents, although parents tend to overestimate their influence in their children's outcomes.

Kathleen Carlsson argues in her 2008 book, *The Case Against Women Raising Children* (New York: Xlibris, 2008), that maternal influence and what amounts to prescriptions for "bonding" and attachment parenting are too intensive and smothering, and the costs too great, for both parent and child.

Although he's not writing on parenting styles but about management, author and expert Bruce Tulgan describes twenty-something employees who enter the workforce and struggle to adapt to criticism, or to embrace a work ethic, and who tend to expect what amounts to hyperparenting—from their bosses. For example, they expect and want their self-esteem to be supported. Bruce Tulgan, *Not Everyone Gets a Trophy* (New York: Jossey-Bass, 2009).

In a personal essay on the future of imagination and literature, Michael Chabon recalls fondly the bicycle adventures of his own boyhood and wonders where the next generation will cultivate its sense of literary imagination and spirit when it spends most of its time within easy reach of wary parents, and rarely ventures forth into the "wilds." See his "Manhood for Amateurs: The Wilderness of Childhood," *New York Review of Books* 56, no. 12, July 16, 2009. This withered spirit of childhood adventure, he speculates, has as much to do with exaggerated parental fears and hypervigilance as it does with the obliteration of our natural, open spaces.

118 **"Just parents"**: *Supernanny*, ABC, air date April 17, 2008.

118 **"We have little commitment to the institution of marriage"**: Sarah Lyall, "For Europeans, Love, Yes; Marriage, Maybe," *New York Times*, March 24, 2002, p. A1.

119 **children measure ahead of American children**: Claude Martin, a sociologist in France, observes "very little difference between being married and cohabitating, and very little difference between children born out of wedlock and those that are born within marriage" in the cultural discourse of Western Europe. (In the United States, to draw a quick contrast, marriage movement minister and marriage educator Mike McManus—one of three commentators paid by the Bush administration to tout marriage education plans—commented that since the children of unmarried mothers are "22 times more likely" to end up incarcerated, single mothers were creating the "next generation of monsters.") Martin is quoted in Lyall, "For Europeans," p. A1; McManus is quoted in Clarence Page, "We'd Rather Get Married than Stay Married," *Seattle Post-Intelligencer*, November 11, 2007, p. B7.

Nor do Western European countries distinguish between married and unmarried parents in their social policies to incentivize marriage, instead focusing exclusively on children's welfare under the rubric of "family policy." Says Maria Lidstrom, the former coordinator for Sweden's family and children's policy, "there is no 'family values' debate, no soul searching for ways to reverse" the trends in her country. Instead, "the discussion has been more focused on how can we help people who want to split up? How can we make it easier for single parents? It's not that the government encourages it. They adapt to make it easier for single parents, single mothers." Email communication with author, July 2008; and Noelle Knox, "Nordic Family Ties Don't Mean Tying the Knot," *USA Today*, December 16, 2004, p. A15.

By several indicia, children in post-marriage European countries outthrive, outsucceed, and outachieve American children. The 2007 UNICEF report of children's well-being in the richest nations finds the United States in the bottom third of rankings for fully five out of six indicators of child well-being: The United States ranks at the very bottom, along with the United Kingdom, on family and peer relationships, subjective well-being, and behaviors and risks. It ranks among the lowest four on the other indicators—material well-being, educational well-being, and health and safety. Sweden, Denmark, the Netherlands, Finland, and Norway, in contrast, score in the top third on almost every measure. The United Nations quality of life survey ranks Norway first and Sweden second overall, while the United States ranked eighth. UNICEF, *Innocenti Report Card* (Florence, Italy: Innocenti Research Center, 2007).

Among other international studies of educational achievement, the Progress in International Reading Literacy Study finds that Sweden, Denmark, Canada, and the Netherlands score higher on fourth-grade literacy than the United States, while France, Scotland, New Zealand, and Iceland score roughly the same.

According to UNICEF, the United States has the highest teen birth rate among the world's rich nations, and about "four times the European Union average." The Netherlands, Sweden, Japan, Switzerland, and Korea have the lowest in the world. Perhaps this higher teen birth rate is due to a lower incidence of abortion in the United States, since it is a less popular or available option here, but according to other research by the Alan Guttmacher Institute, the United States has a just slightly higher abortion rate than Sweden, Denmark, or Norway—as well as a higher teen birth rate. On teen birth rates see UNICEF, *Innocenti Report Card*, no. 3, July 2001; Stanley K. Henshaw, et al., "The Incidence of Abortion Worldwide," *Family Planning Perspectives* 25, supplement, January 1999, http://www.guttmacher/org/pubs/journals/25s3099.html.

119   **"we made a very good wine"**: Lyall, "For Europeans."

119   *Conaway v. Deane*: in 401 Md. 219 (2007).

120   **interpret marriage and family law**: Ian Smith, "The Foundations of Marriage: Are They Crumbling?" *International Journal of Social Economics* 31 (2004), pp. 487–500.

120   **"When I refer to my family"**: Quoted in "Childless by Choice," *American Demographics*.

121   **vertiginous discomfort of boundless choice**: Barry Schwartz, *The Paradox of Choice: Why More is Less* (New York: Ecco, 2004).

121   **When she asked how many wanted to be wives**: Nisa Islam Muhammad, National Healthy Marriage Resource Center, seminar, July 23, 2008. Kai Stewart of Project Future in Atlanta, a nonprofit that assists pregnant teenagers, notes the same tendency for his clients to place a much higher value on motherhood than marriage or the nuclear family per se. Helena Oliviero, "South Leads Trend of Motherhood Without Marriage," *Atlanta Journal-Constitution*, October 13, 2005, p. A1.

123   **the Princess phenomenon**: Peggy Orenstein, "What's Wrong with Cinderella?" *New York Times Magazine*, December 24, 2006. According to retail analysts, the profits from the Disney Princess retail line are $3 billion, which is ten times their 2000 level.

124   **"trapped in a cage of narcissism"**: P. M. Forni, keynote presentation, Medical Library Association, Philaldelphia, October 6, 2009.

125 **Even the quintessential adult act**: For example, 70 percent of men in their twenties say they would trade higher salary for time with their children. Radcliffe Public Policy Center with Harris Interactive, "Life's Work: Generational Attitudes Toward Work and Life Integration," (Cambridge, MA: Radcliffe Public Policy Center, released May 4, 2000).

126 **"Second Running Boom"**: Running USA, Wire 65, August 13, 2008.

126 **The Boston Marathon**: Juliet Macur, "Big Marathons, Already Packed, May Still Grow," *New York Times*, October 28, 2008.

126 **bathroom size has grown steadily**: Modern Danish, "Trends and Considerations When Planning Your Bathroom," http://stores.channeladvisor.com/moderndanish/Store/Tab.

127 **the bizarre affection even for commuting**: Conference Board, "Special Consumer Survey Report: Job Satisfaction on the Decline," August 2002, http://www.consumerresearchcenter.org.

127 **"not just a place to get clean"**: Nouveau Bathrooms, "Bathroom Design Trends," http://www.nouveaubathrooms.com/bathroom-design-trends.

127 **"It's the best part of the day"**: Julia Lawlor, "Why Are These Commuters Smiling?" *New York Times*, May 3, 2000, Technology, p. 1.

CHAPTER 8: MAN-CAVE IN THE PROMISED LAND

134 **I read in March 2009**: Mary Fischer, "Why Women Are Leaving Men for Other Women," CNN.com, April 23, 2009; Jackie Warner quoted in "Women Leaving Men for Other Women," Oprah.com, March 25, 2009.

135 **"child-man:"** Kay Hymowitz, "The Child-Man: Today's Single Young Men Hang Out in a Hormonal Limbo Between Adolescence and Adulthood," *Dallas Morning News*, February 1, 2008.

139 **gave him a sense of "purpose and responsibility"**: Cited in Elaine Tyler May, *Homeward Bound: American Families in the Cold War Era* (New York: Basic Books, 1988), pp. 164, 180.

CHAPTER 9: MARITAL HABITATS

142 **A scant majority of American married couples**: On preferences among marriages and families for the city over the suburbs, and current residential patterns, see Segmentation Company (a division of Yankelovich), "Attracting the Young, College-Educated to Cities," CEOs for Cities National Meeting, May 1, 2006.

143 **"likemindedness"**: David Riesman, "The Suburban Dislocation," *Annals of the American Academy of Political and Social Science* 314, no. 1 (1957), p. 123–46; William Whyte, *The Organization Man* (New York: Simon & Schuster, 1956), pp. 287, 296, 361. Earlier still, in 1907, *Suburban Life* magazine extolled the vibrant community life of fledgling suburbs, such as lakes that attract "nearly all the children and a great many of the older people" in the summer, golf and tennis clubs, and community assembly halls where, for the women's clubs "some well-known personage always speaks on some topic of interest to the majority of womanhood." F. E. M. Cole, "Chicago's Most Unique Suburbs," *Suburban Life*, November 1907, reprinted in Becky Nicolaides and Andrew Wiese, eds., *The Suburb Reader* (New York: Routledge, 2006).

144 **"spaciousness"**: David Riesman, "The Suburban Sadness," in William Dobriner, ed., *Suburban Community* (New York: Putnam, 1958), p. 399.

144 **"claustral" world of the suburbs**: Loren Baritz, *The Good Life: The Meaning of Success for the American Middle Class* (New York: Knopf, 1988), pp. 197, 203, 204.

144 **"collective attempt to live a private life"**: Lewis Mumford, *The Culture of Cities* (New York: Harcourt Brace & Company, 1970; originally published in 1938), p. 216.

144 **The idea of "togetherness"**: In 1954, *McCall's* rebranded itself as not just a women's magazine but a publication aimed at the entire family, together, alone. James Playsted Woods, *Magazines in the United States* (New York: Ronald, 1956).

145 **60 million Americans**: John Cacioppo, *Loneliness: Human Nature and the Need for Social Connection* (New York: Norton, 2009).

145 **"startling evidence" of a decline**: Robert Putnam, *Bowling Alone: The Collapse and Revival of American Community* (New York: Simon & Schuster, 2000), pp. 98, 106. In the mid- to late-1970s a national lifestyle study that Putnam cites found that the average American entertained friends at home fourteen to fifteen times a year. By the late 1990s, that figure had fallen to eight times per year, a decline of almost half in under two decades, and the incidence of going out to see friends had declined as well. Daniel Yankelovich, a prominent social researcher and pollster, also reports a decline of nearly one-third between 1985 and 1999 in the readiness of the average American to make new friends.

146 **"sinister barricades"**: James Howard Kunstler, *Home from Nowhere: Remaking Our Everyday Worlds for the 21st Century* (New York: Simon & Schuster, 1996), p. 94.

147 **modest trend of families opting to live in the city**: It's not that married couples and middle-class families today inherently or essentially prefer the suburban married life. Some do, but some of them simply feel that they don't have many good choices, and that the cities haven't really worked to meet the needs of families.

A Yankelovich survey in 2006 reveals that contrary to conventional wisdom, young married couples with children are just as receptive to urban neighborhoods close to central cities, at 51 percent, as to distant suburbs, at 54 percent. Segmentation Company, "Attracting the Young, College-Educated to Cities." The idea of marriage in the city appeals on general principle, but two severe problems—schools and safety—currently divert from the cities to the suburbs families and couples that otherwise have a robust instinct to be married in public and live in socially vital neighborhoods. However, CEOs for Cities notes that nonurban families do tend to envision attachment, intimacy, and safety through space. CEOs for Cities, "CityKids," 2007.

Absent concerns about these two things, 80 percent of couples would prefer city living, according to a National Association of Homebuilders study cited in Lois Fu, Federal Transit Administration, "The Case for Federal Investment in Major Capital Transit Projects," unpublished white paper, 2003.

A migration of married couples and families back to urban areas seems to be a marital microtrend. In 2008, the American Institute for Architects documented a growing preference against exurban development and toward urban infill housing that is denser, has easy access to transit, and features pedestrian-friendly neighborhoods. Porches, on the other hand, endure as a popular design feature, precisely because they "evoke times with greater neighborhood interaction." See also the projections of much greater desire for urban housing near transit by 2025. See the Center for Transit-Oriented Development, *Hidden in Plain Sight: Capturing the Demand for Housing Near Transit*, July 2004.

Younger marriages start off more connected through the Web and have stayed socially connected. By the intimacy blur of the day, younger married couples might be more apt to blend marriage with friends. In 2003, journalist Ethan Watters wrote about "urban tribes." They're makeshift families that single twenty-somethings knit for themselves before they marry. These tribes, Watters discovered, function more like marriages and families than casual friendships. When members need help in the middle of the night, another friend comes over and—the faux marriage litmus test—feels *obliged* to do so. Ethan Watters, *Urban Tribes: A Generation Redefines Friendship, Family and Commitment* (New York: Bloomsbury, 2003).

149 **Nearly half of all parents worry**: U.S. Census report, cited in Richard Florida, *Who's Your City?* (New York: Basic Books, 2009), p. 259.

149 **this atmospheric dread**: Lenore Skenazy, interview with author, December 11, 2008.

150 **marriage and community are often at odds**: Naomi Gerstel and Natalia Sarkisian, "Marriage: The Good, The Bad, and the Greedy," *Contexts* 5, no. 4 (Fall 2006), p. 16.

150 **Critics such as Kay Hymowitz**: Chris Berdik, "The Greedy Marriage: Two Scholars Argue that Good Spouses Make Bad Neighbors," *Boston Globe*, September 16, 2007, p. D1.

151 **there are ninety co-housing communities**: Cohousing Association, http://www.cohousing.org.

155 **a score of divorced, cohabiting couples**: Cate Cochran, *Reconcilable Differences*, discussed in Anne Kingston, "Upstairs Mom, Downstairs Dad," *Maclean's*, October 29, 2007, pp. 54–55.

155 **"dual master bedrooms"**: National Association of Home Builders, Economics Group, *Home of the Future* (Washington, DC: National Association of Home Builders, 6/7/2010).

156 **"is a pinwheel-shaped mélange"**: Paul Goldberger, "Site Specifics," *New Yorker*, April 2, 2001, http://www.newyorker.com/archive/2001/04/02/010402crsk_skyline; http://www.makcenter.org/MAK_Schindler_House.php?section=1.

157 **"It's not for me to tell people"**: Quoted in H. J. Cummins, "Study Weighs Conflict Factor in Divorce's Impact on Kids," *Minneapolis Star Tribune*, February 26, 2001, p. E1.

158 **Libertarian economics professor Tyler Cowen**: See Tyler Cowen, "Why Don't People Have More Sex?" http://www.marginalrevolution.com/marginalrevolution/2005/05/why_dont_people.html. Cowen is a Harvard-trained economist and a professor at George Mason University.

CHAPTER 10: STORIES OF THE "AFFAIRS" FOLDER

162 **binds a marriage together**: Some courts have agreed that the sexual imperative of monogamy is the mortar of marriage. The 10th Circuit's *Potter v. Murray City*, 760 F.2d 1065 (1985), upheld the firing of a police officer for bigamy on the logic that "monogamy is inextricably woven into the fabric of our society. It is the bedrock upon which our culture is built."

163 **precise figures are hard to come by**: Andrew Greeley notes that even the eminent researcher Helen Fisher had to rely on *Cosmopolitan* and *Playboy* for data on infidelity. Andrew Greeley, "Marital Infidelity," *Society* 31, no. 4 (May–June 1994), pp. 9–13. On the political resistance to conducting research on sexuality see Edward Laumann, "A Political History of the National Sex Survey of Adults," *Family Planning Perspectives* 26, no. 1 (January/February 1994), pp. 34–40. The late arch-

conservative senator Jesse Helms and other legislators resisted asking questions through the national survey, not just about homosexuality but about sex generally.

Researchers struggle to quantify the sexual life of marriage. Husbands and wives give rehabilitating, pro-social responses in surveys and interviews. They redact their own marital records while speculatively exaggerating the perfidy of their friends, neighbors, and ex-spouses; they underestimate strategically; they are not out about their sexual improvisations or exotica. Significantly, in one of these studies, divorced spouses overall reported only a 13 percent rate of infidelity themselves, but no less than 43 percent reported that their *ex-spouses* had been unfaithful to them. Scott Smith and Kim Lloyd, "Spousal Alternatives and Marital Dissolution," *American Sociological Review* 60, no. 1 (1995), pp. 21–25. The trailblazer Alfred Kinsey, making adjustments for reticence in face-to-face interviews with spouses nearby, estimated that about half of married men and about 45 percent of married women had engaged in some extramarital activity before age forty. Alfred Kinsey, *Sexual Behavior in the Human Male* (Philadelphia: Saunders, 1948), p. 585.

163 **A few studies**: David Atkins characterizes infidelity as occurring in a "reliable minority" of marriages, and as a "common phenomenon" that is "poorly understood" nonetheless. See David C. Atkins, Donald H. Baucom, and Neil S. Jacobson, "Understanding Infidelity: Correlates in a National Random Sample," *Journal of Family Psychology* 15, no. 4 (2001), pp. 735–49. See also Michael Wiederman, "Extramarital Sex: Prevalence and Correlates in a National Survey," *Journal of Sex Research* 34, no. 2 (1997), pp. 167–74, for a similar estimate of around 20 percent of spouses, and Edward Laumann, "A Political History of the National Sex Survey of Adults," *Family Planning Perspectives* 26, no. 1 (January/February 1994), pp. 34–40. In *The Social Organization of Sexuality: Sexual Practices in the United States* (Chicago: University of Chicago Press, 1994), authors Edward O. Laumann, John H. Gagnon, Robert T. Michael, and Stuart Michaels estimate the infidelity figure at the lowish end, with 20 percent of wives and 35 percent of married men, but the methodology has been questioned because spouses were interviewed in front of each other. Judith Mackay finds a much higher incidence, closer to other estimates, with half of Americans admitting to having been sexually unfaithful, in comparison to a lower percentage of Germans (40 percent) and Spanish (22 percent). See Judith Mackay, "Global Sex: Sexuality and Sexual Practices Around the World," Fifth Congress of the European Federation of Sexology, Berlin, 2000, http://www2.huberlin.de/sexology/GESUND/ARCHIV/PAP_MAC.HTM. Martin Siegel also estimates a 50 percent incidence of infidelity, in "For Better or Worse: Adultery, Crime and the Constitution," *Journal of Family Law* 30 (1991), p. 55. At the highest end is Shere Hite, *Women and Love: A Cultural Revolution in Progress* (New York: Knopf, 1987).

163 **more reprehensible even than human cloning**: Cited by Pamela Druckerman, "Infidelity No Longer a Death Knell in Politics, *Contra Costa Times*, July 22, 2007. Druckerman's *Lust in Translation: The Rules of Infidelity from Tokyo to Tennessee* (New York: Penguin, 2007) summarizes these attitudes and Americans' stern disapproval in comparison.

163 **Other national surveys**: 2006 Gallup poll summarized in Elizabeth Emens, "Monogamy's Law: Compulsory Monogamy and Polyamorous Existence," *New York University Review of Law & Social Change* 29 (2004), pp. 277–376. Emens's article is tremendously comprehensive and useful, not only for its trenchant legal analysis of adultery statutes and alternatives, but for its review of prevailing attitudes toward monogamy in marriage.

164 **According to a fascinating 1994 study**: Eric Widmer, et al., "Attitudes toward Nonmarital Sex in 24 Countries," *Journal of Sex Research* 35, no. 4 (1998), pp. 359–58.

164 **a simple case of hypocrisy**: Daniel Bell, for example, writing on sexual mores in 1963, called this gap between "stated attitudes and actual behavior" a symptom of the hypocritical, "schizoid nature of sex in America." In Robert Libby and Robert Whitehurst, eds., *Marriage and Alternatives: Exploring Intimate Relationships* (Glenview, Ill.: Scott, Foresman, 1977), p. 383.

164 **"open secret"**: Eve Kosofsky Sedgwick, *The Epistemology of the Closet* (Berkeley: University of California Press, 1990); D. A. Miller, *The Novel and the Police* (Berkeley: University of California Press, 1988), p. 206.

165 **A study in 2008**: Jessica Ramirez, "How to Keep Him from Cheating," *Newsweek*, September 25, 2008, http://www.newsweek.com/2008/09/24-how-to-keep-him-from-cheating.htm. This interview describes research by rabbi and counselor Gary Neuman based on 100 husbands who cheated and 100 who remained faithful.

165 **"four-year itch"**: Helen Fisher's signal work on desire, monogamy, and love is *The Anatomy of Love* (New York: Norton, 1992). Fisher recounts in some interviews that when a married couple reports to be sexually happy and excited after four or five years she's inclined to say, "oh REALLY?" Fisher develops a counternarrative to the adaptive monogamy arguments made by sociobiologists such as Sarah Hrdy in *Mother Nature: A History of Mothers, Infants, and Natural Selection* (New York: Pantheon, 1999). Elizabeth Emens notes in her brief review of Hrdy and other sociobiological works in "Monogamy's Law" that "one can almost hear the sighs of relief emitted by evolutionary theorists when they can conclude that humans are basically monogamous" and choose quality over quantity.

But Fisher delineates the various biochemical processes associated with different phases of love, from the intense desires of the early lust to the oxytocin released during orgasms that bond partners to each other monogamously for a while, to the inducements to a phase of more settled love after two years. Fisher notes the "four-year itch" that inclines us to seek new romantic and sexual objects outside of the settled relationship.

Much earlier, in 1949, anthropologist George Peter Murdock undertook an ambitious study of the marriage and sexual customs of *all* existing societies for which he could find good data, and concluded that a scant 43 out of 238 societies considered "strict monogamy" in marriage to be an ideal. Murdock even deployed gentlemanly grade inflation on monogamy's behalf, classifying as "monogamous a few tribes in which plural unions occur" but are "not *preferred*." The "bias of our own highly aberrant traditional sex mores," confining sex "exclusively within the limits of one social relationship, vested with the responsibility for reproduction," has led to charges of "sexual communism" against "primitive" cultures. George Peter Murdock, *Social Structure* (New York: Macmillan, 1949), pp. 27, 260.

As for monogamous inspirations in nature, the bonobo apes, presumably as natural as any other apes or monkeys that we might look to for marital-biological inspiration and insight, practice rampant nonmonogamy, tend to their offspring collectively (since paternity isn't known), and use promiscuous sex rather than war as a means to work through conflicts between groups. It's a free-love, prelapsarian Eden.

166 **games of dominance and submission**: Esther Perel, *Mating in Captivity: Reconciling the Erotic & the Domestic* (New York: HarperCollins, 2006).

169 **Affairs can and do destroy marriages**: Denise Previti, et al. conclude judiciously that infidelity is "both a cause and a consequence" of marital dissolution. "Is In-

fidelity a Cause or a Consequence of Poor Marital Quality?" *Journal of Social and Personal Relationships* 21, no. 2 (2004), pp. 217–30.

A very useful scholarly review of the "common" but "poorly understood" reality of infidelity in marriage is offered in David C. Atkins, Donald H. Baucom, and Neil S. Jacobson, "Understanding Infidelity: Correlates in a National Random Sample," *Journal of Family Psychology* 15, no. 4 (2001), pp. 735–49. Previti calls it a "remarkable omission" that marriage research pays so little attention to extramarital sex, despite its often consequential frequency, and marriage scholar Roger Rubin found that the three leading textbooks on marriage in 2001 had "virtually no mention" of nonmonogamous lifestyles. Roger Rubin, "Alternative Lifestyles Revisited, or Whatever Happened to Swingers, Group Marriages and Communes?" *Journal of Family Issues* 22, no. 6 (2001), pp. 711–27. Atkins concludes simply that the sparse research on infidelity "has not been commensurate with its prevalence and impact."

Therapists and clinicians view infidelity as one of the most difficult problems to treat in therapy, although it is also one of the ones most commonly reported. In addition, some couples therapists have estimated that 50 to 65 percent of couples in their clinical practices are in therapy as the result of infidelity. Mark Whisman, et al., "Therapists' Perspectives of Couple Problems and Treatment Issues in Couple Therapy," *Journal of Family Psychology* 11, no. 3 (1997), pp. 48–60; Shirley Glass, et al., "The Relationship of Extramarital Sex, Length of Marriage and Sex Differences on Marital Satisfaction and Romanticism," *Journal of Marriage and Family* 39, no. 4 (1988), pp. 691–703.

171 **a small post-romantic marriage trend**: Research on separate bedrooms is from the National Sleep Foundation, cited in Amber Greviskes, "Is the Romance Gone? Couples Increasingly Sleeping in Separate Beds," July 26, 2010, aolhealth.com/2010/07/26.

178 **"infidelity tolerance"**: Jessie Bernard, "Infidelity: Some Moral and Social Issues," in Robert Libby and Robert Whitehurst, eds., *Marriage and Alternatives: Exploring Intimate Relationships* (Glenview, Ill.: Scott, Foresman, 1977), p. 144.

178 **A 2008 survey from Britain**: "Deluded Brides Believe Marriage Will Last Forever," *Express*, April 3, 2008, p. 23.

179 **In Hillary Clinton's case**: On reactions to Hillary Clinton's marriage, see, for example, Sally Bedell Smith, *For Love of Politics: Bill and Hillary Clinton: The White House Years* (New York: Random House, 2007); Jonathan Darman, "Not Really Feeling It: A New Book Tries to Make Sense of the Gripping, Grating Psychodrama that is the Clinton's Marriage," *Newsweek*, October 22, 2007, p. 43; Lisa Miller, "It's Not Her. It's That Marriage," *Newsweek*, March 17, 2008, p. 38. See, among many other articles that document this puzzling contempt, and its origins in Hillary's "sticking it out" after the affair, Michael Powell, "Why Is This Candidate Smiling? In New York, Hillary Clinton's Cool Façade Leaves a Lot of Women Cold," *Washington Post*, August 7, 2000, p. C1; John Harris, "Senator or Soap Star? First Lady's Life Eclipses Her Message," *Washington Post*, January 22, 2000, p. A1; Deborah Mathis, "Clinton Marriage None of Our Business," *Seattle Post-Intelligencer*, October 12, 2000, p. B7; Kathy Kiely, "Scenes from Clinton Marriage Get Airing Before Book Debut," *USA Today*, June 5, 2003, p. A8.

CHAPTER 11: "I CALL IT MARRIED DATING"

185 **"What if we could create"**: this and other comments from Noel Biderman are from an interview with the author, July 9, 2008.

186 **"lack of opportunity"**: David C. Atkins, Donald H. Baucom, and Neil S. Jacobson, "Understanding Infidelity: Correlates in a National Random Sample," *Journal of Family Psychology* 15, no. 4 (2001), pp. 735–49.

187 **Married people who earned**: Alfred Kinsey found in his trailblazing work that 31 percent of women with college degrees had been unfaithful by the age of forty. He also found that infidelity caused fewer problems for more affluent subjects; he speculated that it was because they could afford secrecy, different living spaces, and privacy. Alfred Kinsey, *Sexual Behavior in the Human Female* (Philadelphia: Saunders, 1953), pp. 416, 427. See also Atkins, "Understanding Infidelity."

Conversely, in her qualitative work with poor, single women in Chicago, Philadelphia, and Charleston, South Carolina, Kathryn Edin noted a strong, simultaneous intolerance for and resignation to male adultery. Although her work is qualitative and therefore not as conclusive, her subjects refused to countenance staying with a cheater, viewing a wounded spouse who would put up with it (or, presumably, commit it) as "hopelessly naïve" or "without self-respect." But they fatalistically assumed male infidelity almost as a marital given. "I would like to find a nice man to marry," a white single mother told Edin, "but I know that men cannot be trusted. That's why I treat them the way I do—like the dogs they are. I think that all men will cheat on their wives regardless of how much he loves her. And you don't ever want to be in that position." That narrows the woman's options to non-marriage and self-respect, or marriage and intolerable disrespect from incorrigibly wandering husbands. Kathyrn Edin, "What Do Low-Income Single Mothers Say About Marriage?" *Social Problems* 47, no. 1 (2000), pp. 112–33.

187 **Husbands and wives with graduate degrees**: Atkins, Baucom, and Jacobson, "Understanding Infidelity."

191 **"Facebook is going to be the downfall"**: "Facebook Fuelling Divorce, Research Says," *Telegraph* (London), December 21, 2009, http://www.telgraph.co.uk/technology/facebook/6857918.

192 **this infidelity gender gap is closing**: Atkins, Baucom, and Jacobson, "Understanding Infidelity." On the closing infidelity gender gap, see also Mary Beth Oliver and Janet Shibley Hyde, "Gender Differences in Sexuality: A Meta-Analysis," *Psychological Bulletin* 114, no. 1 (1993), pp. 29–51, which finds no or only small gender differences in sexual behavior in every realm except for masturbation, which males do more frequently than females. Oliver and Hyde note that these differences were wider in the 1950s and have narrowed considerably from the 1960s to the 1980s. Edward Laumann, et al. have conducted some of the most reliable and important research on sexual behavior in the United States with *The Social Organization of Sexuality* (Chicago: University of Chicago Press, 1994), based on a large, representative national database. They find few differences in infidelity between the sexes. Michael Wiederman, in "Extramarital Sex: Prevalence and Correlates in a National Survey," *Journal of Sex Research* 34 (1997), pp. 167–174, reports no differences in incidence or frequency of infidelity for married people over a lifetime under the age of forty. Rhonda Parker, in "The Influence of Sexual Infidelity, Verbal Intimacy and Gender Upon Primary Appraisal Processes in Romantic Jealousy," *Women's Studies in Communication* 20, no. 1 (1997), pp. 1–24, notes diminishing differences by gender as well.

193 **largely invisible audience**: Mike Genung, "Statistics and Information on Pornography in the USA," www.blazinggrace.org/pornstatistics.htm, 2008 data.

197 **doubts that there exists**: Jennifer Schneider, correspondence with author, July 8, 2009. There hasn't been much scholarship on the cyber affair. Alvin Cooper has

published on the prevalence and nature of cyber affairs. See "Online Sexual Compulsivity: Getting Tangled in the Net," *Sexual Addiction & Compulsivity* 6 (1999), pp. 79–104. See also Cooper, et al., "Cybersex Users, Abusers, and Compulsives: New Findings and Implications," *Sexual Addiction & Compulsivity* 7 (2000), pp. 1–25. One limitation with most of this work is that it treats only addictive, compulsive behaviors, as the topic of cyber affairs emerges in clinical and therapeutic settings. Cooper's "Romance in Cyberspace: Understanding Online Attraction," *Journal of Sex Education and Therapy* 22 (1997), pp. 71–84, does look at the topic from a nonpathological perspective, too.

197 **doesn't involve bodies**: Jennifer Schneider, "The Impact of Compulsive Cybersex Behaviors." In only 17 percent of the cases that Schneider discusses did the cyber affairs progress from virtual to actual physical contact.

197 **they "keep secrets"**: Marlene Maheu and Alvin Cooper, *Infidelity on the Internet: Virtual Relationships and Real Betrayal* (Naperville, Ill.: Sourcebooks, 2001). Among their other findings: 9 million users (15 percent of the total Internet population at the time) had accessed the top five adult entertainment sites for pornography. Only 8 percent would characterize themselves as "sexually compulsive," and most spend under ten hours a week in sexual pursuits. Women tend to skip the visual erotica in comparison to men—23 percent of women say they surf for visual erotica, compared to 50 percent of men. But equal numbers of men and women seek sexual and romantic contact in chat rooms. Most all surfers are honest about their sex, although 60 percent say they "occasionally" lied about other biographical details. Twenty percent of the entire Internet-using population engages in some kind of sexual activity online.

CHAPTER 12: ISO (IN SEARCH OF): A BUBBLE

206 **"I found myself making up screen names"**: Jennifer Schneider, "The Impact of Compulsive Cybersex Behaviors on the Family," *Sexual and Relationship Therapy* 18, no. 3 (2003), pp. 329–54.

CHAPTER 13: "THE FIFTY-MILE RULE"

226 **"adultery agreements"**: Ben B. Lindsey, *The Companionate Marriage* (New York: Boni & Liveright, 1927). Bertrand Russell postulated similarly in his 1929 work *Marriage and Morals* (New York: Routledge Classics, 2009, p. 87), "I think where a marriage is fruitful and both parties to it are reasonable and decent the expectation ought to be that it will be lifelong, but not that it will be exclusive of other sex relations." For other studies see James Smith and Lynn Smith, *Beyond Monogamy: Recent Studies of Sexual Alternatives in Marriage* (Baltimore: Johns Hopkins University Press, 1974).

227 **"Partly consciously and partly unconsciously"**: John F. Cuber with Peggy B. Harroff, *The Significant Americans: A Study of Sexual Behavior Among the Affluent* (New York: Appleton-Century, 1965), p. 34.

227 **"merely a set of rules"**: Ibid., p. 34.

227 **"One outgrows adolescence"**: Ibid., p. 158.

227 **"barter in contrived innocence"**: Ibid., p. 35.

227 **26 percent of married women in his sample**: Alfred Kinsey, *Sexual Behavior in the Human Female* (Philadelphia: Saunders, 1953), pp. 416, 427, 434.

227 **"new kind of woman"**: Jessie Bernard, "Two Clinicians and a Sociologist," in Gerhard Neubeck, ed., *Extramarital Relations* (Englewood Cliffs, N.J.: Prentice-Hall, 1969).

228 **"Two nights a week my husband"**: Cuber and Harroff, *The Significant Americans*, p. 160.

228 **Gordon Clanton discovered the same pattern**: Gordon Clanton, *Face to Face: An Experiment in Intimacy* (New York: Dutton, 1975).

229 **"there is nothing against extramarital sex as such"**: Joseph Fletcher, "Love is the Only Measure," *Commonweal*, January 14, 1966, p. 431. Fletcher expanded his view of ethics in *Situation Ethics* (Philadelphia: Westminster, 1966).

229 **"probably a majority"**: Cuber and Harroff, *The Significant Americans*, p. 193.

235 **"If we continue to insist"**: Jessie Bernard, "Infidelity: Some Moral and Social Issues," in Robert Libby and Robert Whitehurst, eds., *Marriage and Alternatives: Exploring Intimate Relationships* (Glenview, Ill.: Scott, Foresman, 1977), pp. 131–32.

236 **access to sex "for free"**: One of the premises of the abstinence movement in the 21st century is that young women "give it away" to boys and men for free, which inhibits romance, sexual commitment, and marriage. In her essay on the "Child-Man" Kay Hymowitz, for example, notes that since young men can get sex for nothing, they're even less inclined to marry (the bargaining chip of our bodies having already been made available to them), which further retards male maturity. Kay Hymowitz, "The Child-Man: Today's Single Young Men Hang Out in a Hormonal Limbo Between Adolescence and Adulthood," *Dallas Morning News*, February 1, 2008. As the old adage goes, "Why buy the cow when you can get the milk for free?"

CHAPTER 14: "WE'RE MAKING IT UP AS WE GO ALONG"

237 **"flat out, no joke don't give an f. about sex"**: Asexual Visibility and Education Network, July 2008, http://www.asexuality.org/home.

237 **dispassion as a "fourth categorization"**: Ibid.

239 **"Young People! Don't Hate Sex!"**: Paul Wiseman, "No Sex Please—We're Japanese," *USA Today*, June 3, 2004, p. 15A. See also "'Asexual Marriage' Website Thrives in China," *Toronto Star*, July 31, 2006, p. E7.

240 **the swinging community has been Googled**: Richard Rayner's brief *New York Times Magazine* article in 2000 includes an interview of Robert McGinley, the president of the North American Swing Club Association. McGinley told Rayner that the group had increased from 150 to 310 affiliates from 1995 to 2000. McGinley said that swinging has become highly organized and institutionalized. Richard Rayner, "Back in the Swing," *New York Times Magazine*, April 9, 2000, pp. 42–43. Terry Gould estimates that there are about 3 million married, largely middle-aged, middle-class swingers or "lifestyle practitioners," as they are now called. This is an increase of almost 1 million since 1990. Terry Gould, "The Other Swinging Revival," *Saturday Night* 113 (1998), pp. 48–58.

According to McGinley, swinging within the last ten years has shown a significant increase, and Susan Wright says that it's grown "exponentially" in the last decade (phone interview with author, September 3, 2008). The mailing list for NASCA had about 12,000 names ten years ago; today, it has around 30,000. McGinley estimates that there are 400 swing clubs today, up from 200 a decade ago. Obviously the Internet and Google have fueled the growth in swinging and ushered in a new era. Couples can explore at home, and they don't have to go into adult bookstores or a club to get information. In the 1970s, 74 percent of swingers found each other through literature, cloak-and-dagger mailing lists, and phone trees, or through swinging magazines. Internet search engines encourage the more casually interested marriage to get more information about swinging without any logistical hardship or the social embarrassment of, say, having to walk in to an adult video store. See Robert Rubin, "Alternative Lifestyles Revisited, or Whatever Happened to Swingers, Group Marriages and Communes?" *Journal of Family Issues* 22, no. 6 (2001), pp. 711–26.

240   **There are more than 500 swing clubs**: Roger Rubin summarizes the state of swinging in "Alternative Lifestyles Revisited."

240   **annual Lifestyles convention**: Interview with Susan Wright, September 3, 2008.

241   **A study in 1985**: Richard J. Jenks, "Swinging: A Replication and Test of a Theory," *Journal of Sex Research* 21, no. 1 (1985), pp. 199–205. Brian Gilmartin found that almost half of a sample of nonswingers would mind if an "otherwise unobjectionable swinging couple moved into their neighborhoods." Gilmartin, "That Swinging Couple Down the Block," *Psychology Today* 8 (1975), p. 55.

241   **Swingers: the Republican base**: Swingers are largely otherwise conventional and politically conservative, with 32 percent in Richard Jenks's research calling themselves "conservative" and 41 percent "moderate." Only 27 percent of swingers called themselves "liberal." Fifty percent of swingers voted for Reagan in 1980 and only 24 percent for Carter. Richard Jenks, "A Comparative Study of Swingers and Nonswingers: Attitudes and Beliefs," *Lifestyles* 7 (1985), pp. 5–20, and "Swinging: A Review of the Literature," *Archives of Sexual Behavior* 27 (1998), pp. 507–21.

247   **Elizabeth Emens provocatively questions**: Elizabeth Emens, "Monogamy's Law: Compulsory Monogamy and Polyamorous Existence," *New York University Review of Law & Social Change* 29 (2004), pp. 277–376.

248   **Something has taken the place**: Joy Davidson, "Working with Polyamorous Clients in the Clinical Setting," *Electronic Journal of Human Sexuality* 5, April 16, 2002, http://www.ejhs.org/volume5/polyoutline.html.

CHAPTER 15: "A PLACE
WHERE A SICK MARRIAGE GOES TO DIE?"

250   **polyamory is not polygamy**: Joy Davidson, "Working with Polyamorous Clients in the Clinical Setting," *Electronic Journal of Human Sexuality* 5, April 16, 2002, http://www.ejhs.org/volume5/polyoutline.html.

250   **"ethical nonmonogamy"**: Elizabeth Emens, "Monogamy's Law: Compulsory Monogamy and Polyamorous Existence," *New York University Review of Law & Social Change* 29 (2004), p. 277.

250   **"Rivals are not allowed"**: Wendy-O Matik, *Redefining Our Relationships: Guidelines for Responsible Open Relationships* (Berkeley, Calif.: Defiant Times Press, 2003), p. 43.

250   **5 percent of marriages were open**: Lillian Rubin, *Erotic Wars: What Happened to the Sexual Revolution?* (New York: Farrar, Straus & Giroux, 1990).

250   **A 2000 survey**: Adam Weber, "Survey Results: Who Are We? And Other Interesting Impressions," *Loving More* 30 (2000), pp. 4–6.

250   **The federal government**: Anita Wagner, correspondence with author, July 2008.

250   **In a 2007 survey of 14,000 people**: Ibid.

252 **"it never _works_"**: In the 1980s, Arline Rubin and James Adams followed up on a 1978 research study. The original sample consisted of 130 respondents in sexually open marriages, and 130 respondents in sexually exclusive marriages. Of the 68 sexually exclusive respondents who were still together in 1983, 62 percent had reported that they had considered extramarital sex, despite their intention to have sexually exclusive marriages, and 28 percent reported having had extramarital sex once or more than once. Rubin and Adams found no statistically significant difference in marital stability between the sexually exclusive and the sexually open marriages. Arline Rubin and James Adams, "Outcomes of Sexually Open Marriages," _Journal of Sex Research_ 22, no. 3 (1986), pp. 311–19.

Nor is there evidence that swinging, or more recreational nomonogamy, affects marital stability. In a 1998 study, Richard Jenks found that more than 91 percent of the husbands and 82 percent of the wives indicated that they were happy with swinging. Less than 1 percent of wives were displeased with swinging; no males expressed any unhappiness. They reported "no change or improvement" in the marriage one way or the other, the swinging activities being intriguingly irrelevant to marital well-being and success. Richard Jenks, "Swinging: A Review of the Literature," _Archives of Sexual Behavior_ 27 (1998), pp. 507–21.

256 **"Our perspective is, you don't avoid"**: "Will Smith Says He Has 'Open' Marriage with Jada Pinckett Smith," UPI News Service, February 8, 2005, http://www.realitytvworld.com/index/articles/story.php?s=1001905.

257 **The "typical" open marriage**: There's very little social scientific research on open and polyamorous marriages. The federal government hasn't been eager to fund research on sexuality generally, to say nothing of untraditional marital forms (Anita Wagner, email interview and correspondence with author, summer 2008). Meg Barker, a British scholar and a polyamorist herself, notes that when a group of academics tried to put together a special issue in the journal _Sexualities_ on the topic of open marriage and polyamory, they couldn't find enough research to do so. Meg Barker, "This Is My Partner and This Is My . . . Partner's Partner," _Journal of Constructivist Psychology_ 18, no. 1 (January–March 2005), pp. 75–88.

What peer-reviewed research does exist is from the 1980s and 1970s and suggests a demographic profile for couples in openly nonmonogamous marriages that resembles the swinging and the infidelity-prone ones. Across several studies from the 1980s, marriages with open arrangements are typically from the ranks of well-educated professionals. In his 1975 study, James Ramey describes that the open marriage group had a mean age of 44 for the husbands and 40 for the wives; all of his subjects were white. Most were in the professions, typically in creative, academic, or managerial occupations. James Ramey, "Intimate Groups and Networks: Frequent Consequence of Sexually Open Marriage," _Family Coordinator_ 24, no. 4 (1975), pp. 515–30. Jacquelyn Knapp, "An Exploratory Study of Seventeen Sexually Open Marriages," _Journal of Sex Research_ 12, no. 3 (1976), pp. 206–20, found that the average age among her 17 couples was 30, and, as in Ramey's larger sample, half of them were employed in academic fields. The rest worked as a nurse, carpenter, pilot, manager, insurance agent, bookkeeper, and secretary. Before entering into an open marriage arrangement, three of the wives and four of the husbands had had illicit, secret affairs. Most had had conservative or moderate upbringings in terms of sex. See also Jacquelyn Knapp, "Some Non-Monogamous Marriage Styles and Related Attitudes and Practices of Marriage Counselors," _Family Coordinator_ 24, no. 4 (1975), pp. 505–15.

Knapp devised a personality instrument in 1982 and found that the composite personality type for a sexually open marriage leans toward partners who are individualistic, academic achievers, creative, nonconforming, stimulated by complexity and chaos, inventive, relatively unconventional and indifferent to what others say, concerned about their own personal ethical system, and willing to take risks. They were not destructive in their relationships, she discovered. Knapp's unpublished work is described in Shelley Ann Peabody, "Alternative Lifestyles to Monogamous Marriages: Varieties of Normal Behavior in Psychotherapy Clients," *Family Relations* 31, no. 3 (1982), pp. 425–35. Knapp concluded that most held to be "especially important" their conviction that no one person can "be expected to satisfy every need." Peabody found that to succeed in a sexually open marriage, the spouses have to be at a "more autonomous level of ego development." Peabody concludes that while it's an unconventional choice, it is a "non-neurotic one" for many.

257 **Warren Buffett**: Warren Buffett, interview with Evan Davis, Public Radio International, BBC World Service, October 25, 2009.

258 **One researcher estimates**: Amity Buxton, "Works in Progress: How Mixed-Orientation Couples Maintain Their Marriages after the Wives Comes Out," *Journal of Bisexuality* 4, no. 1–2 (2004), pp. 57–82; Richard Isay estimates that between 1974 and 1981, 15 to 20 percent of homosexual men were or had been married, although it stands to reason that that percentage would be lower today, owing to greater social acceptance of homosexuality. Richard Isay, "Heterosexually Married Homosexual Men: Clinical and Developmental Issues," *American Journal of Orthopsychiatry* 68, no. 3 (July 1998), pp. 424–32.

261 **Compersion thrives with parity and equity**: Davidson, "Working with Polyamorous Clients in the Clinical Setting."

261 **"limerence" and "NRE"**: Dorothy Tennov, *Love and Limerence: The Experience of Being in Love* (Lanham, Md.: Scarborough, 1999).

263 **after a peek or two**: Marny Hall, in Marcia Munson and Judith P. Stelboum, eds., *The Lesbian Polyamory Reader: Open Relationships, Non-Monogamy, and Casual Sex* (New York: Haworth, 1999). Jacquelyn Knapp's research discovered a minority of open marriage couples who "habitually explored all facets" of their relationships with others, to solidify "the marital bond" between them. James Ramey found that a majority—53 percent—of the couples in "intimate friendship" networks he interviewed said they discussed their encounters "in detail" with each other, and 15 percent "eagerly anticipate[d]" these discussions. Ramey, "Intimate Groups and Networks."

CHAPTER 16: "FREE LOVE 2.0"

265 **A band of Christian sex radicals**: Rustum [Roy] and Della Roy, *Honest Sex: A Revolutionary New Sex Guide for the Now Generation of Christians* (New York: Signet, 1968); "Is Monogamy Outdated?" *Humanist*, March/April 1970, reprinted in Robert Libby and Robert Whitehurst, eds., *Marriage and Alternatives: Exploring Intimate Relationships* (Glenview, Ill.: Scott, Foresman, 1977).

266 **"We had no control over the interpretation"**: Quoted in Judy Gaines Leopard and Dale Wachowiak, "The Open Marriage O'Neills: An Interview," *Personnel and Guidance Journal* 55, no. 9 (May 1977), pp. 505–509.

266 **"potential entrapment of the human psyche"**: Lawrence Casler, *Is Marriage Necessary?* (New York: Human Science Press, 1974). See also Mervyn Cadwallader, "Marriage as a Wretched Institution," *Atlantic*, November 1966, pp. 62–66.

266 **"protest the Establishment"**: Described in James Ramey, "Intimate Groups and Networks: Frequent Consequence of Sexually Open Marriage," *Family Coordinator* 24, no. 4 (1975), pp. 515–30; Larry and Joan Constantine, *Group Marriage: A Study of Contemporary Multilateral Marriage* (New York: Macmillan, 1973).

Jacquelyn Knapp also found in her research that a large number of wives were inspired toward nonmonogamy "by women's consciousness raising activities." Jacquelyn Knapp, "Some Non-Monogamous Marriage Styles and Related Attitudes and Practices of Marriage Counselors," *Family Coordinator* 24, no. 4 (1975), pp. 505–14.

269 **"activist of the heart"**: Dossie Easton, *The Ethical Slut* (San Franciso: Greenery, 1997).

269 **wives, not husbands, often drive the open marriage decision**: Three studies from the 1970s found that women usually broached the topic and initiated open marriages, and were more active thereafter. In some cases they proposed open marriage in reaction to husbands who had already cheated and lied. They wanted to convert extramarital sex into a more ethical, honest, and egalitarian form. In other words, open marriage was in these cases a feminization of infidelity. Jacquelyn Knapp conducted in-depth research on 17 open marriages in Kansas in 1975. In 11 of the marriages the wife first experienced extramarital sex. In another three cases the couple had a first experience together, but it was arranged by the wife. So in all but three couples, the wife took the lead in arranging and initiating extramarital sex. Wives had the first idea in five of the marriages. Knapp interpreted her wives' interest as a desire to remove the double standard of "all right for him but no for me." They also viewed open marriage affairs as less threatening to the integrity of the family and marriage, and they found that "outside relationships allowed them to adjust their own sexual paces, which often exceeded that of their husbands." They felt that comarital relations "allowed them to express affection and to receive affection from more sources, a need that wives often said was to some extent unfulfilled in their marriages." Spouses of both sexes were "relieved" to not have to be the only person required to satisfy "emotional needs." Knapp's sample was not inclined toward recreational swinging but rather toward relationships with "deep friendship" attached.

See Jay Ziskin and Mae Ziskin, *The Extra-Marital Sex Contract* (Los Angeles: Nash, 1973); Ramey, "Intimate Groups and Networks"; Jacquelyn Knapp, "An Exploratory Study of Seventeen Sexually Open Marriages," *Journal of Sex Research* 12, no. 3 (1976), pp. 206–20.

269 **"relish the feeling of owning their desires"**: Joy Davidson, "Working With Polyamorous Clients in the Clinical Setting," *Electronic Journal of Human Sexuality* 5, April 16, 2002, http://www.ejhs.org/volume5/polyoutline.html.

269 **What might extramarital sex look like**: Three of the most prominent guidebooks in the polyamory, new open marriage subculture are Easton, *The Ethical Slut*; Deborah Anapol's *Love Without Limits* (San Rafael, Calif.: IntiNet Resource Center, 1992); and Wendy-O Matik's *Redefining Our Relationships: Guidelines for Responsible Open Relationships* (Berkeley, Calif.: Defiant Times Press, 2003). The most important guideline that emerges in these books is that the "primary" relationship—the spouse—must remain the primary and "rivals are not allowed." Most polyamorous or open relationships insist on this rule. Lovers and mistresses have to be able to accept the limits of the relationship, and not be seeking another spouse, or another primary relationship. These guidebooks also urge couples to specify how much time they would spend with a secondary partner, any limits on sexual behavior they would insist on, and how much they'd want to know about the other relation-

ship. They urge that things should move at the pace of the slowest partner, and some couples want to discuss an encounter beforehand. Some have a twenty-four-hour rule, which holds that each spouse discuss an encounter beforehand, impose a waiting period on a new lust—rather as we do with handgun purchases—and give the partner "veto power" over the encounter. Some couples prohibit relationships among their circle of friends or acquaintances, and most specify that if either partner feels uncomfortable about anything, he or she should bring it up. Almost all of these marriages inspire to an "al fresco" and "no surprises" standard of honesty and consent.

270 **"leading a double life"**: Davidson, "Working with Polyamorous Clients."

273 **And jealousy dimmed even further over time**: The force of jealousy may be overrated. Marriage researcher James Ramey found that jealous reactions had "decreased over time" for 44 percent of the respondents; had never been an issue to begin with for 20 percent; and had stayed the same for the remaining 32 percent. When the primary spouse had a relationship, 60 percent of his respondents had nonjealous, "very" positive (30 percent) or "somewhat" positive (30 percent) reactions. Only 13 percent had "somewhat" negative responses and none had very negative responses. For 19 percent their reaction was "equally positive and negative." Forty-one percent "never" thought their primary relationship was weakened. Ramey, "Intimate Groups and Networks," p. 524.

ABOUT THE AUTHOR

PAMELA HAAG earned a Ph.D. in history from Yale after attending Swarthmore College. She has worked as director of research for the American Association of University Women and as a speechwriter, and has written for the *American Scholar*, the *Christian Science Monitor*, the *Michigan Quarterly Review*, the *Huffington Post*, and NPR, among others. She has held fellowships from the National Endowment for the Humanities and the Mellon Foundation and a postdoctoral fellowship at Brown University.